Eli
Co
als
bar
has
and
cou
Re
edi
Ital
ary

w
ɪ,
n-
he
er
er
ife
he
in
d-
s.

BSCT

Further praise for *Mstislav Rostropovich*:

'This book is a real treasure hoard, not just for cellists, but for anyone with an interest in the music of the past century . . . fascinating insights into life in communist Moscow . . . As a tribute to Rostropovich, this book could hardly be bettered.' *Strad* magazine

'A warm-hearted tribute to her master cellist, and most readers, as a result, will envy the members of Class 19.' Jonathan Keates, *Sunday Telegraph*

'Having already written definitive biographies of Shostakovich and Jacqueline du Pré, her Moscow Conservatoire classmate, Elizabeth Wilson completes a Moscow trilogy with this equally definitive life of her teacher . . . It fills out the life-canvas in fascinating detail . . . The greatest privilege that Wilson enjoyed, as one of his favourite pupils, is what makes her account uniquely interesting. She gives an intimate portrait both of Rostropovich's teaching methods, and of Soviet musical life, with all its splendours and miseries. In the process, she sheds fascinating light on the three composers for whom this cellist was the primary . . . Having read this book, I now listen with new ears to the classic works of the mid-twentieth century.' Michael Church, *Independent*

'The book teems with entertaining anecdotes, of the tricks and new angles which he brought to bear . . . An engrossing read about one of the great characters of the twentieth century.' Peter Spaull, *Liverpool Daily Post*

'An extraordinary book.' *Washington Times*

'Any hint of hagiography is put to rest by the down-to-earth memories of his pupils, who experienced the whirlwind of his intense creativity at close quarters: the sweat, tears, exhaustion and exaltation are memorably described.' Helen Wallace, *BBC Music Magazine*

'A painstakingly researched biography . . . There is . . . a wealth of moving detail that moves the book beyond the hagiographical abstractions or mystifications that "legend" usually suggests . . . It is to Elizabeth Wilson's huge credit that she delivers a biography that is both musically and personally alert but also accessible and as complete as any work on a living subject can be.' Brian Morton, *Sunday Herald*

'Bubbles with the effervescence which seems to have followed Rostropovich wherever he went. The stories of his pranks are wittily retold . . . Wilson has spent ten years researching this book, and her dedication to her subject has produced a volume which should be on every musician's shelf.' Fergus Johnston, *Irish Times*

'As a book in its own right, Wilson's is eminently readable, often moving; I can think of no other recently published book which gives such insight into the moulding of musicians.' Richard Sennett, *Literary Review*

'A valuable new source of information . . . Before Wilson, nobody had described so well the specific context from which Rostropovich emerged.' G. S. Smith, *Times Literary Supplement*

'The publication of Elizabeth Wilson's book is timely, not just for its detailed account of Rostropovich's teaching methods, but as a reminder of what made him special . . . It should be required reading for every performer and music teacher, for it adds up to a manual of musical truth.' Andrew Clark, *Financial Times*

'The most inspiring book I have read in a long while.' Robert Max, *Music Teacher*

by the same author

JACQUELINE DU PRE
SHOSTAKOVICH: A LIFE REMEMBERED

Mstislav Rostropovich

cellist, teacher, legend

ELIZABETH WILSON

faber

First published in 2007
by Faber and Faber Limited
Bloomsbury House, 74–77 Great Russell Street
London WC1B 3DA

This paperback edition first published in the UK and USA in 2021

Typeset by RefineCatch Ltd, Bungay, Suffolk
Printed and bound by CPI Group (UK) Ltd, Croydon, CR0 4YY

A CIP record for this book
is available from the British Library

ISBN 978–0–571–36336–0

Dedicated to the memory of Mstislav Rostropovich
and to my friends, his students of Class 19

Contents

Illustrations

Foreword

Some artists' lives seem to recede into the distance after their death, overtaken by new generations of talents. With Mstislav Rostropovich the reverse seems to have happened – we have become more aware of his colossal stature since his death on 27 April 2007. This perhaps is not surprising, given that Rostropovich always had an eye to the future combined with a vivid awareness of the past, and as such he has lost none of his relevance as cellist, artistic innovator and humanist. Today we cannot think of the names of such composers as Prokofiev, Shostakovich, Britten, Lutoslawski, Schnittke, Dutilleux, Gubaidulina, Penderecki – and others too numerous to name – without thinking of Rostropovich. What other great instrumentalist over the last century has worked so hard for contemporary composers, the creation of new music and for his chosen instrument? Due to his efforts over half a century's performing career, the cello has assumed a more prominent position as a solo instrument, its technical and expressive possibilities infinitely expanded.

Thanks to the continuing reissue and release of recordings, the large number of memorial concerts and festivals, as well as several new documentary films – more details to be found in the Epilogue – Rostropovich's name has remained consistently in the public eye. The maestro basked in worldwide love and appreciation, but few knew how many hours of hard work he spent preparing his interpretations. By the time of his first business appointments – usually a seven o'clock breakfast – he had already been up working at his scores for two or three hours. Time could be found to sleep – either as he admitted 'during long journeys on any form of transport', or 'in the next world'. However, Rostropovich was never shy of publicity and his words and thoughts have been captured in many recorded and filmed interviews. Such material allows new generations of music-lovers to see Rostropovich in action, to appreciate his wit, humour, and energy, and to experience something of the immediacy of his communicative power in live performances.

One of the original aims of my book was to retrieve the more serious and private aspects of Rostropovich's personality, to attempt to define his interpretative principles, and understand the artistic vision and musical knowledge that lay at the basis of his activities as performer and teacher. His students also witnessed at first hand the larger scope of his personality, his intuitive gifts of understanding, his concern for people, and his enormous generosity to many in the most difficult life situations. In this sense, the information and stories in this book remain as relevant as ever today, whether it is read in the UK or the USA or Japan and Russia (where it has appeared in translation).

Because it concentrates on the Soviet years (1927–74), my book makes no claims to be comprehensive – many new works were written for Rostropovich after he had left the Soviet Union, which did not find a place in the scope of this record, any more than the enormous number of concerts and recordings made as cellist and conductor between 1975 and 2006. Nevertheless, his principles as an interpreter of music, as an innovator of his instrument and his vision as a humanist were all formulated in the Soviet period, which I explore in depth.

Rostropovich believed in the absolute necessity of music, as a reflection of the Divine in Man. He also believed, like Shostakovich, in conscience, both musical and human. He realised that there was more to life than music, and knew how important it was to give young people a good chance in life. His commitment to youth was articulated in his creation of opportunity through his Foundations. They were an essential part of his vision for creating a better future. His legacy lives on in the Foundations' enlarged activities, under the direction of his two daughters, Olga and Elena.

It was in Rostropovich's nature to find positive solutions, to give hope, and to find practical ways to manifest his belief in life and music. One only wishes he was here to lend us cheer in these dark times of worldwide pandemic. Looking to his example, we can surely find hope for young and old alike. And to further these hopes I fervently wish that republication of this book will play its part in perpetuating the living memory of the great cellist.

Elizabeth Wilson
Cumiana, Italy. November 2020

Preface

The idea of this book arose some four years ago, when I spent many hours at the Borzhomi festival in Georgia with Ivan Monighetti, fellow cellist and former Rostropovich student. While recalling our student days at the Moscow Conservatoire, we agreed that the influence that Rostropovich exerted on our lives far transcended that of a mere teacher of music or cello, and that during those years of study he had given us food for thought that lasted a lifetime. We believed that for this reason it was important to try and record everything that could be retrieved from memory about Rostropovich the teacher. I have to admit, however, that I was surprised when Rostropovich approved the project and agreed to my writing this book. Although an eminently public figure, he has always been very reticent about his musical beliefs and principles, though willing to share his memories of the great composers of the twentieth century – Prokofiev, Shostakovich and Britten.

It is not an exaggeration to say that the history of the cello in the twentieth century would be unthinkable without the name of Mstislav Rostropovich. His musical personality has dominated the international concert scene for over half a century. And for nearly as long as this, he has seemed to me like a personification of the cello itself. When I was still a complete beginner, my father told me about an exciting young Russian cellist with a nearly unpronounceable name. Rostropovich was one of a series of wonderful Soviet musicians who took Western audiences by storm when they started travelling during the second half of the 1950s. Many cellists were introduced to the instrument through Rostropovich's recordings, as I was; and none of these recordings made more impression on me than his LP of Dmitri

Shostakovich's first cello concerto, made in 1959. I listened to this record day in and day out, captivated not just by the wonderful new music, but by the exhilarating energy of the interpretation, which revealed hitherto unsuspected possibilities of the instrument. As a passionate champion of new music, Rostropovich was responsible for the creation of an important new repertoire. One might almost say that by rising to all the challenges set by the best composers of the day, he reinvented cello-playing – to the extent that when Witold Lutoslawski announced that he was starting work on a cello concerto, Rostropovich could confidently say to him, 'Don't think of the cello, I am the cello.'

In Moscow, however, his fame as a performer was nearly equalled by his reputation as a teacher. Rostropovich taught at his own alma mater, the Moscow Tchaikovsky Conservatoire, becoming a full professor by the age of thirty-one, and head of the cello and double-bass faculty by the time he was thirty-four. He had started teaching during the war at the tender age of fifteen: when his father Leopold Rostropovich died suddenly, the young Slava took over his class at the Orienburg Musical Uchilishche (High School). Even before graduating from the Conservatoire, Mstislav commenced his professional activity as a teacher at the Moscow Central Music School. Shortly afterwards he was taken on the staff of the Moscow Conservatoire itself.

His earliest generation of students, cellists only just younger than their teacher, witnessed Rostropovich's meteoric rise from prize-winning student to internationally acclaimed concert artist. When he was not away on tour, Rostropovich taught regularly on Tuesdays and Thursdays in Class 19, on the third floor of the 'old' wing of the Conservatoire. During twenty-eight years of teaching activity in Moscow, nearly a hundred aspiring cellists passed through his hands. I was extremely lucky to become one of their number when I joined his class in September 1964.

In his quest to popularise the cello and to renew its repertoire, Rostropovich set himself a series of goals. Once he had achieved them, he would soon pass on to the next task. And his own musical activities have not been limited to the cello, for he enjoyed accompanying his wife, the soprano Galina Vishnevskaya, at the piano and later launched himself wholeheartedly into a career as a conductor.

To describe Rostropovich as a teacher is a difficult task. In order to explain the artistic values that he transmitted to younger generations of musicians, I found I needed to examine his background, formative influences and early career, his close contacts with composers, and the special features of his own musical personality, as well as his didactic principles.

The qualities Rostropovich brought to his Conservatoire class reflected the philosophy inherent in his own performances. His capacity for self-discipline and hard work was enormous. To his students he transmitted – with exuberance, wit and compassion – a lasting love of music and a set of ideals that deeply influenced their lives. In doing so, he taught them to believe in their own resources, to think that the impossible did not exist – without doubt his own example served as an inspiration.

One could even say that playing the cello sometimes seemed of less importance to Rostropovich than articulating an approach to music-making that grew out of the creative impulse. Imagery was an all-important tool in his effort to convey an understanding of the musical idea from every angle – emotional, philosophical and structural. As he continues to say, 'Translating my concepts into the real world is very difficult. Often I can only achieve about half of my initial idea.' Hence Rostropovich continuously seeks to reconcile his artistic concepts with the practicalities of performance.

In writing this book, I fervently hope to convey the vast range of objectives that Rostropovich set out to achieve, both for himself and for those he taught. He wished to instil in his students a questing spirit and a sense of vision that should underpin every activity they undertook. In his view, a performance that lacked vision produced mediocre results – just as for Shostakovich a 'mezzo-fortist' was an insipid musician, or for Dostoyevsky, a person who was 'tepid' was guilty of the insufferable sin of indifference.

Rostropovich's students were much affected by the integrity and courage their teacher displayed when he came into conflict with the Soviet regime. In expressing his beliefs through actions as well as words, the cellist was willing to jeopardise his own musical career, and to risk losing the privileges enjoyed by the Soviet artistic elite. Rostropovich's public support of the disgraced writer Aleksandr Solzhenitsyn was motivated by the dictates of conscience; in this he was a follower of the great Russian humanists, for whom moral principles took priority over personal interests.

The authorities reacted to Rostropovich's stand by subjecting him to a subtle and cruel form of punishment, restricting his concert activity within the Soviet Union and banning him from foreign travel. From 1970 onwards, Rostropovich was gradually starved of the possibilities of artistic expression; this deprivation made him appreciate the Moscow Conservatoire all the more as a haven. He retained his position there until his enforced departure from the Soviet Union in May 1974.

He spent the next sixteen years of his life outside his native country, and never accepted another regular teaching position; nor was he able to give any other group of young musicians the kind of continuous rapport that his students from Class 19 were able to enjoy with him. In exploring Rostropovich's work as a teacher from the point of view of his pupils, this book is therefore a document of a unique musical relationship.

Acknowledgements

This book would not have been possible without help from many people. First and foremost, I am infinitely grateful to Mstislav Rostropovich for allowing me to undertake the project. As always, he has been incredibly generous, giving me many hours of his time for interviews, allowing me access to his personal archive and providing me with photographs, as well as giving me assistance of all kinds.

His archive in St Petersburg is housed in a splendid mansion on the Kutuzov embankment, not far from the Hermitage. The curator, Larissa Chirkova – a model of kindness, patience and efficiency – sought out and prepared material that was of interest to me (press cuttings, articles and photographs), and allowed me to use the archive facilities. My deepest thanks to her. The task of reconstructing Rostropovich's concert schedule (an enormous and ongoing project) was entrusted to Mikhail Mishchenko. The list he constructed was invaluable to me, and I express my gratitude to him. My warm thanks too for the invaluable help provided by the archives of the Moscow and St Petersburg Conservatoires; I thank all the archivists concerned. I also wish to thank the Glinka Museum of Musical Culture in Moscow for help and for providing photographs from their collection. My warm thanks to Olga Bochikhina for her help in researching archival collections in Moscow. My thanks to Viktor Akhlomov for the use of his photographs, and also to Alla Vasiliyeva, Natalya Shakhovskaya, Galina Sosnovskaya, Eleonora Testelets, Sergey Kalyanov and Ivan Monighetti for providing photographs and other documentary material from their personal collections.

Years back Mischa Maisky had the idea – very novel at the time – of recording Rostropovich's lessons. The surviving tapes have been of enormous help to me, and I warmly thank him. In my work of collecting material and seeking out reminiscences from ex-students, Mstislav Rostropovich jokingly referred to me as a 'Chichikov', a collector of dead souls. But fortunately the spirit of friendship and devotion to our teacher, and the memory of those wonderfully exciting and thought-provoking class lessons, very much lives on, and provides a strong link between all the ex-students of Class 19 to this day. I have been able to trace the names of well over seventy of them, but I am sure the list is not complete. My intense gratitude goes to all who have granted me interviews, and who have shared their reminiscences with me on the phone and in letters and emails. Their contributions have been fundamental to the concept and content of the book. Their names are listed in the annotated sources. The late Veronika Leopoldovna Rostropovich kindly received me and granted me an interview.

For their many acts of kindness and hospitality, I am most grateful to Ivan Monighetti and his wife Tanya, Eleonora Testelets, Tatyana Melentyeva and Aleksandr Knaifel, Olga Manulkina, Lyudmila Kovnatskaya, Vladimir and Irina Tarnopolsky, and Natalya Gutman.

My sincere gratitude to the Edinburgh International Festival, Lilian Hocchauser, Lucinda Byatt, Oleg Malov and Niel Immelman for helping me in my research.

My warm thanks also to Rostropovich's personal secretaries, Natalya Dolezhall in Moscow, and Natalya Maximova, Olga Maximova and Elena Mashkova in Paris, for their help. On the home front, I would like to thank Francesco Candido, Catherine Wilson and Ann Wilson for giving me support and for their most useful comments and suggestions on my manuscript.

This book has benefited from the expertise of my editor, Michael Downes, to whom I owe a great debt of gratitude. At Faber and Faber, I warmly thank Belinda Matthews for accepting the initial project, talking it through with me, giving valuable advice and for her constant encouragement and interest throughout its preparation. My thanks also to Elizabeth Tyerman for her continuous assistance during the time of writing the book, and to Lucie Ewin for carrying it through production.

Elizabeth Wilson
Cumiana, Italy, 11 October 2006

Notes on the text

Sources and references

A list of the major sources used in preparing this book is given on p. 356. This list includes not only published sources, but also the many interviews I conducted with Rostropovich himself and with his former students. In order not to clutter the text with unnecessary notes, I have not given footnote references where information has been drawn from these interviews. However, I do qualify quotations from interviews that fall outside this category. I have also supplied footnote references to any quoted journals and newspapers, as well as identifying printed publications listed in the bibliography through giving the author's name, an abbreviated version of the title and the page number.

Names

This text follows the familiar Russian convention whereby a single person may be referred to by the family name (e.g. Rostropovich), or by the 'polite' form of name and patronymic (e.g. Mstislav Leopoldovich), as well as by a number of different diminutives or nicknames – the most familiar diminutive associated with Rostropovich is of course 'Slava', while the nickname his students gave him was 'Chef'. The pianist Sviatoslav Richter was also often known as 'Slava', while Rostropovich used to address him by a private nickname, 'Glasha', or by his patronymic, Teofilovich. Rather than standardising names in my text, I have tried to convey the character of my interviewees' recollections by retaining the names or nicknames that they themselves used when I spoke to them.

Educational institutions

There is no exact English or American equivalent of the Russian 'Uchilishche' – it is a college that caters for the period corresponding to the last years of school and the first years of higher education in the English or American systems. I have decided to retain the Russian word Uchilishche in my text, rather than confuse the issue by inventing a term such as 'Musical High School'.

Abbreviations

The abbreviations most commonly found in my text include:
TseMSha (Tsentral'naya Muzykal'naya Shkola) – Central Music School
TseDRI (Tsentral'ny Dom Rabotnikov v Iskusstve) – Central House of Workers in Art.

Transliteration

The system of transliteration is based on that advocated by the Library of Congress. In speaking of *Pyotr Tchaikovsky*, I have used the traditional 'German' spelling, but I have accorded the currently accepted usage of *Chaikovsky* in referring to others with this family name: *Boris Chaikovsky, Mariya Chaikovskaya.*

Introduction

A perspective on the Russian school of cello-playing

From the start of his concert career until his enforced departure from the Soviet Union in May 1974, Mstislav Rostropovich enjoyed enormous prestige as a teacher – in Russia, at least, this brought almost as much fame as his multiple concert activities. His life as a teacher is inseparably bound up with the work of the Moscow Conservatoire, where he studied and subsequently taught for over twenty-five years.

The Moscow Conservatoire is situated in the heart of Moscow, within easy walking distance of the Kremlin. Dating from the 1860s, the imposing yellow-facaded building houses the city's two most famous concert-halls, the Grand and the Small Halls (Bol'shoy i Maliy Zaly). Later an extra wing was built to close the third side of the rectangle of the original L-shaped building, giving onto Bolsh'aya Nikitskaya Street (known in Soviet times as Herzen Street – ulitsa Gertsena). The front courtyard is graced with a statue of Pyotr Ilich Tchaikovsky, the institution's patron, placed there in 1954.

As you enter the old wing housing the Conservatoire's Small Hall, a dark semi-basement corridor leads off to the right from the cloakrooms to various inconspicuous and somewhat shabby offices. One of them, a small, windowless room, houses the archives of the illustrious institution. Here files are held on every individual student and teacher who has ever passed through the Conservatoire's portals.

One of the first documents in the file on Mstislav Rostropovich is an official autobiographical account, written in his own hand for the Department of Cadres of the 'Mosow State Twice Order of Lenin Conservatoire named after Pyotr Tchaikovsky' (as the Conservatoire was formally known in the Soviet era). It is dated 27 November 1948:

I

I, Mstislav Leopoldovich Rostropovich was born into a family of musicians in 1927 in the town of Baku. My father, honoured artist of the RSFSR Professor Leopold Witoldovich Rostropovich, taught cello at the Baku Conservatoire, my mother Sofiya Nikolayevna Fedotova-Rostropovich also worked at the Baku Conservatoire teaching piano. Before the Revolution my father and mother were music teachers. In 1932 the whole family moved to Moscow where my father worked at the Radio Committee, then at the Gnesins' Musical High School, and later at the Sverdlovsk District Music School in the city of Moscow. In 1935 my father started teaching me the cello in his class at the Gnessin school. In 1937 I transferred to the Sverdlovsk District school, from which I graduated from my father's cello class in 1941. In 1937 I was also accepted as a pupil at the Moscow Conservatoire Musical High School, where, without abandoning my cello studies, I started to study composition in the class of E. O. Messner.

In 1941 I was evacuated with the Central Music School to Penza, and then to the town of Chkalov where my parents had been sent in evacuation. In 1942 my father died in Chkalov. In 1943, together with my mother and sister, I returned to Moscow, where I passed the entrance exam for the Conservatoire and enrolled as a student of two faculties, in the composition class of V. Y. Shebalin, and in the orchestral faculty to study cello with Semyon Matveevich Kozolupov.

Since 1944 my mother has been teaching piano at the Sverdlovsk District Music School. In 1945 I was accepted in the ranks of the VLKSM (Komsomol). In the same year I participated in the competition for Conservatoire students for the best performance of a Soviet composition, where I won first prize. Later that year I participated in the All-Union competition for musicians and was awarded the title of laureate and first-prize winner.

In 1947 I took part in the International Competition for musicians in Prague where I won first prize. Since 1946 I have been working as the solo cellist of the Moscow Philharmonic, and in the same year I graduated from the Conservatoire with excellence. My name is engraved on the memorial board of the Moscow State Order of Lenin Conservatoire. Since 1947 I have been working as a teacher at the Central Music School. In 1948 I completed my postgraduate studies in the performers' section.*

Such a report was standard for every Conservatoire student and teacher. Like many Soviet documents, this autobiographical statement records merely the bare facts of Rostropovich's family background, education and early professional life, though these undeniably point forward to a brilliant international career. The final document in the file, however, was anything but standard, and its contents would have been impossible to imagine in 1948. This document is an official

* Moscow Conservatoire archives.

Order signed by the Conservatoire director, N. Kulikov, and dated 6 April 1978:

Rostropovich, Mstislav Leopoldovich is hereby relieved of his duties as Professor and Head of Faculty in connection with his being stripped of citizenship of the USSR according to Statute no. 7 of the USSR Law, formulated on 19 August 1938. Drawn up on the basis of the Resolution of the Praesidium of the Supreme Soviet of 15 March 1978.

In fact, the Moscow Conservatoire was the only institution that stood by Rostropovich during his conflict with the Soviet authorities. He taught there right up until the day of his departure, and his emotional 'farewell' concert, still clearly remembered by certain generations of Muscovite musicians, was given at the Grand Hall of the Conservatoire, when he directed a select student orchestra in a revelatory performance of Tchaikovsky's sixth symphony. Long before then, however, Mstislav Rostropovich's open lessons and masterclasses, given in Class 19, had themselves become a legend.

Of course, Rostropovich's own development owed as much to the circumstances of his upbringing and education as to the extraordinary nature of his talent. Despite the repressive climate of the pre-war Stalinist era, the Soviet Union was a country where the performing arts enjoyed a privileged status. The Soviets aimed not only to maintain the high standards of string playing achieved before the Revolution, but to improve them through establishing an ordered system of music education. Young musicians' needs were catered for by the specialist music schools, and their artistic development was fostered to the point where they were ready to enter the music profession. The Russian pedagogical tradition had always embraced the notion that an artist was responsible not only to the great masters of the past, but towards succeeding generations – a concept coinciding with the social principle of collective awareness promoted by Soviet ideology. Artists were seen as a link in a chain – part of a continuous, living tradition.

This explains why so many great Russian string players placed as much importance upon teaching as on performance: legendary violinists from Leopold Auer to Jascha Heifetz and David Oistrakh were all committed teachers, and the cello had a similar lineage of teaching virtuosi, from Anatoly Brandukov to Gregor Piatigorsky and Mstislav Rostropovich.

By nature an explorer, Rostropovich has been more responsible than any other cellist for shaping the history of the instrument and developing its technical possibilities in the twentieth century. Motivated by a constant need for discovery and renewal, his qualities as performer and teacher defy any standard scholastic definition. Even while he was living in the Soviet Union, he carried his art far beyond the boundaries of any national school.

Indeed, Rostropovich disparages the very idea that there is a contemporary Russian school of cello-playing, let alone a 'Rostropovich school'. For him the concept of 'school' implies rigidity, schematic rules and the force of habit, all features that run contrary to his understanding of Art. He argues that the objective differences that once existed between various national schools of cello-playing have now effectively been erased. Today, the notion of a 'Russian School' has more to do with a shared repertoire and artistic heritage than with a specific technical approach to the instrument. A musician, for example, may gain insights into Russian music by reading Dostoyevsky or Chekhov. Here he can find the key to the national character, which Rostropovich sees as oscillating between extremes of exultation and depression, alternating lofty dreams of unrealisable greatness with periods of alcoholic escapism as sorrows are drowned in vodka.

Despite emphasising artistic values over technique, Rostropovich nonetheless prides himself on being a 'great-grandson' of the founding father of the Russian cello school, Karl Davydov. In turn, when he encounters young cellists who have studied with his students, he greets them as 'my cellistic grandchildren'. Schooled within a tangible tradition, Rostropovich has helped to create a worldwide family of cellists.

Before examining the legacy that Rostropovich has left during a career of more than fifty years, it is worth examining the roots on which it was built. One might define the distinguishing features of the traditional Russian school as an impeccable virtuoso technique harnessed to serve music's emotional impulse. For this reason, mood, atmosphere and a wide range of tone colour are emphasised even when 'technique' is being considered – Heinrich Neuhaus liked to remind his students that the word technique was derived from the Greek word *techné*, meaning 'art'.

Russian string players describe the bow as music's 'soul', for its primary function is to sculpt the phrase and set sound into motion. A freely moving bowing arm helps to transmit the artist's message to the furthest corners of any auditorium. The achievement of a variety of tone and expressive colouring is further enhanced by a natural use of the left hand: shifts can be effortlessly clean, but made emotionally telling through a discreet use of portamento. A performer must be willing to extend his technical skills in order to match his imaginative ideals.

The phenomenon of a 'music profession' is a relatively recent one in Russia, and the notion of a Russian school of performance belongs to the late nineteenth century at the earliest. Long before that, though, European professional musicians came to Russia to seek their fortune at the imperial court of Catherine the Great. Many of them remained and were assimilated into Russian life. In turn, Russian musicians from different levels of society – including serfs belonging to enlightened masters* – were encouraged to travel abroad to receive instruction in Italy, Germany and France. Nevertheless, the influx of foreign musicians continued right through the nineteenth century.

In the early 1800s professional musical education began at the Theatrical Uchilishche or College,† and at the St Petersburg Capella, where most orchestral players and singers received their training. Around the 1850s, the city schools started to teach music, often reaching an excellent level, not only in St Petersburg and Moscow but in the provincial cities. Private music schools also began, many with great success, and the Women's Institutes also provided an idiosyncratic form of training, preparing young ladies for the eminently respectable profession of piano teacher. Rostropovich's maternal grandmother, Olga Fedotova, was one such teacher, who enterprisingly founded her own private music school in Orienburg. There she taught two of her own five daughters before sending them on to the Moscow Conservatoire. On their return they set to work in 'the family business', teaching piano and performing locally.

However, music was not regarded as a real profession for men until the foundation of the Conservatoires of St Petersburg and Moscow in the 1860s. Most of the eminent Russian composers, for example, either had private means, like Glinka, or were trained in other

---

* The phenomenon of the 'serf orchestra' still existed right until the abolition of serfdom in 1861.
† The Uchilishche has no real equivalent in either the British or American education system. It is an intermediate institution or college which caters for the ages of roughly fifteen to twenty, covering the last years of school and the early stages of university training.

professions: as lawyers (Tchaikovsky), scientists (Borodin), in the military or navy (Rimsky-Korsakov, Mussorgsky). The prodigiously talented Karl Davydov graduated as a mathematician before deciding on a career as a cellist, while the pianist Nikolay Rubinstein was a law graduate from the University of Moscow. Despite pursuing music as a profession, he maintained a deep attachment to his alma mater, where he organised 'open classes' for musicians, as well as setting up a prestigious concert series, attracting performers of the stature of Clara Schumann, who enchanted an audience of 1,800 people.

It was through the vision of the Rubinstein brothers, Anton and Nikolay, that the first Russian Conservatoires were established in St Petersburg in 1862 and in Moscow four years later – Anton was the first Director of the former and Nikolay the first Director of the latter. Their intial step had been to found the Russian Musical Society (RMO) in St Petersburg in 1859, with the Moscow branch opening three years later. These organisations hosted concerts by some of the most illustrious performers in Europe, and provided the administrative basis for setting up the Conservatoires. The enormous international prestige of the Rubinstein brothers ensured the loyalty of a staff hand-picked from the best musicians and composers at home and abroad, most of whom had been initially invited to perform concerts.

It was in this way that the cellist Bernard Cossman, taking leave from his post as principal cellist of the Leipzig Gewandhaus orchestra, came to Moscow to perform recitals in 1866. He also performed at the opening ceremony of the Conservatoire, after which he was invited to found the new cello faculty. From modest beginnings – initially only two students – Cossman's Moscow cello class grew steadily during his four-year professorship. Cossman was also responsible for introducing the Schumann cello concerto to Russian audiences, and in 1867 took part in a triumphant performance of Beethoven's triple concerto with Ferdinand Laub and Nikolay Rubinstein. Today Cossman is remembered by cellists for his systematically thought-out exercises for left-hand articulation, which are still widely used despite their aridity. Contemporary reports confirm that he was not just a pedagogue, but a sensitive musician who did much to promote the leading composers of the day. His best pupil was Anatoly Brandukov, who continued his studies with Cossman's successor, the German cellist Wilhelm Fitzenhagen.

A pupil of Grützmacher, Fitzenhagen may have lacked Cossman's stature as a performer, but he was equally sought after as a teacher. In 1870 he turned down Liszt's invitation to teach cello at Weimar in favour of Rubinstein's offer of a professorship at the Moscow Conservatoire. Fitzenhagen performed frequently in RMO concerts, and was reviewed by such noted critics as Hermann Laroche and Pyotr Tchaikovsky, who praised Fitzenhagen's virtuosity though criticising his taste in repertoire. Later Tchaikovsky changed his opinion, and responded to Fitzenhagen's request to compose for him.

A serious and conscientious teacher, Fitzenhagen was devoted to his students, encouraging them to perform in closed evening events and public concerts, in the belief that artists could develop only through gaining experience on stage. He also advocated his students' involvement in chamber music, and was himself a member of the RMO string quartet. Today, however, Fitzenhagen is known primarily as the dedicatee of Tchaikovsky's *Rococo Variations*, and for having collaborated with the composer on some of the revisions to the piece, including a change to the order of the variations and a new finale.*

While Fitzenhagen did much to raise the profile of the cello as a concert instrument, the honour of founding the Russian cello school belongs to his great contemporary Karl Davydov (1838–89), who taught at the St Petersburg Conservatoire between 1876 and 1888. Davydov consciously developed principles that were different both from the German school of Romberg, Grützmacher and Cossman and from the Belgian school of Servais. Although renowned for his filigree virtuosity, Davydov anticipated the modern ideal of an artist whose principal obligation was the communication of ideas through his instrument. Davydov had wide-ranging musical horizons, and was moreover a brilliant mathematician, graduating from Moscow University in that discipline before going to Leipzig to study composition. Meanwhile, he continued his private study of the cello and began giving concerts: a charismatic performer, he achieved immediate success on the concert platform, notably at the Leipzig Gewandhaus. At the age of only twenty-two, he was invited to deputise for Grützmacher as professor of cello at the Leipzig Conservatoire,

---

* The original version was restored and published in 1973 by Izlatel'stvo Muzyka. It has now found its way back into cellists' repertoire, and in 2000 it rather than the usual revised version was set as the obligatory requirement for the final round of the Tchaikovsky competition, a choice that aroused considerable controversy.

and on his return to St Petersburg, Davydov was appointed cellist and soloist to the court of his Imperial Majesty. He was also a noted chamber performer, and played in a string quartet with Leopold Auer.

Davydov's contribution to the development of cello technique involved extending the left hand's flexibility through an innovative use of thumb position. He was also the first cellist to insist on the use of a cello spike, which fixed the instrument firmly in the ground and raised its position (previously it was cradled between the knees). This considerably aided the virtuosity and independence of the left hand. His intention to emulate the freedom and ease of violin technique was evident not only in his easy command of the fingerboard, but also in the brilliance and lightness of his bow strokes. Davydov was equally well known as a composer, and his concert works were designed to please audiences while also displaying his considerable virtuosity. Although his concertos and shorter pieces remain in the cello repertoire today mostly as study works, they are very skilfully written, with a musical sincerity that distinguishes them from the majority of works by nineteenth-century virtuosi. Davydov also set out his ideas in his *School of Cello Playing*, a collection of systematically graded and expressive exercises, which demonstrate the basic techniques of the cello. Although it was never completed, it is still widely used today in Russia.

Davydov's influence extended well beyond the confines of the St Petersburg Conservatoire, and amongst his foreign pupils were Carl Fuchs and Hanus Wihan, the dedicatee of Dvořák's concerto. The renowned German cellist Julius Klengel admitted, 'I only understood what cello-playing signifies after hearing Davydov in St Petersburg in my youth.'* Davydov's s favourite pupil, Aleksandr Verzhbelovitch (1850–1911), followed in his footsteps both as professor at the St Petersburg Conservatoire and as soloist to his Imperial Majesty.

Meanwhile, the Davydov school also began to dominate in Moscow. Although Anatoly Brandukov, one of Russia's best-loved musicians, was considered the obvious choice to succeed Fitzenhagen after his death in 1890, the then director of the Conservatoire, Safanov, thought it advisable to introduce fresh blood from the St Petersburg 'Davydov school'. Brandukov's candidature was overridden and Davydov's pupil, the Estonian cellist Alfred von Glehn,

---

* M. Campbell, *The Great Cellists*, p. 92.

was appointed as head of the cello faculty. Many musicians, not least Tchaikovsky, contested Safanov's decision, for Glehn was perceived as a far less talented musician and cellist than his Moscow rival, whose teaching lacked the vital spark that Brandukov could provide. The young cellist Grigori Piatigorsky reached his own solution to the dilemma by enrolling in Glehn's Moscow Conservatoire class while taking private instruction from Brandukov. Despite such early ambivalence, Glehn came to be respected as an honest and dedicated teacher, who transmitted the Davydov traditions in a meaningful way. He remained professor until he returned to his native Estonia in 1921; he was succeeded by Brandukov, who retained the post until his death in 1930.

Brandukov and Verzhbelovitch came to represent two distinct schools of cello-playing, whose differences were only accentuated by the historic rivalry between St Petersburg and Moscow. The charismatic Brandukov was principally a performer, famed for his expressive musicianship and the great beauty and warmth of his sound. He was an active advocate of Russian music and counted Tchaikovsky and Rachmaninov as close friends. Indeed, he was the dedicatee of Tchaikovsky's *Pezzo Capricioso* and Rachmaninov's cello sonata, and was long remembered for the pathos and noble expression he conveyed in the demanding cello part of Tchaikovsky's Piano Trio, dedicated to the memory of Nickolay Rubinstein. At Brandukov's request, Tchaikovsky arranged some of his most famous compositions for solo cello and orchestra, including 'Lensky's Aria' from *Evgeny Onegin*, the Nocturne, and the 'Andante cantabile' from his first string quartet. Brandukov's influence as an interpreter of Russian music was long-lasting, though he taught only in the last decade of his life.

Aleksandr Verzhbelovitch, conversely, is remembered principally as a successful teacher, for all his qualities as a performer. He can justly be called the 'cellistic grandfather' of Mstislav Rostropovich, whose teachers, Leopold Rostropovich and Semyon Kozolupov, studied with Verzhbelovitch at the St Petersburg Conservatoire. It his to his father, Leopold Witoldovich, that Mstislav Rostropovich has always given credit for his formation as a musician:

My father was a brilliant cellist, and I am certain that I never attained his standard of playing. He was a very modest and unassuming person. He always said, they'll come and ask me to play if they need me. But throughout his life nobody ever came.

Leopold Rostropovich was also an accomplished pianist and a gifted composer: his vision as an all-round musician was the decisive influence on his son. Yet his example also taught the bitter lesson that talent is not enough without the force of character to fulfil it. If Mstislav Rostropovich has on occasion spoken of 'stealing' his success from his father, his words imply an appreciation not only of Leopold's talents, but also of his weaknesses. From an early age, Mstislav learnt to channel his energies single-mindedly to achieve his aims.

In Elena Rostropovich's book marking the seventieth birthday of her father, Mstislav, there is the following account of the family's origins:

The Rostropovich family comes from ancient Polish nobility who lived on the territory of the grand duchy of Lithuania. In 1880 Aleksandr II granted hereditary Russian nobility to the family on the basis of a certificate granted by the College of Heraldry of the Kingdom of Poland testifying to the nobility of Hannibal (Vladislav) Rostropovich (1829–1908). Hannibal's father, Jòzef, was a city judge: he and his wife are buried next to Chopin's parents in the Warsaw cemetery. Hannibal and his wife Florentyna Ssztek (1834–1915) had nine children, of whom Witold (1858–1913) showed musical ability . . . and was sent to study at the St Petersburg Conservatoire. He graduated successfully [as a pianist] and returned to live in Voronezh. Besides giving concerts and teaching, Witold edited music for the Pedagogical Publishing House.*

Witold's son Leopold, born in Voronezh on 26 February 1892, demonstrated prodigious musical gifts in early childhood, and studied piano with his father while simultaneously starting to compose. One day he overheard his father in rehearsal with the cellist A. Lukinich. Overwhelmed by the beauty of the cello's sound, Leopold immediately set his heart on learning this instrument and asked Lukinich for lessons. His progress was so rapid that at the age of thirteen he successfully auditioned for the St Petersburg Conservatoire, enrolling simultaneously in Aleksandr Verzhbelovich's cello class and Anna Esipova's piano class. Verzhbelovich, Davydov's favourite pupil, had already earned a reputation as an inspired cello teacher, but Esipova was even more distinguished. A pupil of the renowned Austrian pedagogue, Theodor Leschetizky (and also the second of his many wives), she had enjoyed a successful performing career before dedicating herself exclusively to teaching. Her class

* Elena Rostropovich, p. 9.

produced various brilliant pianists, amongst them Sergey Prokofiev and Mariya Yudina.

Leopold's contemporaries remembered him as an impulsive and somewhat disorganised student, who emulated his charismatic teacher Verzhbelovich. A natural and exuberant performer on stage, Leopold's outgoing emotionality was balanced by a poetic sensibility. In his four years of study at the Conservatoire, it is reputed that Leopold did not over-exert himself. A romantic dreamer by nature, he relied on his enormous natural talent. Yet he graduated with distinction, and as recipient of the coveted gold medal, his name was inscribed on the marble plaque of the St Petersburg Conservatoire's roll of excellence.

After completing his studies in 1910 Leopold Rostropovich embarked on a concert career, playing recitals and concertos in Moscow, St Petersburg, the Crimea, Tiflis, Baku and in Poland. Amongst his most important engagements was a performance of Davydov's First Concerto under Glazunov's baton. Glazunov had already noted Leopold's 'superlative natural technical gifts' at his diploma exam, when he praised his wonderful tone and phrasing, labelling him 'a great virtuoso and musical talent'.* Towards the end of his life, when exiled in Paris, Glazunov still recalled Leopold's beautiful rendering of the Chopin sonata.

One of his concert tours took Leopold to Paris, where he remained for a few months, spending his concert earnings on consultation lessons with Pablo Casals. It is probable that he had already met the great Spanish cellist in St Petersburg: he would certainly have heard him play there, for Casals performed in nine consecutive concert seasons in Russia between 1905 and 1913. Casals's memorable St Petersburg debut in November 1905 occurred against the background of revolution and chaos. At the instigation of the short-lived Soviet of Workers' Deputies, a series of strikes had broken out, causing disruption and paralysing the railway system. It was something of a miracle that Casals arrived in St Petersburg, for he had been diverted from his original destination of Moscow. The renowned violinist, Eugene Ysaye, on the other hand, did not have the same luck, and was prevented from reaching the northern capital. This provided Casals with an opportunity, for the conductor Aleksandr Siloti was left without a soloist, and called the great Spanish cellist in as a replacement.

* Mikhail Spektor, *Mstislav Rostropovich*, pp. 12–13.

His debut concert on 15 November has passed into legend, since, owing to power cuts, the Hall of the Nobility was illuminated by the flickering light of candles. Among the elegant audience of princes and counts, the musical elite of the city were also in attendance to hear Rimsky-Korsakov's new work *Dubinushka* which was being premiered in the second half. Casals was previously unknown in Russia, but his sensational performance of the Saint-Saëns concerto under Siloti's direction won the hearts of Russian audiences. Significantly, he chose Bach as his encore: the Prelude from the second solo suite. The Bach suites had hitherto been considered insufficiently interesting for public performance, but over the next few years Casals revealed their profound but simple beauty to his Russian audiences.

The effects of his influence were already tangible by 1911, when a Bach solo suite was made a compulsory element of the All-Russian Cello Competition in Moscow. This competition, organised to coincide with the fiftieth anniversary celebrations of the RMO (Russian Musical Society), was the first of its kind in Russia. It was won by Semyon Kozolupov, an older contemporary and fellow student of Leopold Rostropovich.

A Cossack by origin, Kozolupov was born in Orienburg in 1884. At the age of ten he started his musical studies at the Cossack Military Academy, playing in various bands as well as learning the cello. While on tour in Orienburg, Aleksandr Verzhbelovich heard Kozolupov play, and arranged for his transfer to St Petersburg. Kozolupov studied for three years in Verzhbelovich's Conservatoire class, graduating with excellence in 1907.

The following year, he was appointed solo cellist at the Bolshoi Theatre orchestra in Moscow and became a member of the RMO Quartet. Meanwhile, Leopold Rostropovich's career was developing along similar lines, for in 1912 he took up the position as solo cellist at the Mariinsky Theatre orchestra in St Petersburg, remaining there until the upheavals of 1917 effectively closed all the city's theatres. Forced to leave the capital, Leopold found employment at the Saratov Conservatoire, which was founded in 1912 to become Russia's third musical institution of higher education, after St Petersburg and Moscow. The first professor of cello at Saratov was Kozolupov, but he had left in 1916 to take up a position at the Kiev Conservatoire. His position in Saratov was taken in 1918 by Leopold Rostropovich.

I

Beginnings

Mstislav Rostropovich could justifiably claim that he received his musical education within his own family. He was taught cello not only by his father, but by his uncle – for by a strange irony of fate, the musical ties between Semyon Kozolupov and Leopold Rostropovich were strengthened by a familial connection.

A year or two after graduating from the St Petersburg Conservatoire, Semyon Kozolupov returned to his home town of Orienburg. He was due to give a recital, and needed a pianist to accompany him. The Fedotova music school suggested Nadezhda Fedotova, the elder of the two pianist daughters of the school's founder. Kozolupov fell in love with her, and soon the couple were married.

More than a decade later, Leopold Rostropovich likewise came to Orienburg to give a recital. He too requested a local accompanist and the services of Nadezhda's sister Sofiya were provided for him. They too fell in love, and after a whirlwind romance they were married in 1922. Leopold and Sofiya settled in Saratov, where their daughter Veronika was born in 1925. Shortly afterwards, the family moved to Baku, where Leopold and his wife took up teaching positions at the newly founded Azerbaijan Conservatoire.

According to family legend, when Sofiya discovered she was expecting another child, she wished to terminate the pregnancy. As Elena Rostropovich, Sofiya's granddaughter, explained, the family was poor, and as both parents worked, one small child was enough to cope with. A doctor friend prescribed various treatments, including some vigorous sporting activity, but they seemed to have the contrary effect. Indeed Sofia Nikolayevna carried her child for a ten-month term, and on 27 March 1927 she gave birth to a healthy boy.

Later her son Mstislav asked her, 'You had an extra month, couldn't you have given me a better face?' She answered philosophically, 'My son, I was more concerned with your hands . . . '*

The young Mstislav (Slava or Slavka) seemed destined for the cello; his earliest photograph shows him as a tiny infant lying in his father's cello case, which served as his cot. Already as a toddler Slava was fascinated by music, and as soon as he could walk, he would seize a stick and broom to imitate the gestures of his father playing the cello. Later he liked to joke that his first contact with the cello was through the 'music of silence'.

Soon he was able to pick out tunes on the piano. At the age of four, young Slava wrote his first compositions, which included a Polka and a March. As his mother recalled, even as a very young boy her son was always going over to the piano to try out some piece of music, or running to pick up the cello. 'He lived his life through sound.'†

In 1931 Leopold and Sofiya Rostropovich decided to leave Baku and go to the Soviet capital for the sake of their children's education. The family arrived in Moscow with no arrangements made, and no jobs to go to. Leopold's brother-in-law Semyon Kozolupov had advised against the move, and did nothing to help Leopold find a teaching position in Moscow. Though the two cellists were outwardly friendly, their relationship was now shadowed by a rivalry in which Kozolupov always managed to occupy the dominant position.

There was one respect, however, in which Kozolupov envied his brother-in-law. Semyon's three daughters were all gifted musicians, destined to become excellent professionals, but it was evident that Leopold's son Slava was outstandingly talented. Kozolupov could not forgive Leopold for teaching the young Slava himself, and liked to predict that no good would come of this arrangement.

On arrival in Moscow, Leopold initially found work at the Radio committee, but finding accommodation proved more problematic. Family legend recounts that Leopold stood in the middle of the street near the Conservatoire, holding his young son by the hand and accosting passers-by. He pleaded for help, explaining that the family had nowhere to live and that his outstandingly talented young boy needed a musical education. Amazingly enough, an Armenian woman

---

* Ibid. p. 14.
† From TV documentary on Rostropovich made in the Soviet Union in 1968.

named Zinaida Cherchopova was touched by his appeal and took the family in. They lived for nearly a year in a tiny dark room in her communal apartment in Maly Gneznikovsky Tupìk – today the room has been declared uninhabitable and is used as a store cupboard.

The family then moved to no. 2 Kozitskij Pereulok where they occupied a single, dark room. Slava slept on a camp-bed under the Becker grand piano. One day the kind-hearted lift lady informed them that two rooms had become vacant in a communal flat in no. 3 Nemirovich-Danchenko Street – this became the family home until the mid-1950s.

Soon Leopold found a position teaching at the renowned Gnesins' Musical High School, where at the age of eight, the young Slava began his official cello studies with his father. Rostropovich recalls that like many children he was not very fond of practising, but he quickly learnt the advantages of being a good actor. If his parents were out on errands, Slava would stand at the window, waiting for their return. As soon as he saw them approaching, he would run to the cello so that his parents would find him totally immersed in his practice. Naturally his mother would pity the lad: 'My poor boy, you must be tired out. Take a rest now!'

Veronika, Slava's sister, played the violin, but was less committed to music than her younger brother. Their mother would reward the children for a good practice session with a sweet. The young Slava (who had – and has to this day – a sweet tooth) quickly saw how to turn his sister's reluctance to their mutual advantage. Veronika recalled placing her sweet on a chair and saying, 'Slava, half an hour's practice for me and the sweet is yours.' Placing her violin in the upright position of a cello, he 'practised' on it while Veronika played with her dolls under the piano. Sofiya Nikolayevna, listening in the kitchen, was quite taken in.

Slava worshipped his father, and his cello lessons were the high point of his week. Leopold discouraged the idea of routine practice, preferring to develop an imaginative approach to the music, a method that suited Slava. He quickly learned to focus his attention on the musical result, which became inseparable for him from the technical aspects of playing.

Tatyana Gaidomovich, an older pupil of Leopold, also appreciated his inspirational style of teaching. A late starter by Russian standards, the thirteen-year-old Tatyana enrolled at the Gnesins' Institute, where she was advised by Elena Gnesina that it was too late to take up the piano. The cello was suggested as an alternative, and Gnesina dangled a carrot in the form of a brilliant teacher who had recently joined the teaching staff. Leopold Rostropovich agreed to take on the aspiring beginner.

As Gaidomovich recalls:

Leopold Witoldovich was a wonderful person, a combination of a man of his times and a character straight out of a Hoffmann story, with his romantic features and almost Mephistophelean piercing look. [He] was just forty, but he looked much older, whether because of the grey colour of his sparse hair or the deeply etched lines of his expressive face. But he exuded a kind of timeless wisdom, which was in contrast to the Hoffmannesque features, the hidden sorrow of his dark eyes and the ironic fold of his sharply drawn lips. A slight limp did not impede his fast-moving walk.

At our first meeting Leopold Witoldovich questioned me closely. No doubt in my replies he sensed my enormous desire to become involved in music. He promised to take me on and to help find me a cello . . . Then another unexpected thing happened, he sat down at the piano and out poured a cascade of notes, Rachmaninov's C sharp minor prelude, which I knew and loved as my father played it at home.

Leopold Witoldovich hated methodical routine in teaching, and could freely switch from cello to piano during the lesson if he needed to demonstrate a musical point. Sometimes he would sit down and say, 'Enough of the cello for the moment, let me play for you,' and he would perform at the piano a Rachmaninov or Tchaikovsky concerto with enormous artistry and flair.

In class Leopold Witoldovich would reveal his ideas through the rich world of imagery, narrating them with such vividness that even the most indifferent listener or pupil was touched.

Other times after these volcanic outbursts he would distance himself from his pupils. Listening to our playing, making the essential observations, we sensed that our teacher's thoughts were far removed from his real surroundings. On the surface there were few signs of that seething seismic process which convulsed this artist's inner world.[*]

Gaidomovich first met Slava at the Gnesins' Institute and remembered him as

. . . a very pale, thin seven-year-old boy, with marvellous lovely dancing eyes, long spider-like hands and thin legs. The family lived in very poor circumstances. Slava's mother, Sofiya Nikolayevna, was a very sociable, patient and long-suffering Russian woman, who carried the whole household on her shoulders. She had to put up with the passions and stormy outbursts of her husband, and devoted her time to bringing up her children. She herself was a good pianist and sometimes accompanied her husband.[†]

---

[*] T. Gaidomovich, *The Unforgettable*, p. 192–3.
[†] Ibid.

Though Leopold Rostropovich was clearly adored by his family, he was reputed to have a difficult and fiery temper, which was perhaps exacerbated by frustration at not receiving the recognition he deserved as a performer. His family resented Kozolupov, who despite being head of the Conservatoire cello faculty did nothing to help Leopold find a teaching position. Kozolupov seems to have admitted to his sister-in-law, Sofiya Nikolayevna, that he recognised Leopold's greater talent and therefore would not tolerate his presence on the Conservatoire staff.

In terms of character, if not musical ability, Leopold was the weaker of the two men, and tried to avoid conflict with his elder colleague and relative. As Gaidomovich observed:

Despite their being related, or even in some strange way because of this, there was a definite, unspoken rivalry between Leopold Rostropovich and Semyon Kozolupov, who was the undisputed leader of the Moscow school. Kozolupov's authoritative character demanded submission and obedience, and was propelled by great energy and a need for constant activity.

Leopold Witoldovich was of a more nervous disposition, and in certain ways he was an unstable personality. There was an excessively passive side to his nature which was unable to withstand competition.*

Events bear out this interpretation, for after eighteen months teaching at the Gnesins' Institute, Leopold was forced to make way for a protégé of Kozolupov after a dispute with one of the school directors, Elena Fabianovna Gnesina. In 1937, he transferred his main teaching activity to the Sverdlovsk District Music School, which was located on Pushkin Square in the city centre, and Slava followed in order to remain in his father's cello class. At this stage he was making remarkably quick progress; as for the piano, he seemed to pick it up without even bothering about lessons, and his interest in composition was also growing.

Now that Slava had reached the age of ten, Leopold decided to send him for composition lessons with Evgeny Messner at the Conservatoire Uchilishche. Slava's fellow students included Boris Chaikovsky, Kirill Molchanov, Karen Khatchaturian and Evgeny Chugaev. Messner, a pupil of Vissarion Shebalin, was a remarkable teacher of children, who encouraged his pupils to learn through example. In his class they read through numerous scores of different genres and styles: Slava proved unusually quick to assimilate and memorise the music, and his

* Ibid.

phenomenal memory training started here. In 1939 Messner presented the young Rostropovich to Shebalin, who examined the boy's work in progress, a piano trio. Shebalin was greatly impressed by Slava's talent, and visited Leopold to discuss his future, as a result of which the families soon became friendly.

In fact, Slava could easily have become a composer, for when he was twelve, an accident nearly put an end to his cello-playing.

One day my mother made my favourite dish – a vinaigrette salad. Times were hard, and we lived poorly, so for me it was a real treat. She told me to go into our room and not touch anything on the table until she had finished preparing dinner in the kitchen. As we lived in a communal flat, eight other families shared the kitchen, which of course was the scene of daily domestic scandal.

I was so excited at the anticipation of this treat that I started dancing around the dining table. At a certain point I jumped on to the wooden stool which I used to practise on. The stool toppled over, I lost my balance and fell forwards on top of my right arm. I felt a terrible pain in the wrist, and cried out.

On hearing some shouts my mother thought nothing of it, assuming that it was just a normal 'communal flat' scandal. She didn't appear at once, but when she did she was horrified at what she saw. When I got up and disentangled my arms from under me, we saw that there was a break, since my right hand was clearly at a tangent with the rest of my arm. The ambulance was called, and at the hospital it was discovered that I had a double fracture of the wrist. I was operated on under general anaesthetic. When I came to, my forearm was under plaster.

The plaster was removed six weeks later, and I then discovered that I had lost the ability to rotate my wrist and forearm. My hand was turned away from my body and this meant I couldn't make the necessary forearm rotation to allow me to place the bow on the strings. It looked very bad, and it seemed that I might never play the cello again.

A second operation was suggested, but my father wouldn't allow it, as he thought it too risky. Bathing the hand and forearm in hot water was suggested. A little wooden trough was made for this purpose out of an old fruit box lined with oilskin. I discovered that I got relief from these immersions, and continued them three or four times a day for the next six months. Gradually I won back this rotating movement millimetre by millimetre.

In the mean time I got on with my composition studies at the Conservatoire high school. I remember writing some rather good pieces for violin and left-hand piano which I could perform.

Six months later I managed at last to put the bow on the string, even if it was at a fairly odd angle. I have never thought about this, but it might be true to say that this fracture affected my bow position, which always had a hint of outward rotation in it, with the elbow somewhat lowered. It's true to say that as I have long arms, this also makes it natural for me to keep the elbow low.

All in all, this experience was a great lesson to me in life-manship. I realised that it was my intense unflagging desire to play the cello which gave me such dogged determination. Without this desire I would have had to become a composer I suppose!

Slava was quick to recover lost time. By the age of thirteen he had regained such a high standard on the cello that Leopold decided he should complete the cello course ahead of time. Rostropovich recalls: 'When I did my final exams on the cello at the music school in 1940, the commission was very complimentary. One of the teachers, Bezrodny, came up to my father and said, "If it would make all our pupils play as well as your son, perhaps we should consider breaking their wrists too!"'

During the summers Leopold would take his family for holidays to the Ukraïne, leaving the hot dusty city behind:

Father took on work as leader of the cello section in various orchestras for the holiday season. For instance he played in the thermal resort of Slavyansk, where the orchestra played in the park, and he also worked in similar summer seasons in Zaporozhets. Father took me to all the orchestra rehearsals, and I sat in the pit, spellbound, watching and listening. It was then that I dreamed of becoming a conductor.

At Slavyansk I got to know the conductor, A. Stupel, a very kind man who explained the mysteries of orchestral scores to me, showing me how the various instruments of the orchestra were notated, and explaining the system of transposing instruments.

When I spoke to my father about my wish to conduct, he was very strict with me and told me that before becoming a conductor I had first to make a career as an instrumentalist. That was the only way to earn the right to stand on the podium. 'If they know you are an excellent instrumentalist, the orchestral musicians will have a different attitude towards you,' he insisted, 'and they will give you their trust.'

He was absolutely right, and in this way he was able to map out the right path for me. In fact I didn't conduct professionally until 1962, but by that time I had more than twenty years of concert experience as a cellist behind me.

It was at Slavyansk in the summer of 1940 that the thirteen-year-old Mstislav Rostropovich made his professional debut, playing the Saint-Saëns concerto under Stupel's direction in an outdoor concert.

The following year Slava completed his school studies, having finished the five-year course in the space of three years. In the mean time he had been attending the Central Music School (known in Russian by its acronym 'TseMSha') which had recently opened to train exceptionally talented children. Here Slava only studied academic subjects such as literature, maths and geography, while his sister Veronika enrolled as a violin student.

Mstislav was now making such rapid progress that no one had any doubts that he had the makings of a soloist. Leopold deserves credit for fostering a balanced musical education which placed equal emphasis on technique and a wide general musical knowledge.

One of Leopold's favourite exercises to test his own technical mastery of the cello was making transcriptions from the virtuoso piano repertoire, including some of Chopin's Etudes. To please his father, Slava attempted to learn the most difficult of these transcriptions, of the G flat study in octaves, Op. 25, no. 9. He claims that he never matched his father's brilliance in this piece.

Leopold's talents as a pianist were equally prodigious. Once, when Slava declared that he wished to compose a piano concerto, his father brought home the scores of some of the best-known Russian concertos, including Tchaikovsky's first, the Rimsky-Korsakov and Rachmaninov's third. Leopold then proceeded to read through them at the piano, amazing his son by his instant capacity to absorb and transmit the music, even if he was sight-reading.

Everyday life was radically affected by the outbreak of war and the German invasion of Soviet territory in June 1941. As Nazi troops marched rapidly towards the capital in the early autumn, arrangements were made for Muscovite institutions and civilian families to be sent to safety further east. At the end of the summer of 1941 Slava had been enrolled at the Ippolitov-Ivanov Musical Uchilishche in Moscow in order to continue his cello studies with his father, but these plans had now to be abandoned:

When the war broke out I was evacuated to Penza with the students of TseMSha. Then my parents wrote saying that they too were being evacuated and would pick me and my sister up on the way to Orienburg, where our family was to make our temporary home – in those days the town was called Chkalov, after the famous pilot. My sister and I went down to the station in Penza on the appointed day. It was an anxious moment for us, as there were many echelons travelling east, taking people to evacuation. They travelled in cattle trucks, with no windows, just vents to allow the air in. We had no idea which train my parents would be on, and trains kept on arriving and departing. I told Veronika to sit and guard our suitcases while I started searching for them. I ran up and down the platforms, asking which trains had come from Moscow, and searching all the carriages and trucks. People were coming and going, and there was a feeling of total chaos. This went on for several hours; my sister and I were in despair, we were losing all hope of finding our parents. After about twelve hours, while running down the tracks, I suddenly caught a glimpse of my parents standing in the doorway of one of the cattle trucks. We had the most joyful reunion.

The Rostropoviches had chosen Orienburg for their evacuation because they had friends and family there: most importantly, Slava's godmother, Elena Londkevich. She had met Leopold and Sofiya during their courting days in Orienburg; indeed, she was reputed to have been in love with Leopold herself, but when he married Sofiya she magnanimously transferred her affections to his whole family. Now she generously provided a room in her apartment for the family's use, and her kindness greatly eased their difficulties, as Slava recalls: 'She was like a fairy godmother to our whole family, and she encouraged my music-making. Her brother had a rather nice baritone voice, and sang romances. I liked accompanying him on the piano. For instance I remember playing Schumann's "Ich grolle nicht". This served as a stimulus for me, and I learnt to accompany songs in this way.'

Once they had settled in, the Rostropovich children had to get on with their education. Slava attended the 'Second Railway School' for his general education, while studying cello with his father at the Orienburg Musical Uchilishche:

I had had to leave my cello behind in Moscow, so the music school found an old instrument for me in their store room. It had the number '8' painted on it in blue. It was so sturdily built that one could safely sit down on it, which came in handy on train journeys when all the seats were taken. Whenever I wanted to rest, I laid the cello on its side, and sat down on the ribs, near the instrument's shoulder, or else I would squeeze my backside into the carved dip near the F-holes.

One of the best-thought-out strategies of the Soviet civilian evacuation system was to allocate specific towns with one or more important artistic, scientific or educational institutions. This allowed the collective concerned to continue its professional activity, as well as benefiting the host town. In this way, the Leningrad Philharmonic Orchestra was billeted in Novosibirsk, the Bolshoi Theatre in Kuibishev, while the Leningrad Maly Theatre (Malegot) had its temporary home in Orienburg. The Maly's conductors included Boris Khaikin and the young Kirill Kondrashin, and the composers Ivan Dzerzhinsky, Solovyov-Sedoy and Mikhail Chulaki were also attached to the company. This also provided Leopold with the opportunity of chamber music, and soon he formed a piano trio with the pianist Sofiya Vackman and a violinist (S. Gitter) from the Maly Theatre orchestra. They found a job playing at the local 'Molot' cinema, entertaining audiences before the shows.

The impressionable Slava soon fell in love with Vackman:

Sofiya Borisovna was married and some fifteen years older than I was. She would come to our small room to rehearse the trios which they played at the beginning of the film showings. After I finished school I ran along to the cinema, to listen to the trio's performances.

It was incredibly cold in winter, the door would open and close, icy winds howled, and the snow was literally blown through the doors. In fact this is probably the reason why Father fell ill, as he inevitably caught cold. They sat there playing, wearing dark felt boots, coats and gloves and trying not to freeze. Wartime conditions were incredibly hard, there was no food to be had.

I was so taken with Sofiya Vackman that I would try and save her some of my biscuits which I received from a special ration given to schoolchildren. I would surreptitiously transfer the biscuits into her handbag when she wasn't looking.

However, I got very distressed that the public did not always react favourably to my father's trio, probably because the repertoire they played was above the heads of the audiences. I decided that if they were to achieve success then they needed to play pieces that people would enjoy. So I made my first transcriptions for piano trio of popular pieces, like Dunaevsky's march 'Vesyoliye Rebyata' ('The Jolly Lads') and Strauss waltzes. I brought these arrangements to one of the rehearsals, and the trio played them. The audience was delighted, and to my delight I gained the attention of Sofiya Borisovna, who gave me a winning smile.

In April 1942 the fifteen-year-old Slava played in a concert dedicated to works by Soviet composers, appearing in the triple capacity of cellist, pianist and composer. He himself performed his 'Poème' for cello and a 'Prelude' for piano, while his father performed the first movement of his cello concerto, which Slava accompanied at the piano. In a review of the concert by R. Gezler it was noted, 'The three works by Slava Rostropovich are testimony of his great gift for melody, his astute and sensitive use of harmony, and an unerring sense of musical taste. In addition he won over his listeners with his considerable gifts as a performer.'* This was a proud occasion for the

---

* L. Ginsburg, *Mstislav Rostropovich*, p. 7.

Rostropovich family, and the first and last time that Leopold and Slava appeared on stage together:

When my father became ill in the spring of 1942 I took his place teaching at the uschilishe. This position was made official after his death, something that I only discovered recently, when I was shown a document found at the Orienburg Music High School stating that 'Slavka Rostropovich' would replace Leopold. Many of the students were actually older than I was, but already by then I was undoubtedly the best cellist in Orienburg. I was paid by the hour.

I was terribly shaken by my father's death, and I myself fell ill for quite some time. I emerged from this experience as a man shouldering responsibility for the family.

It had been Sofiya Vackman who introduced Slava to the artists of the Maly Theatre, with whom he participated in collective concerts. Vackman agreed to accompany him as well as the singers: 'In between the singers' arias I would play short pieces on the cello (Tchaikovsky's "Sentimental Waltz", Rimsky-Korsakov's "The Flight of the Bumble Bee", and so on). I was paid seventy roubles for each concert. Ten concerts, and I had earned a kilogram of butter, that was the relationship of my earnings in those difficult wartime conditions.' On one legendary occasion, the fifteen-year-old boy, who looked younger than his years, was so warmly applauded that he decided to play an encore. Picking up the nearest piece of music at hand, an arrangement of a piece for violin and piano, Slava placed it on his stand, and stood up to announce its title: '"Torments of Love" by Fritz Kreisler.' The incongruity of these words from a young boy's lips reduced the audience to unrestrained hilarity.

In 1943 Rostropovich was given the opportunity to appear as soloist with the Malegot orchestra performing Tchaikovsky's *Rococo Variations*. In retrospect he judged his performance as not wholly successful: 'I wasn't ready or technically prepared at the time for this work, and later I was forced to rethink my whole approach to it.' Perhaps of even more importance to his formation, though, was the opportunity of seeing opera, for which he developed a passion. The Malegot opera company was one of the most interesting in the country, and had staged Shostakovich's operas *The Nose* and *Lady Macbeth of the Mtsensk District*.

The composer Mikhail Chulaki was the director of Malegot during this period, and was working on his ballet *The Priest and his Workman Balda*, based on Pushkin. Chulaki played a considerable role in Rostropovich's life after his father's death, giving him free composition lessons: Slava composed his first piano concerto under Chulaki's tuition. But the young Rostropovich had to combine study with work, for now he was the family's principal breadwinner:

Money was very tight, and I earned by teaching and playing. My godmother, Elena Londkevich, also helped our family materially. Soon I acquired some carpentry skills, and I started to make small oil lamps from cylindrical glass test tubes. We sold the lamps at the market. But most of the income I earned through playing in collective concerts in factories and smaller towns of the area.

It was on the journey to Orsk that Slava had received some unsolicited help, while part of a 'concert brigade' of artists from the Malegot:

It was bitterly cold, and trains in wartime had no form of heating. It was a long overnight journey, and each of us was handed out a light blanket. When the train started moving, all the lights were turned off, and we lay down on our bunks in all our clothing (mine was threadbare and miserable). I huddled under my blanket, but it had no noticeable effect on my frozen limbs. The temperature was dropping, and I fell into a numbed sleep, where my mind wandered and I thought I would never wake up again. Some hours later I came to because I was feeling hot, and weighed down by layers of covers. I realised then that each of the artists in the compartment had donated his own blanket to provide the extra warmth needed for my survival. They realised it was a case of my need being greater than theirs. To this day I remember their names: Olga Golovina, the pianist Izya Rubanenko, Boris Geft, the tenor, and the dancers Kolya Sokolov and Sveta Sheyina (who were married to each other).

On arrival in Orsk, the artists were given a ration packet with provisions, a useful form of payment in those hungry times:

When I was given some extra rations I usually tried to save the best things to take home to our hungry families in Orienburg. This time in Orsk our packet included some sausages. However, I noticed that they were turning a strange colour, and mould was forming on the outside. My friend, Kolya Sokolov, and I decided the best thing was to sell them at the local market. He came up with a brilliant idea, and suggested washing off the mould, and I duly washed mine down with soap and water. We decided we were in this enterprise together, and we went down to the market and laid out our wares. It was only then that I noticed that his sausages were a different, much brighter colour: mine looked very unappealing next to his shiny ones. Kolya was very good-looking and charismatic, and he stood up and called out, 'And who would like some very appetising *hors d'oeuvres*?' Several ladies came up and pointed to the shiny sausages. 'We'll take those.' 'No, we are selling together or not at all!' When they asked why the sausages looked so different, he looked the ladies in the eye and said, 'Well you see, it's very simple. Mine are smoked sausages, and his are a half-smoked variety!' Once we had got our money, we left. I was a very insecure boy, and felt terribly upset, and almost started crying, thinking that I had been given an inferior variety of sausage. What did this mean, that I was less good than my friends? 'Listen, Kolya, just now you said we were given different kind of sausages? Is that true?' 'Nonsense, Slavka,' he said, 'I just rubbed mine down with Vaseline to make them look better!'

The experience of wartime hardships had a lasting effect on Rostropovich's personality. The way people rallied together in times of difficulty and helped each other provided an unforgettable lesson in life. As Rostropovich has affirmed, 'The kindness I was shown in those years has remained at the base of my great faith in people's goodness.' During the two years spent in Orienburg, Rostropovich's life had changed radically. It was here that he started his professional life as a musician – and 'became a man', taking on complete responsibility for his family.

Orienburg also provided Rostropovich with lifelong friends – including his composition teacher, Mikhail Chulaki, who showed him great kindness:

Chulaki was like a second father in a way, he always kept an eye on me and quietly took note of my family's needs. He believed in my talent and without informing my family he wrote to Shebalin about me. This was instrumental in procuring me a stipend from the Moscow Conservatoire, even before I became a student there. It was worth five hundred roubles a month. It is true that this wasn't much money, not enough even to buy a kilogram of butter.

It was also Chulaki who facilitated our return to Moscow, for it was still forbidden to return to the capital, except under exceptional circumstances.

If Chulaki had become a surrogate father to Rostropovich, Elena Londkevich effectively became a second mother to the boy, sending him a further five hundred roubles each month to Moscow: it was, she told him, 'a scholarship in his father's name'.

2

Studies at the Moscow Conservatoire

By the beginning of 1943, the course of the war had changed, and Soviet troops were now beginning to win back German-occupied territory. Educational institutions in Moscow gradually started to reopen – among them the Conservatoire, with Vissarion Shebalin as its new director.

Thanks to Chulaki's intervention, Rostropovich had been allowed to leave Chkalov (Orienburg) for Moscow: 'I left on 26 April 1943. Trains travelled so slowly at the time that the journey to Moscow took ten days. I arrived on 6 May, and a week later, on 13 May, I took my entry examination for the Moscow Conservatoire. I was accepted as a student in two faculties.' Life in Moscow was an enormous contrast for the young Slava:

After Orienburg, where life was lived on the streets, wounded soldiers abounded and I ran between school and the market, Moscow seemed a picture of gloom. In the evenings the curfew was still observed, windows were closed and the streets unlit. Everything was dark and murky. But during the day throughout Moscow loudspeakers on the streets blared forth piano music, preludes and mazurkas by Chopin, Rachmaninov preludes and Tchaikovsky's *The Seasons*. It was real romantic classical music. It was a way of keeping morale high, and this background of great-quality music added a special spiritual atmosphere to the city.

Rostropovich's official invitation to apply for the Conservatoire, the necessary formality permitting him to return to Moscow, had come from his uncle, Semyon Kozolupov, though Mstislav was initially unenthusiastic about the idea of studying with him:

At one point I had thought of going to study with Aleksandr Shtrimer [Daniil Shafran's teacher] in Leningrad. But in the spring of 1943 Leningrad was still under siege, and its Conservatoire was operating in evacuation in Tashkent. The deciding factor for me was the note my father had left us to read after his death.

He instructed us that under no circumstances were we to sell his cello or the piano, and that he wanted me to study in Moscow with Kozolupov. My family was longing to return to Moscow, and I could not go against my father's will.

In making his dying wishes so explicit, Leopold Rostropovich had shown greater wisdom on his family's behalf than he had demonstrated for himself. There were considerable advantages for Slava in being under the protection of his uncle, the most influential cello teacher in the country. The balance of musical power had shifted since Leopold's own student days: now Moscow rather than Leningrad offered the best opportunities for a thorough training. Moreover, Semyon Matveevich Kozolupov had built a reputation as an excellent and thorough teacher. His pupils found him to be a kind, well-meaning man, albeit rough and ready, in true Cossack style. Though he did not possess the wide cultural background of Leopold Rostropovich, he was dedicated to his students, and went out of his way to help them professionally.

Kozolupov methodically built up his students' technique until they achieved complete mastery of the instrument. Galina Kozolupova, Semyon Matveevich's second daughter and one of his best pupils, recalled that her father believed in developing virtuosity by setting progressively more difficult tasks, ranging from the simplest exercises to pieces of the greatest complexity. Kozolupov's compilation of cello études by a variety of cellist-composers from Duport to Franchomme, from Dotzauer to Servais, became the standard bible of Soviet cello students – it was still in use during the 1960s and 1970s when I studied in Moscow.

Among Kozolupov's students was the future cellist of the Borodin Quartet, Valentin Berlinsky. He had first met Rostropovich in May 1938 at a concert in the Hall of Columns, where a selection of the best pupils from twenty-six Moscow musical schools performed: 'I was then thirteen years old and was studying at the Krasnogvardeiskiy district music school with Kozolupov's assistant, Efim Gendlin. Slava was two years younger than me, but he was already noted for his talent. At that concert we both performed two pieces.'* The two cellists encountered each other again after enrolling in Kozolupov's class in September 1943. Berlinsky characterised Kozolupov as a forceful but immensely charming personality, whose pupils learnt a lot simply from observing him play:

---

* Rostropovich played Bach's 'Arioso' and 'Georgian Dance' by Aivazian.

Semyon Matveevich had the most wonderful hands for the cello. His right-hand technique in particular was incredible; his bow changes were so perfectly smooth that they were completely inaudible, as if he had a limitless length of bow. Yet I would define the greatest feature of Kozolupov's teaching as his immediate ability to see and understand each student's individuality. Thus he was democratic in his approach and didn't force his pupils to play in one particular way. He even encouraged them to go to other teachers for the odd lesson, although by this he intended they go to ex-pupils like his daughter Galina or Sviatoslav Knushevitsky. *

Berlinsky recalls that Kozolupov could also be an obstinate and pedantic teacher.

Kozolupov's conviction that his way of doing things was the only correct one was unshakeable. For instance, in his edition of the Bach suites, one can see his interpretation clearly laid out. He believed the suites should be played only in this way. When one phrased the music somewhat differently or changed the bowings, he would ask 'Why?' To me this was useful as I learnt to defend my views.

But I remember Slava disagreed with me: 'You just try and play to him with different bowings.' In fact I brought Bach's second suite to a lesson with my own bowings, and in this instance Semyon Matveevich let them stand. But when I took the Sarabande of the third suite to a lesson and played the repeat with no vibrato, he put his foot down, and told me categorically that one could not play without vibrato.†

Kozolupov transmitted to his students a strong bow technique, with an immense variety of bow strokes. Great attention was paid to developing the upper part of the bow, often a weak point for cellists. He insisted on using the natural weight of the arm and shoulder, allowing the cellist to remain free while still being able to employ force, at the point of the bow in particular. Kozolupov taught that the basis of all bow technique was a well-rounded *détaché* stroke, to be played on the string in the upper half of the bow.

As regards left-hand technique, he encouraged great flexibility, but first and foremost insisted on precise intonation. Thus certain techniques like left-hand extensions could only be approached once a pupil had secured perfect intonation. Vibrato, however, was considered an essential part of musical expression.

The Kozolupov school was characterised by smooth, expressive phrasing, and an insistence on a beautiful *cantilena* tone. This emphasis on *legato* and *cantabile* suited certain types of repertoire better than

* In interview with E.W., Moscow 2004.
† Ibid.

others, the 'romantics' in particular. But the long seamless lines Kozolupov advocated in the Bach suites, for instance, went against the dance- and speech-like articulation that is implicit in the music, and which lay at the basis of Casals's interpretation. One could argue that the Kozolupov tradition ultimately became a considerable handicap in performing Bach, particularly once it had become frayed through years of thoughtless repetition. Even in the 1970s, the period of the 'early music revival' in the West, the approach to baroque cello style taught in the Soviet conservatoires remained rigidly rooted in Kozolupov's understanding of Bach, which by this stage seemed hopelessly outdated.

Rostropovich, meanwhile, had radically rethought his Bach interpretation in the early 1950s when he first performed the complete cycle of solo suites. One might define his approach as a striving for a large-scale cosmic quality on the one hand and greater intimacy and dance-like charm on the other. His views on Bach were based on a philosophical understanding of the world, which he in turn transmitted to his students.

Notwithstanding its limitations, several generations of fine Soviet cellists came out of the Kozolupov stable, including such excellent performers as Sviatoslav Knushevitsky, Grigori Feigin, Fyodor Luzanov and Natalya Shakhovskaya. This impressive list may be supplemented with the names of the composers Aram Khatchaturian and Sulkhan Tsintsadze, who both studied cello with Kozolupov, something that is noticeable in the consummate ease with which they wrote for string instruments.

Although Mstislav Rostropovich was to become the most famous of Kozolupov's students, he was not a typical product of his class. Even during his student years, he questioned the principles that Kozolupov transmitted. His alert, enquiring mind found Kozolupov's methods to be too narrowly focused on instrumental concerns, and the standard cello repertoire was not enough to sustain his musical interest:

Practically speaking I did not study music in Kozolupov's class. He was undoubtedly a wonderful specialist, but he lived through his intuition. I am of course extremely grateful for what I gained from him, for he knew how to teach the art of cello-playing quite marvellously. But he was not a great musician. For instance Prokofiev's music was beyond him. He would react to it intuitively, saying perhaps to a student, 'What you played just now is very boring, so do something about it.' But he had no idea how to approach a new work.

Rostropovich looked instead to his composition teachers for musical stimulation. He counted himself fortunate to be a pupil of Vissarion Shebalin, who had himself studied with the so-called patriarch of Russian twentieth-century music, Nikolay Myaskovsky. Towards the end of 1942, Shebalin was called back from evacuation and appointed director of the Moscow Conservatoire, a position for which he was eminently suited. His great moral integrity was as much respected as his consummate skill in teaching composition. While his approach was based on Russian classical tradition, Shebalin sought to foster the individuality of each student, as a result of which they evolved very differently: Tikhon Khrennikov and Edison Denisov were both devoted students of Shebalin, yet in both style and aesthetic they represented opposite polarities of Soviet music. Shebalin was totally dedicated to the Conservatoire, and spent his energy not only in raising the level of student achievement, but in finding funds to repair the building, in encouraging concert activity and in attracting fresh staff.

Shebalin's greatest coup was to persuade Shostakovich to join the composition staff in 1943. Shortly after Rostropovich returned to Moscow from Orienburg, Kozolupov arranged for him to meet the great composer. The young Slava was enormously impressed by Shostakovich's impeccable manners and attention to people. Even today he cannot forget how, when he left his coat in the professors' cloakroom, Dmitri Dmitrievich would shake hands and greet by name every single one of the attendants, most of whom were toothless old ladies, and the students sitting on the benches between the different floors met with similar attention. It was with some trepidation, nonetheless, that Rostropovich showed his first piano concerto to Dmitri Dmitrievich: he played it through at an enormously fast speed to hide his embarrassment at its somewhat 'sub-Rachmaninov' style. Shostakovich, however, was impressed, showering Slava with compliments and willingly accepting him in his orchestration class.*

Shostakovich's lessons were the high point of Rostropovich's weekly Conservatoire routine:

I would go to Kozolupov for my cello lesson every Thursday morning sharp at nine o'clock. Then straight afterwards, I rushed up to Class 35 for my orchestration lesson with Shostakovich. The night before I was always busy doing my

---

* E. Wilson, *Shostakovich: A Life Remembered*, p. 215.

homework, often finishing only in the small hours of the night. This meant that sometimes when I played for Kozolupov I was over-tired and did not do my best. I remember how he would sit in the corner of the classroom and listen to his students. Once, when I muddled some fingering, he stared at me and shouted, 'Uncle, just get those spaghetti fingers of yours organised!' He used to call me Uncle, although of course I was his nephew!

Despite his diligence, in his first year Mstislav overlooked the fact that the Conservatoire course involved other disciplines such as harmony, music history and analysis, as well as the obligatory political curriculum:

At the end of my first year disaster struck. Kozolupov called our whole family down to his dacha, and solemnly announced to my mother, 'Your son has seven tails [*syem xvostov*]!' My mother had no idea what he meant, and replied indignantly, 'My son hasn't even got one tail, what are you talking about?' We did not know that a 'tail' meant a failed exam. At the end of each year, students had to take exams in every subject. If you flunked, you got a second chance. However, if you did not pass after retaking the exam a second time, you would be kept back a year, or even risk expulsion from the Conservatoire.

I had somehow failed to realise that these exams were obligatory and I simply had not prepared at all. I only realised how serious it was when I saw the tears welling up in my mother's eyes. With a feeling of shame I reached out for a bottle on my uncle's table; it turned out to be some homemade blackcurrant liqueur. Surreptitiously I drank the whole bottle. I then started feeling very sick, and went out into the garden where I passed out on a bench. Every now and then I would come to because I had to throw up. Then my sister Veronika, who was sitting beside me to keep an eye on me, rebuked me in no uncertain terms: 'You're going to die, you fool.' Then I would sink back into semi-consciousness until another bout of nausea woke me to the accompaniment of my sister's threats. That was my first experience of alcohol.

Afterwards I decided to work doubly hard, and I then started my life pattern of working through the night and in the early morning, training myself to need only three or four hours' sleep in the twenty-four hours of day and night.

In the autumn I disposed of all my 'tails', passing all the outstanding exams.

Rostropovich's new work regime brought immediate results. Berlinsky remembers that the general view that Mstislav's phenomenal talent and capacity for disciplined work destined him for greatness:

Slava stood out from the rest of the students because of his incredible gifts and exuberant nature. He was unlike anybody else and very independent in everything he did. When Slava played, it was as if the cello submitted to him and not the other way round. His whole posture, sound production, the way he held the bow and even his left-hand technique were completely individual.

Kozolupov did not interfere with any of this, since he knew it would be hopeless even to try.

Nevertheless, Rostropovich was ready to modify his ideas when necessary and apply Kozolupov's principles, especially when returning to works he had played previously: 'For instance, when I studied Tchaikovsky's *Rococo Variations* at the Conservatoire I was forced to rethink my right-hand technique, which in the mean time had developed along certain lines. It took me a lot of time and I underwent considerable difficulty, having to relearn the work on completely new technical grounds.'

Rostropovich had a voracious appetite for new repertoire: in his second year as a student (during which he managed to complete three years of the five-year course) Mstislav tackled concertos by Dvořák, Schumann and Glazunov and most of the sonata repertoire, as well as Bach's solo suites. When Kozolupov set him the fifth suite, one of the pinnacles of the canon, he mastered it completely within six weeks.

It was around this time that the young Rostropovich made his first attempt to enrich the virtuoso cello repertoire, when he composed his *Humoresque* Op. 5 for Kozolupov. The piece was a study of fast spiccato technique, somewhat reminiscent of Popper's *Elfentanz* and Davydov's *At the Fountain*, and an appropriate offering for his teacher.

It happened that I saw my fellow students were collecting money to buy flowers. I asked them whom they were to be presented to. 'Oh, they're for Kozolupov's birthday tomorrow.' I had completely forgotten about this date, and felt upset not to be contributing. So I went home and decided to compose a piece for him. I wrote and learnt the *Humoresque* that same night, and performed it – from memory – for Semyon Matveevich in class the next day.

With its innovative harmonic language and its witty and brilliant use of the cello, the *Humoresque* was a wonderfully effective concert piece which Rostropovich often played as an encore. It was published in the late 1960s, upon which many of his students added it to their repertoire.

Rostropovich's ambition to complete the Conservatoire course in three rather than five years involved an extremely busy programme of study. Exam results mattered, for a student's monthly scholarship money could be suspended if his marks were too low. As a recipient of the Stalin stipend, Mstislav was under pressure to do well in his exams, especially the obligatory political subjects that were the bane of every student's life:

I remember in particular my studies of the History of the Communist Party which I took in 1944. Despite the thirteen-year age gap between us, I was very friendly with Svyatoslav (Slava) Richter – my private nickname for him was 'Glasha'.* Because of the war and the facts of his biography, Richter was still a student at the time. He suggested that we studied for this exam together. He would come round to our flat and we set up our books, and took it in turns to read pages of text to each other. But we just could not stop yawning, and soon we realised we were getting nowhere. At a certain point I said to him, 'Listen, Glasha, I simply must pass this exam, it's better I study on my own.' But a few days later he phoned me: 'Slava, I have had a brilliant idea, I have invented an infallible method for studying Party History. Let me come round and explain.' His invention consisted in making me kneel on the floor opposite him. In front of us he placed the very large volume entitled 'A Short Course in the History of the Party' which every student had to know inside-out.† 'You see,' Glasha said, 'if we start to fall asleep, we'll fall forward straight onto the book and hit our faces. This way we'll be forced to stay awake!'

Each exam consisted of questions on a year's study programme. Questions were written down on strips of paper, usually thirty or so in all; on each strip (or ticket) there were two questions, which were drawn at random from a box. Students were required to give oral answers, and the examiner (or commission of examiners) could interrogate them or demand answers to additional questions.

Rostropovich recalls his method for passing his Party History exam:

My first question, on how the Party had helped the partisan movement in the war, was relatively easy, but the second question on the Second International presented me with a considerable problem. The examiner was the organist, Gedike; I think that Kozolupov had warned him that I needed to pass this exam, and asked him to be forbearing, as my stipend depended on my passing. I set off resolutely with my answer to the first question, recounting all I knew about the partisans. Then I noticed that Gedike's head started nodding, and soon he was dozing soundly. It occurred to me that if I showed off my knowledge on the partisan movement at length I could evade the second question altogether. I went on for some time, then suddenly in a very loud voice I shouted out, 'Without the help of the Communist Party the partisans would have achieved nothing. Our Communist Party leads us from one Victory to another!' At this Gedike woke up with a start, and to hide his shame he turned to me: 'You obviously know your stuff, let's give you a four.'‡

---

* Rostropovich also would refer to Richter by his patronymic 'Teofilovich'.
† Its author was reputedly Stalin.
‡ A four was a relatively good mark in this system, where marks ranged from one to five: two represented a failure and five excellence.

My cello exam was an easier matter. I remember that amongst other things I played Paganini's 'Moto Perpetuo', which made a great impression on the exam commission. As a result in the summer of 1944 I was promoted directly from the second to the fifth year.

This jump in level to the final year was an unprecedented occurrence at the Conservatoire. It testified not only to the exceptional artistic maturity and high standard of the seventeen-year-old cellist, but to his hard work and exceptional powers of concentration.

In his parallel studies in composition, Mstislav proceeded at the normal pace. Yet he was considered no less talented as a composer, and in his first year he was awarded the Tchaikovsky scholarship as the most promising composer of the cohort. The composition course involved intensive study of musical theory, orchestration, history, formal analysis, free composition and strict-style counterpoint. The Conservatoire boasted excellent teachers, and Rostropovich received instruction from the best specialists. In particular he was won over by his musical analysis teacher, V. A. Zuckerman: 'How wonderfully he transmitted this apparently dry-as-dust subject! Even now I remember his lessons! And when I perform a Bach suite, I refer back to Zuckerman's analysis of the phrase structures, his teaching of the importance of proportion and his definition of the Golden Mean as the culminative point of the architectonic structure.'*

Mstislav also studied piano and conducting. Although he had had no formal tuition, playing the piano came to him naturally, almost as an extension of his musical being. Now for the first time he took piano as a 'second study' with Nikolay Kuvshinnikov, a former Igumnov pupil.

Rostropovich strove to be on top of whatever subject engaged him at that moment. The notion of 'second study' was meaningless to him, and he wished only to be first in everything. In later years he would remain perplexed by students who did not foster similar ambitions. 'One must always do one's best in everything,' he would explain, adding: 'If I was a lift-boy, I would be the best lift-boy in the world.' Mstislav probably was the best 'second study' pianist of his year, for he could tackle the virtuoso piano repertoire with ease: at his diploma exam he performed no less a work than Rachmaninov's second concerto.

As conducting did not form part of his formal studies, Rostropovich took private lessons with the conductor Leo Ginsburg. For Slava, even

* Mikhail Spektor, *Mstislav Rostropovich*, pp. 20–21.

this was not enough, and he additionally studied the gestural, 'plastic' aspects of conducting with the wife of the composer A. Alexandrov. Chamber music and quartet classes, on the other hand, were part of the required curriculum. Rostropovich was allocated to the class of the brilliant quartet teacher Mikhail Terian, who put him into a young student quartet with Rostislav Dubinsky and Nina and Rudolf Barshai. As Valentin Berlinsky, his successor in this quartet, recounts:

Slava and I have an intriguing ongoing argument, for our memories differ as to how long he played in this student quartet. Slava recalls it as nearly a two-year period, but Rostik and I believed that Slava played in the quartet only for about three weeks. Certainly, according to documents in my possession, by 1944 I was the cellist of this group.

This student quartet started work on two quartets, which became our first reper-toire pieces: Handel's Passacaglia in the arrangement by Aslamazian and Tchaikovsky's first quartet. Then one day Slava brought me with him to a rehearsal at the Dmitrovka student hostel, and announced to his colleagues, 'I can't continue playing in the quartet, as I have so many other things to do just now. So Valka will be replacing me.'*

Thus it was that Valentin Berlinsky started playing in 'The String Quartet of Moscow Conservatoire Students', which achieved world-wide fame in later years as the Borodin Quartet – it celebrated its sixtieth anniversary in January 2005.

Despite his heavy schedule, Rostropovich found time to enjoy student life. Even if his family lived very poorly, they kept a hospitable hearth at their communal flat on no. 3 Nemirovich-Danchenko Street. Mstislav received a small sum every month from the Stalin stipend for talented students, and his godmother also sent him money. Cash was short, and money had little purchasing power during the hungry war years. In generous Russian fashion, it was normal to share whatever meagre supplies you had with friends. The composer Nickolay Karetnikov recalled how Slava would come round to his house, where his mother fed them on whatever she could lay hands on, often only potato peelings: Mstislav was often hungry, and would amaze his hosts with his voracious appetite.

Slava Rostropovich was the life and soul of student gatherings. Most people assumed that his nickname 'Podsolnukh' (sunflower) was given to him because of his irresistibly sunny nature, or what he

---

* In fact, Berlinsky had already played with Dubinsky as violist in a quartet at school, where the two violinists were Leonid Kogan and Julian Sitkovetsky. In interview with E.W., Moscow 2004.

himself defines as 'my striving towards light'. However, his sister Veronika recalled that the nickname derives from the way tufts of hair resisted combing and stuck up disobediently on the top of Slava's head, resembling the petals of a sunflower. But there was no more popular guest than Slava at a party, where he shone with his quick wit and constant good humour and liked to devise games and practical jokes. One of his best known 'party tricks' was to recite a numbered list of a hundred objects, which were noted down by the other guests on a piece of paper. Slava was allowed to glimpse the list only for a few seconds, but hours later he would astound his friends by reciting it in any order, backwards or forwards, or identifying any of the numbered items on it. Rostropovich's phenomenal memory for music had been evident from early childhood, but he deliberately enhanced his general memory (not least in order to perform this feat) by inventing a mnemonic system – unbeknown to him, it was very similar to the so-called 'Theatre of Memory' used in schools of rhetoric in classical Greece and Rome.*

Many of Rostropovich's legendary pranks were still being talked about when I studied at the Conservatoire during the late 1960s, including the tale of a New Year's fancy-dress ball at the house of Elena Bulgakova, the writer's widow. The two 'Slavas' – Richter and Rostropovich – chose to dress as crocodiles: crossing Moscow by taxi in their elaborate fancy dress in the small hours had proved an undertaking, but their reward was a handwritten certificate awarding them first prize for the most original costume. In intervals between lessons or after class concerts, Rostropovich would often regale his students with humorous accounts of his youth. For instance, he liked to tell of the time when he, his sister and a friend took a short holiday on a river boat down the Volga to Gorky (Nizhni Novgorod). They discovered that auditions were being held at the local conservatoire: Slava presented himself as an aspiring beginner-cellist, sitting with the bow in the wrong hand and playing scales in whole tones. The long, convoluted detail of this story always reduced his listeners to helpless laughter.

---

* In brief, the system consisted in having a stable architectural plan, whereby a series of objects or rooms had a permanent function or numeric value in the memory. The numbered objects on the list were placed in the right order according to the permanent fixed plan, and were to be retrieved later. Rostropovich explained, 'It was easy: if no. 7 is always a lamp, and no. 7 on the new list was a teapot, I would just put the teapot on the lamp, and then pick it up when I needed to.'

Rostropovich had a remarkable ability to focus his attention on the matter of the moment, observing small details and illuminating quirks of character – these qualities helped him to become an inspired raconteur.

He applied a similar approach to the process of learning new music, which allowed him to absorb it with enormous ease and rapidity. Even in his second year of Conservatoire studies, Mstislav dreamt of extending the conventional cello repertoire, and his training as a composer helped him to identify immediately with a new work:

Early in 1945 I attended the first performance of Nikolay Myaskovsky's concerto played by Sveta Knushevitsky, for whom it was written. I fell in love with the work, and decided to learn it for an internal Conservatoire competition for the best performance of a Soviet work. Kozolupov was initially not at all enthusiastic, but nevertheless he let me go ahead. I started rehearsing the concerto with his pianist daughter Irina (who was of course my cousin).* To begin with they all thought it was awful music, but gradually they were won round and admitted it was quite a good work. I won first prize at the competition performing this work.†

In the mean time the second All-Union competition for performers was announced: it would take place in December 1945. Because of the interruption of the war, there had been no such competition since 1937, when the cello class had been won by the fourteen-year-old Leningrad cellist Daniil Shafran, a pupil of Aleksandr Shtrimer: Shafran's filigree virtuosity and poetic appearance had caused something of a sensation. Kozolupov decided that several of his pupils should participate in the 1945 competition, including a senior student, Fyodor Luzanov, as well as the younger Berlinsky and Rostropovich.

As Valentin recalls:

Slava and I spent the summer of 1945 together, preparing for the All-Union competition. He came down to live in our dacha at Malakhovka, and occupied the top attic floor, while I had my room downstairs. This meant we could both get on with our practice. But we also had lots of fun. Often we would go and visit our friend, the violinist and composer Leonid Feigin, a pupil of Oistrakh. His father was a famous paediatrician, who rode his bicycle round the village, treating and curing all the local children. Amongst the company which gathered

---

* Kozolupov recalled that Mstislav learnt the concerto in three weeks.
† In April 1944, Myaskovsky had already noted the young cellist. He wrote in his diary, 'Concert of young performers. Rostropovich – very talented.' Sofiya Khentova, p. 37.

in his house was a pianist called Tamara Guseva. Slava was in love with her, and I was in love with another girl. Fortunately we were never competitors in affairs of the heart!

Slava didn't practise a lot, and he didn't need to. However, when he did decide to put in some practice he did so with enormous concentration. I remember him learning Bach's third suite and the Sarabande from the fifth during that summer. He worked in great detail and with painstaking attention.

The 1945 All-Union competition set out to be a special event, with three different categories: piano, violin and cello. The jury, which judged all three sections, reads like a *Who's Who* of Russian music, and included amongst its twenty-two members such illustrious names as David Oistrakh, Konstantin Igumnov, Vladimir Sofronitsky, Aleksandr Shtrimer, Semyon Kozolupov, Dmitri Tsyganov, Lev Oborin and Emil Gilels. Dmitri Shostakovich was appointed chairman of the jury. The upper age-limit for competitors was extended to thirty-two, allowing musicians whose studies had been disrupted by the war to participate. The beneficiaries of this concession included the thirty-one-year-old Sviatoslav Richter: many believed that the rules had been stretched so that he could take part. However, several other competitors had served at the Front, including the twenty-six-year-old Viktor Merzhanov.

Rostropovich decided that he would play Myaskovsky's concerto in the final round of the competition. His choice of a contemporary concerto was far from popular:

Some people assumed that I deliberately chose an 'unknown' modern work. I was accused of lacking the courage to be judged on a well-known concerto from the standard repertoire. After the competition I even had a visit from some discontented competitors who had been eliminated before the final round, including the violinist Lyonya Kogan. These young lads menaced me, and informed me that it wouldn't be safe for me to walk alone on the streets at night. They were indignant that I had 'befuddled the jury's brains' with Myaskovsky's work.

There was a nasty moment for me when during my performance of the concerto the conductor discovered to his horror that the pages of the score had been muddled. At one point he got completely lost, not knowing how to find the right page. Fortunately during the cadenza he managed to sort them out and reorder them. I tried to play slower to give him more time. At the time it looked like an act of sabotage; in any case it was an additional test of nerves which fortunately I managed to surmount.

It was by no means a foregone conclusion that Rostropovich would win the cello category. Berlinsky, who didn't make it to the finals himself, was amongst those who felt that Slava definitely deserved to win. But Kozolupov (who was also one of the jury members) was against awarding first prize to Rostropovich, believing it should go to his long-standing older student, Fyodor Luzanov.

As Rostropovich recalls, the situation was paradoxical:

Most people assumed that my uncle, Semyon Matveevich, influenced the outcome of the competition in my favour. However, if anything he wished to prevent me from winning. We found out about this and about Shostakovich's intervention in my favour through my mother, who frequently visited her elder sister, who was of course Kozolupov's wife. The two sisters liked to indulge in a good gossip and play cards. In this way, my mother picked up a lot of talk. On this occasion Kozolupov returned home straight from a sitting of the jury, looking very upset. He let slip to my mother, 'Your Slavka has grabbed the first prize, because Shostakovich overruled everybody, saying he was head and shoulders above the others. I think it's a mistake; Slavka can wait for a first prize, he's still young.' He added that Luzanov, who had studied with him 'from the roots', should have won the competition. Kozolupov made it clear that he had still not forgiven me for being at least in part a pupil of my father.

As chairman of the jury, Shostakovich had insisted not only that the first prize should go to Rostropovich, but furthermore that no second prize should be awarded. The difference in level between Slava and the other competitors was underlined, and Luzanov had to be content with third prize.

A similar result occurred in the piano category, where first prize was divided between Sviatoslav Richter and Viktor Merzhanov, and again no second prize was awarded. Rostropovich recalls that Richter was late for one of the rounds of the competition. The tension in the hall grew as the jury sat and waited. Finally, Richter appeared together with Prokofiev, and sat down to give an inspired rendering of the composer's eighth sonata. An even more extraordinary event occurred in the second round, as the lights in the hall went out just as it was Richter's turn to play. Candles were procured, and as Richter started to play one of Liszt's *Transcendental Studies* ('Wild Jagd') with phenomenal energy, the candle bounced and bobbed up and down on the piano as if it were alive, conjuring up an image of madness. Rostropovich vividly remembers the quite extraordinary atmosphere in the hall.

Although Richter went on to achieve recognition as one of the most significant pianists of the century, at the time Merzhanov was no less highly considered. He had recently returned from the Front, but managed to restore his pianism to the highest level. His performance of Rachmaninov's third concerto in the final was, by all accounts, outstanding. I remember hearing many heated discussions at the Conservatoire, more than twenty years after the event, about which of the two pianists had played best. While Richter's qualities were self-evident, Merzhanov's playing seemed to echo the wartime sufferings of the Russian people, for whom Rachmaninov's music symbolised nostalgia for a lost world.

In the violin section, meanwhile, no first or second prizes were awarded, and Julian Sitkovetsky won third prize.*

* Sitkovetsky later won first prize at the Queen Elizabeth Competition in Brussels. He married the wonderful pianist Bella Davydovich, but died tragically young. Their son Dmitri has become an outstanding violinist in his own right.

3

The start of a performing career

At the age of only eighteen, Rostropovich was set to begin an illustrious performing career. As an immediate result of his first prize at the All-Union Competition, he was taken on as a soloist by the Moscow Philharmonia. This organisation lay at the top of the pyramid of state agencies responsible for providing entertainment throughout the territories of the Soviet Union. With its offices in the Tchaikovsky Hall, the Philharmonia had access to the most prestigious halls and national concert seasons, where it promoted its roster of acclaimed artists. Fees were established at standard rates payable according to established criteria; these reflected artists' current standing and the awards and prizes they had won, as well as their years of experience. In the 1960s, the top fee remained fixed at 220 roubles per concert – at the time, this converted into approximately a hundred pounds. Rostropovich's first solo engagement under the aegis of the Philharmonia took place in Sverdlovsk, and he was soon playing in the capitals of the other Soviet republics: Vilnius, Kiev, Riga, Tallinn, and Minsk.

Alongside such conventional concerts, however, Soviet musical life also placed great emphasis on the education of the 'toiling masses'. Singers, actors, musicians and dancers participated together in collective concerts which took place in the most varied venues, ranging from the most prestigious halls used for government entertainment, to factories, schools, and workers' clubs. These groups of artists were known as 'concert brigades', a term reflecting the revolutionary aspirations with which they were established. Much of Rostropovich's early professional experience was gained from performing in collective concerts, where artists were given a slot of approximately twenty minutes to perform a selection of short pieces. The cellist understood

41

how useful this experience was, for he had to learn to make immediate contact with an audience, while avoiding the pitfalls of easy success:

I first encountered large audiences as a prizewinner playing in collective concerts. At one of my first performances I played Popper's *Elfentanz*, a very fast and effective virtuoso piece which I had played since childhood. The audience went wild, applauding the speed with which I could play. At the next concert I played even faster. Then a thought flashed through my mind, banal in its simplicity: if they clap so hard, then I'll play faster still. Then at another concert somebody remarked that my tone wasn't big enough, so then I played louder at the next performance. The audiences were thrilled, but I came to realise I was using so much bow pressure that I nearly choked the instrument. I then came to appreciate what Prokofiev said about constantly purifying one's musical taste. This should be a daily exercise like brushing one's teeth. He was perfectly right, and I believe that this form of self-control is extremely important to a musician.*

Valentin Berlinsky observed that Rostropovich worked continuously to enrich his artistic vision and attain new instrumental standards.

With his questing nature, he was eager to develop certain aspects of his cello technique. This search was most evident in his attitude to sound. During the All-Union competition and in the years immediately following Slava was reproached for a certain lack of refinement and warmth in his tone production. As I remember it, he possessed a very large sound but its quality was somewhat harsh and rough. Obviously this was something he was aware of, or else he listened to what people said, for over the next years he worked on developing a much more refined and varied sound quality, and his tone became quite unique. Indeed, certain of his performances remain engraved in my memory for the amazing beauty and imagination of his sound. For instance, I will never forget a wonderful performance of the Schumann concerto with Kondrashin at the Domski Cathedral in Riga. To this day I can still hear Slava's incredible, inspired sound in my head – it came from God.†

Rostropovich was sufficiently confident in his own musicianship that he could absorb and learn from criticism. In listening to suggestions made by teachers and colleagues, he exercised the discrimination which allowed him to evolve his own voice and artistic outlook:

Listening to criticism, however painful, was always useful, for it helped me formulate my ideas and to reinforce them. When I was preparing for the Budapest competition in 1949 I took on board accusations that I was 'squandering my energy' and throwing myself at the music. Others said I was too immature to play Bach, and that my sound did not possess a sufficient depth or beauty.

* Mikhail Spektor, *Mstislav Rostropovich*, p. 26.
† In interview with E.W., Moscow 2004.

Consequently I decided to play a lot of miniatures where first and foremost one must develop a beautiful singing sound and work on filigree, minute details of colour and timbre. To achieve this aim, I learnt various short pieces by Fauré, Debussy, Rachmaninov's *Vocalise* and Prokofiev's Adagio from *Cinderella*.

His own experience was reflected in his later work with his pupils: he set them the same miniatures in class, to ensure that they developed an ear for sound quality in all its diversity. While acknowledging that beauty of sound was not his greatest merit at the time, Rostropovich also understood that it was not something to which he was attracted for its own sake:

After graduating from the Conservatoire I started actively to search for my own style of playing. I needed to evolve my own methods. For instance, when looking to improve my tone production I could have tried emulating Sviatoslav Knushevitsky, who undoubtedly possessed the most wonderful cello sound that I have ever heard. No other player could touch Knushevitsky in regard to beauty and nobility of sound.

But I came to realise that I didn't need this beautiful sound: rather I sought other kinds of expression which suited 'my' repertoire. For by then I had identified myself with new music, and therefore I was already looking well ahead of my time. A wonderfully rich rounded cello tone suited the nineteenth-century romantic repertoire but was out of place in a work like Prokofiev's *Sinfonia Concertante*, where the sound must have other imaginative sources.

Knushevitsky played the Rachmaninov sonata with the lushest cello sound imaginable, something I can never forget. But when I performed the same sonata I was interested in uncovering other aspects of the work, and was not content to merely immerse myself in a wash of romantic sound.

Early in his career, Mstislav Rostropovich set himself the task of bringing the cello to a wider audience. On the one hand, this involved touring to more remote concert venues and performing repertoire that was accessible and easy on the ears, while consistent with good taste. Alongside this, Rostropovich recognised that the cello's status as a solo instrument was inferior to that of the piano or violin. The limited demand for solo cello concerts could be attributed to two reasons: a lack of brilliant, charismatic performers and a shortage of attractive repertoire. While nineteenth-century virtuoso cellists such as Goltermann, Romberg and Davydov all composed for their instrument, their concert works are no match for those of composer-pianists such as Chopin, Liszt, and Rachmaninov. With the possible exception of Offenbach, music by nineteenth-century cellist-composers remains neglected in the concert hall, and has mostly been relegated to class-room study material – not without reason. Rostropovich's burning desire to remedy this situation led him to emulate Pablo Casals, who won new audiences not only through his prowess as a cellist but through his innate musicianship. However, where new music was concerned, Casals did not have either the discerning taste or the good fortune of Rostropovich: the concertos he commissioned from Emanuel Moor and Donald Tovey have not withstood the test of time, and can hardly compare with the works that Prokofiev, Shostakovich and Britten wrote for Rostropovich.

In deciding that he would prioritise the creation of new repertoires and new audiences for the cello, Rostropovich accepted that his own activity as a composer would be pushed into the background. By the late 1940s he had given up writing music altogether, and did not even finish his composition course. As he put it, 'I had to assume the role of secondary personality to the primary personality of the composer.' This role came naturally to Rostropovich, for with his voracious love of music, he empathised with whatever music he was currently involved with. In later years he would instruct his students, 'You must perform the piece you are playing NOW as if it was the best piece of music in the world.' In other words, during the process of performance a musician must forgo personal preferences and cannot allow objective judgements to interfere. According to Rostropovich, a performer – unlike a composer – cannot allow himself strong preferences or active dislikes in musical repertoire. Rostropovich realised that in this, his own temperament was that of a performer. He became convinced that this was his vocation while he was still a student, and listened to much new music by his idols, Shostakovich and Prokofiev:

I remember going to hear the premiere of Shostakovich's eighth symphony in November 1943.* I was so deeply impressed and enormously excited by this amazing music that after the concert I was unable to sleep. I decided there and then to start composing my own symphony. But after I had written a few pages of score, I realised that what I had composed so far somewhat resembled Shostakovich's eighth, only it was far less good.

Then in January 1945 I attended the premiere of Prokofiev's fifth symphony, conducted by the composer. Once again I was shattered by this great music, and again under the force of my impressions I immediately sat down to write a symphony. But it was merely a pale imitation of Prokofiev.

* The first performance of Shostakovich's eighth symphony took place in Moscow on 4 November 1943.

In fact I wrote quite a lot of music during my Conservatoire years, including a string quartet and my second piano concerto. As my active concert career unfolded, it seemed obvious to everybody that my path in life lay as a performer. Nevertheless Shostakovich would often ring my mother and tell her that I should give up the cello and become a composer. I continued attending composition classes, partly because it was important for me to develop as a musician and to widen my horizons, but also because I wished to maintain my contacts with such wonderful teachers as Shostakovich and Shebalin.

When the infamous Decree on Formalism in Music was published in February 1948, it had a devastating effect on Soviet musical life. Rostropovich's teachers, Shebalin and Shostakovich, were removed from their posts, accused of 'professional incompetence'. This had a decisive effect on Rostropovich: 'After the Decree I lost all desire to continue studying composition. I was transferred to Nikolay Rakov's class, but although Rakov was a good teacher, I just stopped going to lessons. It was too much for me to have to witness my idols being trampled on.'

Rostropovich's reputation as a concert cellist had been steadily gaining ground at home, and it spread beyond the Soviet Union as he achieved success in international competitions. In 1947 he travelled abroad for the first time, joining a Soviet team at the International Festival of Democratic Youth in Prague. The festival also hosted various instrumental competitions: Mstislav shared first prize for cello with Fyodor Luzanov.* The Soviets also swept up first prizes in the other categories of violin (Leonid Kogan), piano (A. Kaplan) and clarinet (I. Roginsky). But Rostropovich was the musician who made the strongest impression and received most critical success. In the words of the newspaper *Mlada Fronta*, 'the young student from the Moscow Conservatoire was the sensation of the competition.' For Mstislav it was the start of a reciprocal love-affair with Prague audiences, who took the young cellist to their hearts and welcomed him back on many occasions over the years.

After the young artists' triumphant return from Prague, various concerts were set up to celebrate their success. Amongst them was a prizewinners' concert in Leningrad on 14 October 1947, a date Rostropovich remembers as his debut in the city. The musicologist and writer Sofiya Khentova attended the concert: 'I well remember the day of the twenty-year-old cellist's [debut] . . . at the Large Hall of the

---

* The night before he was due to play, Rostropovich fell ill with a high temperature. Kozolupov was unperturbed, 'You don't know Slava, He'll play. He can manage anything.'

Philharmonia. Judging by the way he strode out on stage with his cello held in front of him like a weapon, with his almost unnaturally straight posture and awkward bows to the audience, one could tell that he was nervous.'* Once again the critics singled out Rostropovich. The article that appeared in *Vechernaya Leningrad* was the first serious review of the young artist to appear in the Soviet press. The critic praised in particular Rostropovich's ability 'to gain the utmost expression from the cello – this most singing of all instruments . . . He has . . . a complete freedom and mastery of the instrument, yet he subordinates his technique completely to the service of the overall musical concept. The great breadth of his artistic interests was evident in the seriousness and depth of his interpretations of Tchaikovsky, Bach and Prokofiev. Indeed Rostropovich is furthering his studies in composition and piano, and in addition is studying philosophy and literature.'†

Two years later, in the summer of 1949, Rostropovich was again nominated to attend the Festival of Democratic Youth, this time in Budapest. Daniil Shafran, the young Leningrad cellist, would also be a participant in this year's competition. Shafran's supremacy as the country's leading young cellist was now being challenged by Rostropovich, four years his junior. Both had already achieved an extraordinary level of artistry, yet they were temperamentally very different. Shafran's attention to detail made him pre-eminent in minia-ture forms: his poetic sensibility and the remarkable palette of tone colours he had at his disposal suited him to romantic and impression-istic repertoire.

Rostropovich's musical vision, conversely, was on a grander scale: his exuberant energy lent his performances an irresistible brilliance, and he was more concerned than Shafran with large-scale structure and formal unity. Beauty of colour and timbral sound effect remained secondary to his underlying identification with the composer's musical impulse. This did not mean that Shafran excluded contemporary music from his repertoire, any more than Rostropovich shunned miniature forms or romantic concertos and sonatas. But their aesthetic and philosophical starting points were very different and in certain ways incompatible. At the Budapest Competition of 1949, Rostropovich and Shafran created a sensation when they were jointly awarded first prize. David Oistrakh, a jury member, wrote that 'Both

* Sofiya Khentova, *Rostropovich*, p. 44.
† Ibid.

cellists are complete masters of cello sound. Their light virtuosity and elegant technique should be the envy of many violinists.'*

By the beginning of the 1950s, Rostropovich had established an ongoing process of setting himself new artistic challenges. One of his first pupils, Tatyana Priymenko, recalls the various phases in her teacher's development:

The late 1940s and early 1950s was a time of searching for Rostropovich, and he experimented quite a lot. I remember three distinct periods in his development. For instance there was a period when he played everything in sweeping monolithic lines, where detail was secondary to the form. Then there was a period when he played using faster tempi, and gave more attention to detail and a refined sonority. Then again he started playing in slower tempi, very spaciously, adding an almost cosmic dimension to his performances.

His older contemporaries, the cellist-musicologists Lev Ginsburg and Tatyana Gaidomovich, remember that Rostropovich's prime concern was to define the philosophical and emotional essence of his interpretation. Gaidomovich noted that in the first years of his concert career, despite his immense temperament, Rostropovich could at times appear emotionally disinvolved, exaggerating the grotesque in his playing at the expense of simple beauty of line. With this came a tendency to stylise certain repertoire.

As he gained in maturity and experience, the cellist began not only to reveal his own sentiments, but to transmit the music's inner emotional message, which he was able to invest with a direct, human simplicity. At the same time, as Ginsburg pointed out, Rostropovich worked on eliminating any hint of 'virtuosity for its own sake', trying to subjugate the personal 'I' to the composer's intentions. His interpretations gained in depth, concentration and scope.†

During the early 1950s Rostropovich started to perform abroad. Initially he travelled principally to the 'Iron Curtain' countries: Poland, Hungary, Bulgaria, Romania, Czechoslovakia, and East Germany. His first trips to the West occurred in 1949 and 1951 when he travelled as part of a Soviet 'brigade' or delegation of artists, first to Finland and then to Norway. His reputation spread rapidly following these visits. Mstislav liked to recount to his friends that his first impressions of the West were irrevocably associated with the aroma of

* See Khentova, p. 45.
† See Khentova, p. 46, and Ginsburg, p. 11.

coffee. The small wooden airport building in Helsinki smelled of coffee, a marked contrast with Soviet airports, which tended to smell of sewage and unrefined petrol! The delegation to Finland included David Oistrakh, the pianists Wolf Yampolsky and Yuri Bryushkov, and two singers, the bass Podtarzhenski and the soprano Valeriya Barsova. The latter had been a favourite of Stalin's at the Bolshoi Theatre, though she was now long past her prime: her wobbly voice and peculiar diction made her a somewhat comic figure. In Helsinki the Soviet musicians were presented to Sibelius. Inspired by this meeting, Rostropovich decided to programme a piece by the Finnish composer at the following night's concert. He acquired the score of Sibelius's *Canzonetta* the next morning, learnt it and – winning a bet with Wolf Yampolsky, his accompanist – played it from memory at that evening's concert.

Perhaps the most important concert in the early part of 1950 was Rostropovich and Richter's debut recital as a duo in March, when apart from premiering the Prokofiev sonata, they performed the Brahms E minor sonata and two Beethoven sonatas, the A major Op. 69 and the C major Op. 102, no. 1. Most of Rostropovich's time during these months, however, was devoted to preparation for the Hans Wihan competition, which took place that May in Prague. Rostropovich's principal task was to develop his interpretation of the Dvořák Concerto, which he had already studied in Kozolupov's class, and which he intended to play in the final round with orchestra.

The contest commemorated the centenary of the birth of the great Bohemian cellist, Hanus Wihan (1850–1920), who had been a pupil of Davydov and therefore had close connections with the Russian school of playing. Much of Dvořák's music was written with Wihan in mind, including the Rondo, the cello part of his 'Dumky' trio and the Cello Concerto, Op. 104 (which was in fact Dvořák's second concerto for the instrument – the first, an early work, is less musically interesting and far less effectively written for the instrument, so is hardly ever performed). Wihan worked alongside Dvořák to revise various passages in the concerto to make them better suited for the instrument. Some recent soloists (Mischa Maisky included) have restored some of the composer's original passagework in their interpretations. Rostropovich disagrees with this decision, believing that changes made by a composer after hearing a piece in the concert hall (whether or not they are suggested by an expert instrumentalist) should be respected. Given that Wihan's suggestions were endorsed by Dvořák, just as Tchaikovsky accepted Fitzenhagen's reworking of the *Rococo Variations*, Rostropovich would never countenance a return to the 'original' edition.

As in Budapest the previous year, Rostropovich and Shafran shared first prize at the Wihan competition and were enthusiastically received by Prague audiences. At the prizewinners' concert on 28 May, Shafran played the *Rococo Variations* (which he had not played very successfully in the final round, by his own admission), while Rostropovich performed the Dvořák. Three days later, the night before leaving Prague, the team of Soviet cellists gave a shared recital, where Rostropovich performed his own *Humoresque* and Grieg's sonata with Wolf Yampolsky.

During July and August 1950 Rostropovich visited Leipzig, Dresden and Berlin as a member of the Soviet delegation for the celebrations honouring the bicentenary of Bach's death – conveniently for the authorities, all these towns associated with Bach were situated within the communist-controlled German Democratic Republic! The other delegates included Dmitri Shostakovich, Mikhail Waiman, and Mariya Yudina. On 29 July Rostropovich performed Bach's fifth suite in a mixed programme given by Soviet artists at the Leipzig Schauspielhaus. As he was preparing to go on stage for the second half, he met Shostakovich looking very distressed. The composer invited him to come and see him at his hotel room as soon as his performance was over; when Rostropovich knocked at his door, he found Shostakovich waiting with some food and a bottle of vodka. It transpired that the composer had agreed to replace the indisposed Yudina in a performance of Bach's concerto for three keyboard instruments. The performance had not gone well, and Shostakovich blamed himself. Since the 1930s he had given up performing all music except his own in public. Feeling slightly anxious, he asked another of the performers, Pavel Serebryakov, to take over a difficult passage from his part. In the concert, Serebryakov played this additional passage, but then forgot to come in with his own part. Shostakovich was mortified, feeling he should not have added this extra burden to his colleague's share. Despite this trauma, the Bach celebrations had the positive result for Shostakovich of inspiring one of his major masterpieces. At the piano competition dedicated to Bach's works, the composer heard the young Tatyana Nikolaeva cause a sensation with her performance of both books of the

Well-Tempered Clavier. On returning to Moscow, Shostakovich was inspired to write his own cycle of preludes and fugues.

Rostropovich, too, had been deeply impressed by hearing so much of Bach's music and by his visit to the Thomaskirche in Leipzig and other places associated with the German master. He returned home with the determination to master Bach's solo cello suites, and performed the cycle as a whole for the first time at the Small Hall of the Moscow Conservatoire on 14 and 21 January 1951, playing the first three suites at the first concert and the remaining three at the second. I remember Rostropovich telling us that he had been particularly concerned about the fourth suite, which he had to learn for the occasion, and with which he opened his second concert. Before going on stage he was in a state of great tension, wanting to give the music his maximum concentration. The performance went successfully, and with this hurdle out of the way, he launched into the fifth suite, which he had played many times previously. But he had underestimated the difficulty of entering into the very different spirit of this profound and complex work, and the performance went much less well than usual. Rostropovich reproached himself for taking the music for granted, and for feeling too sure of himself. The lesson that he learnt from this occasion, and which he frequently cited to his students, was that 'you must be spiritually prepared for each encounter with the Bach suites. You cannot permit yourself to be on intimate terms with Bach, you cannot address his music with the familiar "Thou".'

The act of preparation, he would instruct his students, was sometimes as important as the actual performance. He made a particular point of this once when working with Karine Georgian on the Prelude of Bach's sixth suite, some months before her victory at the Tchaikovsky competition in 1966. As Karine recalls, she had been waiting a long time in class before it was her turn to play:

By the time it was my turn I was probably a bit fed up and anxious. I got up and went over to sit down on the chair in front of Rostropovich. He stopped me, saying, 'Rukha, go back.' I had already played this prelude to him before, and basically it was ready for performance. But he picked up on my inner mood, and wanted to show me it is important to present yourself as an artist from the first steps you take on stage. This image is actually part of the act of performance. He made me go out of the door and walk in about seven times, and was always unsatisfied. I was getting quite upset and angry, thinking, 'What does he want from me, why won't he let me just play?' Perhaps only later did I realise the importance of this lesson: it was not just a question of extending the right image to the audience, but of carrying with you the inner sensation that inhabits the music you are to perform on stage.

It took Rostropovich himself many years before he gained the confidence to record the Bach suites. An early recording exists of the second and fifth suites, dating from the late 1940s, which he soon came to regard as unrepresentative of his views. Rostropovich's interpretation was constantly evolving, and it was only well after his sixtieth birthday that he agreed to fix them on record. Even this recording cannot be regarded as Rostropovich's final statement on the suites, for as he sees it every Bach performance is an act of faith, which reflects the atmosphere and surroundings of the moment as well as the size and acoustics of the hall. Certainly the interpretations on the recordings (which were published both in audio and video) reflect the magnificent romanesque architecture of Vézelay Abbey, where they were recorded.

In March and April 1951 Rostropovich travelled to Norway with a delegation of Soviet artists, performing concerts in several cities. Although he had now travelled to two Scandinavian countries, his first visit to capitalist Western Europe proper was to Italy in June 1951. The artists making up the delegation for this trip were reputedly hand-picked by Stalin to represent the highest level of Soviet culture. The team included David Oistrakh, Emil Gilels, the ballerina Galina Ulanova, and three renowned singers; Rostropovich was its youngest member. The cellist made his Italian debut on 11 June, playing a full recital with Naum Walter at the Palazzo Pitti in Florence as part of Maggio Musicale festival. Their programme included the Brahms E minor sonata and Myaskovsky's second sonata, as well as a selection of effective shorter pieces.

On leaving Florence, the team were put on a train for Milan. When they checked their seat reservations, the Soviet artists found to their surprise that they were divided into pairs, each pair sitting in a six-person compartment. As their journey started, Italians came and filled the other reserved places. The Russians thought nothing of it until the next day, when an article appeared in Milan's *Corriera della Sera* with the headline, 'What Soviet artists talk about'. To their horror, the artists realised that the other passengers were Russian-speaking Italians who had been planted to listen to their conversations. For the most part, the article recorded that Soviet artists abroad tended to grouse about the paucity of their earnings, and in particular about the miserably small *per diem* allowance of western currrency that was handed out to them on tour. Rostropovich recalls that it was lucky that the article did not record the words of his own travelling companion, Ulanova's ballet partner, who had entertained him throughout the journey with frank and detailed accounts of his amorous adventures with many of the Bolshoi ballerinas. Slava had listened in amazed silence – perhaps the stories were too scandalous for reproduction in the Italian press.

During the same trip, as Rostropovich recalls with pride, he made an unusual debut at La Scala, Milan on 25 June. Apart from performing popular miniatures such as Granados's Danzas Espandos no. 5 *Andaluza*, Ravel's *Habanera* and Cassado's *Dance of the Green Devil*, he also came out on stage with Galina Ulanova to play the solo cello accompaniment to one of her most memorable numbers, the 'Dying Swan' from Saint-Saëns's *Carnival of the Animals*. This occasion contrasts with an incident some months earlier, in November 1950, in the town of Cluj, Romania. This time Rostropovich was asked to accompany the ballerina Irina Tikhomorova in a dance based on Saint-Saëns's 'The Swan' from *Carnival of the Animals*. Because the stage was very small, he and the pianist Naum Walter had to play behind the curtain backstage. Things got off to a bad start when Walter played the first three notes of the arpeggio figure that begins the accompaniment, then stopped for a pause lasting two whole beats. Then he played the next bar in the same manner. Rostropovich looked over to Walter, and immediately understood where the problem lay: the piano was in a dreadful state of repair and its keys got stuck as soon as they were played. Walter was frantically pulling the keys back up before striking them again. Given that the whole accompaniment is based on repeated arpeggios, he could only reproduce a small proportion of the piano part underneath Slava's long legato phrases. Soon both musicians were shaking with laughter, for the ballerina, seemingly completely oblivious to the situation, had started her entry, floating across stage with tiny steps, her arms undulating elegantly in imitation of the swan's wings. The whole scene was so comic that the musicians hardly managed to play to the end.

Every artist in those days seemed to have a wealth of stories about their adventures and mishaps on concert tours. Rostropovich was no exception, and he built up an arsenal of anecdotes which served not only to entertain friends, but as lessons in how to cope with the adversity and unexpected events that life threw up. During the same tour of Romania, Rostropovich gave a solo recital in the beautiful hall of the Bucharest Athenaeum. The first piece in the programme was Bach's second suite for solo cello. The cellist, preparing to enter the intensely serious mood of the Prelude with its opening D minor triad, had slowly lifted the bow in an upbeat when a voice in the hall shrieked out with hysterical fervour, '*Traiscà Prietenia Româno-Sovietica*' (Hail the Eternal Friendship between the Soviet Union and Romania). Although the expression of such sentiments was not untypical of the ideological fanaticism of the time, it was so completely out of place in the concert hall that Mstislav dropped his bow in surprise. After that, he would recount to his students, it was terribly hard to start again and to recapture the necessary inner spirit.

Rostropovich would sometimes test his students in class by deliberately trying to distract them and seeing if they could keep on playing. Yuri Loevsky, a student of his Leningrad class, recalls an occasion in the early 1960s when workmen suddenly started walking in and out of the room, noisily carrying buckets of plaster, boards and nails. Loevsky felt he was losing his concentration and could hardly disguise his annoyance at this rude interruption, but Rostropovich cried out to the workmen, 'Continue, make as much noise as you like, he has got to keep playing.' It was obvious that Rostropovich himself possessed the greatest intensity of concentration in performance: he would boast that 'even if an elephant walked onto stage, I would take no notice and keep performing.' This quality of dedication to the moment was one of the features of Rostropovich's musical personality that Shostakovich singled out for praise.

Various other distinctions were coming Rostropovich's way at this time. In 1950 he became a member of the Union of Composers, which entitled him to various privileges, and allowed him to put his name down for an apartment in a newly planned co-operative building in the centre of Moscow, between Ogaryova and Nezhdanova streets.* In 1951 he received the award of the Stalin prize, 'second degree', for achievements as a concert performer. (After 1956, when Stalin's name started to disappear from circulation, this award became known as 'The State Prize'.) At the time Rostropovich was awarded it, the

---

* Today, these streets have reverted to their pre-Revolutionary names: *Gazetny Pereulok* and *Bryusov Pereulok*.

Stalin prize was worth a considerable sum of money – 50,000 roubles – which came in useful as an advance payment on his new co-operative flat. Even more importantly, though, the prize symbolised the State's recognition of Rostropovich's musical success, and ensured his future as one of the Soviet Union's artistic stars.

4

The young teacher

Rostropovich began teaching soon after his graduation in June 1946, in parallel with his work as a performer. His outstanding diploma results had brought him the Moscow Conservatoire's highest award, the coveted gold medal. In consequence his name was engraved on the marble plaque of excellence, which hangs in a prominent space near the entrance to the Conservatoire's Small Hall: Mstislav had matched his father's achievement some thirty-six years earlier in St Petersburg.

It was almost taken for granted that a successful Conservatoire graduate would apply for the three-year postgraduate course. For Rostropovich it was a necessary formality which would allow him to continue drawing a stipend, receive some specialised tuition and continue consultation lessons with Kozolupov while leaving him plenty of free time for his professional activities. Furthermore, the postgraduate degree was a necessary qualification for entry into the Conservatoire system as a teacher. Kozolupov's reference endorsing Rostropovich's application for the course stressed not only his musical talent, but his discipline and reliability:

Mstislav Rostropovich is nineteen years old, and has exceptional talent, with a whole gamut of musical gifts. He is a great cellist, winner of the All-Union competition for performers in December 1945, an excellent composer and pianist. Possessing a good all-round culture Rostropovich has shown himself to be a very organised and disciplined student. He is a recipient of the Stalin scholarship. I consider it also worth noting that Rostropovich is a well-brought-up and modest youth.

Rostropovich's early success as a performer had allowed him to start his career exclusively as a soloist, bypassing the need to play in an orchestra. This was exceptional: both Rostropovich's father and

Semyon Kozolupov had started their professional lives as leaders of cello sections in prestigious theatre orchestras, while in the West, cellists such as Gregor Piatigorsky and Paul Tortelier also started by taking positions as principal cello in important orchestras, the former in the Berlin Philharmonic and the latter in Monte Carlo and Boston, before devoting themselves to solo work. Both Piatigorsky and Tortelier later became dedicated teachers, though it never became their principal activity, as it did for Kozolupov and Leopold Rostropovich.

Because Mstislav was now his family's main breadwinner, there was pressure on him to take on some teaching to supplement the family income. In 1944, alongside her private teaching at home, his mother Sofiya Nikolayevna began a part-time post as a piano teacher at the Sverdlovsk District school, where Leopold had once taught. Meanwhile, Slava's sister Veronika had yet to complete her studies: after graduating she would find work as a member of the Moscow Radio Orchestra.

An opportunity for Slava arose early in 1947, when Galina Kozolupova left her job at TseMSha in order to concentrate on her teaching at the Conservatoire. Rostropovich, still in his teens, was recommended to take over her class, and started his new job in the middle of the academic year. He inherited four of Kozolupova's pupils, aged between fourteen and seventeen: Tatyana Priymenko, Kira Tsvetkova, Georgi (or Yura) Ivanov, and the youngest, Alla Vasiliyeva.*

Rostropovich completed his postgraduate studies in the summer of 1948. Now that he had acquired just over a year's teaching experience, Kozolupov invited him to join the Conservatoire cello staff. On 17 November 1948 the faculty dean confirmed Rostropovich's appointment as assistant teacher to Professor Kozolupov, allocating him a workload of nine hours a week with three first-study students, and six other students whose lessons would be paid at an hourly rate. The position of 'assistant teacher' was the starting point for every teaching career in the Conservatoire. Overseen by the professor, the assistant's duties included sorting out younger pupils' more basic problems, and preparing the more advanced 'first-study' students for

---

* Tatyana Priymenko later became a professor of cello at the Moscow Conservatoire, Kira Tsvetkova played in the Prokofiev String Quartet before her death some years ago, Georgi Ivanov played for many years in the Moscow State Orchestra, and Alla Vasiliyeva became a founding member and principal cello of the Moscow Chamber Orchestra.

the main lesson with their professor. After a few months, Kozolupov allowed Rostropovich to take on responsibility for a few of his own students, who would play only periodically for their nominal professor.

All teaching appointments put forward by an instrumental faculty had to be approved by the various bureaucratic and ideological departments of the institution. On 30 November 1948, the Conservatoire director Aleksandr Sveshnikov (who had recently replaced the disgraced Vissarion Shebalin, a victim of the Decree on Formalism), the Secretary of the Party Organisation and the Chairman of the Local Commission signed a letter confirming that the Dean and Plenum of the Orchestra Faculty had approved Rostropovich's nomination. To finalise the matter, Kozolupov wrote a further recommendation dated 28 December 1948 declaring that Rostropovich had already proved his worth as a teacher and that it was highly desirable to attract him to pedagocial work at the Moscow Conservatoire.

Rostropovich himself was initially uncertain about his teaching abilities:

Although I gave my first cello lessons at the age of fifteen, I never thought that I possessed particular gifts as a teacher. I discovered, however, once I started my regular teaching activity, that I had the necessary analytical faculties to help my pupils. I was able to define where problems lay, and see a way of resolving them.

Generally you can say it's fairly simple to correct a pupil's faults on the cello; either there's something wrong with the bow arm, or else with the left-hand technique. It goes without saying that it is essential to acquire a basis of technological skills on your instrument. There are some rather straightforward rules which must always be adhered to: the bow must remain perpendicular to the string, parallel to the bridge, it must stay straight, and not weave about between the fingerboard and bridge.

But it was also obvious to me that the most important priority was to educate my pupils to love music. And parents should aim to stimulate in their children a love for music and not a love for exercises. Sergey Sergeyevich Prokofiev always said that he was eternally grateful to his mother because she didn't force him to practise the piano, but, being a good pianist herself, she played marvellous music for him, and a lot of Chopin in particular. As a small boy he composed his opera *The Giant* out of love towards music, and not as a revulsion to forced practice and study.

Rostropovich's methods were informed by the principles that his father had handed down to him, where the musical impulse was all-important, and influenced not only attitudes towards the music itself, but the execution of the simplest technical exercise. He often spoke of Leopold in class, and always in the superlative. Thus from the start Rostropovich's approach to teaching was illuminated by the desire to transmit his love of music as much as the wherewithal to play the instrument: 'My special feature as a teacher, which distinguishes me from most other cello teachers, is my musical background as a composer, pianist and later also as a conductor. In my work with my students this broad spectrum of experience means that I approach music not just from the technological or instrumental point of view.' When he first gave cello lessons in Orienburg, most of Mstislav's pupils were older than him, so he had to learn to impose his authority on them. Even in Moscow, Rostropovich was only two or three years older than his first pupils:

This closeness in age meant that the teacher–pupil relationship was based on friendship. I remember after lessons mucking in with my pupils at TseMSha, and we played football in the corridors. I usually acted as goalie, so if I missed a save, I left the school covered in shame.

Most of my pupils addressed me with the familiar *Ty* (Thou) form, but when I started teaching at the Conservatoire I got reprimanded for such unsuitable 'intimacy' with my pupils. I was told that it implied a lack of respect for the figure of the teacher. Duly at the next lesson I used the formal address with my first student, but he took no notice and answered me as before with the intimate 'Thou'. It took some time before I gained enough authority for this 'error' to be corrected.

Alla Vasiliyeva, one of his first and youngest pupils, recalls that in her case, Rostropovich always maintained the formal Vy (You) in addressing her, despite her being younger than him, and that her relationship was tinged by the respect due to a teacher. But the feeling of friendship was also extended to pupils outside school hours:

For instance, once after some exam at school Mstislav Leopoldovich came back to our communal flat, where my mother had prepared a tasty vinaigrette salad, pies and cake. He seemed to always be hungry in those years. I remember him not just eating, but wolfing down the food. 'Mitievna, I just can't eat enough today!' he told Mother. Initially his life had been very difficult materially, and from an early age he had to earn money. I remember he told us that in Orienburg during the war he had once played a concert for a bucket of potatoes.

Another of Mstislav's first pupils at the Central Music school was Tatyana Priymenko:

At the time I started my lessons with Slava I was in my penultimate year at school. Both he and my former teacher Galina Kozolupova were fantastic teachers, but very different. I could term Kozolupova's quality as pure gold, whereas Rostropovich had a diamond's sharp brilliance.

Perhaps the principal difference between them lay in the imaginative aspect of Rostropovich's teaching. For him, it was fundamental that an artist learn to use both his intuition and his powers of logic. Thus, as Priymenko recalls, his whole approach to sound was underpinned by an almost pictorial approach, and he spent a lot of energy on developing the pupil's imagination:

One of the first things Mstislav Leopoldovich gave me to learn was Ravel's *Pavane pour une infante défunte*. He wanted to use a delicate, filigree piece of music to reveal to me a new world of sound possibilities, working both on vibrato and on different ways of using the bow, so as to produce a range of impressionistic colours.

We went through a lot of repertoire in the two years I was with him. I particularly remember how he put me through the hoops with Mozart's horn concerto in Cassado's transcription. He himself was much attracted by this work, and would sit at the piano and get carried away, endlessly polishing details of the phrasing, emphasising the right articulation for every note and small phraselet, while keeping in mind a sense of sweeping structure. He was always very attentive to the overall structure, ensuring that the form dictated the expression, but on the other hand he would also work on the minutest details.

While his musical ideas were enriched by his fantasy, Rostropovich placed emphasis on acquiring the necessary technical handicraft. Priymenko recalls that in order to develop certain aspects of instrumental technique, he set her two of Romberg's concertos, the second and the ninth – works that abound in all kinds of difficulties, from complex bowing strokes to the use of the whole range of the fingerboard. She particularly remembers Rostropovich's imaginative explanation of the spiccato, a bouncing bow stroke:

He used three images that I found very helpful. One was of a typically Russian children's toy, a little round wooden board with chickens attached by strings to a ball. You were meant to move the board with a small wrist movement, so the ball swung underneath it, making the chickens bob up and down, pecking with their heads. Another image was that of a continually bouncing ball, and a third image he used was of 'gogol-mogol', a kind of zabaglione made by vigorously beating up egg yolk and sugar. Here he showed us how to use an energetic rotary movement of the wrist.

In those days spiccato was usually taught with a high wrist, which deprives it of strength and made it somewhat clumsy. But Rostropovich favoured using a low wrist, allowing the bow to find the most elastic point somewhere towards the middle of the stick, where the optimum bounce came naturally. This bow stroke was needed for many virtuoso pieces, such as Popper's *Elfentanz*. He showed us how to adapt the movement so as to increase or decrease the speed of the stroke, giving us complete freedom.

In her last year at school, Priymenko expressed a desire to learn Myaskovsky's cello concerto, having discovered his music through Rostropovich's enthusiastic advocacy of the work.

Slava was genuinely delighted that I liked Myaskovsky's music. Then, when Myaskovsky wrote the second cello sonata for Rostropovich at the end of 1948, we learnt it almost simultaneously with him. It was wonderful for us to hear his first performance, feeling that we were complicitly sharing in its creation.

It was a very interesting time altogether, and we observed the growth of Rostropovich the artist and teacher in those years. When he was given his own class at the Conservatoire, we saw how he organised its work, thinking not only about the individual student, but about the collective work of the class. For instance, he planned very interesting thematic class concerts.

For his young students, hearing Rostropovich play in concert was a lesson in itself. He astounded them with his natural ability as a performer and the phenomenal speed with which he memorised and absorbed new music. As Priymenko recalls:

If Rostropovich didn't practise or play for a period, he had no trouble getting back into form. Another thing that he spoke about a lot was memory. For him it was an extremely important phenomenon. He did not just mean the process of memorising, although he could do this with extraordinary speed, and he expected it likewise of his pupils. But of greater significance was his perception of how to put memory to use. He would advise us, 'Dig around in your own personal experience, you must use images and sensations that are your own, hunt them out in your own memory.' This was the key to an understanding of his use of artistic fantasy. For Slava, images had to be felt with an almost physical sensation, and not viewed in a rational, abstracted way.

Interestingly enough this was similar to Heinrich Neuhaus's approach: he often also provided his students with everyday images from life, some of them seemingly quite banal. But they proved to be very strong in evoking an artistic response.

Tatyana Priymenko spent her last two years at school as Rostropovich's pupil, before enrolling at the Conservatoire in 1949 in Galina Kozolupova's class.

Another of Rostropovich's first pupils, Alla Vasiliyeva, was younger and consequently less advanced than Priymenko, and found

Rostropovich's teaching methods less easy to cope with in her first year with him. Her inhibitions about her level of playing were compounded by the fact that her cello studies had been interrupted at a critical stage:

Soon after I started studying cello, the war broke out and our family was evacuated to Kazakhstan. I had to forget all about music then. When we returned to Moscow, I enrolled at TseMSha, where Galina Kozolupova became my teacher. Despite my relatively low level she helped me gain a sensation of ease on the cello during my three years with her. Kozolupova's method was to demonstrate everything on the cello, and we had to learn through imitation.

Rostropovich gave regular twice-weekly lessons to his pupils; one lesson he would teach at school, and the other at home, in the communal flat on Nemirovich-Danchenko Street where he lived with his family. It was a demanding process, as Vasiliyeva recalls:

If Galina Kozolupova had expected her pupils to imitate and obey, then the defining moment for Rostropovich was his level of interest in each pupil. This determined his desire – or lack of such desire – to work intensely with his student, and affected everything, from his sense of involvement and choice of repertoire to the definition of immediate and long-term objectives.

To begin with I found his approach very difficult, for I lacked the technological resources to satisfy his exacting demands. I felt that he got bored working with me, and that he didn't want to sit down and sort out my basic cellistic problems. Of course he listened with patience to all the things that were required of us: scales, studies and short pieces. But I could see that he enjoyed teaching the older students far more, and was inspired by working on large-scale forms, such as the Bach suites and the great repertoire concertos.

Vasiliyeva's insecurity was increased by her recognition of the high level achieved by the older pupils, with their technical ease, beautiful singing sound and perfect intonation. All this seemed light-years away from the more basic cellistic problems that she was battling with, such as out-of-tune shifts from position to position:

Within the first month, Mstislav Leopoldovich had noted that my musical development was way ahead of 'everything else', meaning my technical possibilities. My twice-weekly lessons soon turned into a kind of torture session for me. Sometimes Rostropovich would take my cello and demonstrate the passages from a Romberg or Davydov concerto that I had been struggling with unsuccessfully. I reached the point when it seemed to me that not only did I not know how to play, I didn't know how to practise or even how to warm up! And Rostropovich played with such unforced naturalness! I was dying to ask him how he did it and what his secret was. But I never had the courage to question him, and I don't think it occurred to him then that I suffered such moments of psycho-logical doubt.

As Vasiliyeva felt her teacher's interest in her dwindling, she even thought of giving up the cello. But in her second year of study she decided to take positive measures to remedy the situation and build up her self-esteem. With the help of her mother, she went back to the basic principles of her very first teacher, Efim Gendlin (Kozolupov's assistant). She studied difficult passages separately and slowly, repeating them over and over again, until she could play them well.

I learnt to practise, and also to appreciate the usefulness of scales. At the same time I realised that I must try and emulate the great model I had in front of me. I went to all Rostropovich's concerts, avidly lapping up everything he did. At that stage I felt that I could learn far more from observing him play on stage. I sat at his concerts in a kind of trance, following all his movements, watching his bow strokes, observing how he distributed the bow, how he phrased with the bow and coloured with the left hand. Then I would come to my lessons having at least in part assimilated my observations, transforming them into technical cellistic terms. I also started to appreciate and understand the unique, all-embracing qualities of this wonderful musician.

As I surfaced from this crisis, I succeeded in reawakening the interest of my mentor. A crucial breakthrough came when Rostropovich decided to set me the Saint-Saëns concerto. I adored this music, and I also adored my idol's interpreta-tion, for I had listened to several of his performances and already knew every note by ear. It was like a ray of light bursting into my school life, and after ten days' hard practising I played it well enough for Mstislav Leopoldovich to consider it 'ready'. Even if my performance was little more than a blind copy of his interpre-tation, nevertheless my hands felt free and I could breathe in synchrony with the music. I learnt for the first time what it was to feel real creative satisfaction.

Rostropovich wished to stimulate his pupils' interest in music, and when time allowed, he would get them to sight-read in class. Indeed, he valued sight-reading as a test of intuition, musical maturity and of the pupil's spontaneous approach to the instrument. It was important to develop the ability to make immediate assessments of the music's character in terms of tempo, articulation and colour, and to translate one's intuitive feelings into technical solutions. Sight-reading requires instant decisions on which bowings and fingerings best transmit the music's requirements, so by emphasising it Rostropovich was training his pupils to react quickly on the instrument. Alla Vasiliyeva was particularly struck by one such occasion where Rostropovich shared his exploration of a new work with his pupils:

One day I arrived at Rostropovich's home for my lesson at the appointed hour. I found Tanya Priymenko and Yura Ivanov were also there already. Mstislav Leopoldovich was busy sorting out a pile of music, placing sheets of manuscript on the floor as if laying out a game of patience. Suddenly some of these sheets found their way on to the music stand. First Yura was asked to read through them, with Slava accompanying at the piano. Then another set of sheets were given to Tanya Priymenko, and it was her turn to play. I was given a third set of sheets. By now it was obvious that these were movements from the same work, and that mine was the finale, which incidentally was the most difficult of the movements. After this session of 'music-making' was over Rostropovich informed us that what we had just played through was Myaskovsky's newly written second sonata. This was before he had played it in public, and well before it was published, so we were reading off the composer's manuscript. One could think of no more difficult test for a young musician.

Vasiliyeva felt that Rostropovich's lessons taught her far more about how to approach music than about the instrument as such:

In the final tenth year at school, Rostropovich started treating me less strictly and gave me more freedom. This helped me listen to myself better, and as a result I started to trust my own ability to sort out my technical and musical problems. I came to realise that it was not enough to imitate, however wonderful a model I had in front of me. Ultimately a copy remains a copy.

Slava's teaching method worked for him not least because he was such an outstanding pianist. Once when I was in the ninth grade he even accompanied me at an exam when our class pianist was ill. In general he seldom talked about how the music should actually be played on the cello. He preferred to teach from the piano, where he would simultaneously explain and play or conduct the music.

Thus I learnt from Rostropovich how to approach a new work, by first realising the structural plan away from the instrument, and then taking the cello and working on detail.

Rostropovich's first students agree that his great merit as a teacher was to engage them actively in the process of music-making, opening up their horizons, and instilling in them a sense of form and style. By the time they left school, they had the means at their disposal to approach different composers, from Boccherini, Beethoven and Saint-Saëns to Dvořák and Myaskovsky.

5

Contacts with composers I
from Glière to Prokofiev

Mstislav Rostropovich was only eighteen when he established himself as a committed performer of new music. While still a student, he felt the need to seek out new works by the best composers and the desire to stimulate new additions to the cello repertoire. Rostropovich's early training as a composer played a significant part in this, for it allowed him to identify immediately with the music of his contemporaries.

The first composer to take note of Rostropovich's compositional talents was his father's friend, Reinhold Glière, who had been Prokofiev's teacher. Once, when Mstislav was six years old, Glière visited the family and was shown the boy's 'compositions'. He asked the young Slava to improvise two characteristic pieces, a march and a mazurka, at the piano. He was impressed by what he heard, and his praise set the seal on Slava's early study of composition. It was appropriate that some thirteen years later, Glière's cello concerto should become the first work dedicated to Rostropovich, even though it had been intended for its first performer, Svyatoslav Knushevitsky:

Early in 1946 I attended the premiere of Glière's concerto played by Knushevitsky at the Hall of Columns in the House of Unions. The concerto is very long and technically it's very hard. I have to say that technique was not one of Knushevitsky's strong points, and on this occasion he simply hadn't studied the work sufficiently. During the performance, he felt things were going badly, his memory failed him and he needed to read off the cello part. He put the music on the floor by his feet, but at a certain point he realised that this wasn't going to solve his problems and he kicked the sheets of paper behind his chair. I thought that Knushevitsky showed an extraordinary power of self-possession to get through the concerto with a modicum of dignity.

After this unsatisfactory first performance, Glière looked for another cellist who could do the work justice. Although Rostropovich was still a student at the time, his performance of Myaskovsky's concerto had made a considerable impact on Moscow composers. Glière invited him to give the second Moscow performance of the work under his direction. Delighted with his excellent execution – naturally Rostropovich played from memory – Glière pointedly dedicated the concerto to him. They went on to give further perfomances in several other cities, including Riga and Vilnius:

Glière enjoyed public recognition; I think he had been awarded no fewer than five Stalin prizes, and he liked wearing his decorations. When he conducted I could hear percussive effects nearby on my left. Soon I realised that it was the jingle of his medals.

Although he directed only his own works, Glière was a mediocre conductor. In one of our concerts together, in Riga, he got muddled and lost control of the orchestra in the second movement. It was only with great difficulty that the orchestra and I managed to get back together to save the situation.

This concerto was the first of a long series of works dedicated to me. I didn't perform it often, since although I respected Glière's musicianship, it is really a second-rate piece.

However, Rostropovich used the concerto as teaching repertoire, feeling it was useful for young cellists to be able to get to grips with a large-scale piece with a lengthy, if somewhat meandering structure. It was a test in stamina and very hard to learn from memory. On occasion, he seemed to set Glière's concerto almost as a punishment for a lazy pupil: 'Right, today is Tuesday, learn the first movement by memory and bring it to me on Thursday. You have two days.' If the student did not succeed in memorising it, Rostropovich would look at him with an air of disappointment and say, 'Just think I learnt the whole concerto from memory in less than a week.'

If Glière was the most senior amongst the eminent living Soviet composers, Nikolay Myaskovsky was the most respected of the following generation. In Rostropovich's own view, his career as a advocate of new music started by performing Myaskovsky: 'The Myaskovsky concerto was the beginning of a definite path in life for me. Myaskovsky led me to Prokofiev, and Prokofiev indirectly to Shostakovich, and through Shostakovich to Britten.'

Myaskovsky and Prokofiev were close friends from their student years, maintaining their relationship through regular correspondence while Prokofiev was living in Paris. Prokofiev, in turn, was the composer, more than any other, whom Mstislav longed to meet:

I fell in love with Prokofiev's music in 1943. Soon after I returned to Moscow from Orienburg I went to see his ballet *Romeo and Juliet* at the Bolshoi Theatre. I was utterly overwhelmed. Over the next two years I never missed a showing of this brilliant ballet. Soon I could play the whole score through on the piano from memory. As a student I attended every performance of a new Shostakovich or Prokofiev work, including the premieres of their respective Eighth and Fifth symphonies.

At last, after imploring one of the composer's friends to effect an introduction, Mstislav was presented to Prokofiev:

Of course he took next to no notice of me, since I was just a boy as far as he was concerned. But after December 1945, when I won the All-Union competition, he started to remember who I was. This was no doubt because I had played the concerto of his great friend Myaskovsky. I then decided to learn his first cello concerto and play it with piano at my solo recital in the Small Hall of the Conservatoire.

Prokofiev's first cello concerto had been cursed with bad luck from the day of its Moscow premiere. Prokofiev completed the work in 1938, and invited Lev Berezovsky to undertake the solo part. Berezovsky set to work with a rehearsal pianist – none other than the young Sviatoslav Richter, who at the time earned his living as a *répétiteur*. The cellist not only had trouble in mastering the concerto's technical difficulties, but found much of the music to be incomprehensible. Nevertheless, when Berezovsky and Richter played the work at an auditon at the Moscow Union of Composers, it was well received, and put forward for performance.

Events took an unhappy turn during the preparations for the concerto's first performance. The conductor Melik-Pashayev had underestimated the difficulties of the score, and had not allowed enough rehearsal time. It was also evident that Berezovsky was not technically secure: at the premiere he played from the music, but even so often drifted apart from the orchestra. The performance was a fiasco, and the concerto was panned by the critics. When Knushevitsky, the best-known Soviet cellist of the time, publicly dismissed the piece as one of Prokofiev's 'failures', any chance of further performances seemed to have vanished. At this stage Prokofiev sent the score to Piatigorsky in the United States, who learnt the concerto and performed it once in 1940. But there too the work was poorly received and quietly forgotten. Few other cellists expressed interest in the piece, although the young Maurice Gendron performed it in London in

December 1945, with the London Philharmonic Orchestra under Walter Susskind.

Rostropovich had not attended the Moscow premiere, but he liked to repeat a story he heard from Richter about Prokofiev's assessment of the performance. When the composer came backstage to salute the artists, Melik-Pashayev tried to break an awkward silence. 'Well, Sergey Sergeyevich, what did you think?' Prokofiev replied with an ingenuous smile: 'Nothing could have been worse.'*

Such stories intrigued Rostropovich, and he decided to learn the cello concerto as a means of approaching the composer. His first obstacle came, however, when he was unable to obtain an orchestral score:

Eventually I obtained a piano score, and was able to learn the concerto. I performed it with piano in my recital programme at the Small Hall of the Conservatoire on 21 December 1947. My cousin Irina Kozolupova accompanied me. Of course I dreamed of being able to show Prokofiev how well I played the cello, and I studied the work hard. Perhaps, who knows, he might actually like the way I play?

Prokofiev did indeed attend the recital performance, and was suitably impressed – though the occasion did not pass without mishap, as Rostropovich recalls:

In those years I never wore glasses when I performed, despite the fact that I am rather short-sighted . . . When I finished playing, I saw somebody with a bald head at the back of the hall whom I believed to be Prokofiev. He kept applauding vigorously and I kept bowing in his direction. In my enthusiasm I played lots of encores, starting with my own arrangement of the 'Dance of the Antillean Maidens' from *Romeo and Juliet*. After the fifth encore I walked into the green room. I was about to go out on stage again, when I was suddenly aware that Prokofiev himself was impatiently standing before me. Through my short-sightedness, I had confused him with my equally bald friend Motkovsky, a cellist from the Bolshoi Theatre, who was sitting in the back row. Prokofiev looked at me quizzically: 'Young man, how much longer are you going to go out for . . .?'

After this scolding, Sergey Sergeyevich congratulated me, and told me, 'You know, I'd like to make some changes in this concerto. Although there is some very good material in the piece, the structure is not compact enough. If you would be

* Information compiled from B. Monsaingeon, *Richter Ecrits/Conversations*, and Solomon Volkov, article in the *New York Times*, 'Tradition Returns: Rostropovich's Symbolism', quoted in Ho and Feofanov, *Shostakovich Reconsidered*, p. 338.

willing to help me I'd be most grateful.' To hear such words from Prokofiev sent me into total delirium. It was one of the happiest moments of my life.

'Of course,' I replied. 'I'm ready to serve for eternity . . . any time of day or night.'

Rostropovich's timing was fortunate, for his performance of Prokofiev's concerto occurred just before an event that convulsed Soviet musical life. On 10 February, less than a month later, the Central Committee of the Communist Party issued a Decree entitled 'On V. Muradeli's opera *The Great Friendship*',* which accused leading Soviet composers of being 'formalist and anti-Soviet'. In the last years of Stalin's repressive rule, such accusations were tantamount to public disgrace, and could have led to the severest consequences. The main culprits were named as Shostakovich, Prokofiev, Myaskovsky, Shebalin and Khatchaturian, and accused of being 'anti-people' and disseminating pessimism and decadence. Rostropovich recalls this grim episode:

Most of their friends distanced themselves from the disgraced composers. Although I was still very young, I understood their enormous significance. They were my idols and I knew that I would never betray them, although at that time it was very fashionable for young performers and musicians to shout criticism from the tribune, and to denounce their teachers. Shostakovich, Prokofiev, Myaskovsky and Shebalin were all shamelessly treated by many of their colleagues and also by some of their pupils. At the Conservatoire, meetings were organised where students and teachers could be heard to make vitriolic statements: 'Thanks to the Communist Party, my ears have at last been opened. We now understand that this is not music, but rubbish.' Such confessions, unfortunately, could be heard rather frequently.

One year before the Decree I started travelling abroad. I had an important career opening out ahead of me. But at the time I never so much as uttered or wrote a single word in which I expressed even the slightest doubt about any of these composers. Naturally their attitude to me was consistent with my behaviour towards them, and they wrote their compositions for me.

In the months after the Decree, the first of the condemned 'formalists' to compose for Rostropovich was Nikolay Myaskovsky, whose second cello sonata dates from this time. The sonata was seen as a work of rehabilitation, and was awarded a Stalin prize. When Rostropovich went to congratulate Myaskovsky at home, the composer wrote a touching dedication into the score: 'To Mstislav Rostropovich, from the not-quite-worthy-of-him Nikolay Myaskovsky.'

* The official title of the Decree referred to the work by Muradeli that had been the initial cause of the debacle. Absurdly Muradeli, who was a mediocre composer at best, was considered a model 'socialist-realist', but one who had inadvertently caused ideological offence.

I gave the first performance of the sonata with Aleksandr Dedyukhin in December 1948. Myaskovsky brought his friend, Prokofiev, to the concert, who came backstage and declared, 'I too want to write a sonata for you.' Prokofiev also made some slightly critical comments about my performance, saying, 'In the third movement when you play the spiccato sixteenth notes on the G string one can't hear a thing.' Here he paused significantly, and seeing my dejected face, he smiled and added, 'But when you play the same passage two octaves up on the A string it sounds absolutely brilliant!'

I must say that Prokofiev put this observation to the test. For in the opening of the second movement of the *Sinfonia Concertante*, the cello starts with a very fast passage on the lower strings. Initially it plays alone without accompaniment, and the orchestra is introduced only once the cello has achieved the higher and clearer register of the A string.

As soon as Prokofiev had completed his new cello sonata he invited Rostropovich down to his dacha at Nikolina Gora, outside Moscow. This first visit was a memorable occasion for the young cellist.

I travelled down by car with Levon Atovmyan. As we drove into the gates of his dacha, I saw Prokofiev coming towards us. He was wearing a raspberry-coloured dressing gown and had a towel tied turban-like on his head. Behind him ran a batch of clucking chicks and cockerels; evidently he had just been feeding them. 'Good day, Sir,' he said jokingly.

I was rooted to the spot in amazement and couldn't get out of the car. When Sergey Sergeyevich saw my dismay, he quipped, 'Pardon me for my country attire.'

I had prepared the sonata well and had also learnt the piano part from memory. By now Prokofiev no longer played the piano so well, and when we read through the sonata I was amazed that he had managed to forget his own music so quickly. He played as if he was sight-reading! I even went so far as to correct him when he played some wrong notes. At this he turned to me: 'Young man, who wrote this work, you or me?' Sergey Sergeyevich suggested that I play the sonata with Sviatoslav Richter, thereby giving his blessing to the start of my duo partnership with 'Teofilovich'.

At the end of the day, towards dusk, he took us with him to visit his dacha neighbour, Nikolay Myaskovsky.

The two 'Slavas', Richter and Rostropovich, first performed the work at a closed concert at the Plenum of the Union of Composers in December 1949, and the official public premiere was given at their duo recital at the Small Hall of the Conservatoire on 1 March 1950.

Rostropovich knew that Prokofiev was in desperate need of money at this time, and decided to play the cello sonata to the committee responsible for acquiring new works for publication. Commissions to composers did not exist as such in the Soviet Union, but money could be paid retrospectively for publication and performance rights. Rostropovich recalls playing the sonata with Aleksandr Dedyukhin in a room on Neglinnaya Street for

Aleksandr Anisimov, the official responsible for the decision. Anisimov was hardly well disposed to Prokofiev, as Rostropovich knew. A choral conductor by training, Anisimov had been director of the Bolshoi Theatre during the mid-1940s, and had immediately removed Prokofiev's works from the Bolshoi's repertoire after the 1948 decree. Shortly afterwards, Rostropovich stopped Anisimov in the Conservatoire corridor. 'Aleksandr Ivanovich, aren't you ashamed to have taken out of repertoire such a brilliant work as Prokofiev's *Romeo and Juliet?*' 'Brilliant?' Anisimov snorted. 'Nothing brilliant there. It's only *dring-dring* from the cymbals and *boom-boom* from the drums!' (The director's box at the Bolshoi is of course situated near the stage, directly over the percussion section!) Despite his hostility to Prokofiev, however, Anisimov passed the cello sonata for publication, but allocated it into the 'B category' of class 1, which meant less money for the composer.

Rostropovich was equally involved in getting Prokofiev's seventh symphony accepted for publication and performance, when he and the pianist Anatoly Vedernikov played it in a four-hand version for the Radio committee, which was made up of various musicologists and composers. It was through the conductor Samosud, chief conductor of the Radio Orchestra in Moscow, and the composer Balasanyan, director of the radio station, that Prokofiev had first been asked to write a 'symphony for children' for the Radio Orchestra. Rostropovich and Vedernikov auditioned the work successfully, repeating it twice, and rights to the symphony were duly acquired. A delighted Rostropovich hurried away to buy a cake and a bottle of champagne to celebrate with Prokofiev. The composer had not attended the audition because of ill health, but as soon as he heard of the successful outcome, he rubbed out the title 'Children's Symphony' from the score. Rostropovich asked him what he was doing, to which Prokofiev replied: 'Since the adults seem to like it so much, let's just call the work the seventh symphony.'

In some ways, it was ironic that Prokofiev's music had caused such political controversy. As Richter had once exclaimed in conversation with Rostropovich, 'When you think of it Prokofiev's music has all the qualities demanded by the authorities: it's melodic and tuneful, and accessible to the people.' Richter remained a loyal supporter of Prokofiev, and showed staunch courage when he refused to play any more concerts until he was allowed to programme the composer's ninth piano sonata. Nevertheless, it was Rostropovich who became closest to Prokofiev on a day-to-day basis. Richter recalled that after they performed the cello sonata, 'Rostropovich latched onto Prokofiev. He was completely entranced by his music. When one saw them together it was quite possible to mistake Sergey Sergeyevich for his father – they were so alike.'* Long after the event, Emil Gilels once implied that Rostropovich had 'latched onto Prokofiev' for opportunistic reasons, an accusation which the composer's widow strongly rejected: 'When everybody else had deserted, the only person who stayed near Prokofiev was Rostropovich. He was the one person on whom we could rely.'† Their relationship was built on firmly musical grounds, for shortly after the cello sonata had been premiered, Prokofiev invited Rostropovich to help him revise his cello concerto:

The first thing Sergey Sergeyevich asked me to do was to bring him some repertoire pieces for cello 'of any quality' which would serve as examples of interesting virtuoso passagework and thereby give him an idea of the instrument's technical and expressive possibilities. I duly took along a pile of works by Popper and Davydov. After a while he returned them to me, remarking sardonically, 'Well, here's the music you brought me – if you can call it that!'

For the next two summers I lived at Prokofiev's dacha and worked with him on the new edition of the concerto. During the other months of the year, I also had frequent meetings with him in Moscow. Therefore I had ample opportunity to observe his compositional process closely.

Prokofiev started the revisions with the second movement. He worked slowly and meticulously, and as he went along, he would show Rostropovich every small change, even if it consisted only of a few bars. Rostropovich frequently recounted a story in class that illustrates this working method. One day he rang Slava and called him over urgently, saying he had made a wonderful discovery in the second movement. Rostropovich rushed over to the composer's flat to find out what the invention was. (At this point Rostropovich always went to the piano to illustrate his story.) Prokofiev started playing through the music as fast as he could from the beginning of the movement with no real rhythm or expression, saying 'this has no importance, and this too has no importance', until he arrived at the loud discords (see five bars before figure 4). 'Here Sergey Sergeyevich smiled broadly, repeating the chords over and over again, exclaiming in delight, "You see what I found. Not bad, eh, don't you think?"'

* Article by S. Richter in Shlifshteyn (ed.) *Prokofiev Materials*, p. 468.
† Mikhail Spektor, *Mstislav Rostropovich*, p. 57.

Having spent so much time with Prokofiev in private, Rostropovich saw how much his music reflected his personality. In his view, it is always important to have a mental picture of the composer when performing his music – in this case, a perception of Prokofiev's sense of humour, almost child-like insouciance and bright inventive mind. Through his vivid descriptions, Rostropovich endeavoured to pass on these images to his students.

Prokofiev had no compunction about saying exactly what he thought, and Rostropovich would recount one particular episode partly as a story against himself and partly to illuminate the composer's personality. The cellist once made a comment about a point of orchestration in the second movement, wishing, perhaps, to show his erudition. It concerned the orchestral accompaniment of repeated quavers which lies well for the chosen instruments in the exposition. But when the passage recurs in the recapitulation, it becomes incredibly low – perhaps too low – for the trumpet. 'What do you mean, Slava, too low for the trumpet?' Prokofiev retorted. 'Just think how the trumpet player will get puffed and red in the face, as he has to blow those low notes.'

For Rostropovich, this anecdote illustrated something essential about Prokofiev's mind: the fact that he visualised orchestration as well as hearing it. Indeed, Prokofiev was often criticised for composing directly into piano score, where he would pencil in indications of the orchestration, without writing out a full orchestral score. Rostropovich would explain that this was not because Prokofiev had any problem in hearing the precise instrumentation he wanted, but because he resented the time spent on a job that others could do. On occasion, Prokofiev requested such 'creative assistance' from Rostropovich:

Occasionally Sergey Sergeyevich would ask me to write a rapid technical passage for solo cello where the texture was specifically instrumental. Maybe it would only be of four or eight bars' duration. He indicated the harmonic framework and the rhythmic patterns.

One time I was rather slow to perform the task he set me and I kept providing excuses for not delivering my few bars. Eventually he got cross and admonished me, 'Well, it appears that you don't even have the talent of Brahms . . . Just think, Brahms could pour out pages of piano studies, and you can't even provide me with a few bars!'

Naturally I was shamed into sitting down that very evening and carrying out the promised task. The next day I took the passage to Sergey Sergeyevich, and observed what he did with it. With pencil and rubber in hand, he looked at my few bars, and then very carefully rubbed out one note here, another one there and substituted different notes in their place. Although he only changed four or five notes in all, it made an incredible difference and brought the whole passage to life. I thought to myself, 'Why didn't I think of that?'

Both Prokofiev and Shostakovich suffered great deprivation after the decree of 1948. Their old works could not be performed, and it was next to impossible to obtain commissions. The only way for a composer to earn was to write patriotic occasional music and music for the films which at the time were little more than propaganda for Stalin. Once Prokofiev phoned Slava to inform him that he had no money to buy breakfast and would have to dismiss his cook as he could no longer pay her. Rostropovich immediately took action and went to the Union of Composers to ask Khrennikov to help out. In his capacity as First Secretary of the Composers' Union, Khrennikov listened politely. He then called into his office a certain Lempert, an official from Muzfond, and ordered him to give some funds in cash to Prokofiev.

It was around the same period that Rostropovich remembers meeting Samosud and Balasanyan to discuss how the Radio Committee might best help Prokofiev. As the three men sat on a bench in Samosud's garden in Nikolina Gora, they came up with the idea that he might consider composing a work on an approved theme, namely the meeting of two great rivers – the Volga and the Don. Such a work would celebrate Stalin's pet projects of reversing the course of rivers and building the Volga–Don canal. For Prokofiev, some appeal could be found in the subject's relationship to nature, if not in its ideological significance. They decided that it would be Slava's job to convince Prokofiev: his success in this task brought life to the overture, and money to its composer.*

Towards the end of 1951, Prokofiev completed his revised version of the cello concerto. Given that the work now bore little resemblance to the original piece, he decided to relabel it as 'Cello Concerto no. 2, Op. 125' – effectively, as he explained, it was a new composition based on material from the first concerto. The first performance of the second cello concerto was to take place in Moscow with the Moscow Youth Orchestra on 18 February 1952, and it was decided that Sviatoslav Richter would conduct the premiere, thereby making his debut as conductor. Rostropovich was happy to have such a committed and excellent performer of Prokofiev's music on the

* The work referred to is *Festive Poème*, '*The Meeting of the Volga and Don*' for symphony orchestra, op. 130.

podium to accompany him, though the engagement had come about only because of an accident. Richter had recently broken a finger on his right hand, which forced him to cancel all his concerts, apart from a performance of Ravel's concerto for the left hand. With time at his disposal, Richter was eager to try conducting, and nothing attracted him more than a new work by Prokofiev. Kirill Kondrashin, the chief conductor of the youth orchestra, agreed to oversee the rehearsals and to give Richter some conducting lessons, and Prokofiev gave his blessing to the idea.

This was not Richter's first involvement with the piece: before the *Concerto*'s performance could be confirmed, it had to be given official approval by a commission at the Union of Composers. Rostropovich had asked Richter to accompany him at the piano for this occasion. Anxious that the work would not be deemed too shocking and dissonant, Richter decided on the expedient of 'simplifying' some of the harmonies: for instance, the repeated discord in the second movement was modified into a simple diminished seventh. Such expedient variants became known as a *vremyanka* (a temporary alternative). Prokofiev wrote '*vremyanki*' for various works of the period, including his seventh symphony, leaving instructions to revert to his original idea when times allowed.

Despite Richter's precautions, the concerto found an unexpected antagonist amongst its listeners when it was auditioned. On hearing the theme in the Allegretto interlude of the finale (figure 15), the director of the Piatnitsky Choir, Zakharov, jumped up and accused Prokofiev of plagiarism. The simple tune, a song with a Byelorussian title, *Byvaitse zdorovy* (known in Russian as *Bud'te zdorovy* and in translation meaning 'Be healthy!'), had actually been composed by I. Lyuban, but Zakharov had arranged it for the Piatnitsky choir. Some confusion exists as to its true authorship, since the melody had become so popular that it was considered a folk song. Zakharov appeared to claim it as his own, and now charged Prokofiev with stealing it, demanding royalties and an apology. When Slava went to Prokofiev's home to tell him of the successful outcome of the audition, he also told him of the 'scandal' that had erupted. Prokofiev laughed and said, 'Well, next time I use it, I'll disguise the tune so well that Zakharov won't even recognise it.' He was as good as his word.

In the mean time, the enterprise of bringing Prokofiev's new work into the world acquired the spirit of hazardous adventure, with the two Slavas as main protagonists, as Richter recalled:

I was full of anxiety over the whole thing. Despite the fact that most of the musicians of the Moscow Youth Orchestra were well-wishing and sensitive in their attitude to me, the rehearsals didn't pass off without conflict. Some musicians would make faces, and could hardly control their laughter behind their grimaces. This is how they reacted to the discords (the augmented sevenths) and the hard terse sound of the orchestra. The cello part, with its unheard-of difficulties and innovations, aroused storms of laughter from the cello section. Kondrashin sat at the back of the orchestra and followed my gestures with a fixed immobile stare. There were only three rehearsals and we only just managed to fit everything in.*

Valentin Berlinsky was leading the orchestral cello section, and had a different perspective on the events in question:

I wouldn't agree with what Richter wrote about the orchestral cellists laughing. In fact I was far too interested in what Rostropovich was doing on the cello to have time to laugh. I was full of admiration for both the Slavas.

This was Richter's one and only attempt at conducting. Of course his musicianship was so great that he transmitted his ideas, and his hands were clear. But it was evident that this was not his emploi, and he himself had no desire to continue.†

It was an enormous challenge to put this large-scale work together on three days of rehearsal, and both Rostropovich and Richter were totally immersed in the music. As Richter recalled, 'It was no joke, and this was a really dangerous undertaking! Sergey Sergeyevich did not attend the rehearsals; Rostropovich felt he would inhibit us by his presence, and he was right. Prokofiev came to hear the work directly at the concert.'

The two artists were in a state of high tension as they walked onstage for the premiere. For Richter, to come out and not see the accustomed piano at the centre of the stage was quite disorientating:

I felt cold all over . . . Where should I go? And then I stumbled against the podium. The whole hall gasped, and after this my fear evaporated . . . We were greeted by furious clapping; I was much angered by this anticipated applause. Rostropovich, however, responded to the public's ovation by continuous bows of acknowledgement. We were being prevented from starting. Fortunately when we

* Monsaingeon, *Richter, Écrits, Conversations*, p. 117.
† In interview with E.W., Moscow 2004.

did begin, what I had been most afraid of didn't happen. The orchestra came in together! Everything else passed as in a dream . . .

Rostropovich and I had made a pact that whatever happened, when he had a pause he would look at me and give me a friendly smile so as to give me moral support.*

Indeed Rostropovich used to recount in class how after the hair-raisingly difficult solo cadenza in the second movement he had to remember to look at Richter. His smile, he said, was more like a monkey's grimace than a token of encouragement. Even so, as he reminded students, it was important that however immersed you were in overcoming technical difficulties, you also had to be able to divide your attention in order to grasp and participate in the artistic whole.

Richter went on to describe the performers' euphoria after having finished the performance.

After we finished we were completely exhausted from the enormous tension. We simply couldn't believe that we had managed to get through the performance. We lost our heads to such an extent that we forgot to call Prokofiev up onto the stage. He came up to the edge of the podium and squeezed our hands from below. In the green room we jumped up and down from joy.

But the concerto didn't enjoy success at the time, and the critics tore it to shreds. But Prokofiev told me, 'Now I can rest happy, for a conductor has been found for my works.'†

The only review of the concert appeared in *Sovetskaya Muzyka*, whose critic Ekaterina Dobrynina dismissed the piece for its 'serious defects and unnecessary complexities'. The performers, too, were criticised. Richter's contribution 'lacked direction and incisive will, his gestures did not convey the necessary tension and expressivity'; all in all, his performance seemed 'insecure and flabby'. As for Rostropovich's interpretation, this was dealt with in one single dismissive sentence: 'The [cellist's] attention was so fixed on overcoming the great technical difficulties which abound in the concerto, that inevitably the quality of his performance suffered.'

Rostropovich always knew how to find humour in a situation: he would complain that it was all made worse because the review in *Sovetskaya Muzyka* contained a photo of himself and Richter smiling broadly, as if to underline their youthful thoughtlessness and total lack of discrimination! For the performers, however, the views expressed by musicians in positions of authority were even more

* Monsaingeon, *Richter, Écrits, Conversations*, p. 117
† Ibid., p. 118.

depressing than the review. The composer Vlasov, who was at the time director of the Moscow Philharmonic, accused Richter and Rostropovich of impudence: 'Those two boys should have the tails torn off their concert dress for daring to play such dreadful music.'

In Rostropovich's view, hardly anybody immediately understood the work's importance. One exception was the Leningrad composer Maizel who was bowled over by its beauty and its innumerable innovations, describing it as 'a bag of conjuring tricks'. Another was Shostakovich, who became devoted to the concerto. Nevertheless, negative sentiments prevailed, for accusations that Prokofiev and Shostakovich were 'anti-People' and 'formalists' still held sway. The hostile climate and barbaric attitudes surrounding Prokofiev in these last years of Stalin's reign undoubtedly cast a shadow over this final period of his life, affecting his health and hastening his premature death.

It was a few days before Rostropovich summoned up the courage to visit Prokofiev – he felt mortified that his performance had not achieved the success he believed the music deserved. However, Prokofiev was totally unconcerned by this aspect of the event: rather, he was grateful that his new work had been brought to life under such difficult circumstances with such a committed performance. But hearing the music in a concert performance, Prokofiev explained to Rostropovich, had made him understand that he still needed to revise the textures and instrumentation. Furthermore he felt that the structure of the final movement would benefit from some changes: in particular he was to radically change the coda.

In the summer of 1952, then, Rostropovich found himself once again working alongside the composer. Sviatoslav Richter suggested at the end of his life that Rostropovich played a large part in some of the ensuing changes to the work, and that these were not all beneficial, but the cellist insists that he did no more than advise: 'Contrary to what is sometimes believed, eight bars of passagework for cello in the first movement were the only bars that I composed in the whole work. Neither did I add anything or interfere in the second definitive revision; the changes all belonged to Prokofiev.' Despite his deteriorating health, Prokofiev managed to complete the second revised version of the concerto later that year. Once again, he decided on a change of title, this time to *Sinfonia Concertante*, which better reflected the work's symphonic scope. But Prokofiev did not change its opus number (Op. 125), thereby clearly indicating that the new version was to replace the second concerto – Rostropovich himself is in no doubt that the *Sinfonia Concertante* represents the composer's final thoughts and that the 'second concerto' is a mere interim stage in the work's development, to which it would be pointless to return. However, the composer himself did not live to hear the work in its final form: by an irony of fate, Prokofiev suffered a similar illness to Stalin, and died on 5 March 1953, the same day as the dreaded dictator.

6

Establishing new performance standards
(1952–62)

With the benefit of hindsight, the implacable logic with which Rostropovich mapped out his concert career can be discerned. By continuously setting new aims for himself – whether learning new works, confronting the peaks of the classical repertoire, or popularising his instrument in the furthest corners of the globe – the young cellist was intent on achieving new standards, if not breaking records. Throughout the 1950s, Rostropovich constantly refined his highly personal interpretations of repertoire works, as well as becoming a standard-bearer for new music.

Rostropovich's 'cheval de bataille' during this period was the Dvořák concerto, which he played frequently and to great effect at home and abroad. At this time, perhaps surprisingly, his concerto repertoire consisted only of three nineteenth-century works: the concertos by Saint-Saëns and Dvořák, and Tchaikovsky's *Rococo Variations*. Prokofiev's second cello concerto (soon to be renamed the *Sinfonia Concertante*) was added to this list in February 1952, and Schumann's Concerto in 1954. Although he had performed two other Soviet concertos in the past, Myaskovsky's was resuscitated only towards the end of the decade, while Glière's long-winded effort was firmly relegated to the Conservatoire classroom.

On 4 June 1952, Rostropovich performed concertos by Saint-Saëns, Dvořák and Tchaikovsky's *Rococo Variations* with the Czech Philharmonic under Karel Ancerl, as a guest of the Prague Spring Festival. This was only the first of many occasions on which Rostropovich performed marathon programmes made up exclusively of cello concertos, something that probably only Casals had done before him. Rostropovich was already a great favourite of Prague audiences, and

79

his performance of the Dvořák concerto in particular won him accolades in the press. As one critic put it, 'His Dvořák is bubbling over with young life, with delight in motion and melody, in places with optimism, and elsewhere by contrast in youthful poetic dreaming. This is a performance that in every bar bears the seal of a great artistic personality, a strong individual, who however respects the composer and bows before him, placing his enormous talent at his service.'*

After his performance in Prague, Rostropovich stayed on to make a studio recording of the Dvořák concerto with the Czech Philharmonic Orchestra under its former chief conductor Václav Talich. The Czech recording company Supraphon was preparing to release several LPs of Dvořák's works under Talich's direction to mark the fiftieth anniversary of the composer's death in 1954. The original plan was to record all the instrumental concertos, the piano concerto with Frantisek Maxiàn, the violin concerto with Alexandr Plock and the cello concerto with Milos Sadlo. In the event, the violin concerto remained unrecorded, and the cello concerto was allotted to Rostropovich – widely regarded as the most exciting young cellist on the international scene, and with a loyal 'local' following in Czechoslovakia.

The major problem for the project concerned the involvement of Václav Talich, for which special sanction had to be obtained. The renowned Czech conductor had been wrongly accused of having collaborated with the Germans during the wartime occupation – this was a tragic misunderstanding, since Talich had in fact done much to defend Czech national culture at the time. Once the Communist regime had been imposed in 1948, Talich was ostracised: though he was still allowed to perform in Bratislava, where he effectively lived under house arrest, he was forbidden to conduct in the Czech lands. As Rostropovich recalls, Supraphon had to appeal to the highest authority in the country, President Klement Gottwald, to waive the restrictions by allowing Talich to come to Prague for the recording. Although permission was eventually granted, public performances were still out of the question.

During his years as its director, between 1919 and 1941, Talich had built the Czech Philharmonic into one of the world's greatest orchestras. His interpretations of Czech music were considered unique, and he was associated particularly with Janáček and Suk, two composers

* *Hudebnì rozhledy* [*Musical Perspectives*], 1952.

with whom he collaborated very closely. Although too young to have worked with Dvořák, he was immersed in the Czech tradition, and was therefore the obvious and ideal conductor for this project. Rostropovich's interest in working with Talich had already been stimulated by a conversation with Evgeny Mravinsky, in which the Russian maestro named Talich as the greatest conductor he had ever heard. Rostropovich was ready to benefit from the insights that the Czech brought to the interpretation of Dvořák's concerto.

During the first playthrough with piano at the hall of the Rudolfinum, as Rostropovich arrived at the beginning of the development section of the first movement, Talich stopped him to suggest that he should observe a slower tempo not only at the *Molto sostenuto* (bar 224), but also at bar 240, where the cello accompanies the flute and oboe. By holding the tempo back and only gradually accelerating and making the crescendo (thereby delaying Dvořák's *animato* for a couple of bars) the climax of this section would have far greater effect. Rostropovich was immediately won over by the musical logic of this suggestion, and asked Talich, 'Would you mind if we start again? Please, maestro, I beg you to teach me all you know about Dvořák.' Talich was happy to oblige, and went through the score meticulously, explaining the circumstances behind the creation of the concerto, the work's structure, and the composer's attitude towards the national traditions of folk melody – the great conductor wished to initiate his younger colleague into the mysteries of Dvořák's spiritual world.

There was an extraordinarily emotional atmosphere during the recording sessions, and Rostropovich recalls that many of the orchestra had tears in their eyes as they played under Talich again for the first time in almost a decade. There were many moments of tension, not least when heavy storms created electrical interference, ruining many of the best takes. The director of Supraphon, Jaroslav Jeda, recalled that the young cellist would repeat whole sections twice, even five times, until he remained satisfied: 'After four hours of intense work, the orchestral members were withering. Now everything depended on Talich. Sweating, he returned from the cabin to the conductor's podium and said with a smile, "That boy wants to repeat it again, and we're going to let him put us to shame?" In the orchestra there was a light rustling. They played once more, and played excellently.'*

* CD sleeve of SU 3825 2. *Vaclav Talich Special Edition 5*.

Listening to this recording, one is struck by the sumptuously rich sound of the Czech Philharmonic. Talich's musical personality is the driving force behind the performance, but Rostropovich's interpretation is totally in sympathy with his conceptual overview. The spacious tempi and the orchestra's warm, opulent tone give full expression to Dvořák's melancholic lyricism, with its all-pervading sense of sorrow and nostalgia. The interpretation underplays the 'heroic' element of the grand tuttis, instead conveying a noble grandeur. The occasional instrumental imperfections in Rostropovich's performance, such as minor faults of intonation, fade into insignificance. One can clearly understand why he prefers this reading to the studio recordings he made of the concerto (conducted by Boult, Rachlin, Karajan, Ozawa and Giulini).

Yet despite the cellist's own view, the objective listener can discern that by 1957, when he made his next recording of the work in London with Sir Adrian Boult and the Royal Philharmonic Orchestra, Rostropovich's musical and technical authority had grown enormously, and his interpretation displays a new stature and complete freedom. Here the cellist's personality dominates the reading, while Boult is happy (and excellent) in the role of accompanist. Meanwhile Rostropovich's two later recordings, made in 1978 with Carlo Maria Giulini and in 1987 with Seiji Ozawa reveal exceptional maturity, depth and interaction between great artists. While Rostropovich to this day gives credit to Talich for his understanding of Dvořák, I would nevertheless suggest that his interpretation of the concerto continued developing, eventually transcending Talich's influence to become a very personal understanding of the score, reflecting a philosophical attitude as much as emotional fervour.

Rostropovich's pupils at the Conservatoire remember some inspired classes on this work given around the time of this 1952 recording. As Alla Vasiliyeva put it:

My lessons with Mstislav Leopoldovich on the Dvořák concerto in my second year at the Conservatoire [in autumn 1952] were particularly memorable. In those days I considered this concerto to be the peak of Rostropovich's interpretive achievement. He went through it with me, illuminating and underlining all the details of the score, talking about the fine nuances and phrasing from the first theme in the introduction to the final coda with its intense, yearning *ppp* as the cello slowly glides down from the heights. This for him was the psychological culmination of the cycle. He amazed us with one revelation after another!

Rostropovich was on a concert tour in Hungary when he received the news of the simultaneous deaths of Prokofiev and Stalin on 5 March 1953. Rostropovich was in no hurry to get back for the dictator's pompous funeral ceremonies, for which all Soviet artists were required in turn to provide solemn music, while Stalin's body lay in state at the Hall of Columns. Unfortunately, Rostropovich also arrived home too late to attend the funeral of Sergey Prokofiev, but before the month was out, he was able to pay a more personal tribute at a memorial concert at the Conservatoire's Small Hall on 21 March. All the artists involved were close to the composer and had come together under the guidance of Sviatoslav Richter, who accompanied his wife, the soprano Nina Dorliak, in various vocal romances, Oistrakh in the first violin sonata, and Rostropovich in the cello sonata, as well as performing the eighth piano sonata.

The most important obligation owed by Rostropovich to Prokofiev's memory, however, was to perform the now revised *Sinfonia Concertante*, but obtaining permission for this to occur required considerable ingenuity. The criticisms launched at the work in its previous guise as the 'second cello concerto' still held sway, and the rehabilitation of Prokofiev only began well after the 20th Party Congress in 1956, when Stalin's crimes were first exposed by Nikita Khrushchev. Ironically, it was easier to arrange a performance of the *Sinfonia Concertante* abroad than at home. When Rostropovich received an invitation to perform in Denmark with the Danish Radio Orchestra, his suggestion of programming the new work in Copenhagen was accepted with alacrity. Now the cellist had to devise a strategy to ensure that this performance would be authorised by the Party authorities in Moscow. There was a firm rule that any new work by a Soviet composer required an audition before an expert commission before it could be sanctioned for performance, particularly abroad. While still awaiting this process, on 7 January 1954 Rostropovich gave a performance of the work, still in its guise as 'second concerto'. The concert took place in Moscow with the Radio Orchestra under its chief conductor, Samosud, one of Prokofiev's greatest friends and supporters. While Prokofiev was still alive, Rostropovich suggested to Samosud making a studio recording for broadcast of the second of the concerto's three movements, which lasts some twenty minutes on its own. Samosud needed no persuasion, but authorisation was required. The support of the composer Balasanyan – head of the radio committee and a loyal Party member, but one who nevertheless understood

Prokofiev's significance – ensured that the recording could proceed as planned.

Next the increasingly politically aware Rostropovich needed to find a sympathetic official who would audition the work for performance outside the Soviet Union, and take responsibility for its 'ideological correctness' and suitability as a cultural export to Denmark. He identified as a suitable choice Mikhail Balaksheev, an employee from the Ministry of Culture who often compèred government concerts, announcing the artists and titles of pieces. Slava maintained good relations with him and discovered that Balaksheev was to accompany him to Copenhagen. At the time, of course, all Soviet artists were required to travel with such a supervisor – usually their official role was that of translator, but they were in fact ideological watchdogs, obliged to report on artists' behaviour outside their homeland. Rostropovich had gauged the situation well for Balaksheev would not want to miss the opportunity of a free trip to Denmark. He decided the best time to stage the 'audition' would be on the eve of an official Soviet holiday, when everybody would be drinking with friends in anticipation of a day off. Rostropovich had made a prior agreement with the studio staff that the recorded second movement would be presented as though it were the complete work. Balaksheev auditioned the music to the accompaniment of Rostropovich's rapturous comments: 'Listen, Misha, what a lovely melody, don't you agree, such a beautiful theme could only be written by a Russian composer? And what richness of orchestration? Isn't it simply brilliant?' After listening to the second movement, Balaksheev had succumbed to the mood of euphoria, and promised to support the authorisation of the first performance. He left in a good mood, free to enjoy the festivities.

In this way, Rostropovich was able to give the world premiere of Prokofiev's *Sinfonia Concertante* in Copenhagen on 9 December 1954, with Thomas Jensens conducting. His next performance also took place outside the Soviet Union, at the Prague Spring Festival on 29 May 1955, under Karel Ancerl. In fact the work was not played in the Soviet Union until 1 February 1956, when Rostropovich performed it in Leningrad under the direction of Kurt Sanderling, the conductor with whom he recorded it the following year.

Thereafter, Rostropovich continued to propagate Prokofiev's great work as frequently as he could. By the time he gave the first Moscow performance on 18 January 1957, again with Sanderling, he had already performed it with the New York Philharmonic Orchestra and the San Francisco Symphony Orchestra during his first American tour in the spring of 1956.*

Between 1953 and 1956 Rostropovich's musical horizons widened enormously as he became increasingly involved with chamber music. By far the most significant partnership was his sonata duo with Sviatoslav Richter. Perhaps because they performed rather infrequently, their concerts were seen as festive events of enormous cultural importance, and were consequently always packed out. On 13 May 1953 they played the complete cycle of five Beethoven cello sonatas for the first time in Leningrad, while on 3 December they performed Myaskovsky's second sonata in Moscow, in the same programme in which Shostakovich's fourth quartet received its belated premiere from the Beethoven Quartet. Over the years, the Rostropovich–Richter duo acquired an extensive repertoire ranging from J. S. Bach (sonatas originally written for keyboard and viola da gamba) to Debussy and Britten, while incorporating romantic sonatas by Brahms, Chopin, and Grieg. Their concerts took place almost exclusively in Moscow and Leningrad, and they almost never exhibited their duo outside Russia. The only exception was their performances of the complete Beethoven cello sonatas in Edinburgh in 1964. Their well-known studio recording of the cycle for Philips was made in Vienna in early June 1962.† Although there was no public performance of the sonatas in the Austrian capital, Rostropovich performed the Dvořák concerto, and Richter played a recital which the cellist remembered for a superb performance of Schubert's B flat major sonata, op. post.: 'I thought Richter's interpretation could not be bettered, it was as if Schubert himself was composing on stage. I remember how upset I was when the Viennese critics wrote that it was bad Schubert playing, which went against all their sacred traditions.'

The two musicians interacted well and derived immense stimulation from working together. Rostropovich freely acknowledged Richter's influence on him, both in terms of his overall cultural knowledge and

---

* He played the *Sinfonia Concertante* with the New York Philharmonic in the Carnegie Hall on 19 and 20 April and with the San Francisco Symphony Orchestra on 30 April.

† The dates given in the LP/CD booklet for the recordings are as follows: Sonatas no. 1, 2 and 5 recorded in June 1962. Sonata no. 3 in July 1961, no. 4 in March 1963. Rostropovich remembers that they were all recorded together in Vienna in June 1962.

through the taut concentrated energy he brought to performance: his interpretations were conceived on an enormous, symphonic scale with a seemingly unlimited range of colour and dynamic. Richter's example was often cited in class, and Rostropovich always pointed to his unusual and vivid approach to the creative process. On occasion he would tell a story against himself about an early rehearsal of the Brahms E minor sonata:

At a certain point Richter turned to me and asked, 'Slava, what do you think the weather was like when Brahms was composing the sonata?' I didn't know what he was getting at and replied without thinking, 'Given that I wasn't around at the time, and neither have I made a study of the weather charts of Vienna in the late 1860s, it is not within my powers to give you a precise answer.' 'Ah,' Richter answered, ignoring my stupid sarcasm, 'but I think it was raining, and perhaps it was a chill autumn day. Brahms, looking out of his window, saw the misty grey drizzle, and composed accordingly.'

Richter's imaginative response gave Rostropovich an immediate key to the melancholic atmosphere of the E minor theme that opens the sonata. This story served as a helpful illustration for a student who approached the work somewhat solidly, or else with too much open romanticism. As Rostropovich taught, creating the initial atmosphere was essential in every piece of music. As a duo, Richter and Rostropovich seldom experienced the problems of balance which tend to occur between two instruments of unequal power. Richter believed that no instrumentalist should ever play with his full strength, but must keep something in reserve. If the muscles were stretched to maximum tension, then this was adversely reflected in the sound. The physical vibrations of the sound waves would no longer be free.

Rostropovich believed in similar principles on the cello, and was able to express them with a succinct phrase, as when he told Natalya Gutman at her first lesson with him, 'Natasha, give me an angle, and I'll give you sound.' He meant that even when playing at the point of the bow, the elbow must never be completely stretched out, but bent at an angle, so the free weight of the arm could still be used to produce sound. For Natasha it was impossible to forget this simple formula, which did indeed unlock the secret of producing a large sound.

The following story of the duo's rehearsals of the Beethoven C major sonata (Op. 102, no. 1) illustrated how to create an illusion of great power without forcing the sound or becoming overbearing. In the A minor Allegro second movement, the cello and piano play the

86

marcato dotted opening theme together in fortissimo octaves, where the cello's single voice is pitched against the piano's four voices. Rostropovich recalls that he felt completely drowned out by Richter's powerful fortissimo:

I asked him, 'Teofilovich, would you mind playing a bit less loudly?'

'*Pozhaluista* [please], of course, just as you wish,' he replied and then proceeded to play the passage equally loudly. This happened several times; I was wondering how to overcome a potentially difficult situation, when I hatched an idea. 'Tell me, how many voices have you got?' 'Four.' 'Yes, and I have one. You see, you are the army, and I am the general.' Richter liked this concept of the cello emerging as leader; he took on the role of 'infantry', hunching his back in tension and giving the illusion of unlimited force. But he actually played with less sound, allowing the cello to come through the texture clearly.

In fact, as Rostropovich has stated, 'Richter could open the piano lid fully, but he would never allow any discrepancy in the balance. He was trained in his duo with Nina Dorliak, and his delicacy in regard to his chamber partners was irreproachable, he never drowned them. Altogether he had the most brilliant feeling for ensemble-playing.'

By the 1950s Richter was already a legendary figure in the Soviet Union, and his reputation preceded him long before he first travelled to the West. Because of his origins and the fact that his mother had left Russia with a German officer during the war and now lived in Germany, Richter's travel was limited to the Eastern European satellite countries until 1960. He was regarded as a force of nature, sometimes completely unpredictable, a law unto himself. There were occasions when Richter would suddenly feel inspired to play. In Moscow, it was enough for him to make his wishes known, and often enough a concert was organised and announced on the same day, provided a suitable hall was available. Word of mouth would ensure that audiences appeared in their hordes. In his non-conformism, sometimes taken for deliberately cultivated eccentricity, there was an element of role-playing. He could profess ignorance of 'Soviet reality' and might refuse to play in a factory until the red banners with their slogans were taken down. Once he was heard to say, 'What does a one-rouble note look like, I've never seen one before? Ah, is that one? I didn't know they were so little.' Such attitudes could seem ingenuous or irritating, but they allowed him to stand on the periphery of society.

Rostropovich, by contrast, maintained an acute sense of his real surroundings, devising ways of coping with Soviet officialdom through deft intelligence and an intuition that allowed him to keep several steps ahead of everybody else. Their diverging attitudes to everyday life did not affect the artistic relationship of these two giants, however, and in music their common ground was far greater than any differences.

Richter's name was synonymous with artistic integrity, and many stories circulated about the dedication with which he could work at some minute detail of technique or a single musical phrase. He was known to practise ten or eleven hours a day, although he himself reputedly claimed that three hours' daily practice was sufficient, unless one was learning a large amount of new repertoire. Aza Amintaeva, the pianist who worked in Rostropovich's class from 1959, lived in the Composers' Union building on Nezhdanova Street in the flat above Richter. Sometimes she would hear him play the same few bars, or even four or five notes, over and over again; sometimes she might even fall asleep for a few hours, to find he was still practising the same bars when she woke up! Of course, Richter could also hear Aza and her next-door neighbour, another accompanist at the Conservatoire, when they practised. On one occasion when Aza was preparing a difficult new work, Richter was at home and suffered in silence. But the next day he transmitted a message: 'Please tell Aza that if she doesn't change her fingering she'll never get that passage right.' Aza had a wonderfully infectious laugh, and when she told the story she chuckled until tears came to her eyes, though at the time she was rather put out: 'Why couldn't he have lifted the telephone and told me which fingering would have worked better?'

Despite the large number of recordings each made, neither Richter nor Rostropovich was temperamentally suited to the recording studio. Richter resolved the problem in part by taking a recording team on tour with him, thus acquiring several recorded versions of the same concert programme taken from a series of recitals; this enabled him to select the best performances to make up the LP recording. Rostropovich only adopted this idea much later in life, when he came to appreciate the wisdom of the approach taken by 'Teofilovich'. The cellist confessed that he would often feel inhibited in the presence of the microphone, particularly during live concerts. However, this inhibition did not seem to affect the quality of his recordings, and was probably a subjective impression – once he was in the studio, his professionalism was unparalleled, and it is difficult to detect any sense of unease or restriction in his recordings. Perhaps, though, it was fortunate that he was unaware that most of his Moscow concerts, at least in the 1960s, were recorded by the radio, apparently unofficially for the archive. The radio and televised concert broadcasts that survived and have subsequently been issued on CDs and DVDs do testify to Rostropovich's unique energetic charge in performance, that particular 'buzz' between him and the audience which made his concerts unforgettably exciting.

Apart from the Beethoven cycle, the Richter/Rostropovich duo left recordings of the two Brahms sonatas and the Grieg sonata. Additionally two versions of their interpretation of the Prokofiev sonata are extant: the studio recording made for Melodiya in 1957, and a radio recording from the very first performance in 1950, which is an important historic document. As Rostropovich recalls, the microphone was placed on one side of the hall, which favoured the piano:

I don't think the sound in this recording represents what was heard in the hall. But it does convey the special atmosphere of the occasion, the presence of Prokofiev, and the whole musical elite of Moscow gathered in the Small Hall of the Conservatoire. One can sense my agitation (it was the first time I played with Richter), but more than that the festive spirit of the occasion. It was one of those few concerts which had an undefinable something in the air – a concentration, thick with intense human emotions, of great expectations, a special energy. If one had thrown a handkerchief into the hall it would have hung in the air, suspended in mid-flight. At one point the audience could not overcome their emotion and broke into applause after the end of the scherzo, with its brilliant upward-running passage, sounding like cats scampering up the keyboard. Naturally, this rather sophisticated audience knew perfectly well that it shouldn't applaud between movements, but it was unable to resist the spontaneous urge. When I listen to this recording now, it is as if a projector illuminates this memorable moment of my life: I vividly see the faces in the hall, and smell the atmosphere. I even sense Prokofiev's perfume which he loved using so much (using perfume, incidentally, was something he taught me to love). This recording has that aromatic flavour which resurrects the past for me.

Of course, over his long career Rostropovich played recitals with many excellent pianists. In Russia these included Naum Walter, Wolf Yampolsky, Frieda Bauer (who also played for his class) and Mariya Kondrashova. Nevertheless his first loyalty lay with the pianist with whom he worked regularly from his student years until he left Russia: Aleksandr Dedyukhin, who followed him not only round the world but to the remotest corners of the Soviet Union, and who was always ready to rehearse at any time of day or night, frequently learning new concertos with Rostropovich, so he could play the orchestral score at the piano.

In autumn 1953, Rostropovich also formed a piano trio with Emil Gilels and Leonid Kogan. Their first concert took place at the Small Hall of the Moscow Conservatoire on 25 October 1953: the programme consisted of a trio by Saint-Saëns, Schumann's first trio in D minor and Beethoven's 'Archduke', Op. 97. The group existed for the best part of seven years, providing competition for the long-established and better-known trio of Lev Oborin, David Oistrakh and Sviatoslav Knushevitsky, though in fact Rostropovich's trio played only a handful of concerts and never achieved the popularity of their rivals. Their performances were characterised by a polished elegance, which reflected the primary role of the piano in the formation, enhanced by Gilels's impeccable instrumental skills and beautifully rounded sound. However, it was Rostropovich's ebullient personality that stood out in the group, assuming a dominant role – this, at least, was how the London critics judged the trio in 1960 when reviewing their concerts at the Royal Festival Hall. This led to considerable dissatisfaction from Rostropovich's partners, who accused him of 'playing to the gallery' and disrupting the group's equilibrium. But by this stage the trio's days were numbered, not least because Rostropovich had discovered that Leonid Kogan had acted as an informer, reporting on his behaviour and things he had said on a previous trip to London. This threw all Rostropovich's foreign travel plans into jeopardy.

This unfortunate incident has to be understood in the context of the difficult times in which these artists worked. Kogan had evidently been caught having social contact with some Americans who came to Moscow after the end of the war. As a result, he was 'recruited' by a sympathetic officer of the Soviet security forces, who thereafter protected his career, but expected information. On discovering what had happened, Rostropovich took his wife with him to confront Kogan about the matter. Kogan was unable to provide any reasonable explanation for what had happened – the trio was finished. Unfortunately, few recordings of their partnership remain, but those that do include a BBC studio broadcast of Shostakovich's second trio, where the second-movement scherzo is taken at a breathlessly fast speed, and the D major Haydn Trio (HXV no. 16). The trio occasionally expanded into a piano quartet with the addition of the viola player

Rudolf Barshai, and on other occasions dispensed with the pianist to perform as a string trio.

Throughout 1955, in fact, Rostropovich gave a remarkable number of chamber concerts with a great variety of repertoire. On 3 March he joined forces with members of the Taneyev Quartet to perform Arensky's quartet for the unusual combination of violin, viola, and two cellos at a concert in Leningrad. (Two years later Rostropovich performed the same work in Moscow with the Beethoven Quartet. He would often recount how he arrived at the first rehearsal, having forgotten to bring his part. To his colleagues' amazement, he sat down and rehearsed without recourse to his part, proving himself able to play the whole piece from memory.) On 27 March, his twenty-eighth birthday, Rostropovich performed the three Bach sonatas (originally written for viola da gamba and cembalo) with Richter at the Small Hall of the Moscow Conservatoire. A few weeks later they played there again, performing both Brahms sonatas and the Grieg A minor sonata. In the intervening days Rostropovich was on tour, performing Shostakovich's cello sonata with the composer at the piano. Other concerts that year included performances of Tchaikovsky's sextet *Souvenir de Florence* in October, and in a formation with viola (Barshai), flute and guitar, a programme of Haydn flute trios, Beethoven's Serenade for flute, viola and cello and a Notturno for the four instruments together, wrongly attributed to Schubert. (In fact, it was the composer's arrangement of a work by Wenzel Matiegka.)

One might expect that his increasingly busy concert schedule would have led Rostropovich to neglect his Conservatoire students, but on the contrary, he was now preparing his best pupils for their own concert careers. In May 1955 he took four cellists (including two of his own students) from the Moscow Conservatoire to the Prague Spring Festival to compete in the cello competition that he had won only five years earlier – now he was acting as a jury member. By far the most significant event of this trip, however, was Rostropovich's meeting with Galina Vishnevskaya, herself a renowned artist, and already one of the Bolshoi Theatre's principal sopranos. They had in fact been introduced a little while before at a reception in Moscow – but in Prague, as soon as Rostropovich set eyes on Vishnevskaya, he was determined to conquer. Later he recounted that his best weapon was his wit, and that he had worn Galina down through laughter! Their whirlwind romance in the beautiful Prague spring led to their 'unofficial' marriage only four days after they had met. When

Rostropovich was asked recently whether he had ever entertained any doubts about the speed of their courtship, he answered with characteristic decision, 'Yes, I wasted three days of my life.'

The Prague honeymoon was cut short when Vishnevskaya had to travel on to Yugoslavia. Rostropovich in the meantime had a busy schedule to fulfil in Czechoslovakia. On 20 May he played a recital with Frieda Bauer, then on 26 and 27 May he performed the complete cycle of Bach suites for solo cello in two concerts. Two days later he gave a performance of Prokofiev's *Sinfonia Concertante* with the Czech Philharmonic under Karl Ancerl, while on 3 June he performed the Saint-Saëns concerto in Bratislava.

On her return to Moscow, with a good deal of theatrical drama, Vishnevskaya moved into the Rostropovich family flat on Nemirovich-Danchenko Street. Shortly afterwards they registered their marriage quietly. In March 1956, their elder daughter Olga was born, and a few months later in December, they moved into the co-operative apartment that Rostropovich had bought in the Composers' Union block on Ogaryov Street.

1955 had been an extremely eventful year in Rostropovich's life both romantically and musically: it was crowned on 20 October when he was awarded the title of 'Artist of Merit of the RSFSR', a high tribute for an artist still in his twenties. It was the following year, however, that saw the start of the cellist's brilliant international career, with his first appearances in the 'capitalist' countries of the West. Invitations to Soviet artists to appear in the USA and the UK owed a lot to the changing political climate. The concept of exchange had recently been implemented under the more liberal leadership of Nikita Khrushchev, ending the Soviet Union's years of isolation under Stalin. Exchange, from the Soviet point of view, was not just about opening up markets in trade and benefiting from advanced Western technology, but also involved demonstrating the ideological superiority of the Soviet system. Culture and science were regarded as embodying the highest Soviet achievement, and thus Soviet artists, orchestras and ballet companies represented their country's honour abroad.

Before now, Rostropovich's performances outside the Eastern bloc had been limited for the most part to the neutral Scandinavian countries. Nevertheless his reputation had preceded him, and he was eagerly awaited by audiences in England and the USA.

In February 1956 he travelled first to France, making his debut with Aleksandr Dedyukhin in recitals in Paris, Bordeaux and Lyon. On 3 March he made his debut at the Royal Festival Hall in London, performing the Dvořák Concerto under the direction of Hugo Ringold. Immediately afterwards he recorded the Myaskovsky and Saint-Saëns concertos in EMI's Abbey Road studios with the Philharmonia orchestra directed by Sir Malcolm Sargent.

Rostropovich's first long coast-to-coast tour of the USA began in early April: he made his American debut on 4 April at New York's Carnegie Hall, where he performed with Dedyukhin Brahms's E minor sonata, the Shostakovich sonata and various shorter pieces, arrangements of Debussy piano music and his own *Humoresque* – plus Bach's sixth solo suite for good measure. Rostropovich's American orchestral debut took place in Cleveland, where he performed the Saint-Saëns and Dvořák concertos. Other performances followed in Washington, New York (with the New York Philharmonic), Los Angeles and San Francisco. Everywhere he went, he was greeted with enormous acclaim, from critics and audiences alike. Sol Hurok, the legendary American impresario of Russian-Jewish origin, who looked after all Soviet visiting musicians, immediately booked him for a return tour.

Soviet artists worked hard for small rewards, for most of their foreign-currency earnings were taxed at exorbitant rates by the Soviet state. Moreover, artists effectively had no independence, and could not decide their own programmes, let alone negotiate their fees. Soloists of the calibre of Oistrakh and Rostropovich were lucky to be left with as much as a hundred dollars or so of the large fees demanded on their behalf – though at home, anybody earning even small sums of foreign currency was envied, for this allowed them the luxury of buying desirable foreign products, unobtainable in the Soviet Union.

Hurok was of course aware of the bureaucratic restraints on Soviet musicians, and told Rostropovich that naturally this time he would deal directly with the Ministry of Culture, but in the mean time he asked for the programmes and repertoire for his next visit. A few months later Rostropovich was called to the Ministry: 'How dare you give the programmes to Hurok's office for your American tour? You are aware no doubt that this is our job, you must have our permission for what you play!' Rostropovich replied: 'Well, the music I play is instrumental and has no texts. I don't know what there is to object to. I just gave Hurok my normal repertoire.' The cellist was given a considerable talking to, and told to put his programmes in writing. 'I'll phone them through,' replied a furious Rostropovich.

A couple of weeks later, he rang the Ministry of Culture, ready to dictate his American programmes to the official responsible: 'I think I'll start with some Bach, the suite no. 7 in F minor, then perhaps something classical – what about a Mozart sonata for cello and piano?' 'Alright. Which one will you play?' 'The fourth sonata.' 'Good.' Then Rostropovich continued, 'We'd better put in something Russian, what about Scriabin's sonata for cello and piano?' The unsuspecting official wrote down these lists of non-existent works for cello, and blithely sent them off to Hurok's New York office. When this prank was exposed, the Ministry of Culture sought out Rostropovich. 'What is this, are you making fools of us all?' But they had to admit defeat, and an official conceded that 'Rostropovich has ridden over us like a tank!' – an expression soon repeated throughout Moscow. This incident was one of many in which the cellist was able to outwit the petty cultural officials, while ostensibly adhering to the rules.

After his return from his first American trip Rostropovich wrote a lengthy article* describing his impressions, which were for the most part unconnected with his own performances. He was deeply impressed by the high quality of the US orchestras, their concert halls and the enviable conditions that American musicians worked in, and most particularly by the wonderful facilities he saw in conservatoires, and the music departments of colleges and universities. Rostropovich often joked that cultural exchange would flower 'if only we could use the wonderful American facilities and fill them with our Soviet musicians!' He was amazed by the friendliness and open-mindedness of the Americans he met, among whom were many whose families originally came from Russia. In particular, he wrote of his meeting with Rachmaninov's friend Alexander Grainer, from whom he learnt much of interest about the great Russian composer. While in California, Rostropovich visited the Hollywood studios, and accepted an invitation from the composer Lucas Foss to the University of California, where he met with teachers and students, and heard a concert of works by William Schumann. The Russian cellist was curious to discover as

* Published in *Sovetskaya Muzyka*, no. 8, August 1956.

much as possible about new American music, and for his part willingly imparted the latest news about Soviet composers and their work.

Rostropovich was always eager for new encounters, and they were not limited exclusively to musicians. He was informed that the writer Leon Feuchtwanger had wanted to attend his Los Angeles recital, but could not come because of ill health. With characteristic generosity, Rostropovich proposed that he should go and play for the writer in his home outside the city. His article recounted some of the linguistic difficulties he experienced in establishing contact with Feuchtwanger:

I had only learnt a little German in my middle-school years, and my knowledge of the language is extremely poor. Nevertheless it's true that through German I can express just about everything I need to, but without recourse to grammar. This means that whomsoever I am talking to can understand everything except for one detail: whether I am speaking about the past, the present or the future! From the first minute of my meeting with Feuchtwanger I felt so depressed at my poor knowledge of German, that I was afraid to open my mouth, and tried expressing myself with my eyes, gestures, and mime. But Feuchtwanger was so natural and charming that within about ten or fifteen minutes he had put me so much at ease, choosing such simple German words, that he managed to convince me that my knowledge of German was no worse than that of any great German writer. Soon I caught myself with an outrageous thought: it was I who spoke excellent German, while Feuchtwanger was having to stop and search for words.*

Rostropovich played solo Bach suites for the writer and his wife. Afterwards he stayed for dinner, and they conversed long into the night. Feuchtwanger explained the importance of music in his life: 'It seems to me that music can create such atmosphere, such a condition of the human soul, that it prepares the ground for that sensibility and awareness which brings out the very best in man . . . '

Back at the Moscow Conservatoire, Rostropovich regaled his students with stories of this American visit, and shared his impressions with a large circle of Moscow musicians at a packed-out meeting of the Conservatoire Student Circle. It is difficult to imagine just how thirsty Soviet musicians – young and old – were for information about life abroad. Naturally they were particularly curious about the United States, then the great unknown. Rostropovich recounted his meetings in Los Angeles with such legendary names as Gregor Piatigorsky and Jascha Heifetz, musicians regarded by Soviet Russians

* Ibid.

as part of the great national artistic patrimony that had been lost to them in the wake of Revolution. Heifetz had come backstage to congratulate him after one of his Los Angeles concerts, pronouncing with certainty, 'Young man, you will be famous for your bow arm, not so much your left hand!' This judgement from the God of all string players may have been somewhat disconcerting at the time, but it proved that Heifetz had been duly impressed by the cellist's innovative approach to the instrument, which lay in his attention to colour and sound and in the enormous power and flexibility of his bowing technique. In Los Angeles, he immediately established a relaxed relationship with Grigori (Grisha) Piatigorsky, which soon developed into a warm friendship. Rostropovich willingly answered Piatigorsky's questions about his Moscow friends, whom the elder cellist hadn't seen since leaving Russia in 1924! Piatigorsky's brother, Stogorsky, was a well-known Moscow cellist and teacher, who had changed his name rather than be associated with his emigrant brother.*

Piatigorsky invited Rostropovich to his home, showed him his cello, the world-famous 'Batta' Strad, played his recordings of sonatas by Hindemith and Samuel Barber, and spoke a lot about Rachmaninov, who like him had lived for many years in Los Angeles and with whom he had frequently performed. At the end of the evening, Piatigorsky made Rostropovich a gift of a beautiful Satori bow, together with some of his own transcriptions of pieces for cello.

Rostropovich was always eager to learn from distinguished fellow cellists, particularly when they might suggest innovations that extended the possibilities of the instrument. For example, in the early 1960s, when the French cellist, Paul Tortelier, invented the bent cello spike which raised the body of the cello to a more horizontal position, Rostropovich was eager to try it out. He agreed with Tortelier's claims that this gave the cello better projection, since it allowed the 'f-holes' on the front of the instrument to direct the sound upwards and into the hall. Certainly acoustics suggest that the more traditional 'vertical' position of the straight cello spike means that the sound waves get absorbed as they fall downwards towards the ground, rather than being bounced back from the walls or ceiling of the hall. The raised position of the cello that the bent spike allowed also made it much

---

* 'Piatigorsky' means 'of five mountains', whereas Stogorsky means 'of a hundred mountains'.

easier to play in the high positions. The potential disadvantage was that if the cello became too high, it was awkward to play in first position – but as Rostropovich quipped to Tortelier, 'you and I don't need first position'.

Initially Rostropovich adopted Tortelier's patented spike, which was made up of three separate pieces. However, there was an inconvenient aspect of the patented spike, since it didn't retract into the cello (as is the case with a straight metal spike) and it could not be fitted into standard cases. Furthermore, since the middle section was made of wood, the spike had less resilience, and if the cello was played energetically the wood tended to split. Soon Rostropovich designed an improved version – a single piece of metal which was bent in a specific way and could be lengthened – and had it made up for him in Paris. With this innovation, he felt that he gained in comfort and freedom: it seemed a natural extension of his previous sitting position, unlike the almost exaggeratedly high horizontal position of the cello that Tortelier adopted. Naturally the 'bent spike' was soon being used by Rostropovich's pupils.

1956 also saw the addition of a new work to Rostropovich's concerto repertoire. While the Schumann concerto is his personal favourite amongst all the romantic concertos, he sees it as interpretatively the most difficult. In order to come to terms with the piece, he played it with piano accompaniment in one of his early Moscow recitals, but was not happy with his performance. In 1954 he made a recording of the work, conducted by Samosud, but it was only in December 1956 that he gave his first performance of the concerto with orchestra in Lodz, Poland. Even then he did not feel ready to present it in more important venues. He would recount to his class how he searched for the key to an interpretation of this late piece, listening to other works of the period and studying Schumann's biography. The concerto was conceived while the composer was beginning to be afflicted by mental illness, and his vulnerable psychological state is evident throughout the work, where the balance between fragile poetry and questing spirit represents the two sides of Schumann's nature – Florestan and Eusebius in their latter-day transformations.

Rostropovich was well aware that home audiences can be among the most mercilessly critical – even if, paradoxically, they can also be staunchly loyal – so he waited another four years before performing the Schumann concerto in Moscow under Gennadi Rozhdestvensky's direction. This was in November 1960 – in fact he had played it the previous season in Vilnius and Sydney. But from then on it became one of his major interpretive achievements, just as the Dvořák concerto had been in the previous decade. Valentin Berlinsky recalls being amazed at the incredible sound-world Slava had conjured up in a stunning performance of the Schumann concerto in Riga in August 1963. For Berlinsky, it was in this work that Rostropovich reached the summit of his achievement in the classical repertoire.

Meanwhile, Prokofiev's *Sinfonia Concertante* continued to dominate Rostropovich's concert schedules. In 1957 he introduced the work in London (with Sargent), Milan and Venice, as well as recording it for the Soviet label *Melodiya* with the Leningrad Philharmonic Orchestra under Kurt Sanderling.

Perhaps the most significant new musical departure of the year, however, was Rostropovich's debut as a pianist, accompanying his wife. Incredible as it may seem, when they got married, Galina and Slava had never heard each other on stage. If their attraction to each other initially lay outside their art, their partnership was soon consolidated by their mutual musical understanding. They played their first concert together in Tallinn on 13 September 1957 – Vishnevskaya had suddenly found herself without a pianist, and Rostropovich gallantly offered his services as replacement. The couple's first duo recital included opera arias from Mozart to Wagner and Verdi, and lieder by Schumann, Richard Strauss, Fauré and Granados. This was not the repertoire with which their partnership was associated, but reflected rather Vishnevskaya's wide range of roles as principal soprano at the Bolshoi Theatre. It was evident from the start, however, that their music-making was fuelled by a dynamic rapport resulting from the unified vision of two strong and volatile artistic personalities who were nonetheless able to waive any interpretative differences. It was not always easy to get Slava to find time to rehearse, as Galina has vividly described – he always wanted to learn the programme from memory before they started work together, though often this was achieved only at the last minute. Yet all the tensions that accumulated during this frenetic process invariably melted away on stage, and they felt absolutely free in their music-making.

The partnership was undoubtedly strengthened by their mutual willingness to learn one from the other. Not only was Rostropovich drawn to the world of opera, which he had loved since his encounters with the theatre in Orienburg, and the rich literature of vocal romance, but he understood how to enrich his instrumental approach by borrowing from vocal techniques. Vishnevskaya, for her part, adopted many aspects of Rostropovich's philosophical approach to music, coming to favour spacious tempi and great contrasts of mood and dynamic. Rostropovich's piano playing was characterised by the most wonderful refinement of sound and enormous range of colour, which was tinted by his intimate knowledge of the orchestral palette. His sensitive gifts as an accompanist proved just another facet of his enormously talented musical personality.

Nevertheless, for the moment his priorities lay with the cello, and he continued to enrich his repertoire, learning Richard Strauss's symphonic poem, *Don Quixote*, in January 1958. A performance of any work by Richard Strauss was quite an event in Moscow at the time, for during the Stalinist period his works (like those of Debussy, Berg, and Britten, among others) were labelled 'decadent and bour-geois'. Even when the political situation somewhat eased in the mid-1950s, it was necessary to have written permission to withdraw a score by Debussy, Schoenberg or Richard Strauss from the Conserva-toire library. It was through persistent nagging that performers such as Rozhdestvensky and Rostropovich helped to win back the right to perform much repertoire considered standard in the West, although for the most part the Second Viennese School and any form of Western modernism were not tolerated.

The musicologist Manashir Yakubov, head of the Conservatoire student circle, an organisation with plenty of curiosity and granted some autonomy, recalls Rostropovich's difficulty in getting permission to perform *Don Quixote*. The student circle invited him to come and talk about Strauss's work, and Rostropovich accepted with alacrity. Classroom no. 47 was packed out in anticipation, as Yakubov remembers:

To start with he unfurled his thoughts on this wonderful youthful work of Richard Strauss – perhaps his best of that period, recounting them with capti-vating and interesting imagery, using all the artistry at his disposal. He explained *Don Quixote* with enormous relish, brilliantly demonstrating at the piano, revealing all the wonderful innovations of the harmonic and instrumental textures, and the remarkable orchestration. He himself took such delight in every detail, in the composer's flights of fantasy and humorous orchestral imagery – the fight with imaginary windmills, the bleating of sheep and the whining chant of pilgrims. His enjoyment, which I can only compare to that of a great gourmand, was so infectious that we were entranced by the reading of this musical novella. Then he took his cello and played the whole work through, accompanied on the piano by Aza Amintaeva, his faithful Sancho Panza.*

By the end of the 1950s, Rostropovich had established himself as one of a handful of the most prestigious Soviet performing artists. His achievements both in playing new Soviet work (dealt with in a separate chapter) and in introducing many Western works to home audiences were of inestimable importance. For instance, in the 1958/59 season he added the Elgar and Honegger concertos to his repertoire, as well as performing Haydn's D major concerto for the first time. He remained sensitive to the demands of audiences, catering to public taste on the one hand while educating it on the other. Rostropovich always thought very carefully about what to play, where, and for whom. A typical recital programme would offer one or two classical sonatas (usually Beethoven or Brahms) and some attractive short pieces, which provided easier listening. In a venue with a consolidated tradition of classical music, he would also play a contemporary work, either the Shostakovich or Prokofiev sonata, or a sonata by Hindemith. He regarded himself not only as a pioneer for new music, but for the cello itself.

In order to achieve his self-appointed task of popularising his instrument, Rostropovich set out to gain completely new audiences in the furthest parts of the Soviet Union, often playing in places so remote that they could only be reached by boat. It was a normal feature of a Soviet artist's life to play the odd concert in factories or workers' clubs, but Rostropovich carried ideological guidelines to the letter, bringing Art to the people in a far more radical way than any of his colleagues. In February 1958, for example, having created an unusual formation of musicians dubbed 'Masters of Art', Rostropovich set out with his new colleagues – the bayan-player Yuri Kazakov, the singer Vitali Kil'chevsky and the actor Lazar Petreikov who recited various texts – to perform in the 'virgin soil' regions of the distant Altai steppe. The small group of musicians had the flexibility to play in any venue, not just in some village hall, factory or collective farm, but also on the back of a lorry or in an aeroplane hangar. The bayan, a Russian accordion-like instrument with a

* M. Yakubov, article 'Don Quixote' written for this book.

large range of pitch and colour, proved an adaptable accompanying instrument, often imitating a piano or an organ.

In July and August of the same year, the group undertook an extended tour of Siberia and the Polar Regions, often travelling by river. They played in large cities such as Novosibirsk, Irkutsk, and Krasnoyarsk, as well as visiting the mining town of Norilsk and smaller settlements such as Khatanka and Dulinka. In Krasnoyarsk they hired a small boat, and sailed down the great Yenisey river, stopping off at small muddy villages, landing where the fancy took them, sleeping in the boat or in accommodation provided.

The repertoire was aimed at people who had never heard classical music before, and included such appealing miniatures as Tchaikovsky's *Nocturne* and *Sentimental Waltz* arranged for cello and bayan, and a transcription for bayan of Dunaevsyky's overture to the popular film *Children of Captain Grant*, as well as vocal romances and popular operatic arias. The actor recited verse and took on the role of compère. On this extended trip the singer was Alexei Geliva, a bass from the Bolshoi Theatre. A very handsome man, Geliva enjoyed considerable success, not least with the ladies. The programmes had been carefully thought out, and ended with a romance by an anonymous composer for bass accompanied by bayan and obbligato cello with the significant title, 'I have no words to express my sentiments . . .'

At a certain point in the tour Geliva announced that he was tired, and would from now on cut out the final number. His partners surmised that he did not want to share his triumph with them, and decided to get their own back. At the last concert of the tour, Rostropovich and Kazakov insisted on reinstating the romance. Reluctantly Geliva agreed. As they walked onto the stage Rostropovich warned, 'My friend, tonight you're really not going to be able to express your sentiments very much . . .' Then he and Kazakov, his partner in crime, started playing the romance a fourth lower than usual; the singer couldn't even begin to find his notes, which were now of course out of his range, and his mooing attempts to find the right pitches reduced the audience to irreverent laughter.

The whole experience naturally provided Rostropovich with a rich fund of entertaining stories, many of them involving the sort of jokes and pranks typical of musicians on a 'working vacation'. A comic episode, however, could also have had its instructive sides.

Rostropovich often liked to tell of the time when he was playing in a small village hall somewhere upstream on the Yenisey. The villagers walked in and out of the hall, talking all the time:

I noticed some of the men at the back pointing at me, and loudly exchanging comments across the hall: 'Look at that musician, that balding chap there, sawing away with the stick, he's not bad eh?' Then they would poke each other in the ribs and they continued exchanging remarks. The louder they talked, the louder I tried to play. But the only result was that they just raised their voices all the more. I tried playing with more sound, but soon I understood this was a losing battle. Then I changed tactics, and suddenly played very quietly, with a real pianissimo. The result was magical, a sudden hush fell on the hall, and the men at the back were left gaping with their mouths open, they fell silent from astonishment. That was a great lesson to me. If one plays loudly all the time, it becomes very tedious for the listener; soft playing can have a far greater effect. A musician must know how to draw the listener in towards him.

Rostropovich's popularity grew year by year, and he used his artistry to conquer every continent of the globe. In May 1958 he visited Japan for the first time, and in the autumn of 1959 he made a second, prolonged tour of the USA and Canada. In July and August 1960 he travelled to New Zealand and Australia, performing with orchestra and with the pianist Dedyukhin, while Galina Vishnevskaya joined him for the second half of the tour.

In 1961 he made an extended tour of Latin America, playing forty-nine concerts in the space of fifty days, between 9 March and 30 April. Apart from his performances in prestigious halls in cities such as Mexico City, Havana, Caracas, Buenos Aires, Rio de Janeiro and Montevideo, Rostropovich brought his art to people of all walks of life, playing in schools, polytechnic institutes and 'friendship clubs'. In Cuba he performed in concert halls, at tobacco factories, town squares, sugar plantations, hospitals and workers' clubs, as well as travelling by lorry to the people's militia points in the hills, often giving three performances a day. Not surprisingly he was greeted throughout the country as a hero, an artist who represented the best of the democratic Soviet spirit.

During this period of his life, Rostropovich kept a detailed tally of his concerts and the programmes he played in every venue. It was not without pride that he noted the number of concerts he played each year: in 1959, 94 concerts; in 1960, 125 concerts; by early November of 1961, 99 concerts. This intense performing activity, together with a notable number of LP recording releases both in the Soviet Union and in the West, ensured Rostropovich's reputation as the world's leading cellist. By establishing new standards of cello-playing and enriching the instrument's repertoire, he had become recognised as a major force in classical music.

7

An independent teacher

The promotion of Mstislav Rostropovich from assistant to *dotsent*, or independent teacher, was recommended by a vote of the Moscow Conservatoire's council of teachers in November 1952, and officially ratified by the Ministry of Culture of the USSR on 23 March 1953. In five years as Kozolupov's assistant, Rostropovich had gained valuable experience, and had put his ideas to the test. He had already assumed effective responsibility for several Kozolupov students, including his former pupils from the Central Music School, Alla Vasiliyeva and Yura Ivanov. Nonetheless, as the youngest teacher on the Moscow Conservatoire staff with his own class, the twenty-five-year-old Rostropovich still had to prove himself and to overcome scepticism from certain quarters.

Kozolupov had been responsible for the rise of the Soviet cello school, having taught over a hundred graduates himself, and now his best pupils perpetuated his didactic methods, occupying prominent teaching posts throughout the country in the most important conservatoires and schools.* Kozolupov had facilitated this process by arranging the publication of books and study materials. His leading position remained unchallenged in the cello faculty, which also boasted other respected professors, not least the charismatic Sviatoslav Knushevitsky; initially at least, Rostropovich would be given mainly students the other professors did not want. Soon, however, word spread that he was an inspirational teacher whose growing experience on stage gave him the confidence and capacity to

* The organisation of 'faculties' at the Moscow Conservatoire (one for each string instrument, one for woodwind, brass, etc.) dates from 1936. Kozolupov was head of faculty from 1936 to 1954.

impart his deep interpretative insights. Students discovered that he was interested above all in transmitting the musical message, and did not believe that technique could be separated from it.

Rostropovich began his new position with a 'half-load' of about half a dozen students, and consequently received half the normal monthly salary, which at the time amounted to a thousand 'old' roubles. The size of his class gradually grew, however, until at its peak in the 1960s, it numbered sixteen students. From 1956 he had also started teaching postgraduates, whose three-year course was compatible with work in the profession. Some postgraduates lived in different cities, where they might have a part-time teaching job or a position in an orchestra, but they were allowed time off to study and to travel to Moscow for periodic guidance from their professor.

The Moscow Conservatoire boasted many renowned performers on its staff, and it was understood that their concerts took precedence in their schedules. If a concert tour was particularly extended, part of the musician's teaching salary would be deducted, but this loss of earnings was usually made up by Gastrolbureau, the institution responsible for the remuneration of Soviet artists' concert activities. Teachers were required to give written notification of their absences, so Rostropovich's file in the archives, with its many handwritten requests for leave of absence, provides a rather precise record of the dates and locations of his performances. A full professor could rely on his chosen assistants to take over and prepare students during his absence. Rostropovich, who had not yet attained this status, allowed his students to go to other teachers while he was away, usually leaving them to make their own arrangements. But a quick perusal of archival documents makes it abundantly evident that as soon as Rostropovich returned to Moscow – if only for one or two days between tours – he always found time to make up the lessons his Conservatoire students had lost.

Some considered Rostropovich's frequent absences to be disruptive for his students, but any lack of regularity in their lessons was more than compensated by his energetic and concentrated style of teaching. In one single lesson he might give sufficient food for thought for the next two months, setting both short- and long-term aims.

Rostropovich's phenomenal memory also worked to his advantage: even after a long gap between lessons, he knew how to pick up the threads of his work, remembering exactly what his last instructions to each student had been. In addition he seemed to have a 'sixth' sense which allowed him immediately to identify a student's weak points and suggest how to remedy them. However strict and demanding he was, Rostropovich's attitude to his students was always constructive: he allowed them to feel that it was possible to achieve anything they aimed for. However, should he sense any lack of commitment from the pupil, he could be mercilessly critical.

Rostropovich's very personal style of teaching was clearly inextricably connected to his experience as a performer. He encouraged all those who were willing to learn, and his overriding aim was to instil in every pupil, whatever the level of his or her talent, a genuine love of music. Qualities such as perfect pitch, a developed memory or disciplined technique were not ones that Rostropovich considered to be interesting in themselves, for they could be acquired through training. Artistic flair, on the other hand, was a natural gift, even if not always immediately evident. He proved to have a very shrewd instinct in identifying a student's potential for artistic development, in uncovering the 'jewel' hidden behind a dull exterior.

Rostropovich's principal aim was to stimulate his students to stretch their horizons and aim much further than 'the four strings of the cello'. Psychology played a large part in his approach: while ensuring that his students had sufficient technical means at their disposal, he insisted on the fundamental rule that they should know what they wanted to achieve before tackling any task. This maxim applied equally to practising a simple, slow scale or in shaping the interpretation of an entire concerto. For Rostropovich, and hence for his 'disciples', having doubts implied knowing how to overcome them. The possibility of failure was banished from the learning process. In order to acquire the tools of his trade, a student needed a pragmatic intelligence and the ability to stand outside himself. Imagination, tied to emotion (which together made for artistic intuition), defined his whole approach to music.

When listening to a cellist play for the first time, Rostropovich formed an immediate impression of his overall personality and musical outlook. As he would put it, 'I can tell you everything about a student's character after hearing him play for less than two minutes.' He was quick to diagnose the cause of problems, and would try to offer remedies that were built on some positive features of the student's talent. This meant adapting his approach for each individual

The birth of a cellist: Leopold Rostropovich with his son Mstislav
Semyon Matveevich Kozolupov
Aspiring young musicians: Veronika and Mstislav Rostropovich

First-prize winner at the All Union competition, with Mstislav Rostropovich's inscription to his godmother, E. Lonkevich: 'To my dear "second mother", Kokochka, from Slava Rostropovich', 23 January 1946
Rostropovich demonstrating to his class at the Central Music School, *c.* 1947. Left to right: Alla Vasilyeva, Tatyana Priymenko (seated), Georgi Ivanov, class pianist and Kira Tsvetkova

Rostropovich's orchestral debut in Leningrad, Grand Hall of the Philharmonia, 1947
The young Rostropovich shows off the stretch of his left hand, *c.* 1948

A remarkable duo is born: Rostropovich and Richter, 1950
Recording the Dvořák concerto with Václav Talich, Prague, 1952
Friend and disciple: Rostropovich with Prokofiev, 1951

Arriving in Prague for the Hanus Wihan competition, May 1955. Left to right: G. Chaplygin, delegation leader, Yura Ivanov, Mstislav Rostropovich, Frieda Bauer, Mikhail Khomitser, Tatyana Priymenko and Medeya Abramyan

Bringing music to the people, Altai Steppe, February 1957. Rostropovich with Yuri Kazakov (bayan) and actor. The backdrop shows the graph of the Five-Year Plan, with slogans appealing to the workers to produce a thousand combine harvesters by June

Sailing down the Yenisey River. On tour with the 'Master of Arts' ensemble, Eastern Siberia, 1957

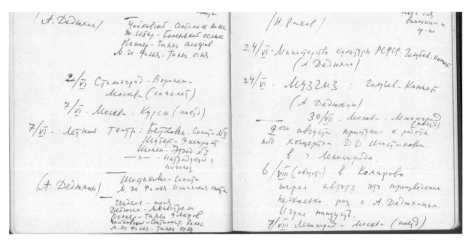

With Shostakovich after first Moscow performance of his first cello concerto, October 1959. Standing behind them, Stefan Kalyanov and the conductor Aleksandr Gauk

Pablo Casals conducting an ensemble of cellos. Amongst the players are Zara Nelsova, Mstislav Rostropovich (bottom left-hand corner), Gaspar Cassado, Antonio Janigro, Martita Casals, Mexico City, 1959

Rostropovich's concert diary entry for August 1959, indicating dates when he learnt Shostakovich's first concerto

Rostropovich with cello ensemble made up of fifteen students and ex-students at the Grand Hall of the Conservatoire, *c.* 1958. Left to right: Rostropovich, Aleksandr Damurjan, Ilarion Sheshvili, Lev Evgrafov, Valery Zelenyak-Kudreiko, Alla Vasilyeva, Miron Yampolsky, Kseniya Yuganova, Peter Zimmerman, Alla Khatsko, Dzhemil Mamedov, Viktor Apartsev, Lyubov Pyatnova, ?, Galina Sosnovskaya, Alexei Esipov
Performing the Aria from Villa-Lobos's *Bachianas Brasileiras* no. 5, Small Hall of the Leningrad Philharmonia. Rostropovich with members of cello class and the singer Kira Izotova, *c.* 1959/60
A day off with Aza Amintaeva (right of Rostropovich) and class members visiting Leningrad, *c.* 1959/60

Rehearsal of Britten Cello Symphony, Stockholm, January 1966

student, and finding the key to unlock any physical or technical 'block'. This often involved distracting attention from a specific problem, and opening up other channels: the rich associative images that he liked to employ played an essential role both in cutting through emotional reticence and in stimulating the student's own imaginative resources.

In Rostropovich's view, developing the overall personality was as important as perfecting the technical training and fostering artistic maturity. In many cases his teaching produced unexpectedly good results, and weaker students made progress in a way that his colleagues had not believed possible. Rostropovich avoided any standard or predictable formulas in his lessons, and consciously sought to undermine the image of an authoritarian professor dictating to his students. The key to the student–professor relationship, in his view, was to combine an informal, personal approach with relentlessly high demands. At the start of the lesson Rostropovich would aim to put his student at ease, whether through teasing, jokes, exhortations, or even at times through feigning a lack of interest or employing tactics of distraction. Sometimes, to break through the tensions, he would approach a student's weaknesses through a psychological back door. It was difficult not to feel inhibited by the force and brilliance of Rostropovich's personality: his students needed to learn to take from their teacher, and the most stimulating lessons came from adopting a 'duelling' technique, where sharp reactions produced a reciprocal give and take. Rostropovich willingly admitted that his failures occurred precisely when he had been unable to establish this kind of contact with a student, though this was a very rare occurrence.

From the start Rostropovich believed in the concept of the open class, which allowed students to learn from observing each other, from discussion and constructive criticism. This did not preclude him from giving lessons on a one-to-one basis, which usually took place in his home. At one time or another, almost every student received a private lesson or two from their professor. In certain rare cases, he would teach a postgraduate student almost entirely outside the class situation.

Rostropovich welcomed students from all over the Soviet Union into his class, nevertheless, much of the best talent came from his TseMSha class. Some students, like Alla Vasiliyeva and Viktor

Apartsev, remained with Rostropovich from their school years right through to the end of their postgraduate studies, staying with him for as many as fourteen or fifteen years. Other of his TseMSha pupils enrolled with other Conservatoire professors – with Semyon Kozolupov (as did Kira Tsvetkova) or his daughter, Galina Semyonovna (as did Tatyana Priymenko, for example).

Rostropovich did not take on beginners, but one pupil who came to him at a very early stage was Miron Yampolsky, the son of the well-known pianist Wolf Efimovich Yampolsky. A soloist of the Moscow Philharmonic, Yampolsky had acted as Oistrakh's principal accompanist, and also performed with other leading soloists. When Miron's parents decided to start their son on the cello, they discussed which teacher would be the best for him. At the time Knushevitsky was the most famous cellist in the Soviet Union, but having recently played with the young Rostropovich Yampolsky announced to his wife that as far as cellists were concerned, there was no question – 'This is IT!' At the age of eight, then, the young Miron followed in his brother Viktor's footsteps at TseMSha, enrolling as a pupil of Rostropovich in 1952. Miron recalls that at least one of his two weekly lessons was held in Rostropovich's home on Nemirovich-Danchenko Street:

Often we were greeted at the door by Sofya Nikolaevna, Rostropovich's mother. She was a formidable figure, and her fragile aspect – she was small and very thin, with a long white braid – belied her force of character. She dressed in a large man's shirt (from her late husband's wardrobe) and was a chain smoker. I was quite intimidated by her and would cling to Mother's skirts, while the women stopped to chat. Sofya Nikolaevna would sometimes complain about her son to Mother: 'Slava's chasing ballerinas at the Bolshoi when he should be practising!'

As Miron recalls, Rostropovich's class at TseMSha was quite numerous, and included many talented cellists. But not all of his pupils persevered with the cello; some went on to become conductors or singers. Those who didn't pass the 'transitional' exams, held twice within the ten-year school curriculum, passed into other professions.

In 1955 Rostropovich stopped teaching at TseMSha, although he retained contact with the more talented young cellists and oversaw their development, listening to them periodically in his Conservatoire class. Miron Yampolsky was one of the few pupils of the school class who continued with Rostropovich after 1955, although he officially graduated from TseMSha under Stefan Kalyanov, who had by then become Rostropovich's assistant.

Rostropovich often helped his graduate students to find their first jobs in the profession. For example, he recommended Alla Vasiliyeva for a post at TseMSha. The first year she started as his assistant, which meant that while she did most of the teaching, the pupils were still overseen by Rostropovich. In her second year, she taught an independent class, inheriting his pupils and acquiring new ones. A few months before she graduated from his class in June 1956, Rostropovich provided her with another introduction, telling her to ring Rudolf Barshai, the well-known viola player from the Tchaikovsky Quartet. Barshai duly informed Vasiliyeva that he was organising a select new chamber orchestra and invited her to join it. Her talents proved ideally suited to the demanding and scrupulous work that he expected of his musicians, as she combined a soloist's attributes with the discipline and sensitivity of a chamber musician. Barshai, who initially led the orchestra from a playing position before becoming its conductor, built up the Moscow Chamber Orchestra into one of the world's best ensembles of its kind. From the time of its brilliant debut early in 1956, Alla held the position of principal cellist for some forty years, achieving the record as the orchestra's longest-serving member.

Rostropovich had intuited that this opportunity would suit her individual talent, and satisfy in particular her interest in baroque music, an area largely ignored in Russia at that time. While working with the orchestra, Alla continued her postgraduate studies with Rostropovich. For her, it was his insight into interpretation that were the most valuable aspect of his teaching, rather than what she learned about the mechanics of cello-playing:

The deepest and brightest impressions from my time as Slava's pupil were, first and foremost from listening to him in concert, and from our work on two concertos: the Myaskovsky and particularly the Dvořák . . . Rostropovich was without peer in works of large-scale form, with their weightier significance. An intimate knowledge of the orchestration was essential to the perception of the whole work and to the interpretation of the cello part. Through his wonderful set of associations, he could illuminate every point, as if projecting images on to a screen. When he talked about musical structure, he insisted that repeated material should always sound different, so when the same theme occurred in the recapitulation it was to be viewed through the prism of its development, having undergone transformation both in its emotional and philosophical aspect. Since my father was an architect, these explanations of the architectonic structure of music appealed to me greatly.

For Vasiliyeva, Rostropovich's musical explanations served to push her to find her own instrumental solutions – in the long term, independence of thought is the most useful gift a teacher can make to a pupil.

Lev Evgrafov was another student who transferred to Rostropovich at TseMSha after the death of his former teacher David Borisovich Lyubkin, Kozolupov's assistant:

The first thing I studied with Mstislav Leopoldovich at school was Mozart's Horn Concerto in Cassado's transcription. I remember his inspirational accompaniment at the piano, he got completely carried away by the music. Without stopping me to give his instructions, he showed the musical flow and phrasing at the piano, while simultaneously talking and singing. He fantasised with the most wonderful images, often inventing theatrical dialogues with great comic effect. One had to follow and try to absorb his suggestions as one was playing: 'Lev, do this, now try that.' There was no time to sit back and think things over. Everything had to be instantaneous.

Rostropovich often left the student to work out just how he was to implement his suggestions, and he would usually just brush aside any questions: 'Think the music and you'll find a way. Play with your nose, as far as I am concerned.' To begin with many of his students were perplexed by such advice, but they gradually realised that the power of the idea would ensure the success of the search for solutions. As Evgrafov concluded, 'Being taught by Mstislav Leopoldovich was a fantastic experience, his methods were unlike anybody else's. He set his students aims and tasks that required attitudes which differed completely from the conventional schooling that we had received before. In particular, his manner of thinking in associative images was so striking that it affected our whole approach to life.'

Rostropovich was only a few years older than his Conservatoire students, so they could easily relate to his example as an artist, as Evgrafov recalls:

Mstislav Leopoldovich dazzled us with his performances of new works. I remember hearing the first performance of Prokofiev's Second Concerto before it underwent its final revision as the *Sinfonia Concertante*. Whatever he performed left the impression of an extraordinary virtuoso feat, one simply couldn't imagine how many of the passages could be played on the cello at all. Later when one saw the score, one realised that it was all possible to play, and even not as difficult as one had first imagined. Rostropovich had this wonderful capacity of imparting brilliance to everything he touched.

Rostropovich believed that the musical concept of a piece should generally be worked out away from the instrument, and put to the test in the context of the whole, so that any dividing line between the initial idea, the technical means and the overall result was obliterated. In an interview with me he expressed this teaching philosophy very succinctly:

I have never believed in the kind of 'false pedagogue' who explains technique in a dry, systemised way. For me it is essential that a musical impulse is behind everything the pupil does, and that his brain is alert when playing. I believe a teacher should avoid instilling the idea of repetitive, 'unthinking' habit in the hours of practice. This is why I like giving pupils difficult combinations to try out in scales and studies, so as to sharpen their reflexes and develop their flexibility.

And even with less advanced pupils, who perhaps need to concentrate on acquiring the means and wherewithal to play the instrument, I tried never to separate the musical reasoning from the technical aspect in giving advice. I might say, for instance, 'you need a hard sound here, try to play near the bridge.' Instead of saying to the pupil, 'play sul tasto' (on the fingerboard), I would say, 'play very softly as if there is air between the string and the hair of the bow.' The musical image in this way stimulates the pupil to find the technical means and helps him remember through association.

Of course it is also important to ensure that a pupil has a thorough technical grounding, playing scales, studies and study concertos. But the idea of the kind of sound you want must be there from the start, even if only playing an open string.

Despite his aversion to a mechanical study of technique, Rostropovich nonetheless guided students to an understanding of the instrument and its technical possibilities. He would suggest transferring technical problems encountered in repertoire pieces to scales and studies. A 'trick' that was useful in learning a passage was to repeat them with slight variations, for instance accenting and lengthening one of the four notes in a group of semiquavers, starting with the first, then the second and so on. An even more complex task was to apply triplet phrasing to groupings of four semiquavers, or vice versa. Inventing different bowing combinations made the task more intricate still. A student who played through a difficult passage in ten or more different ways developed quick mental responses.

With the same purpose, Rostropovich often set his students Cossman's conventional studies in double-stop patterns, as a means to develop finger strength and velocity, but also in order to instil mental agility. He was adamantly against routine repetition, for it dulled the senses. Furthermore, repetitive movement could result in muscular strain. Rostropovich used the Cossman studies rather to build up both physical and mental stamina by inventing a variety of exercises derived from them – making the two voices move in different rhythms, duplets against triplets, and harder still, triplets against four semiquavers, constantly changing the function of the voices.

Rostropovich taught his students to know their physical limitations and never to force the pace. The muscles had to be warmed up gradually, and he encouraged changing from one set of movements to another so as to avoid the muscle contraction and cramp resulting from repetitive gestures that can lead to problems like tendonitis. His students were taught to follow the principles used by sportsmen, respecting the physique through regular work and gradual build-up of stamina.

Once certain fundamental principles had been imparted, Rostropovich preferred not to interfere with his pupils in their 'kitchen work' (as he described this basic technical process); beyond a general insistence on quality rather than quantity of practice, he believed that each person must develop their own recipe for study. Sometimes Rostropovich would invite his pupils to practise at his home, knowing that many of them lived in cramped conditions, and that in the hostels and the Conservatoire they often had to queue for practice rooms, while competing with the noise of musicians in neighbouring rooms. Usually he left the student alone, but sometimes he would listen in to check how he was working. Afterwards he might comment: 'Why did you need to repeat that phrase, when you already played it perfectly well the first time? What were you trying to achieve by that?'

Rostropovich himself believed in maximum efficiency, declaring, 'I only practise the things I can't play, not the things I can play.' This attitude required an ability to stand back and analyse one's defects, directing one's energy very precisely. He disapproved of 'playing things over and over', dismissing it as an exercise in 'idiotic self-complacency'. Indeed, on rare occasions Rostropovich even forbade pupils to practise, if they were working too many hours without producing tangible results.

An essential part of the Conservatoire training was the regular exhibition of students at 'class evenings', as these concerts were known, which were always held in the beautiful Small Hall of the Conservatoire. From the start Rostropovich turned these class evenings into events shaped by a guiding idea, thinking carefully about the order of pieces and seeking connections between them. His programming ideas for the class concerts often reflected his own current interests and achievements, such as his first cycle of Bach suites cycle in 1950, or his performances of the complete Beethoven sonatas with Sviatoslav Richter. Once his class had expanded in the 1960s, the programmes often reached marathon lengths. Two or three consecutive concerts might be dedicated to one particular theme, such as Soviet cello music. Back in the early 1950s, however, each concert was shared between Rostropovich's four or five students, as Evgrafov recalls:

To begin with, the class was so small that each of us might play as much as a quarter of the whole programme. At one of the first of Rostropovich's class concerts I played three movements from Bach's fourth suite, some small pieces, and the first movement of Davydov's first concerto.

After these 'class evenings', Mstislav Leopoldovich would invite all the students who had participated back to his flat to celebrate, and we always had lots of fun. He would organise a wonderful supper, helped by his mother and sister, Veronika. After we had finished eating, a kind of post-mortem was held on our performances, but this was done in a totally original manner. Mstislav Leopoldovich had a tape recorder and devised a kind of radio programme, in which his sister Veronika acted as announcer: 'This is Radio Moscow transmitting the Latest News! Tonight Rostropovich's students X and Y and Z performed at the Small Hall of the Conservatoire . . .' Then followed a careful analysis of each of our performances. Mstislav Leopoldovich's penetrating comments were not only interesting but full of humour, one might say even black comedy. I remember several such occasions at his home at Nemirovich-Danchenko Street, before he met and married Galina.

With his dislike of schematic models, Rostropovich enjoyed using the element of surprise in all things: surprise stimulated the reactions and brought humour to a situation. Often students were unexpectedly put to the test, and Rostropovich might ask them to transpose a piece into a different key, or else improvise a passage. On other occasions he would suddenly demand to hear a scale played in a myriad of complex bowing combinations. The Armenian cellist Medeya Abramyan's first experience of playing for Rostropovich was typically disarming. She had been sent to Moscow as a representative of the Armenian Soviet Republic for auditions for the World Youth Festival in Bucharest, and Rostropovich was on the panel of judges. Medeya recalls:

We were introduced backstage, where he congratulated me and informed me that I had been chosen to go and play in Bucharest. To my great surprise and dismay,

Mstislav Leopoldovich then suggested that I transfer my studies to his newly formed class at the Moscow Conservatoire. Until that year he had officially been Kozolupov's assistant. I was then in my second year at the Erevan Conservatoire where my cello teacher was Levon Grigorian.

Rostropovich invited Medeya to his home so that they could discuss these ideas further and he could review her repertoire:

I remember how nervous I was before this meeting; as I walked down the street I kept repeating his difficult-to-pronounce name and patronymic. The very first thing that Mstislav Leopoldovich asked was, 'Just play a scale for me.' I found this something of a shock, as if I was being put on the spot; it was not a pleasant moment. Later I came to realise just how useful scales can be, and that they are an essential part of the cellist's learning process.

Rostropovich facilitated Medeya's transfer, writing letters to placate the relevant authorities and reassure her mother. He started work with her on the programme for her concerts in Romania, which was selected chiefly from effective miniatures and virtuoso pieces. Rostropovich's principle of 'perception through images' fundamentally influenced Medeya's artistic development.

Abramyan's transfer from Erevan to Moscow reflected the kind of difficulties that many students from the outlying republics encountered at the beginning of their studies, ranging from the tedious bureaucratic procedures to the emotional demands of getting acclimatised to a large and foreign city. Medeya faced many such problems after enrolling as a third-year student at the Conservatoire in September 1953:

To start with there was the question of finding accommodation in Moscow, then getting used to the food, and the climate. I discovered that I had an incredibly full study schedule, with an enormous quantity of lectures and theoretical material. Apart from my cello studies I played in an 'all-female' string quartet, a piano trio and other ensembles as well as in the student orchestra. With such a full programme it wasn't easy to find enough time to practise the cello. My working day lasted from six in the morning to midnight. I scheduled three practice sessions: from seven to ten a.m., from two till four in the afternoon, and from nine to eleven in the evening. I needed all this time to prepare between one lesson and the next, since Rostropovich required me to learn an enormous quantity of new repertoire, all from memory.

To begin with he set me works that went 'against the grain', pieces which I found particularly hard to learn and assimilate. He worked a lot on my right-arm technique, and I soon discovered that the bow was indeed more important than the left hand.

Fellow students remember Medeya Abramyan as an outstandingly talented cellist, with a strong musical personality and an exceptionally beautiful sound. She and Georgi Ivanov were the first Rostropovich students to play at an international competition, as participants at the 1955 Hans Wihan competition in Prague. Rostropovich sat on the jury of the competition he had won five years back, as well as heading the Soviet team of four competing cellists, the class pianist, Frieda Bauer, and the 'head of the delegation', the inevitable 'accompanying' official from the Ministry of Culture.

The other competitors included Tatyana Priymenko, who had already participated in the string quartet competition at the Prague Spring Festival of 1950, when her group had won first prize:

In 1955 the Soviets had a very strong team: Mikhail Khomitser, Knushevitsky's favourite pupil, myself, Yuri (Georgi) Ivanov and Medeya Abramyan, the last two being Mstislav Leopoldovich's pupils. Medeya had a very striking musical personality, and her playing was full of emotion and passion. With its rich variety of vibrato, her sound was very individual. As an artist she certainly attracted attention to herself. However, the first prize was divided between Khomitser and Sasha Vechtomov, a Czech cellist who had studied with Semyon Kozolupov. Medeya and I shared the second prize.

It was during the competition that Mstislav Leopoldovich met Galina Vishnevskaya, and their lightning romance unfolded under our eyes. Galina Pavlovna was singing as part of a team from the Bolshoi Theatre. I remember once going into her hotel room to see her sitting on her bed, legs tucked under her in oriental style, and Slava on a chair beside her, practising the cello.

Rostropovich sat on the jury with such distinguished colleagues as Milos Sadlo, Kazimierz Wilkomirski and Paul Tortelier. From his carefully written notes on all the competitors, which served as a private *aide-mémoire* during jury discussions, one can see that he more frequently found fault with the competitors' musical judgement than with their technical attributes. He clearly did not appreciate the musical taste of the joint winner, Khomitser – his notes include barbed criticisms such as 'he performs the music as if it was a Gurilyov romance'. In more specific terms, his comments suggest an excessive use of sentimental glissandi, too many sudden 'nauseous' crescendi, and uneven bumps in the legato cantilena. But Rostropovich also gave credit where it was due – to Khomitser's 'very good' beginning of Dvořák's *Rondo*, for example, although the rushing of the Polka section was deplorable.

Whatever disappointment he felt at Medeya not achieving the top prize had to be put into the perspective of the whole learning process. Medeya suffered from occasional lapses of memory when she played, which Rostropovich put down to her exclusive reliance on 'tactile' memory – memory of the fingering rather than the notes. Memory is an essential element in a musician's life, particularly since convention requires that soloists play from memory on stage. Some have more natural mnemonic gifts than others, but memory can be trained and reinforced. Rostropovich defines its three physical aspects as visual, auditive and tactile, but emphasises that above all the musical memory must predominate. For instance if your musical memory is secure, you can improvise fingerings and bowings on stage, should you depart from the model learnt. He himself usually commits a score to memory before he starts learning the cello part. His last memory check is to see whether he can play the cello part through on the piano, where the physical patterns required to produce the sounds are completely different. During performance, any hesitation or distraction can affect the cellist's memory and trip him up. Reactions on stage differ from those in the practice room or in the classroom, so for Rostropovich it was very important to analyse one's reactions during a concert performance. After every class concert, he expended a lot of time discussing students' performances in every aspect, and asking them to work out the reason for any error that occurred.

The stress of playing in a competition is still greater than that of a concert, for inevitably the musician is aware of being judged. The Soviet conservatoires were extremely competition-oriented, not least because a 'laureate' (a national or international prizewinner) was guaranteed concert work, and with luck was able to travel abroad, a rare privilege in those years. At this stage, having students who succeeded in competitions was also important for Rostropovich's own career, as Alla Vasiliyeva points out. Medeya became his first prize-winning student, and two years later Vasiliyeva was the first of his students to gain a first prize: 'I won the gold medal at the Moscow Youth Festival competition in 1957 which I shared with Natalya Shakhovskaya, who at the time was a student of Kozolupov. Just after I won this prize Slava was appointed full professor. The Conservatoire took note of his students' successes.'

Anatoly Nikitin was one of the first 'outside' students to enrol as a postgraduate in Rostropovich's class. After graduating from the

Leningrad Conservatoire, Nikitin joined the Leningrad Philharmonic Orchestra, then in its heyday under Mravinsky, but also wished to study contemporary repertoire under Rostropovich. On one of Rostropovich's visits to Leningrad, Nikitin met him and requested lessons. It was decided that he should first enrol as a postgraduate at the Leningrad Conservatoire, and then transfer his studies to Moscow. Nikitin continued to work with the Leningrad Philharmonic Orchestra and later became section leader. He also became a distinguished teacher and head of the cello department at the Leningrad/St Petersburg Conservatoire, a position he still occupies today.

Nikitin has defined Rostropovich as a kind of 'musical Leonardo da Vinci' because of the universality of his approach:

As a performer Rostropovich was great, and in his capacity as a teacher he was no less great. Nevertheless as a pupil one had to know how to study with him, one needed talent to receive from him, and to put the knowledge he imparted to good use. I would not call him a professor of cello, but a professor of all the disciplines of music. His aura and the atmosphere of his class was extraordinary – just to be in his company was a wonderful experience, one learnt from him all the time.

For his lessons, Nikitin usually travelled down to Moscow just for twenty-four hours on his day off from the orchestra:

I had most of my lessons at Rostropovich's home, since it wasn't easy for him to squeeze me into his busy schedule. When my free day coincided with his Conservatoire class I would play for him there; one also learnt a lot from hearing him teach other students. I would participate in the class concerts too.

In my years with Rostropovich, I studied many works, often bringing them to him just one time. I was given the opportunity to play Prokofiev's *Sinfonia Concertante* with the Leningrad Philharmonic, and Slava agreed to prepare me for this performance. He was, I think, the only performer of the work at the time. In any case he lent me his music, for it still had not been published. Similarly I learnt the Tchaikovsky *Rococo Variations* with him to play with the Philharmonic. He would encourage me: 'Anatole, go and play!'

Anatoly was amazed that Rostropovich went to the trouble of writing in fingerings and bowings for his students. He suggested that Slava should just write them into one part and let his students copy them out as need be. Rostropovich saw the wisdom of this idea, but only implemented it once Stefan Kalyanov became his assistant and took the task on. The disadvantage of this system was that by the 1960s the annotated scores had acquired the status almost of a sacred untouchable text, a notion whose rigidity went against Rostropovich's more flexible approach. The 'Rostropovich edition', with the master's fingerings and bowings carefully copied in, certainly served the purpose of giving the student a logical and coherent instrumental approach to the music, but when the fingerings went against the physical build of a particular hand, or the student's individual idea of the piece, Rostropovich was the first to encourage change. Anatoli recalls:

After my lessons with Slava, I wrote down everything he had said, I didn't want to forget any details. In fact Rostropovich often changed his ideas, there was nothing fixed or fossilised about his approach. He would never say, 'You must play like this,' rather he would help you search for solutions. Perhaps a month later he would say something different to a student about the same work. In this he set an example: as a great master he shied away from fixed definitions.

But the one thing he couldn't bear was indifference in performance. For him music represented the expression of something, a sentiment, or a mood, and if one played without expressing one's own relationship to the music he found it intolerable.

Rostropovich's great merit as a teacher was to help each of us discover our own attitude to the music. With his flights of fantasy, he provided many interpretive revelations. He had this unique ability to address the music on intimate terms.

The continuous evolution in Rostropovich's approach to music meant that his cello-playing did not carry the stamp of a particular school. As Nikitin observes:

He was in a completely different class from any other professors and teachers, he operated within a different framework. One learnt a lot simply from observing him play. There were many aspects of his instrumental approach which lay outside the conventional formulation of any school, he invented his instrumental technique as needed to suit his musical ideas. He was not really interested in handing down any particular tradition of cello-playing.

Furthermore Rostropovich evolved a style of playing which was comfortable and natural to him. Once a well-known cellist observed to me that actually Rostropovich's playing position was 'incorrect'. I could only answer, 'Well, if only everybody played as "incorrectly" as he does!'

In fact, Rostropovich was acutely aware that his arm and hand positions were highly individual, possibly as the result of his boyhood accident. It was partly for this reason that he preferred demonstrating at the piano in class, for he never wanted his students to imitate him in a parrot-like fashion. Moreover, with his extraordinary memory and wonderful pianism, he could display his musical ideas with ease at the piano – his students often found themselves playing with two pianists, the class accompanist playing the printed part and Rostropovich simultaneously demonstrating.

The class accompanists themselves were of an exceptional calibre, as Lev Evgrafov recalls:

We were lucky to have the most wonderful class accompanists, Mariya Abramovna Stern and Frieda Bauer, who later became Oistrakh's pianist. Bauer was a favourite pupil of Igumnov, and she played divinely. I have never heard anybody else play certain things so well: for instance the way she filtered the sound in diminuendo in the third movement of the Rachmaninov sonata was unforgettable. Bauer possessed a unique filigree quality of sound and mastery of dynamic control.

Another pianist who for a time worked in the class was Evgeniya Seidel. In 1959 Aza Amintaeva became the class pianist; she was totally devoted to Rostropovich and his class, and remained in this position until he left Russia in 1974.

The Conservatoire timetable included at least one hour's rehearsal with the class pianist, who was expected to know the whole repertoire, including the piano scores of every concerto. Furthermore, most class pianists were willing to devote as much time to students as needed, on occasion preparing whole concert programmes with them. Rostropovich himself played concerts on occasion with both Frieda Bauer and Aza Amintaeva, thus endorsing them as artists in their own right. Students could in a sense regard them as teachers too.

Rostropovich taught his students that every working relationship with another musician must be based on respect and cultivated through mutual understanding. He often used to recount a comic incident that occurred just before he and Vishnevskaya gave their first joint recital in Tallinn. Two days before their departure he went to collect their train tickets and sleeper reservations from the Philharmonia. He was handed two separate envelopes, one of them with a first-class 'soft' sleeper berth, the other with a second-class 'hard' berth. 'What's this?' he exclaimed. 'Why two separate bookings in different classes?' The explanation was humiliating, although its simple logic was irrefutable. 'Vishnevskaya is the soloist, so for her the soft berth, and the accompanist is booked in the hard berth!' Rostropovich used this story as an illustration that there could be no question of thinking the 'accompanist' as inferior: the pianist was an essential component of every singer and instrumentalist' recital.

Rostropovich's democratic approach meant that he would often participate as a performer in the class concerts, giving his students the opportunity to feel – at least for an evening – on an equal footing with him. This helped his class to retain the spirit of a close family gathering, as one of his students, Valery Zelenyak-Kudreiko, recalls:

When I was studying in Rostropovich's class from 1955 to 1960, it hadn't quite reached the high level of recognition it did later. The atmosphere was more relaxed and we felt less inhibited with our teacher, who after all was still quite close to us in age. I was some ten years younger than him, and in a certain way he felt like an older brother to me. He knew all our families, would visit us at our homes, perhaps to celebrate after a class concert. He was friendly with my parents, and on special occasions like 8 March he would quite likely ring my mother to wish her and my grandmother a 'Happy Women's Day'.

Rostropovich was still making his mark as a teacher at this stage, and when he was away on concert tours, he suggested that we ourselves ask for lessons with other teachers – he still had no assistant. During his absences, then, I would have lessons from such cellists as Knushevitsky, Sergey Shirinsky and Sergey Aslamazian. Rostropovich was very open-minded, and he encouraged us to be curious too.

This curiosity consisted not just of listening and learning from other cellists, but from other instrumentalists too, and particularly singers. Rostropovich encouraged students to study recordings by great opera and lieder singers in order to identify with a particular voice, trying to define what kind of sound quality they preferred. This partly reflected the influence of Galina Vishnevskaya on Rostropovich's artistry, particularly on his enhanced concept of sound. When speaking of the variety of expression needed in cello sound, he would frequently ask his students to emulate the human voice, both in terms of phrasing and breathing, and through techniques such as vibrato, portamento and glissando. The bow, he suggested, could be equated with a singer's breathing, creating a myriad of nuances in the phrasing and shaping the musical line; the left hand, he suggested, performed the function of the vocal cords, dictating pitch and, through the vibrato, colour.

The short length of the bow can easily seem an impediment to string players, imposing restrictions on the musical line through the necessity of changing its direction. In imitating the long line and breath control of a great singer, Rostropovich was able to cultivate a 'seamless' bow change: his aim was to 'eliminate the bow's existence from one's mind' through a process of sublimation. He would also explain the differences between different kinds of voices, perhaps asking a student to emulate the sound of a dramatic tenor, with a wide amplitude but somewhat slower oscillation of vibrato, or else a lyric tenor, using a narrower and faster vibrato to attain a warm, rounded but less forceful sound.

Operatic declamation could be achieved through the careful use of portamento in the bow, while through judicious left-hand shifts one could reproduce different types of vocal expressivity, which meant knowing exactly when and how much glissando to use. Another technique Rostropovich suggested was the substitution of one finger for another on a repeated note, producing a kind of *parlato* articulation while varying the pitch of the note by microtonal intervals – something that a singer would do naturally. (An example of this technique can be found in Rostropovich's recording of Casals's transcription of Fauré's *Après un Rêve*.)

Rostropovich's approach to cello technique was founded on the necessity of overcoming the limitations of the tools at our disposal. He frequently calls the bow an imperfect accessory to the instrument: looking forward to a time when it will be radically improved, he would share with his students his utopian dream of inventing a continuously moving bow, which would revolve round the body like a hula-hoop. Even should such a radical solution be realistic, however, it could only help with bowing long, legato phrases, not with other types of stroke. For Rostropovich, however, the concept of an endlessly long, smooth line was less a practical proposal than a philosophical metaphor for taking music out of the fixed boundaries of time. While music is created within the concept of tempo and rhythm, nevertheless there exists the idea of stasis, that timeless atmosphere which Rostropovich so often succeeds in transmitting in his own performances. He liked to prompt his students to aspire beyond the dimension of real time, with its metronome markings and inexorable divisions into ticking seconds and minutes.

The high demands Rostropovich set himself in the concert hall were carried into the Conservatoire classroom. His authority as a teacher grew in tandem with his brilliant concert career, and by the end of the 1950s he became the obvious candidate to take over the position of head of the cello faculty. In 1954, after nearly twenty years in the position, the ailing Semyon Kozolupov had been succeeded by Sviatoslav Knushevitsky, his most eminent pupil. However, Knushevitsky was temperamentally unsuited to the administrative work the post required, and he simply did not have the drive or energy to make a good department head.

On 22 May 1958 Rostropovich made a formal application to the Conservatoire director Aleksandr Sveshnikov for the head of faculty position. However, he had still not been promoted to the rank of full professor, and consequently his candidature could not be considered, although his vision and energy ideally suited him for the job. During the same month, in fact, Knushevitsky was promoting Rostropovich's candidature for a professorship, and signed a letter of support on behalf of all members of the cello faculty. As the first step in a long bureaucratic procedure, Rostropovich was nominated as a candidate-professor in June 1958. A year later his nomination as a full professor was confirmed by the Conservatoire council, although his academic title was finally confirmed by the Ministry of Culture only on 21 April 1960.* His wage was set at 350 new roubles a month, over three times his initial teaching salary (this in a country where – officially at least – inflation did not exist). The relatively high salary reflected the prestige associated with academic education in Soviet times – professors were an elite caste! Nevertheless, many material items remained beyond the reach of a normal professor: a car, for instance, cost about six thousand new roubles.

It was at this stage that Rostropovich needed to resolve the pressing question of finding an assistant, in view of his intensive concert activity, large class and full teaching load. Several of his postgraduate students felt that they were being groomed for this job, including Vasiliyeva, Nikitin, and Evgrafov. No doubt Rostropovich saw a gift for teaching in each of them: he firmly believed that young artists should be encouraged to teach, since apart from anything else it was a way of clarifying one's own ideas. He often asked postgraduates such as Vasiliyeva and Evgrafov to help look after talented students at the various Moscow music schools. His eventual choice of assistant, however, was Stefan Timofoeevich Kalyanov – a decision that caused surprise and some consternation. Kalyanov had studied with Galina Kozolupova, and while never becoming a performing cellist, he was extremely interested in methodology and enjoyed teaching children. He passionately admired Rostropovich and attended all his concerts,

---

* The Council approved the professorship of both Rostropovich and the famous violin teacher Yuri Yankelevich on 16 June 1959.

thus drawing attention to himself; Rostropovich for his part felt sympathy towards Kalyanov and wished to help him.

It is probable that Rostropovich preferred to have an assistant without a strong independent artistic personality, but who was happy to fulfil his orders and suggestions obediently while also taking on the functions of secretary. Many, though, came to view Kalyanov as a bureaucrat, the 'man in the grey suit', rather than a worthy assistant to one of the world's greatest cellists. Kalyanov's simultaneous career within the administrations of the Conservatoire and Central Music School (of which he became director for several years) would undoubtedly have brought him in close contact with Party bureaucracy: whether or not he was requested to report on Rostropovich and his class, it is generally understood that this is what happened.

For many of the better students, lessons with Kalyanov seemed an unnecessary and tedious formality, but weaker students who were behind with their technical preparation found him to be a very thorough and helpful teacher. Certainly in my own case, I am grateful to him for his dedicated work: Kalyanov found the time and energy to give me five lessons a week in my first year of study in Moscow, when my technique needed radical reform and building up anew. Even for those at more advanced stages of study, however, Kalyanov exerted a calming influence, preparing them before they were exposed to the merciless demands made by Rostropovich in his open masterclass.

Kalyanov's appointment was confirmed on 10 October 1959 – until this point Rostropovich had been thinking of reducing his teaching to a half-load, but the presence of an assistant made it practically possible for him to cope with his relatively small class of six students and two postgraduates. In spring 1961 Aleksandr Sveshnikov asked Rostropovich to apply again for the position of head of faculty. After Kozolupov's death earlier in the year, and Knushevitsky's retirement due to ill health – or, as some believed, because of his penchant for the bottle – the cello faculty was without a head. A year earlier, when the matter had been put to a secret ballot, most faculty members voted for Rostropovich, despite his relative youth, but Rostropovich freely admitted the problems he faced:

It was a difficult moment for I had to 'leap over' this generation gap. True, it was not so much me but those who felt they were being surpassed who saw this as a 'psychological hurdle'. Everybody was used to the idea that I was a 'talented youngster'. My older colleagues Svyatoslav Knushevitsky and Galina Kozolupova were gradually forced to leave me some space, although it was only a fissure through which I could barely crawl. This led to a lot of bad feeling towards me, which made me suffer deeply.

Certainly Rostropovich's successful careers as performer and teacher provoked much envy – and also some downright malice. Rumour was rife, and it was whispered that reckless ambition had led Rostropovich to trample over other faculty members. Some went so far as to hint that not only was he responsible for ousting Knushevitsky from his position as faculty head, but that he had hastened his demise. Further unpleasant rumours followed, amongst them hints that Rostropovich was keeping Daniil Shafran out of the Conservatoire and hindering him from performing abroad.*

All these rumours were totally unsubstantiated. Knushevitsky had stepped down of his own accord, and Rostropovich had always spoken of his admiration for his mastery as a cellist and artist: any rivalry that had existed between the two piano trios they played in ended when in 1960 the Gilels/Kogan/Rostropovich trio stopped its activities. Nonetheless, the rumours persisted to the point where Rostropovich decided that the best solution all round was to step down from his position and leave the Conservatoire – he had plenty of other things to keep him busy! He decided to seek advice from Krasnaya Presnaya district judiciary tribunal as to whether he could exercise his right to retire. However, Aleksandr Sveshnikov would not hear of it, and intervened personally. He understood Rostropovich's indispensability to the Conservatoire, and confirmed his appointment as head of the faculty of cello and double-bass. Rostropovich would fully prove his worth, bringing in innovations, raising standards and adding to the Conservatoire's prestige in many ways.

* See Mikhail Spektor, *Mstislav Rostropovich*, p. 56.

8

Contacts with composers II
Shostakovich and his successors

At the time of his death, Prokofiev had been working on seven new works simultaneously. Two were pieces for cello, both intended for Rostropovich. The three-movement concertino for cello and orchestra was virtually complete in piano score, and the composer had marked into the margins clear indications of the instrumentation he wanted. The concertino was not specifically designed as a 'concerto for youth' – a popular and characteristically Soviet genre of which Kabalevsky was the leading exponent – yet with its simple, compact form and its melodious style it was potentially widely accessible both to listeners and competent young performers. Rostropovich had suggested a neoclassical work to Prokofiev, and had brought various pieces as possible models, such as transcriptions of short pieces by Handel and Gluck. However, such suggestions had not enticed Prokofiev to return to the style of his 'Classical' symphony; rather he drew on his inherent melodic gift to compose a work with long 'Russian' lines, particularly in the lyrical second movement.

The concertino also took up an unusual challenge stemming from Zakharov's accusations of plagiarism in the finale of the *Sinfonia Concertante*. Prokofiev reacted with characteristic humour, telling Rostropovich that he intended at some point to disguise beyond recognition the theme *Byvaitse zdorovy*; the theme was actually attributed to I. Lyuban and not to Zakharov, despite his claims. In the concertino he did just this, using it as the principal thematic material of the final movement: with its complex chordal writing, it is a far more convoluted version of the theme than that used in the *Sinfonia Concertante*. After Prokofiev's death Rostropovich collaborated with Dmitri Kabalevsky in completing the orchestration of Prokofiev's concertino. He considered Kabalevsky the most suitable choice because of his love and knowledge of Prokofiev's music: his admiration for the deceased composer was unstained by the envy he showed towards Shostakovich.

Shortly before he died Prokofiev had also started another work for unaccompanied cello: a four-movement sonata, of which he completed only the exposition of the Andante first movement. This opens with a liltingly lyrical B minor theme, whose ballad-like character contrasts with the scherzo-like second subject (in D major), where the main voice is accompanied by a staccato figure. Prokofiev also left some sketches for other movements, including an Allegro, which as Rostropovich recalls was to bear 'a minuet or gavotte-like character'. The composer also started a second Andante movement, whose slow introduction was to lead to a four-voice fugue. Here Prokofiev aimed not to leave out a single note of the theme or counter-subject in each of the statements and inversions. This involved some intricate double-stoppings, and Prokofiev had asked Rostropovich to show which combinations of notes were feasible on the cello. Interestingly enough, the fugue subject is close in its intonational structure to the *Byvaitse zdorovy* theme used in the concertino and the *Sinfonia Concertante.**

Prokofiev's music played a prominent part in Rostropovich's fast-developing international career, and the cello sonata and the *Sinfonia Concertante* had provided a unique calling card when he made his debuts in various Western countries: the very fact that a composer of worldwide repute had created significant new works for a cellist still in his mid-twenties spoke volumes. Rostropovich introduced Prokofiev's new works at every opportunity; for instance, in February 1956, he included the sonata in his recital programmes with Aleksandr Dedyukhin in Paris, Bordeaux and Lyon during his first concert tour of France, and he played the *Sinfonia Concertante* at major venues in the United States as well as around Russia. However, after Prokofiev's death, Rostropovich had to wait several years for a new work of comparable significance to appear. It took more time still before the cellist's reputation had spread sufficiently to prompt composers from outside the Soviet Union to write for him. The next contemporary cello concerto that Rostropovich added to his repertoire was by Mieczyslaw (or Moisei) Weinberg.

* From V. Blok's article 'Nezavershennaya sonata', in *Sovetskaya Muzyka,* no. 4, 1969, pp. 68–74.

The three-movement concerto, Op. 43 in C minor, in fact dated from 1948, the year of the infamous attacks on the 'formalism' of leading Soviet composers. The criticisms in the Central Committee's Decree had harrowing consequences for musical life in the Soviet Union: composers began to write their most important new works for 'the drawer', leaving them dormant in the hope of better times. Just as Shostakovich's violin concerto, completed in February 1948, had to wait seven years for performance, so too did Weinberg's cello concerto.

In common with many of Shostakovich's works of the time (*From Jewish Poetry*, the fourth quartet, and so on), Weinberg's cello concerto is saturated with the intonational melos of Jewish folk song – indeed, Weinberg strongly influenced Shostakovich's interest in Jewish popular music. Weinberg's own biography makes this subject matter poignantly significant. A refugee from German-occupied Poland, he had fled to the Soviet Union in 1939, and completed his musical studies in Minsk. In 1941 he was evacuated to Tashkent, where he met the famous Jewish actor Solomon Mikhoels and married his daughter Natalya (Tala). In 1943 he came to the attention of Shostakovich, who helped him return to Moscow. Tragically, on the night of 7 January 1948 Mikhoels died in Minsk, the victim of a set-up 'accident'. Ironically, having escaped Nazi-controlled Poland, Weinberg once more found himself in a country with an organised campaign of anti-semitism. (Tala Mikhoels' uncle, Dr Vovsi, was one of the doctors arrested in the final sweeping purge of Stalin's reign, the so-called 'doctors' plot'.) When Weinberg himself was arrested in February 1953, Shostakovich proved a courageous and loyal friend, writing to Lavrenti Beria, the former head of the MGB (as the KGB was then known), to intercede for Weinberg. However, his release in May that year was more likely simply a consequence of Stalin's death.

Weinberg was delighted when Rostropovich expressed interest in his cello concerto, and participated actively in the rehearsals during late December 1956 and early January 1957. He helped Rostropovich in his meticulous preparation, accompanying him at the piano. Tala Vovsi-Mikhoels recalls that the cello concerto was first performed in Leningrad, and was most enthusiastically received.* The Moscow premiere took place on 19 January at the Grand Hall of the Conservatoire, under the direction of Samuil Samosud. Weinberg was so

* Telephone interview with E.W., 2006.

overwhelmed by Rostropovich's brilliant interpretation that he dedicated the concerto to him. He was undoubtedly struck by the cellist's conceptual understanding, as well as his close identification with its inner emotional world. For his part, one of the things Rostropovich most valued in the concerto was Weinberg's ability to set up every change of mood, skilfully preparing the transitions and evolving connections within the overall development.

Although Weinberg had not studied formally with Shostakovich, he considered himself a Shostakovich disciple – and the great composer in turn highly respected Weinberg's talents. Shostakovich's influence was a manifest feature of Soviet musical life, and Rostropovich maintained close contact with many of his former composition students, amongst whom Yuri Levitin, Galina Ustvolskaya and Boris Chaikovsky were all to compose works for cello at his behest. In the mean time, Rostropovich deepened his musical relationship with Shostakovich himself through their shared performances of the 1934 cello sonata, Op. 40. Rostropovich had learnt the piece while still a Conservatoire student:

As soon as I mastered the cello sonata, I took it to Shostakovich and asked if he would listen to me. He agreed, so I played it through with him at the piano. Of course I was very nervous, and, following advice from my teacher, Kozolupov, I tried to play in a rather dry manner. Dmitri Dmitriyevich made very few comments. But I was very happy when in the slow movement, he actually asked me to play with more rubato, particularly in the phrase where there are the fast decorative melismas. Yet in the recapitulation, when the piano has the same material, he himself refrained from using much rubato, as if he found it a little embarrassing.

On 8 November 1954 Rostropovich performed the sonata with its composer for the first time at a collective concert dedicated to Shostakovich and Shebalin at the Small Hall of the Moscow Conservatoire. The following spring they played it several times during a concert tour, which included the cities of Tallinn, Minsk and Riga. The programme was entirely dedicated to Shostakovich's music, the other works being the vocal cycle *From Jewish Poetry* (which had received its belated premiere that January in Leningrad), and a selection of Preludes and Fugues from Op. 87.* Shostakovich's personal

---

* For instance, the concerts in Minsk and Riga took place on 6 and 7 April 1955, and the programmes were repeated in Leningrad and Tallinn. Rostropovich and Shostakovich also performed the sonata at smaller collective concerts in workers' clubs.

support of Rostropovich was shown by the fact that he also performed the sonata in Rostropovich's own cello recital at the Small Hall of the Conservatoire on 17 April – for the rest of the programme, Dedyukhin was the pianist.

Two years later Shostakovich and Rostropovich laid down their interpretation in a studio recording. This version vaunts very fast speeds in the outer movements, testifying to the way in which the sonata itself had evolved: the original edition (published in 1935, the year after its composition) had slower metronome markings and tempo indications than the later 1960 edition (prepared by the dedicatee Viktor Kubatsky). Shostakovich's stated intention had been to write a classical sonata in four movements.[*] In a radio interview in 1938, he stated that the sonata's second movement was a minuet;[†] one can perhaps see an analogy with the second movement of Brahms's E minor cello sonata. As time went on, however, performances of the sonata – many with the composer at the piano – accumulated speed, and the 'minuet' acquired the characteristics of a fast and energetic scherzo. As Rostropovich recalls:

Each time we played the sonata, we performed it differently; however, we had never before played it as fast as we did in our recording. I think that this was because Dmitri Dmitriyevich was in a dreadful hurry to get away to see some relatives, who were all invited to his sister's dacha outside Moscow. That meant that his chief concern was to get the recording finished as quickly as possible; it was a beautiful day and he couldn't wait to join his friends and down a glass of vodka. He certainly did not have the feeling that this recording was supposed to be a document for posterity. Rather it was: 'Come on Slava, let's get it done quickly, I need to leave soon.' No doubt because he was in such a hurry, Dmitri Dmitriyevich kept missing the four chords that precede the cello triplet passage in the finale. He splashed them every time! I suggested to Dmitri Dmitriyevich that we ignore that place for the time being, instead keeping going and finishing recording the rest of the movement. After that, we sat down together at the piano and quickly recorded the chords in question using four hands. We played them about twelve times: I played the left-hand part and he the right-hand part, both of us using two hands! This solved the problem of these two bars very nicely! In fact,

---

[*] In the original edition, the first movement (in sonata form) was marked Moderato with a metronome marking of crotchet = 116; the second Moderato con moto, crotchet = 152. The third movement Largo gives a metronome marking of 69, and the finale, an Allegretto 184 (both markings also refer to the crotchet pulse).

[†] Andrey Kryukov, article ('For the information of future chroniclers') in L. G. Kovnatskaya (ed.), D. D. *Shostakovich Collection of Articles for the 90th year of his birth*, St Petersburg, 1996, p. 164.

the piano part is very hard, and later when his hands started to weaken, Shostakovich complained that he couldn't manage all the notes in the very fast scale passages played in octaves.

Shostakovich was an excellent pianist, although somewhat reserved in his range of emotional expression. He favoured a dry, percussive touch, particularly in the high registers of the piano. As Rostropovich explained, this was a 'composer's' interpretation, whose principal aim was to allow the listener to perceive the precise nature of the written score and the musical construction. Shostakovich had previously recorded the sonata in 1946 with Daniil Shafran, with whom he also performed it in public several times in 1946 and 1947. Shafran likewise testified to Shostakovich's unusual musical generosity and flexibility: 'No matter what I asked or suggested about the text of the sonata, Shostakovich unfailingly listened to every word, giving me his undivided attention; as a rule he agreed to any new details regarding the performance, even those which went against his original notation in the score. Of course these were relatively insignificant "corrections" of this superb composition.'*

The differences between Shafran's 1946 recording and the 1957 recording with Rostropovich are comparable to those between the various editions of the published score: the original Triton edition of 1935 and the three later editions from 1960, 1964 and 1971, the last of these edited by Kubatsky. The later editions were a result of changes that had emerged in successive performances and are reflected in the new tempi and dynamic markings. Rostropovich's 1957 recording formed the basis of the interpretation that he passed on to his students – though of course he allowed them freedom to deviate from his reading, since he was opposed to the idea that any interpretation should be rigidly codified.

The next large-scale Soviet work that Rostropovich added to his repertoire was the concerto by Evgeny Golubiev, best remembered today as the teacher of Alfred Schnittke (who had great respect for his qualities as a composer). After giving the first performance in Saratov on 31 May 1959, Rostropovich returned to the concerto a couple of times, playing it in Moscow and Kiev, and also assigned it on occasion to his students. However, Golubiev's work was entirely overshadowed

---

* Viktor Yuzefovich, conversation with Daniil Shafran, *Sovetskaya Muzyka*, 1978, pp. 74–85.

by another new concerto written for Rostropovich shortly afterwards. The first the cellist heard about it was in an article in *Sovetskaya Kultura* on 6 June 1959 entitled 'Creative Plans of Dmitri Shostakovich', in which the composer declared that he was writing a cello concerto with a 'march-like' first movement. Rostropovich had always dreamed of his former teacher writing for him, although he had never expressed this fervent wish to Shostakovich:

Shortly after I won the All-Union competition in December 1945, I went down to the Ivanovo composers' retreat, at Shostakovich's suggestion. His family were also staying. One day I went skiing with Nina Vasilyevna, Dmitri Dmitriyevich's wife. I touched on a sacrosanct issue by asking, 'Nina Vasilyevna, since you know your husband so well, please tell me what I should do so that he writes something for cello?' She looked at me attentively and said, 'Slava, only if I tell you, you must promise not to speak about this with anybody else.' In expectation of the magic formula I started to tremble like a dog ready to pounce on some wild game. 'Alright, Slava, if you really want him to write for you, then NEVER ask him about it!'

After reading the article in *Sovetskaya Kultura*, Rostropovich's curiosity was greatly aroused, but he continued to maintain his silence. Then towards the end of July he received a postcard from Shostakovich, inviting him to perform the newly completed concerto. Anxious to receive the score as soon as possible, he travelled up to Leningrad with his pianist Aleksandr Dedyukhin to meet with Shostakovich, who was staying at his dacha outside the city in Komarovo:

I arrived from Moscow on 2 August with Dedyukhin, and that same evening Dmitri Dmitriyevich invited me to his sister, Mariya Dmitriyevna's town flat on the fifth floor, opposite the Kazan Cathedral. On the upright piano that stood there, he played me the cello concerto for the first time and then gave me the score. As he played the second movement, he even shed a tear or two. He told me that this work was extremely dear to him. Then came a very strange question, but in leading up to it he went through terrible convolutions. It was literally as if he was torturing me when he kept repeating, 'Please tell me, do you like this work? No, please tell me the truth, do you really like it? It is very important to me.' I insistently reassured him that I was absolutely shaken to the core, I was so impressed by the concerto. Eventually he conceded the argument, and said, 'Then there remains just this one question. If you really like it so much, then will you please permit me to dedicate it to you?' I can never forget this. No other composer, not even the most humble or untalented, had ever addressed me like this. It set a seal on my whole life. Of course I permitted it!

Rostropovich thereupon locked himself in his room at the Evropeiskaya Hotel, opposite the Philharmonic Hall, and on the morning of 3 August he sat down to practise. He practised for ten hours that day, ten hours the day after, and during the third day he worked for eight hours.

The day after Dedyukhin and I went out to Dmitri Dmitriyevich's dacha at Komarovo. Everybody was very agitated, so we sat down for a little, but I was impatient to start playing. Then came one of the great moments of my life. Dmitri Dmitriyevich said, 'Just hold on, Slava, I'll look for a music stand and bring it for you.' 'It's not necessary,' I replied. 'What do you mean, not necessary, what do you mean?' 'I'll play from memory.' 'Impossible, impossible!' I then played through the concerto for the first time with Dedyukhin at the piano – from memory.

This first performance was evidently an extraordinary and unforgettable occasion for all who witnessed it – mostly members of Shostakovich's family. In the words of Shostakovich's son-in-law, Evgeny Chukovsky:

The people gathered in this small room yielded to a state of superficial numbness, although passions smouldered within each one of them. They were captives to the will of the composer, who sat there tensely listening to the music which previously he alone had heard . . . I thought to myself, 'Who if not God has given the author such power over people?' As for the author, he said of his work, 'I took a simple little theme and tried to develop it.'*

Shostakovich was overcome with delight, as Rostropovich recounts:

His mood became radiant. 'Let me ring my friend, Isaak Davydovich [Glikman],' he exclaimed, and he promptly asked him to come over at once. While Glikman was on his way (and he needed at least forty-five minutes to make the journey) I played the concerto through again, just for Dmitri Dmitriyevich. After that we broke open a bottle of vodka – it served as combustible fuel. For my part, there was no question of resistance, and Dmitri Dmitriyevich and I polished off the bottle between us. And while Glikman travelled and we waited, the vodka was gradually getting sucked into my organism. When Isaak Davydovich arrived, Shostakovich asked me to play the concerto again. I have no idea what I played then, but it probably didn't bear any relation to Shostakovich's concerto, perhaps it got mixed up with the Saint-Saëns. I had gone completely floppy, I was in such a state of euphoria, I imagine it was like being high on drugs. In my extreme happiness I had no sensation of myself nor of the music. Dmitri Dmitriyevich kept saying, 'This is all simply marvellous.'

* Elizabeth Wilson, *Shostakovich: A Life Remembered*, 2006, p. 368.

The story of Rostropovich learning the work in three days has become legendary, but even more striking, to my mind, was the way he so quickly and deeply identified with the new work. The cello concerto follows the structure of the first violin concerto, written for Oistrakh in 1948: a four-movement arch with the central slow movement leading to an extended cadenza which follows directly on to the finale. The concerto is full of contrasts, but the predominant mood is one of energetic vitality, with the character-istic overtones of irony and sarcasm evident in the outer movements, whereas the more philosophical slow movement expresses moods ranging from quiet meditation, to acute inner sadness, from angry protest to a sense of full-scale tragedy.

Amongst the hidden ironies of the concerto was the subtle disguising of Stalin's favourite song, 'Suliko'. Rostropovich recalls how once Shostakovich set him a riddle:

'Can you guess, Slava, where I have hidden the theme of "Suliko"?' I answered, 'Dmitri Dmitriyevich, I thought I knew the concerto really well, but honestly, no, I haven't found it.' He then sat down at the piano and showed me the place where the motif sounds for the last time in the finale, when the basses play the first part of the phrase (and here he sang), 'And where is my . . .' and then in an extreme register with a shrill screech of the piccolo, its continuation: '. . . Suliko, Suliko?' This para-phrase of the song is really a piece of musical hooliganism, very daring and provoca-tive at the time. Nevertheless it was next to impossible to uncover this quotation and make this association; certainly I was not able to without it being pointed out to me.

Shostakovich had ridiculed this song already, using it in its original form in his ironic satire *Rayok* (variously translated as 'Peepshow' or 'Little Paradise'), which had been composed, at least in part, during 1957, two years before the concerto. *Rayok*, an imitation of Mussorgsky's satirical work of the same name, is basically a home entertainment, a ferocious parody of the idiotic bureaucratic language and simplistic musical taste of Stalin, his ideological expert, Andrei Zhdanov, and his petty functionaries – the very people who had made life a misery for Shostakovich by instructing him how he should write music. Rostropovich remembers how around this time, when he visited Shostakovich at home, the composer often used to hum a tune while looking at him quizzically. Only many years later was he able to identify the melody with the moment in *Rayok* where the figure of Dvoikin – a cipher for Zhdanov – sings the injunction from his 1948 speeches: 'Music must be beautiful . . .' Rostropovich admits, 'At the time I didn't ask Dmitri Dmitriyevich what he was singing. But now I wonder if perhaps by humming these strange melodies he was provoking me to ask this obvious question; but through my stupidity I didn't do so.'

The opening motif of the concerto's first movement is an equally well-disguised allusion to an earlier piece: 'Procession to Execution' from the film score to the *Young Guard*. In the concerto, however, the motif is transformed to become a minor triad resolving into the key of E flat major, in a fast jaunty tempo; in the original, it was a C minor triad followed by a dissonant chord in a slow, heavy tempo.

Rostropovich also liked to point out the connections between Shostakovich's first concerto and Prokofiev's *Sinfonia Concertante*, even if these works were essentially very different:

Shostakovich went to listen to all my performances of the *Sinfonia Concertante*. After I recorded it, he once told me, 'Slava, I have played the LP so many times, that now it's so worn out, and the disc only issues a sort of hissing sound.' And indeed, as he was writing his first concerto, Shostakovich remarked in an interview how much he had been influenced by Prokofiev's *Sinfonia Concertante*. I emphasise this, since in certain publications it has been written that they were antagonists. But this is complete nonsense. It is true that they were not real friends either, they were very different personalities; but each of them held the other's music in enormous respect.

Shostakovich borrowed some specific ideas from Prokofiev in this concerto – for example in the way both the first movement and the finale end with loud timpani blows:

When I first played the Prokofiev *Sinfonia Concertante* there was a one-legged timpanist, a war veteran who played in the orchestra. At the very end of the finale, the cello ascends the heights as if spiralling to the very summit of a domed roof; on reaching the highest note it is silenced by one bang of the timpani, which puts an end to this frenzied madness. This remarkable player stood on one leg (he had no artificial limb to support him) and struck that note. After the concert Dmitri Dmitriyevich joined us to celebrate. 'Slavka, how that one-legged guy thumped his drum! He called everything to a halt with that final blow!' At the end of his own cello concerto there are seven rhetorical bangs on the timpani. Undoubtedly Shostakovich borrowed this idea from Prokofiev's *Sinfonia Concertante*.

Interestingly enough, Shostakovich admitted having studied all the famous cello concertos while composing his own. Rostropovich recalls being somewhat surprised when Shostakovich announced,

'Slava, do you know which of all the cello concertos is the best, in terms of structure, duration and orchestral balance? Undoubtedly the Saint-Saëns!' The French composer skilfully uses the cello's register and dynamic range to perfection, always allowing it to project over the orchestra without requiring the cellist to force the sound. For Rostropovich, the other notable example of a well-orchestrated and well-balanced concerto for cello is Elgar's.

There was an established tradition that Shostakovich's new works received their premieres in his native city: Rostropovich first performed the concerto to an ecstatic reception on 4 October 1959 in the Hall of the Philharmonia, with Evgeny Mravinsky directing the Leningrad Philharmonic Orchestra. The first Moscow performance followed a few days later, directed by Aleksandr Gauk. In class we often heard the story of how Gauk announced to Shostakovich that he had 'found the clue' for the opening motif. For Rostropovich, the anecdote illustrates how dangerous it is to try to define music in words, or to apply specific texts to it:

I have to say that Dmitri Dmitriyevich did not particularly like Gauk as a musician or as a person. Once, during a rehearsal for the Moscow performance Gauk enthused, 'What a wonderful first theme, you know I feel that it even has a hidden text: "We're all for peace" [my vse za mir], ta-ta tà, ta-ta tà! We're all for peace!"' Shostakovich immediately responded, 'Quite correct, quite correct! Of course, that's right, that's how you should hear it!' In general Shostakovich never bothered to correct a fool, saying 'Those who have ears can hear!'

Rostropovich also recounted the origins of the concerto's metronome markings, which he does not observe, as he freely admits. The story reveals Shostakovich's flexible attitude to tempi and his dislike of metronomes:

One of my first performances was recorded privately, and Dmitri Dmitriyevich asked me if he could mark into the scores the metronome markings taken from this performance. Of course I agreed. But very soon, as my interpretation developed, I decided to play both the first and second movements somewhat faster. By the time I went to America and recorded the concerto with Eugene Ormandy in November 1959, I was playing the work with more forward impetus. Shostakovich attended these performances and recording sessions, and he told me that he preferred my slightly faster tempi. But he never bothered to go back and alter the original metronome markings in the score, even though they were derived from a performance of mine.

Rostropovich's interpretation won immediate popularity for Shostakovich's cello concerto wherever he played it. It sealed his reputation as a performer capable of winning new audiences for new music. Meanwhile, other young cellists were clamouring to learn the concerto. One of the first to do so was the seventeen-year-old Leningrad cellist Aleksandr Knaifel, who had fallen in love with the piece at its first performance. In the absence of any published score, Knaifel transcribed his own part and a piano reduction of the orchestral score after hearing a radio recording. Enormously impressed by this feat of enthusiasm, Rostropovich took Knaifel into his Moscow class partly on the strength of the achievement.

Alongside his work as a soloist, Rostropovich had also been building up a repertoire of new chamber works by Soviet composers. On 2 January 1957 he played four of Yuri Shaporin's five pieces for cello and piano, giving the premiere of the entire sequence a month later in Leningrad. The final piece in the set, 'Scherzo', an effective virtuoso piece using spiccato bowing strokes, achieved considerable popularity and was often played independently from the cycle. It made use of a device Rostropovich had suggested to the composer in order to heighten the impression of velocity and virtuosity: this involved writing principally fast, repeated pairs of notes, only occasionally breaking into passages of single notes.

On 2 March the same year, Rostropovich gave the first performance of Boris Chaikovsky's attractive cello sonata in Moscow, accompanied by the composer, and the performance was repeated in the Small Hall of the Leningrad Philharmonia six days later. Both performances formed part of extended recitals in which Rostropovich's pupils joined him for Villa-Lobos's *Bachianas Brasileiras* nos. 1 and 5 for eight cellos, no. 5 also featuring his wife Galina Vishnevskaya as soprano soloist. Programmes such as these were typical of Rostropovich's flexible and imaginative approach, and they allowed postgraduate cellists and the best undergraduate students a chance to be involved in prestigious public concerts.

Another new cello sonata was written for Rostropovich later in 1957 by Yuri Levitin; it was premiered on 20 November 1958, again accompanied by the composer. It was characteristic of Rostropovich's enthusiasm and generosity that he did not keep new works back for his own exclusive performance, but often asked his students to prepare the new pieces he himself was learning. Only a month after Rostropovich's premiere of the Levitin sonata, on 18 December, one of his students played it at a class concert at the Small Hall of the Moscow Conser-vatoire. During this programme, thirteen students (ranging from Miron Yampolsky, still a student at the Central Music School, to Alla Vasiliyeva, his oldest student, and the Leningrad-based postgraduate Anatoli Nikitin) performed a marathon programme of pieces by Shaporin, Kodály, Piatigorsky, Martinu and Handel, concertos by Honegger, Elgar and Prokofiev (both the concertino and the *Sinfonia Concertante*), and ending with *Bachianas Brasileiras* no. 1.

Meanwhile, Rostropovich needed a different kind of repertoire when he was playing in remote places to new audiences, as when he toured the Altai and Eastern Siberia with his group 'Masters of Art', or travelled all over the Soviet Union with his loyal pianist, Aleksandr Dedyukhin. As a duo, they not only performed recitals, but took part in collective concerts. Once Rostropovich and Dedyukhin arrived in the small and remote town of Dzyomgi, situated near the Amur river, not far from Komsomolsk, and only five kilometres from the Chinese border. The concert was to be held in an enormous aircraft hangar which could easily accommodate four thousand people, but Rostropovich and Dedyukhin arrived to discover that the organisers had cancelled their concert because only five people had turned up. However, Rostropovich found out that these five men and women had trudged many kilometres over the taiga especially to hear him play: they were former ZEKs (political prisoners), who had served long terms in the camps and were still living in distant exile. Without hesi-tation, Rostropovich told the organisers that he would play for this small audience without a fee: he asked for five chairs, invited the men onto the stage and played his full programme for them with Dedyukhin, adding as many encores as they requested.

Rostropovich gave a great deal of thought to the sort of repertoire that was suitable for smaller scale concerts. In an article in *Sovetskaya Muzyka* in July 1959, he made a heartfelt plea to young composers to write short, effective concert pieces. Why, he asked, were instrumentalists still forced to play salon pieces from the late nineteenth century, most of which were of poor quality? Why did today's composers all wish to write grandiose concertos and imposing sonatas, ignoring the tastes of a less educated public? He naturally cited examples of wonderful composers like Liszt, Weber and Chopin (and more recently Bartók, Prokofiev, and Villa-Lobos), who had drawn on folk music and popular song to compose excellent, innovative pieces in short forms which were well suited to the instruments they were written for. Rostropovich reluctantly came to the conclusion that many young composers had a poor knowledge of instrumental technique, as was evident in their ignorance of matters such as bowing instructions when writing for strings. He threw down a challenge for young Soviet composers, and equally for the Ministry of Culture, who could easily have organised an initiative to stimulate composition in 'popular' styles.

Rostropovich solved the problem in part by performing (and sometimes also making) many brilliant transcriptions for cello of atmospheric and effective virtuoso pieces for other instruments, but he also continued to add new large-scale works to his repertoire. In 1961 he conceived a series of concerts in Moscow made-up exclusively of new Soviet works. Such 'conceptual programming' was quite unusual in the Soviet Union at this time, and represented an urge on Rostropovich's part to educate his audience as well as simply catering to popular taste. In Moscow at least, Rostropovich's very name was a guarantee to audiences, and people flocked to his concerts, trusting in his judgement. In six concerts given at the Small Hall of the Conservatoire between 1 October and 7 November, the cellist played works by Prokofiev, Myaskovsky, Boris Chaikovsky, Shaporin, Levitin, Weinberg, Golubiev, Knipper, Rakov and Shebalin. He was accompanied by various pianists, including the composers of works specially written for the series. Amongst the new works were Weinberg's first solo sonata in D minor (first performed on 4 October) and his second sonata for cello and piano (first performed on 15 October), both dedicated to Rostropovich. Another significant addition to the sonata repertoire came from Shebalin, a close friend and contemporary of Shostakovich, who had taught Rostropovich composition at the Conservatoire. Shebalin lived in retirement, having been considerably incapacitated by a stroke. He still managed to compose, even though his right hand was paralysed: by sheer force of character, he trained his left hand to write down music. Rostropovich had commissioned the new cello sonata as a mark of his respect and gratitude to a significant composer of great musical integrity: he was well aware that Shebalin had been marginalised from Moscow musical life, of which he had been the mainstay for many years.

Less substantial new works in the series included Golubiev's attractive 'Concert Aria', Lev Knipper's 'Kirghiz Song' and Nikolay Rakov's pieces for cello and piano. True to his belief that the public also needed some attractive lighter fare, Rostropovich also performed some short pieces by Prokofiev, including his own arrangement of the March from *The Love for Three Oranges*, and the composer's original arrangement of the Adagio from the ballet *Cinderella*.

Amongst those whom Rostropovich had originally commissioned to write for him was the Leningrad composer, Galina Ustvolskaya; indeed, her name featured in the posters for the series. In 1960 she wrote her highly original *Grand Duo* for cello and piano, and played it through for Rostropovich in Leningrad:

Galina was outwardly very shy, almost exaggeratedly so. She was a good-looking woman, and I knew that she and her teacher Dmitri Dmitriyevich had enjoyed a 'tender' relationship. In fact there was an enormous contrast between her musical personality and her everyday behaviour. With extreme diffidence, feigning timidity, she eventually agreed to play the *Grand Duo* for me. But the moment she sat down at the piano she was transformed, and threw herself into the music with unbelievable ferocity, striking the keys with enormous force, hammering out this loud and percussive music. I understood that in the political climate of the time, the *Grand Duo* would not receive permission for performance. In fact to play it in public would be positively dangerous, and I did not want to be responsible for her being thrown into prison! Only many years later, in 1996, did I play and record this work, which she had dedicated to me.*

Rostropovich's growing reputation as an advocate of new music meant that composers from all over the world soon started to send him their compositions, and he had to become more selective. The composer Yuri Falik, one of Rostropovich's first postgraduate students in his Leningrad class, recalls seeing his teacher sorting out a jumble of large scores into piles in his Moscow flat: 'Slava explained that these consisted of new works that had been sent to him, and he was looking through them. The first, rather smaller pile was a selection of scores he was interested in performing; the second, by now almost a mountainous heap, was made up of the new works he had rejected.' The amount of effort expended in learning a new score is enormous, all the more so if the artist wishes to commit it to memory, as Rostropovich invariably did. Several of the works he learnt he only played once. I remember Mstislav Leopoldovich telling me that good new works seemed to come in waves of seven – one excellent work for

* The *Grand Duo* actually received its first performance in Leningrad on 7 December 1976, given by Oleg Stolpner and Oleg Malov. Soon afterwards they recorded it for *Melodiya*.

six which would be forgettable. Indeed, the list of Soviet composers who wrote concertos for him in the early 1960s is almost like a roll-call of obscure musicians now consigned to neglect and oblivion: S. Moralyov (1960), I. Finkelshtein (1961), L. Knipper (1962), M. Rauchverger (1963), Y. Levitin (1963).

Throughout the 1960s, Rostropovich continued to add to his repertoire not just new concertos but also chamber works by Soviet composers: sonatas by Kabalevsky (1962), Karen Khatchaturyan (1966), and Eduard Mirzoyan (1967), and an interesting work by Boris Chaikovsky – Partita for cello and small chamber ensemble (1967).

By 1968, however, Rostropovich's attention had turned to conducting, and although he remained very busy playing cello concertos and accompanying Vishnevskaya, he necessarily almost stopped commissioning new sonatas and chamber works from his compatriots.

Nonetheless, his first series of concerts of Soviet chamber works had been hugely significant, for numerous reasons. It provided the evidence of involvement in the creation of new Soviet art that justified Rostropovich's candidature for the prestigious Lenin prize in 1962. It was also a precursor of the cellist's grandiose 1963/64 cycle of eleven concerts, during which he performed practically the whole extant concerto repertoire for cello and orchestra, as well as giving several significant world premieres, including works by 'foreign' composers such as Britten's *Cello Symphony* and Henri Sauguet's *Concert-Mélodie*. It was the success of this gruelling marathon that led to the eventual award of the Lenin prize in 1964: in the eyes of the world, it established Rostropovich as a unique performer, who at the age of thirty-seven had done more to enrich the cello repertoire than any previous player.

INTERLUDE I

Natalya Shakhovskaya

In the life of every creative person, certain meetings at the right time can have a decisive role. My musical formation was influenced by my contacts with certain great personalities, such as Mariya Yudina, with whom I had the good fortune of playing. However, Rostropovich was a special chapter in my life, and it was he more than anybody who completely changed my outlook on life, both as an artist and as a human being.

I transferred to his class in my second postgraduate year, just before the auditions for the Prague Spring competition, for which I was a candidate. I came to him equipped by Semyon Kozolupov with excellent schooling and a solid technique. I had played all the important repertoire, and I was already a first-prize winner in the Moscow Youth Festival of 1957. At the Conservatoire I was regarded as a fully-fledged artist in my own right.

I well remember my first lesson at Rostropovich's flat, when I brought the Schumann concerto. Mstislav Leopoldovich sat down at the piano, and started accompanying me; our work began. I was sucked into a vortex of new ideas, as he opened up before me vast new musical horizons. I nearly choked from my admiration and delight, but at the same time I seemed to shrink to the size of a tiny mosquito. It seemed that I knew nothing, and very soon I understood that I simply didn't have the means to realise the vision that he had imparted to me, with its overflowing palette of colours and nuances, where the entire concept of the musical structure was revealed in all its contrasts of relief and fantasy. I played neatly and cleanly, but that was that. I had no way of grasping everything he told me, let alone finding the wherewithal to express it.

From the start Rostropovich had an enormous emotional effect on me. His lessons were often conducted from the keyboard, where he immediately became involved in the process of music-making. The more he himself loved the work, the more inspired he would become. Naturally this happened with the Schumann concerto, and perhaps even more so when he was teaching works that had been written for him. Sometimes Mstislav Leopoldovich got so carried away that it seemed he was no longer aware of the student. You were blown along under the hurricane force of his personality. He took endless enjoyment in his own discoveries, showing the melodic flow with its undulating rubato lines, pointing to a beautiful harmonic modulation, some detail in the secondary voice, and so on. His own enthusiasm was so boundless that one was hypnotised by it, and inevitably one succumbed to this excitement.

Nevertheless, after such an inspiring lesson, I had to come to terms with the revelations offered. I needed to get down to the long and difficult task of realising these new ideas, and evolving a scheme of work.

The morning after my first lesson on the Schumann concerto I had to play it at the audition. I was completely bowled over by all the novel ideas that Rostropovich had conveyed to me, and I wanted to express myself in the light of these discoveries. However, I didn't have time even minimally to digest them. Goodness only knows how I played. Galina Kozolupova came up to me afterwards and looked at me with disdain: 'Natasha, what has happened to you?'

I had a few more lessons after this, and the next thing I knew was that Mstislav Leopoldovich left on a long tour abroad for several months. Suddenly I found myself alone.

I cannot tell you how complicated things got then. They even wanted to throw me out of the Conservatoire. The reason was simple jealousy, since I had left my long-standing teacher, Semyon Kozolupov, but I had not gone to study with either of his favourites, Knushevitsky or his daughter Galina Semyonovna. It was felt that I should present myself at the competition in Prague as a Kozolupov student, not a Rostropovich student.

The competition programme included a contemporary work, and it was decided that I should play it at an audition while Rostropovich was away, to see if he had done his job properly – new music was considered his speciality. But I had no intention of playing without *having first studied the piece with him; there hadn't been time to do so before his departure. I excused myself, saying that my hands were hurting, I couldn't play. Then the Conservatoire commission became insistent, and told me that in this case I should go back to Kozolupov for lessons. I couldn't possibly do this, as he would have undone the work that I had started with Rostropovich on the rest of the competition programme. In the Dvořák concerto, for instance, I had changed all my fingerings and bowings, and I knew that this would upset Kozolupov, who would imagine that I was deliberately discarding all he had taught me over the years. After only a few lessons with Rostropovich, I was incapable of going back to my old style of playing, and I didn't want to make such a pretence.*

This refusal caused me eventually to be thrown out of the Conservatoire. The day I was expelled I came home to find a man from the Ministry of Culture waiting for me. The Conservatoire director Sveshnikov had already demanded that the Ministry strike me off the list of competitors for Prague. I then explained the situation to the Ministry official. All in all the Ministry of Culture were understanding, and told the Conservatoire to reinstate me, for they were not at all sympathetic to the cello department intrigues.

So it was that I went to play at the Prague competition. Galina Semyonovna Kozolupova was sent as a jury member representing the Soviet Union. The first prize went to Natasha Gutman, who was a pupil of Kozolupova, and who of course proved to be a marvellous cellist and musician and fully merited the prize in her own right. But I was told that when the jury had suggested that the first prize should be divided between us, the only person to vote against it was Galina Semyonovna.

On his way home from the USA, Rostropovich flew in to Prague especially to hear the prizewinners' concert. When he learnt about the proceedings, he said to me, 'To hell with the competition, it's time for you to come home and start working!' Afterwards he had a terrible row with Galina Semyonovna, as he asked to see the documents of the competition, and I think she resisted.

Then the following year (1961) the All-Soviet competition was announced, as a prelude to the 1962 Tchaikovsky Competition, where the cello was represented for the first time. It was also the first time that the All-Soviet national competition had been held since Rostropovich had won it in 1945. Mstislav Leopoldovich prepared me for both these competitions.

I worked hard and prepared well for my lessons with him. I played with great temperament, and thought that I was doing fine. But I was often proved wrong. He would suddenly ask me, 'Did you hear what happens at this moment in the piano part? You are not reacting to the harmony. Have you noticed that in the exposition, the value of such a note was a minim, but here in the recapitulation it's an eighth note?' In other words he demanded a complete knowledge of the score and of the music. With his heightened perception he was forever uncovering a host of new details.

As a rule Rostropovich never worked on one piece with me more than once or twice. This meant that I covered a very large repertoire with him. Often the lessons were concentrated in a very short space of time. He might be in Moscow just for three days between tours, and I would be called up to have a lesson at ten in the evening which might finish at midnight, and the next lesson would be the morning after at nine, often with a new work.

If I protested, 'But Mstislav Leopoldovich, how will I have time to prepare?' he would reply, 'Well, that shouldn't be a problem, you have eight hours of free time ahead of you, time to learn three whole concert programmes!' I would pout and grumble, but to no avail. He did this to test me and to check out my reactions. He remembered everything. If he changed things like bowings and fingerings, he would ensure that I had learnt and assimilated them in a musical way, and that I was capable of fulfilling his demands. I felt that he was in a sense checking my whole being, to see what I could achieve, how well and fully I could concentrate and assimilate ideas quickly.

I was certainly put to the test in our lessons on Prokofiev's Sinfonia Concertante. *It seemed to me that I had prepared it really well, that I had got into the spirit of the music, understood the concept, and I felt confident. I came to the lesson with the class pianist, Aza Magamedovna Amintaeva, who subsequently became my accompanist and duo partner. When the lesson started, Mstislav Leopoldovich decided to check just how well I really knew the piece. 'Play me the second oboe part in these bars, now here the solo horn . . .' During that lesson I didn't get to play my own part at all. So I went away and studied the score intensely. The next day, I came back, but before I was allowed to play there was more interrogation: 'Now, Natalie, play me the viola part in these bars in the finale.' Each lesson ended in tears, and so it went on until I really did know the score inside out. Of*

144

course when Rostropovich saw the rivers of tears running down my face he only scolded me: 'You shouldn't drink so much tea, Natasha, it's coming out both ends I see.' There were so many insults, but I had to submit to them.

Only when I really knew the whole score did he start talking to me normally and allow me to play the cello part. And of course it meant I could respond when he said, for instance, in the finale, 'Listen to the oboe theme (the same theme that Prokofiev used again in the concertino), now you answer, enter into dialogue, but play smoothly and not with the oboe's articulation.'

Later I was terribly grateful, since I understood that it was not just a question of knowing the score, but of actually being initiated into the act of hearing. If, for instance, one listens to the texture of the piano part, then one can choose to blend into the texture, or perhaps, on the contrary, play in opposition to it, with contrasting colour or articulation.

Another thing that Rostropovich did was to enlarge the horizons of my sound-world. He thought that my playing was too small-scale, too focused on the requirements of chamber music, and he worked for quite some time with me on vibrato. He felt that my vibrato was too narrow, and this, he told me, took away from the overall scale of my sound, and restricted my ability to project. He spoke about under-standing vibrato on the cello as an emulation of the human voice. He explained how the sound could grow and develop on one note, a tech-nique used by singers. If you stand right next to certain singers, you hear their voice has an enormously wide vibrato which oscillates from a quarter-tone to a semitone. Yet in the concert hall this same voice gives the impression of a fully rounded tone, with pure intonation, spot on the middle of the note.

I considered myself fortunate that Rostropovich never worked with me in the class, but always alone in private. There were no witnesses. I think he made an exception for me, since he knew I was terribly vulnerable, and sometimes he said some horribly cruel things to me. But this was his way of getting the best out of me. Probably he didn't want to humiliate me in front of people, given that I was reputed to be the Conservatoire's 'star' cellist and there was enormous pressure on me to succeed in the Tchaikovsky competition.

A few weeks before the competition started, the Ministry of Culture arranged that all the Soviet competitors could stay in a group of dachas at Serebryany Bor, an exclusive settlement in a green area of Moscow near the river. We were given the best imaginable working conditions, where we could enjoy some peace, fresh air, no interruptions to our work. And in addition we were well fed.

I had a room next to Valya Feigin, and I could hear that he was always practising. But I was not going to be outdone. I decided to get up earlier than he did, at six in the morning. In the end I was practising eleven hours a day!

When I returned to Moscow I was to have my final lessons with Rostropovich. I had barely started playing, when he stopped me. 'Natalie, what's happened to you?' Evidently he immediately intuited that I had been overdoing it; the life had gone out of my playing. I confessed that I had been provoked into practising like a maniac. Mstislav Leopoldovich said, 'Natasha, put your cello away right now. You'll leave it here in my flat for the next twenty-four hours. Go out and think about other things.'

I was horrified, for the competition was to start in two days' time, and I didn't know what to do with myself. But he was right, it was better to be fresh and spontaneous, rather than play like an automaton.

Rostropovich was interested in everything about my presentation: how I walked on stage, how I was dressed, how I took my bow. He regarded it all as part of the artistic act. He called in his wife, Galina Pavlovna, to help. She was very generous, and gave me a piece of material to make a concert dress and lent me a pair of shoes, as well as giving me advice on how to behave on stage.

One of the features introduced at the Tchaikovsky competition was a specially written new piece given to the candidates to learn specially for the second round. In our year the piece was by Vladimir Vlasov and was entitled 'Improvisation'. After the competition Vlasov asked Rostropovich to play it at a concert devoted to his works. Mstislav Leopoldovich had of course seen the score when he worked on it with the students in the class. But he only started preparing the piece himself just one hour before this concert.

We had agreed that I should drop by his flat around six in the evening and that we would go to the concert together. I found him sitting with his cello, putting in bowings and fingerings, and playing through the work slowly. As we were walking down the street to go to the concert, I started chatting and asking various questions. He turned to me and said, 'Natalie, let me be for the moment, I have to carry this music to the concert.' And so it was, he arrived and played this ten-minute piece from memory, having spent only one hour learning it. Such was the force of his concentration.

I think that Rostropovich has a unique capacity to see, hear and understand things through his fantastic intuition. It doesn't matter if he perhaps has not studied so many disciplines, or is not even very widely read. His perception of the surrounding world and of other people is hypersensitive. This is evident in his manner of giving advice, for he knows how to give his entire attention and thought to the person in front of him and to the problem in hand. I can never forget his eyes when his thoughts are taken over like this, when he appears to go into a particular state of attention. I remember once asking his advice about a programme. He seemed to dismiss the question. Then about half an hour later, I observed his eyes move somewhere else, as if seeing something in the distance, and I understood that his thoughts were completely concentrated on formulating his answers. It was a process that allowed him to identify totally with the single individual at that moment in time.

Most importantly Mstislav Leopoldovich taught his students to extend their vision beyond the four strings of the cello. 'You must know more, you must aim for greater things,' he would tell us. 'This will mean that your sound, even within the physical dynamic limits of the instrument, will acquire greater depth and volume.' The belief that the musical vision has to stimulate your quest for instrumental solutions is what made Rostropovich such a unique and convincing artist. And the emotional impact he has on audiences is so great because he himself is always searching for something that transcends his present vision: throughout his life he has never stood still.

9

Popularising the cello

Rostropovich brought his characteristic drive and forceful energy to his new position as head of the cello and double-bass faculty at the Moscow Conservatoire. He was responsible for many innovations, for raising standards and revitalising the somewhat antiquated approach to repertoire and performance employed by his predecessors. Not least amongst his achievements was his insistence that the cello should be added to the instrumental categories represented at the Tchaikovsky competition. Another was to reform double-bass tuning and notation, abandoning the transposing 'soloist' system in order to establish 'natural tuning' as the standard method throughout the country.* Sorting this out at the various levels of musical education helped orchestras to achieve better intonation and performers to grasp scores more easily. However, the reform required new editions of both didactic and orchestral literature, most of which hitherto had only existed using the transposing system; Rostropovich, supported by the double-bass section leaders of the major Moscow orchestras, raised this issue at the highest levels.

Not long after his appointment as faculty head in Moscow, Rostropovich received an invitation to teach at the Leningrad Conservatoire. After the death of Aleksandr Shtrimer early in 1961, Pavel Serebryakov, the director of the Leningrad Conservatoire, wrote to Rostropovich inviting him to take on a class of postgraduate students. As he explained, there existed no teacher in Leningrad who could

---

* The 'solo tuning', from bottom up, was F sharp – B – E – A, whereas the standard orchestral tuning, as today, was E – A – D – G (sometimes with a bottom fifth string tuned to either B or C). In solo literature, before the 'reform', the double-bass transposed so that a written G would be heard as A, etc.

effectively replace Shtrimer or provide the level of tuition necessary at postgraduate level. Attracted by the high level of students he was offered, Rostropovich agreed to take on a half-load, provided that the Moscow Conservatoire did not object. In September, the Ministry of Culture decided 'to make an exception' in confirming his position as Professor at the Leningrad Conservatoire. The only person previously to hold a professorial position at both Conservatoires was Shostakovich, and this only for a brief period in the mid-1940s. In fact, after his ignominious dismissal from both institutions in 1948, Shostakovich gave up teaching altogether, but Serebryakov scored another 'triumph' when he persuaded him to return to his alma mater to teach a select class of postgraduates in 1962.

From Rostropovich's point of view, his new position was compatible with his other activities: it involved seeing his students on a monthly basis, entailing perhaps six or seven lessons spread over the year. During the five years he taught at the Leningrad Conservatoire, he worked with a total of ten postgraduates, beginning with just two in autumn 1961. One of them was Yuri Falik, who had also graduated as a composer. Falik acknowledged Shtrimer as an excellent teacher and a refined musician, but he had been frustrated at his professor's ignorance of the contemporary cello repertoire: Shtrimer was not interested in teaching it, and could only point Falik in Rostropovich's direction. As fate would have it, Falik did indeed eventually become his pupil:

Genna Gennovker and I were Rostropovich's first postgraduate students. I was now able to realise my dream to study contemporary repertoire, and I studied with him concertos by Honegger, Hindemith, Prokofiev and Shostakovich. When Mstislav Leopoldovich came up for our first lessons in October 1961, he displayed enormous interest in everything I did: 'I hear that you compose. Do show me your compositions.' He discovered that my diploma work was a symphony for strings and percussion and he said that he would take the score to the conductor, Gennadi Rozhdestvensky, who was interested in contemporary music. He was as good as his word and introduced me to Gennadi Nikolayevich. He also presented me to Shostakovich, with whom I formed friendly relations. This was such a change from Shtrimer's indifference to new music. Every time we met over the years, Slava's first question to me would invariably be: 'Tell me, what new works have you written?'

To begin with, Mstislav Leopoldovich came up to Leningrad quite often. If he wasn't playing a concerto himself he would work with us from midday to late at night; lessons could last between two and two and a half hours each, for he never looked at the clock. It was an enormous contrast from the rather dry, academic style of Shtrimer's teaching. Rostropovich was so uninhibited in his manner, his teaching was so lively – vivid and entertaining, full of humour. Often he would grab hold of my cello and demonstrate how to play something, then he might sit down at the piano, saying, 'Do you remember that bit in this Tchaikovsky symphony (or it might be a quotation from Brahms, Prokofiev or Shostakovich) – please find a unified image for this section you are playing.' Mstislav Leopoldovich possessed a phenomenal erudition, but he never showed it in a boastful way. But just from a small comment of his, or the way he played a phrase, one was aware that everything he said and played was backed up by profound knowledge and understanding.

It was a time of renaissance at the Leningrad Conservatoire. At the same time Shostakovich resumed teaching a postgraduate class, and Mravinsky also accepted a professorship. All their lessons were open, so students would run from one class to another. Rostropovich's class was always chock-a-block full of people; not only cello students, but pianists, conductors, violinists rushed to hear him teach.

I remember an impressive concert in 1962 in Leningrad to celebrate the centenary of the founding of the St Petersburg Conservatoire. Salmanov wrote his Ode for massed orchestra of cellos, double basses, trumpets and timpani. This anticipated the events put on by the cello club, where we played at the Large Hall of the Philharmonia.

Slava was active in making things happen in Leningrad; before, its musical life was like a stagnant pond, but he came and stirred up the waters. When he was around, people found themselves walking on their heads, for he radiated such energy through the force of his personality.

The idea of popularising his instrument by creating ensembles and orchestras of cellos had come to Rostropovich during his first trip to the USA. Before his American debut at Carnegie Hall on 4 April 1956, he found himself with two free days in New York. The evening before his recital, he accepted an invitation from a group of New York cellists in the home of an amateur musician. They told him of their intention to set up a cello club, similar to those in existence already in London and San Francisco. Indeed, on his next trip to the USA, in 1959, Rostropovich was invited as Gregor Piatigorsky's guest to the foundation ceremony of the New York violoncello society; Piatigorsky and Bernard Greenhouse were the founding patrons, while Pablo Casals was elected as the club's honorary president, and later Rostropovich himself took on this role.

In the mean time, during this first American tour, Rostropovich enjoyed several opportunities for informal music-making in private homes. For instance, in Washington, Rostropovich played chamber music with members of the Budapest Quartet. In Los Angeles he played the Schubert C major quintet with Jascha Heifetz and Piatigorsky, amongst others, and was also invited to the home of Viktor Gottlieb, where a group of cellists performed the *Bachianas Brasileiras* no. 1, presenting him with copies of the score and parts.

By the time he arrived in San Francisco at the end of April, his appetite for cello ensemble music had been awakened, and he accepted an invitation from the famous local cello club with alacrity. Immediately after performing Prokofiev's *Sinfonia Concertante* with the San Francisco Symphony Orchestra, Rostropovich was taken to a specially organised meeting, where a gathering of over a hundred cellists welcomed him. He heard cellists of all ages and stages play in various formations and large ensembles. When asked to play, he decided to dilute the 'massed bleating' of cellos with a performance of some preludes on the piano! At the end of the evening, he was asked as guest of honour to cut the sumptuously decorated cake: it was a full metre in length, and on the top, his name and the opening bars of Bach's third suite had been inscribed in icing sugar.

Rostropovich returned to Moscow with a suitcase of music for cello duo, quartet and larger ensemble, which he immediately gave his students to learn. The pieces were presented in class concerts, which were usually crowned with a rendering of *Bachianas Brasileiras* no. 1 for eight cellos, or no. 5, which also included a solo soprano: Galina Vishnevskaya would add to the glamour of these events by singing the solo part in no. 5, though usually performing only the Aria, the first of the two songs which make up the piece. The Villa-Lobos performances were so popular that they soon became a regular feature of concerts not just at the Moscow Conservatoire, but also in other venues and cities. When the poet Anna Akhmatova heard a performance of the Aria from *Bachianas Brasileiras* no. 5 on the radio in December 1961, Vishnevskaya's interpretation inspired her to write a poem:

> A woman's voice rushes like the wind,
> black, moist and full of night,
> and whatever it touches in flight
> is instantly transformed.
> Light shines through faceted diamond,
> And for an instant the glimmer of silver,
> The rustle of some enigmatic robe
> Of fabulous silks.

And this enchanted voice
Evokes such powerful force
That before us emerges not the grave
but a mysterious flight of stairs.*

I too had the good fortune to hear a performance of *Bachianas Brasileiras* no. 5 with Rostropovich and Vishnevskaya (this time with an orchestra of over a hundred cellos) in the Large Hall of the Leningrad Philharmonic in May 1966. On that occasion I sat next to Jacqueline du Pré, who was likewise thrilled and enchanted by the performance, and wrote home enthusiastically about hearing 'two of the world's greatest artists'. In the same concert, the cello orchestra played Davydov's *Hymn*, which Jackie regarded as a special tribute to her as the current owner of the famous Davydov Stradivarius cello.†

By the late 1950s, the class cello ensemble started performing outside the Conservatoire, participating in collective concerts at such prestigious venues as the Kremlin Palace of Congresses, on occasion joining forces with other groups such as the Conservatoire harp ensemble. As Valery Zelenyak-Kudreiko recalls:

Twice at least Mstislav Leopoldovich took the whole class to Leningrad in the late 1960s. Once we played at the Academic Capella, the other time at the Maly Zal (Small Hall) of the Philharmonia, where we performed a programme of duets and trios, as well as larger ensemble pieces. We always finished with the *Bachianas Brasileiras*. For instance I played the Handel sonata for two cellos as a duo with Viktor Apartsev (it was an arrangement, but a very good one), and other students played duos by Couperin and Boismortier. All these pieces were quite unknown in the Soviet Union, and audiences enjoyed them as interesting novelties.

Now that he was head of the cello faculty, Rostropovich had an administrative base from which to initiate a series of meetings and concerts dedicated to cellists and the cello, which often took place at the TseDRI (Central House of Workers in Art) Hall. The first such event was dedicated to the memory of Kozolupov, and shortly afterwards, in January 1962, he organised a concert to honour Casals's eighty-fifth birthday. The cello faculty also played host to Piatigorsky and other distinguished

* EW's translation.
† Elizabeth Wilson, *Jacqueline du Pré*, 1998, p. 193.

jury members at the time of the Tchaikovsky competition in April that year.

The logical progression from such projects was to create a club open to a wider circle of cellists, whether amateur or professional. In the autumn of 1964 Rostropovich opened the first such cello club in Moscow, and a few weeks later founded its sister organisation in Leningrad. His aim was to create a chain of such institutions across the country, which would cater for cellists of all levels. In addition, Rostropovich encouraged cello ensembles in local music schools: his occasional visits to such schools would entail a master-class, a meeting with teachers and pupils where he recounted the latest events in the 'cello world', and a concert by the school ensemble, in which he might inspire through example by participating as an 'extra'.

The 'solemn opening ceremony' of the Moscow cello club was held on 21 September at the TseDRI Hall. As the critic Braginsky noted,* the occasion hardly merited such a description, for it was festive and joyful from start to finish. Rostropovich initiated the evening by reading out greetings from Pablo Casals, then presented the new club with a collection of signed photographs from such famous musicians as David Oistrakh, Sviatoslav Richter, Dmitri Shostakovich, Herbert von Karajan, Zino Francescatti, Josef Szigeti, Igor Stravinsky, Eugene Ormandy and Jascha Heifetz, and even celebrities such as Marcel Marceau and Yuri Gagarin. After this Rostropovich recounted his own plans, and talked of the new concertos written by Boris Tishchenko, Tikhon Khrennikov, Dmitri Kabalevsky and Sulkhan Tsintsadze – he was shortly to give premieres of the first two. Professor Lev Ginsburg followed with a well-prepared lecture about the state of the cello today. The climax of the evening was a performance of the 'Toy' symphony (attributed to Haydn) in which distinguished colleagues from the Conservatoire cello faculty sat down to play cuckoo, whistle, triangles and drums under Rostropovich's direction.

Rostropovich asked his postgraduate student Mark Drobinsky to keep records of the meetings and act as a kind of secretary. As with everything he did, Rostropovich wanted to make the Soviet cello clubs the best, the most active, and the most popular in the world. The way he set about collecting signed photographs was typical of the

---

* Article in *Sovetskaya Muzyka*, no. 12, 1964.

obsessive single-mindedness with which he approached any new project: a list compiled in January 1969 showed that Rostropovich's personal contacts had led to some two dozen or so signed photos being added to the cello club's original collection, amongst them greetings from Marlene Dietrich, Otto Klemperer, Charlie Chaplin, Yehudi Menuhin, George Szell, not to mention many of the best-known contemporary cellists. (Throughout his life Rostropovich has taken joy in establishing such collections: for instance, friends and students always knew that a porcelain figurine of someone, whether angel, man or pig, playing the cello would be an acceptable gift, for he had an enormous collection at home. Later he started collecting antique furniture: Vishnevskaya's memoirs include comic accounts of his searches for 'hidden treasure' across the country.)

Once formally established, the cello clubs of Moscow and Leningrad took over the kind of events that had previously been mounted under the auspices of the Conservatoire cello faculty. These included celebrations of such world-famous cellists as Pierre Fournier (who was in Moscow for his sixtieth birthday), and Gaspar Cassado: my circular invitation to the latter was addressed to 'brothers and sisters of bow and spike'! In the winter of 1966, I attended a cello club evening with Jacqueline du Pré, held to celebrate the finals of the national All-Union competition. Additional attractions included the showing of western films, nothing to do with the cello, but considered a worthwhile bonus. On that occasion the film, *Italian Divorce* starring Gina Lollabrigida, was shown. Afterwards Rostropovich invited his whole class back to his apartment, where many toasts were drunk; then, showing a new side of his talents, he entertained us all by playing tangos at the piano, and we danced as he played. The post-graduate student Mark Drobinsky recalls that particular evening:

I remember how Jacqueline [du Pré] danced at this party with such joy and complete lack of inhibition. At some point I asked her to dance with me, and found it impossible to restrain her or hold her – the force of her nature was really larger than life! Altogether Jacqueline left an indelible impression on us all, and I can never forget her extraordinary temperament and wonderful playing.

On another occasion, as Silvija Naruňaite recalls, Rostropovich invited his students back to supper after a class concert. While they were sitting at the dining table, he put on a disc by the jazz pianist Erroll Garner. About twenty minutes later, he slipped out of the room, perhaps to turn the LP over. Another ten minutes passed, and suddenly Silvija realised this was not Garner playing, but Rostropovich – he had sat down at the piano and seamlessly continued Garner's improvisation.

With Knushevitsky's death in December 1962, Rostropovich found himself to be the senior cello teacher in the country – in status if not age. He had taken over many students from his elder colleagues' classes, and needed to make new appointments. One of his first actions as faculty head at the Moscow Conservatoire had been to invite Daniil Shafran to join the teaching staff. To make the offer more attractive, Rostropovich planned to transfer some of his own best pupils to Shafran, but he nonetheless declined – indeed, he never taught at any institution, although later in life he proved an inspiring teacher in masterclasses. Rostropovich held Shafran in great esteem as a cellist and musician, and had previously recommended to the Ministry of Culture that the next invitation he received from America should be reassigned to Shafran, believing that it was only fair that American audiences should be allowed to get to know this remarkable talent.

Rostropovich's ebullient confidence in his own qualities allowed him to be unusually and genuinely generous to other colleagues; sadly, the emotionally vulnerable Shafran continued to hold Rostropovich in part responsible for his having been 'pushed into the shade' by comparison.

In autumn 1962, Natalya Shakhovskaya was given her own class at the Moscow Conservatoire, and shortly afterwards so were Mikhail Khomitser and Natalya Gutman. In fact, Gutman started teaching while officially still a postgraduate student in Rostropovich's Leningrad class. At a speech at her final graduation in June 1967, Rostropovich received a storm of applause when he said, 'Natasha is an example to all you Leningraders. You see, you shouldn't complete the Leningrad Conservatoire without already having a class at the Moscow Conservatoire!' These appointments helped to widen the choice available to students in the Conservatoire cello faculty. Shakhovskaya, a thorough and dedicated teacher, centred her career on the Conservatoire, becoming head of faculty after Rostropovich's departure. Natalya Gutman, on the other hand, concentrated on concert performance, but like Rostropovich, always combined playing with teaching. With Rostropovich installed as faculty head, there was a period of greater stability at the Conservatoire. The difficult period of petty intrigue came to an end, harmful rumours floundered where they had started, as nothing more than idle gossip. For the most part teachers and musicians were fully aware that Rostropovich's energies and gifts would be of enormous benefit to the Conservatoire in general, and that he could do more than anybody else to elevate the cello's standing and to create opportunities for young cellists.

For Rostropovich, competitions were an important means of achieving this status for his instrument. Of course, competitions were a way of life at the Conservatoire, and nationally too, the cello had established its place in the leading contests, but Rostropovich dreamed of creating a new international cello competition in Russia. The first international competitions were instituted for pianists and violinists well before the Second World War. The first Chopin competition, for example, was held in Warsaw in 1927, and the Ysaye competition (the predecessor of the Queen Elizabeth Concours in Brussels) was instituted in 1937. The correspondence of the young Shostakovich, writing home from Warsaw as a participant of the 1927 Chopin competition, reveals the nationalistic spirit demonstrated both by the Soviet team and their Polish rivals.

During the isolationist period of Stalin's rule, opportunities to travel to any form of contest in the West were so rare that participants felt almost obliged to succeed. Soviet violinists and pianists swept up top prizes at the Concours Eugène Ysaye in Brussels before the war. Laureates such as David Oistrakh and the young violin prodigy Boris Goldstein in 1937 and Emil Gilels, winner of the piano competition in 1938, returned from Brussels as conquering heroes and were met by cheering crowds at the Bielorussky station. Stalin himself fêted the victorious artists at Kremlin receptions: the story of how he promised to visit the home of young Busya Goldstein to drink tea became the talk of the town. The prodigy had been clever enough to turn the Leader's promise to good advantage: 'Josef Vissarionovich, it would be a great honour to welcome you, only I don't know where we could drink tea as we live in a communal flat and share the kitchen with ten other families.' Within days the Goldstein family was allocated a separate town apartment, without having even to apply.

More opportunities for Soviet musicians to travel came after the war with the creation of 'Festivals of Youth and Friendship' in the Eastern Bloc countries, and during the 1950s, the Soviet Ministry of

Culture empowered the Moscow and Leningrad Conservatoires to select young Soviet instrumentalists to participate in competitions in the West. Soviet pianists and violinists won prizes in Brussels at the Queen Elizabeth Concours and at the Marguerite Long and Jacques Thibaud competitions in Paris. As more competitions were instituted, so 'competition fever' grew to become an ingrained feature of the Soviet conservatoire system. In Rostropovich's eyes, though, the cello continued to lag behind the violin and the piano in status, and there still existed no 'first division' competition for the instrument. This perception was reinforced when the Tchaikovsky competition was established in 1958 without a category for the cello.

Rostropovich's rich personal experience as competitor and jury member had led to a firm belief in the benefits of competitions: they provided an opportunity for young cellists to pit themselves against their peers and to compare experiences with fellow instrumentalists from all over the world. In 1957 Rostropovich was invited to serve on the jury of a newly founded competition for cello, the first Concours International Pablo Casals, held in Paris in October 1957, and he returned to judge the second Casals competition in Mexico in January 1959. The first Casals competition was created to mark the world-famous Catalan cellist's eightieth birthday; it had to be postponed from June to October because of Casals's recent heart attack. The distinguished panel of judges was made up of Pierre Fournier, Enrico Mainardi, Maurice Eisenberg, Gaspar Cassado, Milos Sadlo, John Barbirolli, and Rostropovich, while Paul Bazelaire acted as jury chairman. Casals declined involvement as a judge, but attended all the sessions, encouraging and stimulating the young competitors through his presence.

Three excellent Soviet cellists had been selected to participate, none of whom were current Rostropovich students. The favourite was Valentin Feigin, a pupil of Semyon Kozolupov, who came from a well-known Moscow musical family. Another strong candidate was Aleksei Lazko, a student of Shtrimer at the Leningrad Conservatoire. Tatyana Priymenko, one of Rostropovich's very first pupils, was the third cellist on their team. But this time it was not the Soviet team which won the top prizes; the outright winner was the American cellist, Lesley Parnas, while the German Angelika May received second prize. Feigin and Lazko were awarded third and fourth prizes respectively.

In the December 1957 issue of *Sovetskaya Muzyka*, Rostropovich gave a detailed account of his impressions of the competition. It got off to an unpromising start when a strike of electrical workers led to blackouts throughout Paris and the city's transport system ground to a halt. The first round, scheduled to begin in the morning, was delayed, but even by evening the Salle Gaveau was still without electricity, so the competitors played by candlelight and torches were shone on to the pianist's stand.

Rostropovich vividly described his first prolonged meeting with Casals. He was invited to his hotel room, where he presented the veteran cellist with various gifts, scores and recordings of new Soviet music. As a final gesture – made in honour of those Russian musicians who still remembered Casals's concerts given in Moscow and St Petersburg before the Revolution – Rostropovich gave him a wooden figure of a bear playing the cello, carved by a renowned Kostroma craftsman. Touched to the heart, Casals was overcome by memories of his meetings with Rimsky-Korsakov, Glazunov, Rachmaninov and Siloti. Although Rostropovich did not mention this, Casals must surely also have recalled Leopold Rostropovich, his one-time student. Next, though, it was Casals's turn to make a gift to Rostropovich. He asked for his cello to be brought to him. Playing for almost the first time since his recent heart attack, he performed two pieces of unaccompanied Bach, the Prelude from the second suite and the Sarabande from the fifth. Rostropovich enthused:

Apart from the wonders of his interpretation, I was amazed by the precision of his intonation and the strength of his fingers – at eighty years of age! Casals plays Bach as if conducting a live conversation. His frequent rubati are a unique feature of his performing manner. After playing a phrase, he would glance at me, and then go on to the next phrase as if responding to the first. In all this he found a great inner equilibrium to the music.

At a farewell party given by Paul Bazelaire, Casals again played Bach both on the piano and the cello. When he finished performing, he handed his cello to Rostropovich, and commanded 'Play!' A shy, almost reluctant Slava was persuaded by Bazelaire, who offered to accompany him in the second movement of the Brahms F major sonata, proving to be an excellent pianist. The friendships Rostropovich made with jury members such as Gaspar Cassado and Pierre Fournier were to be consolidated in the future when Rostropovich invited them to Moscow as judges for the Tchaikovsky competition.

Despite the convivial atmosphere, the competition results in Paris came as a disappointment to the Soviet team and required explanation. Rostropovich's article touched on a weakness of Russian interpretative style when he observed that 'our youthful performers should pay greater attention in their study and approach to the performance traditions of Western classics. I do not doubt that had works by Tchaikovsky, Myaskovsky, Khatchaturian and Prokofiev been included in the selected list of concertos to play in the final, our candidates would have received higher prizes.'

In this instance Rostropovich noted that Feigin, while a favourite of the audiences, had miscalculated by choosing to play Schumann's concerto and had been marked down for stylistic lapses. The issue of Soviet ignorance of Western traditions could be attributed in part to the long period of isolation from the rest of the world, but also to a tendency to approach music instinctively, relying more on emotion and fantasy than on powers of analysis. Certainly Soviet performers were often criticised for their lack of understanding of the classical tradition, whether interpreting Haydn and Mozart or Beethoven and Schubert.

I remember how surprised I was when I first went to Russia that so few musicians had any knowledge of Haydn's great symphonies, for example – they were hardly ever performed. Religious music was proscribed, depriving Soviet listeners of the opportunity to hear or study the choral masterpieces of Bach and the oratorios of Handel, let alone Mozart's *Requiem* or Beethoven's *Missa Solemnis*. My astonishment was complete when I attended my first lecture on music history. Unable to believe my ears, I heard the musicologist explain that 'the hero' of an unnamed work of Handel (a composer of 'social-democrat' leanings forced to work for 'aristocratic' patrons) was 'the People', represented by the choir. Only when the 'Hallelujah Chorus' was played to illustrate the point could I identify the work in question as *The Messiah*. The lecturer had spoken about the work without once mentioning the biblical derivation of its texts!

By way of compensation, the Russians' strength lay in their interpretation of the romantic virtuoso repertoire and of new Russian music. When it came to setting the programme for the Tchaikovsky competition, Rostropovich ensured that the repertoire included works by Shostakovich, Prokofiev, and Khatchaturian, in which Soviet cellists could deliver interpretations that could be considered authentic.

For the second Casals competition in Mexico in 1959, Rostropovich, once again a judge, intended to take one of his own students, Medeya Abramyan. Despite her arduous preparations for the competition, disappointment awaited her and the other Soviet candidates when the authorities withheld their permission to travel, at the last minute and for no apparent reason – such were the injustices and tribulations to which young Soviet musicians were subjected. Casals was once again in attendance in Mexico, although as before he chose not to sit on the panel of judges. The jury was similar to that in Paris, with the addition of André Navarra, Zara Nelsova, Adolfo Odnoposoff from Cuba and the Brazilian composer Heitor Villa-Lobos. Rostropovich formed a friendship with Villa-Lobos who declared his intention to write a concerto for three cellos and orchestra which would reflect the three great personalities of the chosen dedicatees, Rostropovich, Fournier and Cassado. Unfortunately, Villa-Lobos died shortly afterwards, and did not have time to fulfil his promise.

The private juror's notes that Rostropovich preserved from this competition refer primarily to questions of musical judgement. Although severe in condemning competitors' technical weaknesses (for instance, a Guatemalan cellist's 'completely mad fingering' in a Boccherini sonata and 'catastrophic' intonation), he was merciless when it came to lack of musical taste. Thus a German candidate was charged with having a 'sound like a vibraphone', while an American cellist, dismissively classified as an 'orchestral player', was accused of using 'revolting' glissandi; a third cellist was mocked for making his cello sound 'like a gopher plucking a guitar'. One of the participants, the young Ana Bilsmer, later became a pioneer of baroque performing techniques. Rostropovich defined his performances as 'technically strong', although he regretted his 'prosaic sound'. The winner in Mexico was a French cellist, Aleth Lamasse, whom Rostropovich particularly praised for her interpretation of Bach. To celebrate the conclusion of the competition, Casals directed the jury members and his young wife, Martita Casals, in a performance of his own *Sardana* for massed cello ensemble.

In 1958, between the two Casals competitions, the Ministry of Culture invited Rostropovich to perform Tchaikovsky's *Rococo Variations* at the gala opening of the first Tchaikovsky competition. The authorities were dismayed by his adamant refusal, but it was a matter of principle: 'How can you expect me to be seen playing at an event of such importance when the cello has been excluded? And it is not as if the repertoire is lacking, for Tchaikovsky wrote several wonderful original works for cello.'

The considerations that lay behind the creation of the Tchaikovsky competition went beyond the purely musical. As the first international music contest to be held in the Soviet Union, it was conceived as an event of political importance which enacted the policy of 'peaceful co-existence' with the West on the one hand, while simultaneously aiming to prove Soviet supremacy. A sense of rivalry was inherent in the concept of cultural exchange: the Soviets wished to prove that their musicians played better through 'ideological enlightenment'. 'Overtaking America', a slogan that originated in the early 1930s (and was now stridently claimed by Mao Tse-tung during 'the great leap forward' in China), proved to be an unrealistic struggle in economic terms, whether the gauge was steel production or harvests of wheat or maize. But the Soviets claimed equality, if not superiority, in the arts and sciences, as a result of the undoubted excellence of their education, training, and research facilities – and of the enormous resources invested in these fields by a benevolent socialist system. The competitive spirit between the two principal superpowers was symbolised in the public eye by the 'space race'. The language of lunar exploration seeped over into descriptions of cultural events: thus Rostropovich was portrayed by the Western press on more than one occasion as an artistic equivalent of Gagarin, and at the 1962 Edinburgh Festival critics dubbed him 'the fifth man in space'.

No efforts were spared to make the first Tchaikovsky competition a triumph, and the biggest names in the country were put at its disposal: Shostakovich was appointed president of its artistic organisation committee, responsible for the choice of repertoire, appointing the jury and establishing the rules. Oistrakh and Gilels, also members of that committee, would head the juries of the violin and piano competitions respectively. For Muscovites, the access that the Tchaikovsky competition provided to musicians from the West and to different interpretative styles was of enormous significance. In 1958, the violin competition was won by Valeri Klimov, a student of Oistrakh, whereas in the piano section the young American pianist, Van Cliburn, carried off the first prize. A 'capitalist' victor was a political thunderbolt, yet was an enormously popular choice, for Muscovites fell under the spell of Van Cliburn's charisma, virtuosic prowess and sincere romantic musicality. A joke circulated in Moscow for some years afterwards: 'What did 'Kliburn and Klimov have in common?' (The answer being: 'Both their names start with "V" and "K", and neither of them can play the violin' – a cruel judgement that reflects Russians' ecstatic attitude to foreigners rather than any serious critical capacity.)

The only problem with the competition, as far as Rostropovich was concerned, was that the cello had been overlooked. The experience of sitting on the jury at the two Casals competitions fuelled Rostropovich's ambition to create a competition in Moscow which would exceed them and all others in significance. Having successfully petitioned for the inclusion of a cello category in the second Tchaikovsky competition in 1962, he aimed to prepare an unbeatable team and to appoint a jury of unparalleled quality, made up of the world's best cellists.

In order to prepare for the Tchaikovsky competition itself, a series of national contests was set in motion, culminating in the 'competition of Cellists of the USSR' held early in 1961. This was effectively the first such 'All-Union' competition held since Rostropovich won first prize in the contest of 1945. Its jury included all the leading Soviet cellists: Kozolupov, Knushevitsky, Galina Kozolupova, Vladimir Vlasov, Sergei Aslamazian, Artem Georgian and Rostropovich himself. This was the period in which two extraordinary female cellists, Natalya Shakhovskaya and Natalya Gutman, were emerging as great talents. Shakhovskaya, until recently a student of Kozolupov, had shared first prize with Alla Vasiliyeva in a competition at the Moscow Festival of Youth in 1957, but had lost out to the younger Natasha Gutman, a student of Galina Kozolupova, at the Prague Spring festival in 1960, by which time she had switched to Rostropovich as a teacher. The All-Union competition served as a final filter in selecting the team for the Tchaikovsky competition, and only those who won awards or who were already laureates were allowed to participate. Amongst them were five Rostropovich pupils: Viktor Apartsev, Maris Villerus, Evgeny Altman, Yuri Falik, and Natalya Shakhovskaya. The other competitors on the Soviet team comprised prizewinners like Mikhail Khomitser, Valentin Feigin and Natalya Gutman. Thus the level proved to be extraordinarily high.

The second Tchaikovsky competition itself opened in early April 1962, and the cellists commenced their first round on 7 April. The sixteen-member jury, with Rostropovich as its chairman, included such illustrious cellists as Gregor Piatigorsky, Maurice Maréchal, Gaspar Cassado, Pierre Fournier, Sviatoslav Knushevitsky and Daniil Shafran. The Ministry of Culture had made participation in the Tchaikovsky competition very attractive to foreigners, paying all hotel expenses and the candidates' air fares to and from their country of origin. (In 1966, the New Zealand cellist Ross Pople told me that this was a deciding factor in his participation!) Amongst the many excellent 'foreigners' was a strong team of cellists from the United States – Lesley Parnas, Toby Saks, Douglas Davis, Daniel Domb, and Lynn Harrell; only the latter two did not reach the finals. The Soviet team boasted three or four potential winners: the two Natalyas (Shakhovskaya and Gutman), Valentin Feigin, and Mikhail Khomitser. Rostropovich had invested so much energy and effort in creating the competition that it was automatically expected that one of his students would win, and of them Shakhovskaya was the strongest candidate.

Natasha Gutman recalls that 'I never expected to be the victor myself, but Valya Feigin was definitely a candidate for the top prize; in those days he played superbly.'

The jury was asked to vote on a point system, grading candidates from one to twenty-five, and to indicate after each round which candidate they thought should be the victor. After the first round ten members abstained from an opinion, while the other six votes were divided equally between Feigin and Shakhovskaya. At the end of the second round the situation had changed, and ten jury members indicated that Shakhovskaya should win. Her successful performance in the third and final round meant that she had maintained her leadership throughout the contest.

When I asked Rostropovich what were the qualities he looked for in competitors, he emphasised the performer's relationship to the music far more than the technical side of cello-playing. 'Although sometimes one hears cellists with such awe-inspiring techniques, that one cannot but be impressed. But for each member of the jury, listening is very individual. I have never insisted on anything during the voting.' Rostropovich's jury sheets for the 1962 Tchaikovsky competition show that he gave top marks (twenty-five) to Gutman,

Feigin, Shakhovskaya and Khomitser in the first two rounds (while also recording his continuing doubts about the latter's stylistic taste), and he also awarded Lesley Parnas with maximum points in the second round. In the third and final round, held between 11 and 14 April, twelve selected candidates – six Soviet cellists, and six 'foreign' cellists – each played two concertos with orchestra: Tchaikovsky's *Rococo Variations* plus a concerto of their choice. The two Natalyas both selected Prokofiev's *Sinfonia Concertante*.

Some complained that the results had been predictable from the start: Shakhovskaya, in first place, was followed by Parnas and Feigin in joint second, and the third prize was shared between Gutman and Khomitser. The fourth to sixth prizes were given to non-Soviet cellists. Many musicians believed that Lesley Parnas had all the qualities to repeat Van Cliburn's victory, while others would have preferred another of the Soviet candidates to win. Rostropovich recalls that Parnas possessed such incredible beauty of sound that through it he won over his audiences: 'He also had a a wonderful cello, but the spell of his sound was so great that actually one became less concerned about the interpretive quality in his playing.' For his part, Piatigorsky spoke exclusively of Natalya Gutman's qualities in an interview he granted to a Soviet newspaper. But overall, Shakhovskaya's victory was unequivocal, and for the most part endorsed by critics and audiences. The violin section likewise had a Soviet first-prize winner, Boris Gutnikov, while first prize in the piano competition was shared between the Soviet pianist Vladimir Ashkenazy and the British John Ogdon.

After the final, Rostropovich took the jury members out to celebrate at the Aragvi restaurant, renowned for its excellent Georgian cuisine. After the main courses were over, he had a surprise in store. After slipping unobtrusively out of the room, he returned dressed as a 'Kapellmeister' in a sumptuous baroque wig, holding a handful of children's percussion instruments. Two Conservatoire students were invited to aid this 'improvised' performance of the 'Toy' symphony – a wonderful photo records the cream of the world's cellists sharing out their toys and playing under Rostropovich's direction.

All in all, Rostropovich could claim that he had maintained his promise to create a competition of the very highest standard: the Tchaikovsky competition had won its credentials as the world's most important cello contest.

From this point onwards, participation in competitions became integral to Rostropovich's classes both in Moscow and Leningrad. He selected students according to their talent, experience and seniority, and during the frequent national competitions he took careful note of new talents and also observed how older students reacted under pressure. Rostropovich encouraged a philosophical attitude towards competitions, and both winners and losers had to regard them as a test of one's abilities and a useful learning experience. When Rostropovich started working with Yuri Falik, his first postgraduate student in Leningrad, he suggested preparing him for the Tchaikovsky competition. Falik recalls:

I was the only Leningrad cellist to pass through the various preparatory selective competitions and to be chosen to play at the Tchaikovsky. Throughout these contests there reigned a great competitive spirit, the traditional rivalry between Muscovites and Leningraders, but also students from the same teacher contending against each other. Rostropovich still regarded me as a 'Shtrimer' pupil, for I hadn't yet managed to entirely assimilate his approach towards music, although I strove towards it with all my force. From the start I was completely won over by Rostropovich's whole approach. As it turned out too many of his pupils played at the Tchaikovsky competition, and inevitably not all reached the finals, myself included. It was typical that when Rostropovich greeted me after the second-round result, he started by saying something positive: 'You know, Piatigorsky really liked your playing, and he wants to give you his photo as a present.' He asked me to look at the result in a constructive light. 'You know, imagine that you have been a victim of an accident – an ordinary person walks out into the street, and suddenly that day a car runs him over. You played well, you had good votes in the first and second round, and then bang, you were struck off the list of finalists.' Shafran also told me I had played well, but somebody had to be sacrificed, for the contest was taking on the character of another All-Soviet event.

Rostropovich assured me that there would shortly be another opportunity for me. 'There's going to be a competition this summer at the Helsinki Youth Festival, you can go with more or less the same programme,' he told me. 'I'll be in the jury, everything will be alright.'

Indeed, immediately after the Tchaikovsky competition was over, auditions for the Helsinki contest were announced in Moscow. Falik and Tamara Gabarashvili (a very talented third-year student whom Rostropovich had inherited from Kozolupov) were selected as the two Soviet candidates. Another cellist who participated in these selective auditions was Eleonora Testelets, who had recently graduated from the Riga Conservatoire:

At this stage my teacher Berezovsky encouraged me to do my postgraduate studies with Rostropovich. I went to Moscow for the Helsinki auditions, and was put onto the reserve list. Afterwards Mstislav Leopoldovich invited the selected candidates (Tamara, Yura Falik and myself) back to his home. He went into his kitchen to grab something to eat, and called me in. I was shaking all over, but never the less took my courage in hand and asked him, 'Please, I really would like to study with you. Would you take me in your class?' 'Yes, I'll take you,' he answered to my enormous happiness. I returned to Riga feeling that I had won something more important than a competition.

The third Casals competition was scheduled to take place in Budapest in 1963. A strong Soviet team had been selected, including Mikhail Khomitser, now appointed as a teacher at the Conservatoire. There was a general perception that he needed to enhance his reputation by winning an international competition after his relative failure at the Tchaikovsky contest. Lev Evgrafov was another of the selected candidates. He was now officially a postgraduate student of 'cello theory' under the guidance of Lev Ginsburg, although he continued to have occasional lessons from Rostropovich. However, Rostropovich concentrated his efforts on this occasion on two of his class students, Tamara Gabarashvili and Maris Villerus. Whereas Khomitser and Evgrafov won first and second prizes respectively, these two students were awarded fifth prize and a diploma.

Back at home the competition results were disputed. Rostropovich had not gone to Budapest, so was not directly involved in the stories of intrigue and in what certain candidates felt to be 'discriminating results'. However, there was a feeling that Rostropovich's power within the Conservatoire cello faculty was so overwhelming that when his absence gave an opportunity to promote other teachers' students it could not be passed up – this, at any rate, was how some interpreted the relatively poor performance of the students he had nurtured.

Meanwhile, the Tchaikovsky competition had been established as an event that would occur at four-yearly intervals, although it was moved from April to June, a time that fitted in better with the Conservatoire schedule since it allowed students to complete their end-of-year exams before competing. Preparations for the next Tchaikovsky competition started in 1965 with a series of national competitions – the All-Russian, the Trans Caucasian, the Baltic states, and others – and the All-Union competition was held in February 1966. In order to prepare his students for the Tchaikovsky competition, Rostropovich freed his schedule so that he could remain in Moscow for five months between January and June. By coincidence, this was also the period when the twenty-one-year-old Jacqueline du Pré came to study with him in Moscow, taking time off from her own busy concert schedule to do so. She had no desire at all to participate in the competition, and neither did she need to, given that her brilliant career to date had seen her highly successful Carnegie Hall debut and her renowned recording of the Elgar concerto with Sir John Barbirolli for EMI. Nobody who attended Rostropovich's classes could forget his lessons with Jacqueline, for they did not resemble any traditional form of instruction, but rather a voyage of discovery by equal masters, an inspired dialogue between two extraordinary artists. Indeed, despite the very high level of the 1966 Tchaikovsky competition, every other cellist was put into the shade by du Pré. Once again there was a close struggle between Soviet and American students – or more precisely, between students of Piatigorsky and those of Rostropovich. Karine Georgian proved to have all the qualities of a winner – temperament, artistry, and that complete concentration which allowed her to maintain an impeccable standard of playing throughout – and consequently she overshadowed Rostropovich's other students, Tamara Gabarashvili, Eleonora Testelets and Mariya Chaikovskaya. The Americans had a formidable team of Steven Kates, Laurence Lesser and Nathan Rosen, and the Finn, Arto Noras, a favourite ex-student of Tortelier, was seen as another possible candidate for first prize.

The preparations for the contest did not lack for tension and rivalry – nor were they without moments of drama, even of farce, as Eleonora Testelets recalls:

A month or so before the competition we were sent by the Ministry of Culture to stay at Serebryany Bor to give us the optimum conditions to prepare. We could practise to our hearts' content, and we were very well fed. 'Play, play, and play,' we were told. You could compare it to the hyped-up training for a sportive event. We were constantly reminded that Soviet candidates had to shine, and most particularly over the Americans. The shock of Van Cliburn's victory in the first Tchaikovsky piano competition was never to be repeated; the Ministry of Culture refused to countenance such errant loss of face! We lived in small cottages (or dachas), and I shared one with Tamara Gabarashvili. I had a separate entrance to my part on the left side, hers was on the right. Mstislav Leopoldovich had warned his three female students, 'On no account are you to receive husbands or lovers.' In fact I had recently got married, but my husband was in Riga, so I lived by the rules, and got on with my work. But young people have their passions, and the other two girls had recently fallen in love with their future husbands. One night around midnight Mstislav Leopoldovich and Aza Amintaeva paid us an unexpected 'inspection' visit. I was already in bed when they knocked, but put on a dressing gown and opened the door. 'Can we come in for a cup of tea?' Rostropovich asked. When he knocked at the other cottages, the situation was different. One of the young men managed to jump out of the window and hide, I believe, whereas Tamara's young man felt it beneath his dignity to move off the couch. Mstislav Leopoldovich was very angry with her. Aza was totally devoted to Rostropovich, worshipping the very ground he stood on. Coming from Dagestan with her eastern temperament, it was in her character to see everything in black and white, there were no gradations of colour, or of good and bad for her. She had always adored Tamara and would do anything for her, but from now on she was dead set against her.

But when it was my turn to get into trouble during the actual competition, Aza was very kind and took pity on me. We became very good friends. All competitors, both foreigners and Soviets, were housed in the Budapest Hotel. And there a flirtation I had started with an American candidate developed into a passionate romance. After I played the second round, this news had flown around Moscow and became known to the authorities. It was considered an absolute disgrace to have such a relationship with a foreigner (and worse still, an American). They wanted to punish me and throw me out of the competition. Poor Mstislav Leopoldovich had to come to the rescue and use all his powers of persuasion to ensure that I would be allowed to play in the finals with orchestra. He insisted that I leave the hotel, and asked Aza and Natasha Shakhovskaya to help. So I stayed in Aza's flat, sleeping on a camp bed. Aza cooked for me, Natasha ironed my clothes, and I started to recover my senses. I was touched by their support, and even managed to play quite well at the final round with orchestra. I remember that even Galina Pavlovna paid me a compliment. She rarely praised Mstislav Leopoldovich's students, but this time, she came up to me and said, 'Molodets, Ella, well done!' I was awarded third prize, and I was pleased to have done so well. In particular I was delighted when Wilkomirski said that of all Rostropovich's pupils, I was the one whose playing had the character and strength that reminded him most of our teacher.

Although the jury sessions were closed, information about any disagreements seemed to leak out quickly. In the voting after the second round, it appears that Piatigorsky felt that his students were being marked down. He reputedly stood up and said, 'I really don't know what I am doing here, I have such a lovely villa in Los Angeles overlooking the Pacific. I might as well go home.' A scandal was about to erupt, and silence descended, but Rostropovich was not lost for an answer: 'Grisha, you haven't seen my dacha outside Moscow yet. You don't know how beautiful it is out there!' Rostropovich succeeded in pacifying all parties so that the jury could proceed amicably with the voting. The gold medal was eventually won by Karine Georgian, with the silver shared between Arto Noras and Steven Kates. Eleonora Testelets and Ken Yasudo divided the third prize, and Laurence Lesser and Mariya Chaikovskaya the fourth. Somehow the right political compromise was found, with an overall Soviet first-prize winner, but more top prizes won by 'foreigners' so that the jury did not appear to be too biased.

The 1970 Tchaikovsky competition coincided with the centenary of Lenin's birth, which was celebrated with due ceremony throughout the Soviet Union. Before the competition, the chairmen of the various juries, Gilels, Oistrakh and Rostropovich, were summoned to the office of the Minister of Culture, Ekaterina Furtseva, and warned, 'You understand that this year, there can be no question but that OUR artists win; absolutely no foreigners for first prize.' Rostropovich, feigning innocence, asked, 'Is there any particular reason for this?' 'How could you forget, it's the hundredth anniversary of Ilyich's birth!' Without losing his aplomb for a moment, the cellist promptly replied, 'In that case why don't we postpone the Tchaikovsky for a year so that we can have a fair competition?' Furtseva glared at him, while Gilels and Oistrakh could hardly restrain their laughter. Once again it was the talk of Moscow that Rostropovich 'had ridden over the authorities with a tank!'

In the event, Furtseva's wish was fulfilled when, for the third time running, the Tchaikovsky competition was won outright by a Rostropovich student, David Geringas – with three of his other students, Victoria Yagling, David Grigorian and Vagram Saradzhan, also receiving top prizes. But by June 1974, when the next Tchaikovsky competition took place, the situation had changed drastically. Just a week or so earlier, Rostropovich had left the Soviet Union, having applied to Brezhnev for permission to live and work abroad for a two-year period after a series of humiliations and cancelled concert tours and recordings. It was perhaps predictable that under these circumstances, no Rostropovich student could hope to win the competition. As his former student and favoured candidate, Ivan Monighetti, was well aware, his chances of top prize were compromised. (Though Monighetti had recently enrolled as a postgraduate student of cello theory with Lev Ginsburg – not because he wished to disassociate himself from Rostropovich, as some speculated, but because there were not enough vacancies at the

Conservatoire for postgraduate cellists – Rostropovich continued to regard him as his own student.) The competition was ultimately won by the Leningrad cellist, Boris Pergamenshikov, who succeeded on his own merits – but many felt that Monighetti had played equally well, and could at least have shared the first prize had pressure not been exerted on the jury by the Ministry of Culture.

Over the last difficult years, the Moscow Conservatoire had always given its support to Rostropovich, and the director was willing to accept his application for a two-year sabbatical, keeping the position of head of faculty open for him to resume on his return.

Indeed, he was not technically dismissed as professor and head of faculty until March 1978 (as the last document in his Conservatoire file reveals), when Rostropovich and Vishnevskaya were deprived of their Soviet citizenship. The decision of the Conservatoire director to discharge Rostropovich from his duties was an inevitable consequence of that decree. Just as the great cellist was deprived of all his honours and medals by the Soviet government, so he was relegated to oblivion by the institution which had nurtured him and where he had spent the best years of his life, educating new generations of cellists over nearly thirty years. Natalya Shakhovskaya was appointed in his place as head of the cello faculty.

INTERLUDE 2

Aleksandr Knaifel

I first heard Rostropovich in a concert in Leningrad, when I was still very young. It was during the 'reign' of Shafran, and there was a definite sense that the newly emerging Rostropovich 'camp' was somehow in opposition to the well-established Shafran camp. Daniil Shafran, like his teacher Shtrimer, was a hypnotic artist, and the complete antithesis of what Rostropovich represented. He came from a tradition of performing that was much admired by the older generation of music-lovers, but it was a kind of music-making that didn't really appeal to me.

Slava deserves credit for bursting away from that tradition. Admittedly, by comparison with Shafran's, his playing wasn't quite as refined or polished, not quite so 'intellectual', not so mysterious – but it had some deeper quality which sought out an inner musical truth.

Throughout my schooldays and my student years at the Conservatoire I did not understand what I was doing in my surroundings. The world around me seemed foreign and hostile, and I sat in class as if I was in a cage, frightened of everything, thinking: 'What have I done, what am I guilty of, to deserve this?' That feeling of terror when a teacher looks at you, and you acknowledge that you know nothing and can never know anything. It felt as though this kind of knowledge was superfluous to what I believed was important in life.

I arrived at Rostropovich through Shostakovich, and my serious study of the cello began with the first cello concerto: I was probably the first person after Slava to perform it. I learnt the whole cello part by writing it down from an illegal radio broadcast made in late 1960 or early 1961, without ever seeing the music. Then the orchestral score was published and I got hold of one, and asked the composer Gennadi (Genna) Banshchikov to play it with me. It was quite something! Genna, a contemporary of mine at school, was a brilliant sight-reader at the piano. We played it for Slava when he came up to Leningrad and he was quite amazed.

Genna Banshchikov and I decided we would both take the auditions for the Moscow Conservatoire. We made a pact that if we got in he would write a cello concerto and I would play it. This is exactly what happened. When we played at our auditions we both passed as top of our respective lists, making the Muscovites tremble. Then I had an incredible experience at the exam. The composer, Edison Denisov, was one of my examiners, even though he himself was still only a postgraduate student. He had heard of my Shostakovich exploit and decided to give me a hard time. He asked a thousand questions, probing what I knew, and he discovered that I really did know everything written by Shostakovich – all his chamber music and symphonies. He gasped and said, 'I don't know what you are doing here!' We soon became the greatest of friends.

I found my initial contact with the Rostropovich phenomenon to be quite strange and unsettling. To begin with, I experienced the high level of energetic tension that he carries within him as something very perplexing and frightening, almost unbearably so. But at the same time I was drawn to it, and understood that it was not something aggressive and alien, as was everything else that I had met in my years of education. The phenomenon of Rostropovich was in itself instructive, in some way. I started to understand myself better, and to be able to define my aspirations.

I sensed that when Rostropovich worked in class, he wished to awaken a genuine sense of music within me. I started to perceive music according to the laws responsible for its conception and birth, and to understand the purpose for which it is created. I became interested in the textures and material in Bach and Beethoven. Inevitably, at the beginning all this carried the character of imitation – an imitation that came from vigilant attention to Rostropovich's work in class. However, imitation – in its best sense, and correctly understood – can be life-enhancing and instructive, since it provides a key to one's approach to culture and tradition. It's like being in a congregation in a church: you only enter into the spirit of the matter after beginning with imitation.

Initially, I thought I wouldn't be able to cope with the pace and intensity of the work in Rostropovich's class, but then I began to open out and find my wings, thanks to the very fact of his existence. When you were studying with him, it was a matter of survival, keeping your head above water. He was here one minute, then the next he would disappear on his travels. When he reappeared on our horizons, zooming in from the great velocity of his orbit, everything would change for the better: it seemed that one's perception was enhanced, one's life speeded up and one's feelings intensified. Everybody virtually stopped sleeping when Slava was around – his type of music-making, his whole attitude to life had that effect on people.

Gennadi Banshchikov wrote me the cello concerto as we had agreed: it was an amazingly good piece, especially if you consider it was the work of a first-year student! I played it for Slava, and he liked it so much that he asked Banshchikov to write another concerto for him. Then I performed the concerto with orchestra at the Grand Hall of the Moscow Conservatoire. Banshchikov went on to write four cello concertos, including the one dedicated to Rostropovich – these were heady times for us all.

In many ways I came down to Moscow against my better judgement – I disliked the city, I felt it as alien and hostile, and the whole atmosphere of the Conservatoire was completely foreign to my nature, with its emphasis on competitions and prizewinning. I knew with certainty that this was not my world, and I could not become part of it. So although entering Rostropovich's class was an opportunity for me, at the same time I thought, 'Well, that's it.' And in a sense it was the end of me. But with his sensitive antennae, Mstislav Leopoldovich detected that I was leading some kind of double life, and all the time he would ask me, 'Well, old man, what are you up to?' Later he admitted that 'I always felt that you erected a screen in front of you, and I wanted to peep behind it, but you never let me in!'

During my two years with Rostropovich I studied a lot of standard classical repertoire – and moreover, influenced by Rostropovich's excellent pianism, I went through a phase of being greatly attracted to the piano. In particular, I loved the great romantic virtuoso repertoire with its technical challenges, octaves and passagework. One day I came to the class before anybody else and sat down at the piano and started playing Rachmaninov's Humoresque. *I was playing and playing, and all of a sudden I felt that something strange was going* on. I became aware that Rostropovich was standing by the door, listening to me; in fact, quite a crowd of people had by now gathered around him, their curiosity awakened by seeing Slava outside the class. He had no doubt been about to enter, but on recognising me he was intrigued – 'What on earth is Shurik up to?' He must have stood there quietly for over ten minutes.

This was an example of the kind of unspoken understanding that hung between us: Slava probably realised that although I had no real secret, I was involved in some other world. It was like having a stranger among friends, and a friend among strangers, as the saying goes. Rostropovich knew that I could be captured only with the net of my musicianship.

Although I was not studying composition at the time, I did go and have some lessons at the Conservatoire with Balasanyan, who was a wonderfully sensitive composer, while also being outgoing and responsive. In fact, I composed quite a bit while I was in Moscow, including several early pieces for piano. I then decided to present my works for the entrance exams for the composition faculty of the Moscow Conservatoire. What happened next was unprecedented. The examiners told me, 'You know all kinds of music exist – good music, bad music and indeed, very bad music. But what you have shown us doesn't even qualify as music!' My friends, Sofia Gubaidulina in particular, were terribly upset by this: 'What's this, how can they do this to you?' But I answered, 'Don't be upset – on the contrary I'm happy since it's given me the right to go back home.'

I decided to switch to studying composition: I took the entrance exam for the Leningrad Conservatoire entrance exam and was immediately accepted onto the third-year composition course. My 'swan song' in Class 19 at Moscow was the Dvořák concerto, which Slava had asked me to learn very quickly, between one class and the next. I sat down, practised like mad and learnt it from memory in three days: I was able to meet the musical challenge, but the physical strain was a disaster for my arms. I played it all the way through to him in the class with Aza accompanying me. Then somebody important came into the class and he asked me to play the whole concerto again. God knows why he did this to me, it was the finishing touch. By the end my arm was completely numb: I had no feeling in it at all and it hung by my side, limp, like a dead weight. I was diagnosed with inflammation of the nerve and told to rest completely; I couldn't use my arm at all, let alone play the cello. It took at least a couple of months before it recovered, after various treatments, including acupuncture.

Later I realised that the injury was sent by God, because giving up the cello allowed me to realise myself as a composer and not a performer. I was able to leave Moscow, which I had never come to like, and return to Leningrad, where I enrolled in Boris Arapov's class. As for my cello, I sold it later with no qualms, and bought a grand piano on the proceeds.

Despite this outcome, my period of just under two years with Rostropovich was of inestimable importance and provided me with lifelong inspiration. I never had the feeling that this was just a relationship between teacher and student: it was a bond that had a lasting effect on me, through the years, for ever. It's like when you meet a woman and immediately recognise that it's going to affect you for all your life, as in Aleksandr Blok's Neznakomka (The Unknown Lady) – a chance meeting, but it changes what you are for good. So it was for me with Mstislav Leopoldovich: he became part of me – and as life has shown, our fates were indeed intertwined.

There are performances of his that I can remember to this day. For instance the Brahms F major sonata with Aleksandr Dedyukhin – I remember how they both walked out on stage carrying the mood of the music, conveying a huge sense of decision and direction. Dedyukhin reached the piano while Slava was still walking, and started playing while in the act of sitting down at the piano. Slava literally had to fall into his chair to answer the challenge of the piano's tremolo. This was no circus act, but a genuine outburst of artistic energy. Only Richter could do something similar, as when he played the Shostakovich D flat major fugue: the repeated dominant and tonic chords at the end had such momentum that his gestures continued after the music had stopped – he bounced in his chair and 'played' the chords in the air or on the wood of the piano. That was born of the impetus and abandon of his energy – such moments are unforgettable.

No less wonderful were Rostropovich's concerts with Vishnevskaya, where they wove spells on their listeners with their rendering of romances by Glinka and Tchaikovsky, recreating an intimate and delicate world lost to us in the mists of nostalgia. Some of their recordings I have played so often, yet they still seem fresh and bring tears to the eyes.

All of Slava's music-making is filtered through his understanding of the world: you can play music this way or that, in one style or another, but it is the perception behind what you do that counts. This is how he gets his wonderful abstracted slow tempi, as in his unforgettable conducting of the overture to Evgeny Onegin at the Bolshoi, where he conjured up the sound as if from another world, cutting through years of stagnant tradition.

But Rostropovich's music-making was built on the foundation of everyday experience. I mean this in the way that Metropolitan Anthony Surozhsky, the great Christian writer, talks about Christianity representing materialism in its fullest sense. Slava's playing is materialistic in this way, and you can feel that it stems from firmly planted roots. When a person is full of his own individual message, then for better or for worse he puts himself at the forefront. For me this imposition of 'I' – the self – is not of interest, and can only be of interest if your 'I' and my 'I' happen to coincide and carry the same meaning. For Rostropovich, however, perception of 'self' is immersed in the action of transmitting the text, of carrying the material in its primal state, almost emphasising its fundamentally unchanged character. That is why he likes slow tempi, so that not one note escapes his understanding, and so that he captures the subtext in the deeper sense of the musical material that is implied between the notes. His music-making is shimmering and alive, and this comes from an inborn feeling of submission towards the text and its message. It is a quality that cannot be invented or developed. You have to be born with it.

One sees this even in the way Rostropovich greets somebody, throwing himself towards him to embrace him. In that moment of time that person means everything to him and gives sense to his very existence. I believe that this is right. It is wonderfully put again, by Surozhsky, one of my religious teachers in life: 'When you see somebody approaching, prepare yourself and say – a meeting is taking place.' A person must be prepared with the maximum of attention.

Of course you can interpret this in a different way, like a rather bad joke – his wife has been known to say, 'Slava throws himself on a person like a long-lost friend and then comes up to me and says, "Galya, tell me who was that?"' Of course you can look at his behaviour as an amusing anecdote or simply as a matter of habit, but that would be wrong, since his action stems from a genuine feeling of joy. And if he did not throw himself to embrace the person, if he *did not feel the absoluteness of that particular meeting, it would be lost in the stream of everyday routine. But for him it is something to treasure, and his joy is not calculated or premeditated. It is the same when he looks at you with a penetrating look that cuts through everything – that signifies an inexplicable quality of attention, equal to an expression of love, at that particular moment.*

I was always struck by this amazing combination of strength and energy, on the one hand, with a kind of nervous animation, a palpitating attention. His strength acts through his tenderness, a tenderness that is rooted in the ground, in everyday life. This is Slava's absolute element, when you can be softer than the softest, tenderer than the most tender; you can hear this in his fabulous pianissimi *and in the yearning tenderness of his sound, as he pours out his soul on the cello, as if singing with a human voice.*

10

The early 1960s

The 1960s saw Rostropovich at the height of his powers and international fame as a cellist. He was popular wherever he played, but outside his own country, he found his warmest and most appreciative audiences in Great Britain. Pivotal to the 'love-affair' between the Russian cellist and his British public was the creative relationship that Rostropovich and Vishnevskaya developed at this time with Benjamin Britten.

In 1960, Rostropovich paid his first visit to the Edinburgh Festival, where he played a recital with Dedyukhin on 7 September. The following day he gave the UK premiere of Shostakovich's cello concerto with the Leningrad Philharmonic orchestra under Gennadi Rozhdestvensky, and on 21 September the same combination repeated the performance at London's Royal Festival Hall. Some BBC television footage survives of the rehearsal in the hall, at which Shostakovich was present. In the fragment of the final movement that was recorded, one sees the dynamic energy exuding from Rostropovich as he seems to attack his instrument, curling around it like a tiger. Here is a musician of commanding authority, master not only of his instrument but of the whole performance, constantly urging the orchestra on with a glance here, a body gesture there, while maintaining disciplined contact – and a certain air of complicity – with the conductor.

Shostakovich accompanied the Leningrad Philharmonic orchestra throughout this tour, during which Mravinsky also conducted performances of the eighth symphony. At the evening concert where Rostropovich performed, the composer found himself sitting in a box next to Benjamin Britten, and afterwards they went backstage to greet the artists. This was how Rostropovich first met the English composer who was to become so important to him, a tale he has often recounted:

Shostakovich came up to me and said, 'Slava, I want to introduce Benjamin Britten.' I was rather startled, for the only piece of Britten's that I knew was the *Young Person's Guide to the Orchestra* [which incidentally opened that evening's programme] and I associated his name with that of Purcell. I said to Shostakovich – in Russian of course, but in front of Britten – 'But I thought Britten had died ages ago.' 'No,' Dmitri Dmitriyevich replied, 'this is him before your eyes.'

Later that evening Shostakovich complained to his younger friend, 'Slava, do you know I am aching from so many bruises along my side.' 'What happened, Dmitri Dmitriyevich, did you fall down?' 'No, but at the concert tonight, every time Britten admired something in your playing, he would poke me in the ribs, and say, "Isn't that simply marvellous!" As he liked so many things throughout the concerto, I am now suffering!'

Rostropovich there and then asked Britten if he would consider writing for cello. Britten's reply was encouraging: the matter needed serious discussion. They agreed to meet the next day at the Prince of Wales Hotel, the rather modest hotel in Kensington where all Soviet artists lodged when visiting London. Rostropovich asked Gennadi Rozhdestvensky to help out as interpreter.

Britten had indeed been overwhelmed by Rostropovich's mastery, and declared that he had never before heard such cello-playing. Britten assured Rostropovich that he was not interested in any form of commission as such, but if he were to write the sonata, he would impose one condition – that Slava came to the Aldeburgh Festival to give the first performance, and he would partner him at the piano. The warm friendship that sprang up spontaneously between the two men was based not only on mutual admiration, but on great human empathy. Rostropovich felt much freer with Britten than he did with Shostakovich, for he could express his emotions to him fully on the one hand, and at the same time indulge in gentle teasing and jokes. As Galina Vishnevskaya put it, 'From the beginning I felt at ease with [Ben]; I am sure that everybody who had the luck to know this charming man must have felt the same sense of simplicity and natural-ness in his company.'*

* G. Vishnevshaya, *Galina: A Russian Story*, p. 304.

Britten started composing the cello sonata early in the autumn while on holiday in Greece. He was intrigued by Rostropovich's innovative approach to the instrument and also appreciated his deep musicianship. The five-movement sonata explores various aspects of virtuoso technique to great effect. As a viola-player himself, Britten had a deep understanding of string instruments, and despite its complexities, the sonata lies comfortably under the fingers. The witty second movement, 'Scherzo-Pizzicato', is a study of plucking techniques, with guitar-like chords and fast repeated notes using the right hand, as with a mandolin. The finale, meanwhile, is a highly effective *moto perpetuo* based on *saltando* bowing, in which the 6/8 rhythm is constantly subdivided into more complex patterns of five and seven.

Rostropovich received the score of the new sonata in Moscow early in February, and immediately rushed to his music room to 'study its beauties'. He was thrilled by the new piece, and without delay sent a telegram to Britten expressing his delight. Anxious to play it through with the composer at the earliest opportunity, he arranged to stop over in London on the way to Mexico. Given that Soviet artists could travel abroad only to authorised destinations on concert tours, this was easier said than done, but somehow he succeeded in arranging to change flights at Heathrow, where he landed on the afternoon of 5 March.

Rostropovich headed straight off to the flat in St John's Wood where Britten was staying. Once installed in the small music room, the two men were overcome with nerves, and both seemed too shy and reticent to sit down and start playing. Slava recalls that Britten solved the dilemma by proposing a drink, and with one glass of whisky (or more) inside them, their inhibitions dissolved, and they were able to sit down at their instruments and play through the sonata, not just once but several times. Britten's ability as a pianist was legendary, and the sound he produced from the instrument seemed to transcend all notions of instrumental technique and go straight to the heart of the music. Rostropovich often said that 'Ben plays the piano just like he composes' – by this he meant that Britten not only created music, but involved himself in the same manner in the 're-creative' act, allowing a fragile link to be forged between sound in its metaphysical, 'abstracted' state and its embodiment in the real physical world.

As an accompanist, Britten showed astonishing sensitivity to his partners as well as to the smallest details of the score: sometimes, however, he risked inadvertently stealing the show, for his compelling rendering of a simple accompaniment figure could hypnotise listeners and almost distract them from the principal line. As Imogen Holst observed, 'He used to accompany Schubert songs with such intimate concern that the music sounded as if it were his own'* – the same could have been said in relation to any of the music he chose to perform. Galina Vishnevskaya recalls being so entranced by Britten's beautiful rendering of the introduction to Tchaikovsky's duet from *Romeo and Juliet* (which she was performing with Peter Pears at the Aldeburgh Festival) that she felt unable to open her mouth and come in. She turned round and looked at Ben, her eyes conveying an apology and the request to 'play it again!' Rostropovich told a similar story about recording Schubert's 'Arpeggione' sonata with Britten in the studio. After Ben had played the piano introduction, he felt paralysed and unable to put bow to string: 'Excuse me, Ben, but if I am to come in, could you please play that again . . . a little bit less beautifully! Otherwise I simply can't play!'

From the start, composer and cellist immediately felt the closest creative rapport. They played the new sonata through several times, until Britten suggested dining at a nearby restaurant. They ate in concentrated silence, but as Slava noticed, Ben kept humming the first movement's enigmatic second-subject tune, which in the composer's words 'rises towards and falls away from a pianissimo harmonic'. The harmonic is arrived at by way of a questioning upward glissando, which is answered in the second half of the phrase. Rostropovich inferred that the humming had a purpose:

I realised that Ben was tactfully teaching me how to play this phrase, to make it a little freer in rubato, and he showed just how to gauge the small crescendo and diminuendo and exactly where to start the glissando. I captured the spirit of this theme by imitating the way he had hummed it. Ben would never give explicit instructions, and in fact we never talked about how his music should be performed. Everything sorted itself out in the process of playing. But I had to learn to grasp at hints like this.

The lack of a common language could have been an obstacle to communication, but Rostropovich and Britten soon established a private lingo in the form of a garbled German which was soon dubbed 'Aldeburgh Deutsch'. No doubt this description covered a multitude

* Humphrey Carpenter, *Benjamin Britten: A Biography*, p. 402.

of linguistic sins, as my father discovered once in the late 1960s when he had the temerity to intervene in a conversation between the two men. On overhearing Rostropovich make an arrangement to meet Britten on Thursday afternoon, he suggested, 'Ben, surely Slava means *Donnerstag*, not *Dienstag*.' But Ben quickly retorted, 'Don't you know that in Aldeburgh Deutsch *Dienstag* IS Thursday!' Rostropovich could be just as linguistically resourceful: Peter Pears recalls that he once described a nuclear physicist (his dacha neighbour, Sakharov) as one 'mit kochende wasser zu tun.'*

At their first working meeting in London, the two men decided on their recital programme for the festival: Schubert's 'Arpeggione' sonata (which Rostropovich had to learn for the first time), Debussy's sonata, an unaccompanied Bach suite, and finally the premiere of Britten's new sonata. In addition to the duo recital, Rostropovich would perform the Schumann concerto with the London Symphony Orchestra under Britten's direction.

Shortly after this meeting, Britten wrote to Vishnevskaya to invite her too to participate in the festival, for he had recently heard her recordings and was enormously impressed.

Rostropovich's first appearance in partnership with Britten at the piano took place on 4 July at the Jubilee Hall, Aldeburgh – their interpretations were widely regarded as revelatory and the recital was a triumphant success. Britten's cello sonata, with its five contrasted movements, had an immediate appeal for audiences. From the outset, many musicians perceived it as a musical portrait of the mercurial Rostropovich, reflecting the characteristics described by the *Times* critic, William Mann: 'Gay, charming, an astonishingly brilliant executant, but behind these qualities a searching musician with the mind of a philosopher.'

Soon, however, it was the turn of Galina Vishnevskaya to take Aldeburgh audiences by storm. Her UK recital debut at the Jubilee Hall, accompanied as ever by Rostropovich, was a programme of extraordinary length and variety. It included opera arias, romances and lieder, capped by Mussorgsky's cycle, *Songs and Dances of Death* – proof of the singer's artistry, versatility and remarkable stamina. For the surprise encore, Rostropovich switched from piano to cello while Britten went to the keyboard, and together they performed

---

* Peter Pears, *Travel Diaries*, p. 148.

an arrangement of the Aria from Villa-Lobos's *Bachianas Brasileiras* no. 5. Vishnevskaya was hailed in the press as 'the Russian Callas' and 'the female Chaliapin' – she and her husband had irrevocably won the hearts of the Aldeburgh festival audiences. From now on, 'Slava and Galya', as they were affectionately known, were welcomed back to the festival almost annually.

After the Aldeburgh festival was over, Britten and Rostropovich recorded the new cello sonata for Decca at London's Kingsway Hall on 19 and 20 July. Schumann's *Fünf Stucke im Volkston* and Debussy's sonata were included on the same LP. In the same period, Vishnevskaya and Rostropovich made their first recordings of Russian romances for EMI – in his days as a Soviet artist, and indeed after he left Russia, Rostropovich had no exclusive recording contract.

Once Britten had heard Vishnevskaya perform in person, he immediately identified her voice as what he wanted for his *War Requiem*, the work he was currently writing. He was delighted when she agreed to take part, and in March 1962 he sent the completed score to the couple in Moscow. Rostropovich lost no time in perusing it, despite being laid low with flu: from his sickbed, he wrote to Britten that 'It is a profound and highly powerful work. It is majestic!' In the same letter he complained of his ill health, telling Ben that only one doctor could cure him: one who lived at The Red House, Aldeburgh – 'Only he can bring me back to life by composing a brilliant cello concerto!' Peter Pears had a point when he jokingly complained that Rostropovich was something of a bully, who wanted Ben to write exclusively for him.

In his keenness for Vishnevskaya to sing in the *War Requiem*, Britten had not reckoned with the Soviet authorities: to Galina's chagrin and fury, permission was not granted for her to sing at the premiere in Coventry Cathedral on 30 May 1962. The *War Requiem* was considered politically provocative, as was the plan to place a Soviet artist on stage next to a German soloist, the baritone Dietrich Fischer-Dieskau. For Britten there was a poignant symbolism in the idea that Galina, a survivor of the Leningrad blockade, should sing alongside Fischer-Dieskau, who had served as a soldier in the war and started his singing career in a prisoner-of-war camp. The third soloist, Peter Pears, had declared himself a pacifist, like Britten, and spent the first years of the war in the USA. The soloists' different biographies were, for Britten, part of the statement he wished to make about peace. However, the Soviet authorities refused to regard Britten's masterpiece as a condemnation of war and a call for reconciliation: they believed that they had the monopoly on '*Mir i druzhba*' (peace and friendship) – a hackneyed phrase that was transliterated by a wit at the British Embassy as 'beer and rhubarb'.

Despite this setback, Britten did not ignore Rostropovich's touching request for a 'therapeutic' work, and by November 1962 he had produced the first movement of a substantial concerto 'very much shaped like a symphony'. It was originally planned to hold the first performance in Moscow in March 1963, when Britten was due to visit Russia under the auspices of the British Council for a festival of British music. In the event, he only finished the work in May, and the rescheduled premiere at the Aldeburgh Festival was cancelled because of Rostropovich's illness. The premiere of the *Symphony for Cello and Orchestra* thus did not take place until March 1964, when Britten fulfilled his promise to return to Moscow to conduct the premiere. Rostropovich had had to content himself in the mean time with cadenzas that Britten wrote at his request for the first and second movements of the newly rediscovered Haydn C major concerto (Hob VIIb I).

Rostropovich had given the first Russian performance of Britten's cello sonata with Sviatoslav Richter on 26 December 1961 at the Small Hall of the Moscow Conservatoire, in a programme also including the Chopin and Debussy sonatas. Richter had been introduced to Britten by Rostropovich a few months previously, but he didn't play at the Aldeburgh festival until 1964, after which he returned almost annually until 1970. Britten and Richter struck up a friendship that was underpinned by their extraordinary four-hand duo partnership, which arose as the result of a spontaneous impulse during Richter's first visit to Aldeburgh.

Rostropovich was delighted to be able to return to Aldeburgh for the 1962 festival, where his performances included the Shostakovich cello sonata (with Britten), and Beethoven's clarinet trio (with Britten and Gervase de Peyer). As he recalls, Britten had not reckoned with the pianistic difficulties of Shostakovich's finale, and was quite cross about having to practise so much. Ben got extremely nervous before the concert, but he brilliantly overcame all the technical complexities, taking an unimaginably fast tempo in the finale's semiquaver scale passages without dropping a note.

Alongside Rostropovich and Vishnevskaya's warm relationship with Britten and Pears, they also formed a friendship with Lord Harewood (then director of the Edinburgh Festival) and his first wife Marion (later to become Mrs Jeremy Thorpe), and established an important connection with the London impresarios, Victor and Lilian Hochhauser. These relationships helped to make Great Britain a favourite place for the couple to visit, and recognition came from the Royal Academy of Music in London when it awarded Rostropovich its gold medal in March 1962.

Visits to the Aldeburgh festival left a particularly profound impression on Rostropovich, who adored its informal spirit and the domestic intimacy of music-making between a group of friends whose level of performance was always superlative. He also admired the festival's unique approach to programming, which reflected Britten's erudition and wide-ranging taste. Aldeburgh audiences, then as now, comprised not only visiting music lovers but also local inhabitants, many of whom were actively involved in aspects of the organisation. When not performing himself, Rostropovich enjoyed attending other performances, and was always in the audience whenever Britten's music was played. *The Turn of the Screw* made a profound impression on him, and likewise on Shostakovich when he heard it shortly afterwards in Moscow. Rostropovich enjoyed the ambience of the Suffolk town, and going down to the shingle beach to watch the fishermen bring in their catch. All the images he soaked up in that first visit helped him identify more closely with Britten's work, and to visualise the setting of so many of his operas – first and foremost *Peter Grimes*, from which Rostropovich would play extracts for his students back home. At the time Russians were still largely ignorant of Britten's music, although the advocacy of Rostropovich and other Russian champions of Britten gradually changed this.

Rostropovich's experience of Aldeburgh also fuelled his determination to create his own festival in Russia. Hard as it is to believe today, there were no music festivals at all in the Soviet Union at that time. In January 1962, in a short article written for *Sovetskaya Kultura* and entitled 'What will music be in the future?', Rostropovich proposed the creation of 'temples of art' throughout the Soviet Union, where new music would be lovingly nurtured. The rhetorical question – would music be tonal or atonal? – is brushed aside with the comment that 'If it is atonal, at least things will be easier for students: they won't have to trouble themselves studying scales.' Rostropovich continued his article with an optimistic vision of the future:

A performer, like yours truly, travels around the country giving concerts. In some far-flung city, he is met by the town administrator, a passionate music lover, who implores him not to play 'The Hillocks of Manchuria' or some such trite song, but to perform instead an unaccompanied Bach suite or a sonata by Kara Karayev (for surely by then this composer will have written a cello sonata!). The administrator then shows the artist a marvellous hall with a wonderful concert grand piano . . . In rural areas, imagine some village hall, where after a hard day's work bringing in the harvest, the local workers' music club will show films of operas by Prokofiev and Shostakovich, which by this time will have become immensely popular.Ï

The article concluded on a wistful note: 'What a wonderful thing it is to dream!'

A month later, *Sovetskaya Muzyka* published a longer and more serious article entitled 'Love for Art, Love for the People', in which Rostropovich begins by acknowledging the positive achievements of Soviet music: a network of first-rate concerts exists throughout the country, the teaching system is excellent, and state subsidy of composers is generous – particularly compared with their Western colleagues, most of whom find it difficult to survive financially by composition alone. Rostropovich goes on to pose the question, 'How can we artists improve our services to the people?' His answer begins by deploring the lack of any organised festivals of new music in the Soviet Union, and cites Aldeburgh as a prime example of a festival in a small town which aims to involve – and educate – the local populace. Its resident composer leaves a particular personal imprint on the programming, which could be described as 'music through the eyes of Benjamin Britten'. There is much work to be done if Soviet musical life is to provide opportunities on a par with the new music festivals existing in the West. At home, Rostropovich somewhat acidly complains, any events connected with new music occur haphazardly and suffer from mediocre presentation.

Once again Rostropovich sets out a utopian vision for his readers, this time of a contemporary music festival in some distant town, Yakutsk, Murmansk or Nalchik. This was the fourth such festival, presided over by Shostakovich, and featured the best Soviet performers playing Soviet music from Prokofiev to Ustvolskaya. Successive festivals would tackle different themes: for instance, music from other Eastern bloc countries. As Rostropovich points out, since the Soviet Union spends more on the arts than any capitalist state, it should therefore have superior means at its disposal for creating cultural events. What distinguished Soviet composer or performer would refuse the chance, if offered, to set up a festival? In conclusion Rostropovich defended the maxim that love of music goes hand-in-hand with love of the people for whom it is played and created. Nonetheless, he advised, Soviet artists should give more thought to the ethical role of music in society.

Rostropovich's vision of 'a musical education of the masses' was certainly in line with the ideological guidelines of the State, something that would be taken into account when he was a candidate for the coveted Lenin prize. He had already earned credit with the authorities by dedicating a series of concerts (described in Chapter 8) to new Soviet works, and now composers and Conservatoire colleagues published articles in support of his candidature. It came as a surprise to all when he was not chosen as a prizewinner in 1962. However, he was nominated again in 1964 and this time was successful. The prestigious Lenin prize brought money and privilege to its holders. Rostropovich would jokingly call the red wallet-sized prizewinners' card 'Slavik's card': brandishing it in front of officials or shopkeepers was like waving a magic wand, allowing the holder to receive otherwise unobtainable consumer goods, or to buy first-class train tickets without a prior reservation.

Despite recognising his outstanding qualities, Rostropovich's musician friends were highly sceptical when it came to realising his dream of creating a festival of contemporary music. On 13 January he found himself in the town of Gorky, playing Prokofiev's concertino and the Saint-Saëns concerto under the direction of his friend Israel Guzman. During his trip, Rostropovich held a conversation with Guzman and the orchestra's director, Nikitin:

'You know I'm thinking of setting up a contemporary music festival,' he informed them. They replied, 'Thinking's not much good, a bit of action is what's needed.' So I said, 'Fine, let's take action. Let's have the festival here in Gorky.' 'All words, and no action,' was their reply, and I fell for the bait: we laid bets as to whether it would happen, and effectively agreed to organise the festival together. When it opened, and I was driving through the main street of Gorky, which was bedecked with banners and flags, I remember thinking to myself, 'I'll probably end up in jail for setting it up. They'll say, "Just think, for some piece of nonsense we went and decorated the town with flags."'*

* Elizabeth Wilson, *Shostakovich: A Life Remembered*, pp. 377–78.

The festival took place in June 1962 and consisted of five events. Rostropovich performed in three of them – the first a mixed chamber recital on 11 June, where he played Kabalevsky's cello sonata with the composer and accompanied Vishnevskaya in Prokofiev's Akhmatova songs and Shostakovich's *Satires*. The concert also involved two recent Tchaikovsky prizewinners, the violinist Boris Gutnikov, and the cellist Natalya Shakhovskaya; the latter led a group of local cellists under Rostropovich's direction in the Aria from Villa-Lobos's *Bachianas Brasileiras* no. 5, with Vishnevskaya as soloist.

On the following two evenings, Rostropovich performed, under Guzman's direction, Shostakovich's concerto and Prokofiev's *Sinfonia Concertante*. The programmes also presented orchestral works that were new to local audiences such as Bartók's *Concerto for Orchestra*, Britten's 'Sea Interludes' from *Peter Grimes*, and Hindemith's *Metamorphosen*.

The orchestra and town of Gorky now occupied a special place in Rostropovich's affections, and he felt it would be the ideal place to schedule a special concert dedicated to Shostakovich, in which both he and the composer could test out their conducting skills. Shostakovich agreed to conduct the first part of the concert, consisting of the *Festive Overture* and the first cello concerto with Rostropovich as soloist. The cellist would then exchange bow for baton, after the interval directing the four entractes from *Lady Macbeth of Mtsensk* and finishing with a new orchestration of Mussorgsky's *Songs and Dances of Death*, with Vishnevskaya as soloist – Shostakovich had completed this in August 1962 while on honeymoon with his new wife, Irina Supinskaya. Rostropovich's motives in scheduling the concert were typically altruistic: he knew that Shostakovich was experiencing difficulty playing the piano, due to a debilitating illness affecting his hand and legs, and was anxious to create an opportunity for him to perform. Although Shostakovich conducted the programme excellently, despite considerable nervousness, he did not pursue the idea of conducting his own works. Rostropovich, on the other hand, was increasingly attracted to a métier which opened up new musical horizons to him.

The Gorky concert took place at a time when Shostakovich's star was in the ascendant, as Aleksandr Knaifel, well known for his feat of learning the first cello concerto from a radio transmission, recalls:

I was completely under the spell of Shostakovich. In the year and a half I spent in Moscow there were three events of fundamental importance for me. Firstly, the production of *Lady Macbeth of Mtsensk* in the new version (*Katerina Izmailova*) at the Nemirovich-Danchenko Theatre. I attended every rehearsal, all forty of them, and every performance. Similarly I attended all of Kondrashin's preparatory rehearsals of the fourth and thirteenth symphonies, as well as the concert performances. Then there was also Stravinsky's return to Russia in 1962. These were occasions of unique significance.

The events Knaifel refers to did indeed have an enormous impact on Moscow musical life. Although Shostakovich composed his fourth symphony in 1936, he had effectively been forced to withdraw it, and had waited for twenty-five years for a first performance. When they finally heard it, audiences were overwhelmed by the force and originality of its ideas and its grandiose, Mahlerian framework. Meanwhile, the recent thirteenth symphony, a setting of five poems by Yevtushenko, was controversial because of its texts – particularly that of the first poem, *Babi Yar*, which was an outright condemnation of anti-semitism. Rostropovich and Vishnevskaya had heard the composer play it through shortly after it was written, and Galina had suggested a bass soloist who would be suitable for the large solo part. (Her first choice refused on seeing the explicit nature of the texts.) When Evgeny Mravinsky withdrew from conducting the first performance, Rostropovich was indignant at what he perceived as a betrayal of Shostakovich. From now on his relations with the conductor cooled considerably, and were severed completely in 1966, when Mravinsky 'postponed' the premiere of Shostakovich's second cello concerto without consulting either Rostropovich or the composer.

From the early 1960s onwards, Rostropovich sought to be involved in performances of Shostakovich's music whenever it was possible. Thus he decided to join the orchestra as leader of the cello section at the premiere of the new production of *Katerina Izmailova* given in January 1962 at the Nemirovich-Danchenko Theatre. As he recalls, the conductor was so overcome by his presence in the orchestra that he always tactfully looked in the other direction, rather than having the temerity to indicate an entry to such a famous artist. However, even the supremely confident Rostropovich was slightly intimidated by the situation: 'I was all the more nervous, since I knew that if I were to make a mistake or play badly, Shostakovich would nevertheless come back stage and say in a distinctly sardonic tone of voice,

"Thank you for helping out!"' This, incidentally, was the first and last occasion on which Rostropovich played in an orchestra.

Katerina Izmailova was a work with a deeply personal significance for Shostakovich, as is evident from his self-quotation in the eighth string quartet. This quartet, too, had overwhelmed Rostropovich when the composer first played it through to him on the piano in summer 1960, shortly after completing it. The cellist recalls that Shostakovich turned to him at the end and said, with tears in his eyes, 'Now there's a piece which can be played at my funeral.' Some time later, after the premiere of the eighth quartet by the Beethoven Quartet (shortly followed by the Borodin Quartet's superlative interpretation), Rostropovich gathered together his Leningrad friends, Mikhail Vaiman, Boris Gutnikov and Yuri Kramarov to learn the quartet with him. They first performed it in a concert of Shostakovich's works at the Small Hall of the Leningrad Philharmonic on 11 March 1962. At the rehearsal, as Rostropovich recalls with pride, the composer started weeping silently on hearing the *pianissimo* cello solo at the end of the fourth movement. The melody is a quotation of '*Seryozha, khoroshiy moy*' (Seryozha, my handsome one), the aria that Katerina sings when she approaches her lover in the transit prison in Siberia in which they are both incarcerated: she pours out her love for him, not realising that he has already betrayed her.

From now on, the many strands of Rostropovich's musical activity were increasingly interwoven. In Moscow he tended to organise his concerts into series or cycles, under a specific banner or overarching programming concept. Similarly class evenings, both in Moscow and Leningrad, were usually programmed according to a particular theme, and both classes continued to be at the heart of his activities with the cello ensemble, and later the cello clubs.

With projects multiplying in number and complexity, Rostropovich showed a rigorous discipline and amazing capacity for work: it sometimes seemed as though he must lead an enchanted existence, with forty-eight hours at his disposal every day. His incredible stamina seemed proof of a very strong constitution, but even so, his schedule sometimes took its toll on his health: in the early 1960s he would often complain of an irregular heartbeat, pains and mental fatigue, compounded by insomnia. Fortunately the right medication was found for this minor heart complaint, which had been blown up in the

West into stories of heart attacks. Rostropovich's 'Napoleonic' quality of being able to survive on very little sleep (he claimed only to need three hours in every twenty-four) worked in conjunction with an ability to feed off work and his contact with people to produce a capacity for continuous regeneration through music. Despite his restless nature, Rostropovich did not convey an impression of hurrying or of agitation, whatever the activity he was engaged in: his ability instantly to 'switch in' to any situation was remarkable, and he always focused his attention absolutely on the task in hand.

Rostropovich once explained his approach to life and work to me. It was, he told me, like having a powerful and efficient 'motor' which for the most part just ticked over quietly, but was ready to take off with a sudden burst of energy at the moment required. One had to remember to service and check the motor at regular intervals – in other words to be both self-aware and aware of others. This gave one clarity in one's approach to work and relationships. The quality of self-knowledge and the ability to pace oneself were things he tried to convey to his students, so that they made the best use of their inner resources and learnt to achieve the maximum amount within the minimum time.

These attributes were at the fore when Rostropovich embarked on his most ambitious project to date, his cycle of eleven concerts over the 1963/64 season. This series practically constituted a comprehensive overview of the concerto repertoire for cello, forty-four works in all. It took place in the Grand Hall of the Moscow Conservatoire in collaboration with various Moscow orchestras and six different conductors, not counting the composers who conducted their own compositions. For good measure, Rostropovich repeated seven of the eleven programmes in Leningrad during the same season, mostly accompanied by the Leningrad Philharmonic.

Versions of the cycle were repeated around the world in the years that followed. In summer 1965, he gave a series of nine concerts over four weeks at the Royal Festival Hall in London. This cycle concluded with a performance of Britten's *Cello Symphony* conducted by Rozhdestvensky: when the composer appeared on stage to acknowledge the applause, Rozhdestvensky handed him his baton, and the final movement was encored, this time with Britten conducting. A further variant of the series was performed in New York over two weeks in early 1967: this cycle included two new works by American composers, a concerto by Lucas Foss and *Variations* by Walter Piston.

The original cycle in Moscow included repertoire that spanned three centuries from the baroque and classical periods to contemporary works. Many works were unknown to Russian audiences: Rostropovich could claim Soviet premieres of three Vivaldi concertos, Haydn's C major concerto, Respighi's *Adagio and Variations*, Glazunov's *Concert-Ballade*, Bloch's *Schelomo* and Hindemith's concerto of 1940. Fourteen works had been specially composed for the cycle, all dedicated to Rostropovich, including pieces by Henri Sauguet, Benjamin Britten, Lyubomir Pipkov, Arno Babadjanyan, Lev Knipper, Boris Chaikovsky, and Vladimir Vlasov. Aram Khatchaturian's *Concerto-Rhapsody* was given its Moscow premiere on 14 January 1964 during the fourth concert of the cycle, dedicated to Russian concertos, while another novelty was Shostakovich's new orchestration of Schumann's concerto, executed at Rostropovich's request.

At the start of the 1963/64 academic year, Rostropovich decided to set his students some of the new works he had programmed, wanting his class to feel actively involved in the exciting enterprise. In the past his students had played new works more or less immediately after their teacher, but now they would learn them simultaneously, and even, on occasion, ahead of him, as Lev Evgrafov recalls:

Rostropovich's great cycle included a concerto by Lyubomir Pipkov, who was considered a kind of 'Bulgarian Khrennikov'. One day in the autumn of 1963 Mstislav Leopoldovich asked me, 'Lev, please can you learn this concerto and record it with piano by next week.' I managed to fulfil his request, although it was a long and difficult work on a symphonic scale. Pipkov was expected in Moscow, and Rostropovich needed to show him a recording of the work, which he himself still hadn't had time to learn. He probably used my recording for this purpose.

At the time many students were surprised that Rostropovich should give a new work to a pupil to learn before he had played it himself. But in later years, when they themselves started teaching, they understood the wisdom of the concept, for knowing the new work from the outside gave Rostropovich a better perspective on it.

The way in which works were allocated to students was sometimes something of a lottery: one student could draw a baroque concerto, another a completely new work. It fell to Karine Georgian to have to learn Pipkov's *Concerto-Sinfonia*: she recalls the process as something of a struggle, which caused some laughter in class, though she accepted it with good humour. Mariya Chaikovskaya, meanwhile, set out to learn Henri Sauguet's new work, entitled *Concert-Mélodie*. A lesson on this piece was recorded for a Soviet television documentary about Rostropovich: the excerpt included in the surviving video recording vividly captures his teaching style, even though the atmosphere was rather more formal than usual, given that this was a special demonstration class for cello teachers from all over the Soviet Union.

The first-year students were for the most part exempt from learning a new work; usually they needed to concentrate on sorting out technical problems. Nevertheless Rostropovich would give them a series of challenges, and with this in mind he set his first-year student David Geringas the small C major concerto attributed to Haydn (which was actually a work by David Popper using material from various different Haydn works). Geringas had gained his place in the class thanks to the withdrawal of Knaifel, and was pleased to have a 'real' piece of music to work on. When he brought the concerto to class in the spring of 1964, Rostropovich unexpectedly exclaimed, 'You know what, this concerto will solve my problem.' It turned out that Tikhon Khrennikov's concerto, which Rostropovich had been due to play at the next (and final) concert of the cycle, was still not completed. Given Khrennikov's powerful position as First Secretary of the Composers' Union, Rostropovich could hardly complain, even if it was the second time that the composer had missed his deadline! On the first occasion Rostropovich had resolved the problem by swapping its place with another work in the cycle, but now he was left with a dilemma. Because he had virtually played his way through the entire cello repertoire, it was no easy matter to find a substitute work. It occurred to him, therefore, that this Haydn–Popper concerto, although not authentic, was a sufficiently attractive work which he could rustle up with a few hours' practice.

For students like David, to hear their professor perform the piece that they had played in class a few days previously was in itself an instructive experience. During the performance, Rostropovich unexpectedly missed a few harmonics in a short closing cadenza. Backstage after the concert, he caught David's eye and said, 'Well, old man, you see what can happen: I was too self-assured, and I slipped up.' This ability to admit his mistakes was a refreshingly human aspect of Rostropovich's personality: he rarely expressed satisfaction with his playing (at best sardonically saying that 'it wasn't bad'), and while he was always happy to accept congratulations and hug his admirers after a concert, in general he preferred not to discuss his performances. Humility towards one's art, he felt, should be practised rather than preached.

For Rostropovich's students the cycle afforded a unique opportunity to hear their teacher in an enormous range of repertoire. Rostropovich encouraged his pupils to reach their own judgements about the repertoire they heard and to identify with some particular work they wished to play. Natalya Shakhovskaya, for instance, added Knipper's *Concerto Monologue* to her repertoire and later recorded it. Hearing the master bring a new score to life was an important part of the learning process, as the experience of Vagram (Vago) Saradzhan, not yet a student in the class, shows. Saradzhan was in Erevan when Rostropovich played the world premiere of Khatchaturian's *Concerto-Rhapsody* during spring 1963, and recalls being 'in complete shock' after the impassioned rendering of the work:

To start with I had never heard such a wonderful sound on the cello. I was so impressed by the way Mstislav Leopoldovich played the principal theme that I rushed home, carrying this sound in my ears. I was determined to reproduce it myself, and I stayed up with my cello till four-thirty in the morning, trying to capture the colour and character of his tone. In doing so I recalled his image, and worked on the width and intensity of the vibrato, using flatter finger pads, and also experimented with the bow pressure and speed, imagining his arm position with the free weight of shoulder at play, and a slightly lowered elbow. I was so intent on transmitting this sound, because I carried it within me, it rang in my inner ear. I then realised the truth of the dictum – it is the ear that dictates sound quality. Over the years I learnt a lot from Rostropovich simply by observing him play.

The composer of the work that so impressed Saradzhan, Aram Khatchaturian, was in Rostropovich's estimation a wonderful musician and a fine, generous human being. However, he did have an endearing weakness, which was his well-developed sense of self-importance. Rostropovich likes to tell the story of how he learnt the work as a surprise for Khatchaturian. It grated on the Armenian composer's nerves to know that while Slava had learnt Shostakovich's concerto four days after he obtained the score, when he received the manuscript of the *Concerto-Rhapsody*, he never seemed to have time to learn it. Khatchaturian implored him to play the new concerto with piano accompaniment at a concert dedicated to his works in the Small Hall of the Moscow Conservatoire. Rostropovich discovered that he had another engagement that evening in the Grand Hall, and that he therefore could not accept. When he saw Aram Ilyich's doleful brown eyes and large, pouting mouth, Rostropovich realised that he had caused serious offence. He quickly calculated that there would in fact be time to rush from one hall to the other in time to fulfil Khatchaturian's request. He kept his plan secret from the composer, and sat down to learn the new concerto.

The events of that day provide a snapshot of a working day in Rostropovich's Moscow life. In the morning he rehearsed with the orchestra for his evening concert, then he went to the Conservatoire class to work with students. He auditioned David Grigorian, a young cellist from Erevan, whom he invited with his father to come and listen to his rehearsal of the *Rhapsody-Concerto* with Aza Amintaeva in one of the larger Conservatoire classrooms. Three Armenian cellists were present in the select audience, who had all been sworn to secrecy; they were thrilled to have witnessed the birth of a work by their nation's most distinguished composer. After rushing home to grab some food and to change, Rostropovich returned to the Grand Hall to play his official concert, after which he dashed over to the Small Hall for his surprise appearance at Khatchaturian's concert. This earned him the undying gratitude of the Armenian master, and further enhanced Rostropovich's already legendary reputation at the Conservatoire.

The two concertos from the cycle that became particular favourites with students and were frequently featured in class concerts were those by Boris Chaikovsky and Arno Babadjanyan. The former, a substantial four-movement work written in an attractive idiom, shows the influence of composers as diverse as Stravinsky, Britten, and Lutoslawski, while also featuring elements of popular song, jazz and dance rhythms. As one might expect from a student of Shostakovich, the work is beautifully balanced, always allowing the cello through, and Chaikovsky's orchestration is dazzlingly inventive. The work also has its own distinctive humour which contrasts with the sarcasm and irony at work in Shostakovich's music. The virtuosic cello writing is offset by unusual combinations in the orchestral scoring, while the theatrical element throughout the work gave ample scope for Rostropovich's love of drama and impersonation. Perhaps for this reason, he was particularly enthusiastic about Boris Chaikovsky's new work and announced him to be a 'composer of genius', the most interesting of his generation in Russia.

From an objective standpoint, the concerto has some minor musical defects – at times its invention is thin, its structural balance uneven – but any awareness of these was swept away by the effervescence of Rostropovich's performance. Chaikovsky's cello concerto had a deep impact on its listeners, Shostakovich among them: after the first performance, he asked Rostropovich to lend him the score so that he could 'study its heavenly beauties'. Rostropovich championed the work at home and abroad, and also asked Chaikovsky to write a new chamber work. He showed him some Messiaen scores, and suggested to Chaikovsky that he would love to have a Russian equivalent of the *Quartet for the End of Time*. Messiaen's influence was tangible in the effective new work Chaikovsky produced some years later. Entitled *Partita*, it was scored for the unusual combination of cello, electric guitar, piano, harpsichord and percussion. Ultimately, however, Rostropovich's championship was not enough to win any genuine interest for Boris Chaikovsky outside the Soviet Union, nor indeed enduring popularity at home.

The concerto by the Armenian composer, Arno Babadjanyan, also represented a highly progressive variant on a 'classical' Soviet-style work, but in this case it was based on elements of national folklore. It is a forceful and appealing work, written in a single tautly structured span without division into separate movements. The noble rhetoric of its introduction was ideally suited to Rostropovich's expansive temperament, and the fast section that follows is built on a lively ostinato 5/8 rhythm with a decorative element borrowed from Armenian chant. The influences on its style range from Carl Orff to Bernstein, from Stravinsky to Khatchaturian, yet the originality of Babadjanyan's voice is demonstrated in his remarkable skill in reconciling features of modernist experimentation with a national idiom. Still remembered in the former Soviet Union as a wonderful pianist and extremely talented composer, Babadjanyan's early death deprived him of the recognition he deserved. Today his music is hardly performed outside Armenia.

Programming so many new works within one season was something of a gamble, and not all of them found a stable place in the repertoire. Russian audiences tended to be more curious about foreign composers than those from the Soviet Union, and when Rostropovich secured the presence of both the Parisian Henri Sauget (who conducted his *Concert-Mélodie* in the fifth concert of the cycle, which was dedicated to French music) and Benjamin Britten (who conducted his *Cello Symphony*) the halls in both Moscow and Leningrad were packed out. In Leningrad, Rostropovich arranged for Sauget to meet Conservatoire students so he could talk about his work and about new musical developments in France; Rostropovich illustrated the lecture by playing through the concerto with his Leningrad class pianist Viktoria Bogdashevskaya.

Undoubtedly the greatest single masterpiece to emerge from the cycle was Britten's *Symphony*, a work of enormous complexity and great originality of structure. The symphonic character of the piece influences the various roles that the cello soloist is required to adopt, whether as initiator of dialogue, accompanist, leader of the cello section, or as part of the orchestral texture. In the first movement, for instance, Britten handles the thematic material in a masterly way as the cello line weaves in and out of the musical fabric, its function constantly changing. The second movement, a burlesque-like scherzo, inhabits a shadowy world – haunted, it would seem, by 'ghosts' of the *War Requiem*. The heart of the matter lies in the majestic slow movement, which culminates in an extended cello cadenza that serves as a transition into the finale, written in Britten's favourite passacaglia form.

The premiere of the *Cello Symphony* may have caused some dismay to the average Moscow concert-goer, unfamiliar with its idiom, but it was given an ecstatic reception by the many young students present. It also made a profound impression on members of the musical community, from Shostakovich to Emil Gilels. David Oistrakh told Rostropovich that he was vastly impressed, not just by Britten's music, but by Slava's feat in memorising such an intricate solo part. Shostakovich, who had followed the score closely, afterwards tackled Britten on a technical point: 'You know, Ben, the fermati [pauses] in the second movement? It's all very well when you are conducting and Slava is playing, but other musicians might ruin everything simply because they won't know how long these pauses should last. Why don't you write in the precise value of each of these fermati, mark them in as rests. You know one simply can't rely on the judgement of performers!' Britten laughed, but in the end he did not adjust anything in the score. Perhaps, he felt that the recording of the *Cello Symphony* that he and Rostropovich were about to make would provide the necessary authoritative statement.

The work's success was repeated in Leningrad. This time it was the Conservatoire students who had prepared a surprise for Britten, inviting him to a performance of the first half of the *War Requiem* which they had prepared themselves. Considering that the work was in effect banned, and the material was next to impossible to find, Britten could not but be enormously impressed by the devotion and enthusiasm of the young Leningrad performers.

Given the unique nature of this cycle, one might have expected that Rostropovich's schedule for the year would have been completely devoted to learning new cello concertos. It is true that apart from a two-month tour of America between mid-October and mid-December 1963, he did little travelling over the season, and that for the most part his concert activity was divided between Moscow and Leningrad. But far from being content to restrict himself to performing a mere thirty or so cello concertos, he also found time to learn several new programmes with Vishnevskaya, which they performed both in Leningrad and Moscow. One programme was dedicated to Mussorgsky songs, another to Tchaikovsky romances, and a third shared between songs by Rachmaninov and Stravinsky. Nor did he neglect other aspects of the cello repertoire, continuing to perform duo recitals and chamber concerts. To honour Shostakovich's fifty-seventh birthday, Rostropovich participated in a concert of his works on 22 September 1963 at the Small Hall of the Leningrad Philharmonia, playing in the second piano trio and eighth quartet as well as accompanying Vishnevskaya in the *Satires* and extracts from *Lady Macbeth*. In Moscow on 28 March 1964, meanwhile, he joined the Beethoven Quartet for a performance of Schubert's C major Quintet.

Even at this peak of performing activity, Rostropovich did not neglect his students in Moscow and Leningrad, and he ensured that they performed their full quota of class concerts. It was certainly an extraordinary time for the many musicians who had contact with him at this time, for Rostropovich carried with him such infectious vitality that people within his radius seemed to discover hidden resources and new energy within themselves. When working with him, nothing but the best was good enough. As Natalya Shakhovskaya put it:

Rostropovich had an almost hypnotic effect on everything and everybody in his surroundings. When he walked into the Conservatoire, the atmosphere there changed perceptibly, it became charged with energy. It wasn't just the smell of his perfume which was transmitted, but a new life would start, full of unexpected things. His enormous temperament, the phenomenal energy of his artistic nature attracted and involved everybody!

Shostakovich was responsible for drawing Slava's attention to Boris Tishchenko, a twenty-seven-year-old postgraduate student in his Leningrad class. In the autumn of 1965, Tishchenko, now in his final year, responded to Rostropovich's urgent request for a new work. At first, Shostakovich was not entirely pleased to discover that his student had embarked on a cello concerto; evidently he had not been consulted and this composition fell outside the scheme of work planned for Tishchenko's diploma. Yet when he saw the completed piece, he could not but express his admiration. He expressed some minor reservations, and suggested that Tishchenko reconsider those places where the cello might have difficulty coming through the orchestral texture. The concerto was scored for an unusual formation of solo cello, seventeen wind instruments (both woodwind and brass), accordion and percussion.

It may have been no more than coincidence, but just as Tishchenko's cello concerto was receiving its first performance in Leningrad in February 1966, Shostakovich too conceived the idea of a new work for cello. Rostropovich told his students something of his part in the genesis of the work that became the second cello concerto. In 1965, he had spent New Year's Eve as usual at the Shostakovich family dacha in Zhukovka. As a game, each person played or sang their 'favourite tune', and when it was Shostakovich's turn, he sat down and played an Odessa street ditty: '*Bubliki, kupite bubliki*' (Bagels, buy my bagels) which he had referred to in his youthful opera *The Nose*. Rostropovich was amazed to discover, a few months later, that the composer had used this simple melody as the principal theme of the concerto's second movement.

Shostakovich started writing the concerto immediately after completing his eleventh string quartet in February 1966. To begin with, he thought this new work might become his fourteenth symphony* – and indeed he later confirmed that the cello concerto could be described as a 'fourteenth symphony with solo cello part'.†

---

* Shostakovich, letter to Isaak Glikman dated 16 February 1966. Glikman, *Story of a Friendship*, p. 126.
† Letter to D. Shepilov dated 21 September 1966. Quoted in Rubtsova, *Tikhon Khrennikov: on his times and himself*, Moscow, 1994, p. 142.

In April Shostakovich went down to the Crimea with his wife, where they stayed at the Nizhnaya Oreanda Sanatorium near Yalta, and he worked intensively on the concerto.

Exceptionally, Shostakovich had shown Rostropovich this work in its unfinished form – it was unusual for him even to speak of a composition before he had completed it. Seeing the cello part before it was complete meant that Rostropovich could give the composer 'one clever piece of advice', about playing double-stops in fourths across three strings, something that the composer incorporated into the finale. Shostakovich also consulted Rostropovich about the feasibility of writing the second-subject melody in tenths, an interval that does not usually feature as part of a cellist's technical armoury. Rostropovich remembers:

In such moments I seem to have good fortune, for I said to Shostakovich it would be fine, and to demonstrate I took my cello and played the tenths in question very cleanly and confidently. Afterwards I regretted this success, for every time I perform the work in public and arrive at that spot I get nervous, I have to pray that I wouldn't miss that first chord. Dmitri Dmitriyevich suggested that he could give the lower voice to the violas, but I persuaded him to leave it the way he had first written it.

Shostakovich completed his second cello concerto on 27 April and its first performance was planned in Moscow for 25 September, the composer's sixtieth birthday. The new concerto became a personal favourite of Rostropovich's, and it became firmly established in the cello repertoire from its very first performance.

Only a month later he performed it again, and I recorded my impressions of his interpretation in a letter to my parents:

Rostropovich gave another performance of Shostakovich's second concerto which was truly brilliant – he played so marvellously this time, that we were all moved en masse. It was really a better performance than the premiere. Afterwards we went and said goodbye to him . . . Rostro is once more off on tour.

As I wrote in the same letter, only two days earlier I had attended another concert celebrating the seventy-fifth anniversary of Prokofiev's birth. This time Rostropovich appeared as a pianist, playing the piano part of the sextet version of the Overture on *Jewish Themes* with the 'brilliant' Borodin Quartet – 'this was so wildly acclaimed that they had to play it again as an encore.'

In the autumn of 1966 Rostropovich stated in an interview: 'Shostakovich's new [second] cello concerto has a duration of thirty-seven minutes. If by the thirty-eighth minute other cellists start performing it, I will be delighted.' This, in fact, is more or less what happened, for I well remember students bringing the concerto to play in class within weeks of its first performance. The 'Bubliki' theme became so popular that one could hear the cellists in class playing it in an improvised arrangement for several cellos while they awaited our professor's arrival. Everybody in Rostropovich's class fell in love with this marvellous work, agreeing that although it was far darker and more introspective than its predecessor, it was every bit as interesting.

The concerto was the last work Shostakovich wrote for solo cello, but a year later he composed his *Seven Verses of Aleksander Blok* with both Vishnevskaya and Rostropovich in mind, in response to their request for some vocalises for voice and cello. Shostakovich did in fact restrict himself to this combination in the first piece of the cycle, 'Ophelia's Song', but eventually abandoned the idea of keeping it for the whole piece: 'You see, Slava, I tried to satisfy your request, but when I started writing the second movement with a whacking pizzicato in the cello, I realised that I didn't have enough instruments.' At that stage he decided to add piano and violin to the instrumentation. While Shostakovich remained Rostropovich's idol at home, the relationship he developed with Benjamin Britten was of no less importance. The *Cello Symphony* received its UK premiere at the 1964 Aldeburgh festival, and shortly afterwards Rostropovich and Britten recorded it for Decca in Orford Church together with the Haydn C major concerto. Immediately afterwards, they were due to drive to the North of England for a concert in the Seckers Theatre in Rosehill in Cumberland, planning to spend one night en route at Harewood House in Yorkshire, home of the Princess Royal, Lord Harewood's mother.

Rostropovich's story of this event has entered the annals of musical history, but is nevertheless worth retelling again – if only one could bring it to life as dramatically as he did for the students in his class!

As a Soviet citizen, one did not get much opportunity for meeting a real princess. For Rostropovich, princesses came either from Hans Christian Andersen or from Tchaikovsky's ballets – young and beautiful, fairy-tale stuff. During the intervals of their recording session, Rostropovich would be seen slipping out into the graveyard of Orford Church, where he seemed to perform some strange acrobatics. When Britten caught sight of this, he asked him what he was up to. Slava explained, 'Ah Ben, you see I am practising my *kliksen*, my curtsy, *la riverenza*.' 'Whatever for?' 'Well, when I meet the Princess Royal I must behave in the most respectful manner.' Britten was perturbed, but initially took no notice. When he observed that Slava's 'gymnastics' were becoming more and more elaborate, with the addition of flourishes and falling onto knees, Britten started to be alarmed. He tackled the issue when, together with Peter Pears and Marion Harewood, they started their drive up North.

'Slava, you were of course only joking. You are not going to behave like that in front of the Princess Royal, are you?' 'Oh no, I am completely serious.' 'But you see, the Princess Royal is rather old, and she might get a fright. If she had a fit or a heart attack, then you, a Soviet citizen, will be held responsible, and it could turn into an unpleasant diplomatic incident. Surely we don't want a scandal.' Rostropovich objected: 'Well, I'm not going to give up my curtsy now, after practising it for so many hours.'

When they stopped in Lincoln for lunch, Britten asked Slava to abandon all thoughts of such behaviour; it really might have serious consequences. 'Alright,' Rostropovich said, 'I'll restrain myself, of course, that is if I manage to, but on one condition.' Britten asked what it was. Slava now played his trump card: 'Three new works for cello in exchange for me giving up my *kliksen*.' However much Britten protested, Slava remained adamant. There and then a contract was drawn up and written onto the menu. Britten put his signature to the promise of three new works for cello, and Rostropovich signed his part of the agreement. As he recalls:

Naturally Ben grumbled afterwards and I could hear him muttering words about 'Damned blackmailer'. And of course I played my role to the last; even as we were being led in to the Princess, I would make as if to curtsy and fall on my knees, but then stopped myself while wagging my finger to Ben and whispering, 'Three new works!' My disappointment was indescribable when I actually met the Princess Royal; by now she was far from being the young and beautiful princess of my fairy tales. She was wizened, old, and very formidable. I doubt if I would have ever had the nerve to curtsy or kneel in front of her. When Ben and I played some Schumann pieces, I remember her looking up at me quizzically as she paused for an instant from her crocheting.

Britten proved to be a man of his word. Three suites for solo cello, the result of this strange contract, were written in 1965, 1967, and 1971 respectively. Before that, however, Britten wrote a vocal cycle entitled *The Poet's Echo*, on verses by Aleksandr Pushkin. Dedicated to Vishnevskaya, he composed it while holidaying with the Rostropovich couple in Armenia during August 1965. The events of the holiday are described in detail in Peter Pears's travel diaries. Armenian hospitality was fabulous, and the best it could offer was put at the disposal of the illustrious party at the Composers' Union rest house in Dilizhan, in one of the most scenic parts of the country. Rostropovich had helped the Armenian composers' union set up a small festival of Britten's music in Erevan, where he had agreed to perform the *Cello Symphony*. To his mortification, the conductor (Yuri Aranovich) simply hadn't bothered to study the score or prepare the orchestra properly. Rostropovich tried to save matters at the first rehearsals, but realised the venture was doomed. He had time to warn Britten that things weren't going well, but did not prevent him from coming to the dress rehearsal. Slava played as best he could, and corrected the conductor, who did not seem to notice the mass of errors being perpetrated by the orchestra. At a certain point Britten got up and walked up to the ramp by the stage, thumped it with his fist, making an enormously loud bang, and addressed the conductor. 'Young man,' he said, trembling all over with rage, 'this is a travesty. I forbid you ever to conduct any of my works ever again.' Rostropovich had never before witnessed Britten's wrath, and could not have imagined that he was capable of such anger.

Apart from this incident, the holiday was relaxed, happy and creatively successful. Aza Amintaeva, who was staying with Slava and Galya in their Dilizhan cottage, told them that a distant relative of hers was the curator of the Pushkin memorial museum at Mikhailovskoye, the estate near Pskov, where the poet had spent several years of his exile. A plan was hatched to take Britten and Pears there immediately on their return to Moscow. They arrived in the late afternoon at Mikhailovskoye, and after supper, late in the evening, Britten and Pears performed the new song cycle. When they reached the song 'Insomnia', in which the composer perfectly depicts the ticking of the clock in the piano part, they were amazed to hear the clock from Pushkin's study next door striking midnight, in perfect synchrony with the rhythm of the song. Both Rostropovich and Aza would repeat this story to us in class as an instance of a mystical experience, in which some supernatural power joined together the great poet and the great composer for an instant in time.

Students at the Moscow Conservatoire were fortunate to witness the first 'unofficial' performance of the first Britten suite for unaccompanied cello, which Rostropovich played in the large Classroom 21 on the eve of his departure for the 1965 Aldeburgh festival. I can never forget my impressions of that occasion: in the packed-out classroom, we were sitting almost on top of our professor, and not only seeing, but positively feeling, the power of his concentration as he played through this marvellous and complex work for the first time. For me, watching his brilliant handling of the virtuoso variations of the Last Canto was like witnessing the impossible.

Britten's first suite quickly made its way into the repertoire of the better students; I remember Jacqueline du Pré brought it to class in spring 1966, observing the similarity of the fugue subject to that of the opening C major fugue from Bach's *Well-Tempered Clavier*. Natalya Gutman soon added the suite to her repertoire, performing it with great effect.

I had the good fortune to hear private performances of all three suites, for Rostropovich learnt the second during his journey from Leningrad to Tilbury by boat in June 1968. As I accompanied him on the journey home for the holidays, I discovered that three days on a ship were all that a great cellist needs to learn a new work. True, a delay caused by fog in the Thames estuary gave him some extra hours, although many wondered if the fog wasn't in the captain's head. (The night before, the skipper had challenged my professor to a drinking match, though I never discovered who won!)

In April 1971, I was privileged to hear Britten play through the recently composed third cello suite on the piano to Rostropovich and Shostakovich during his visit to Moscow. Knowing the full story of Slava's support for Solzhenitsyn and his precarious relationship with the Soviet authorities, Britten only agreed to come to Moscow for the 'Days of British Music' festival on the condition that Rostropovich was allowed to play the *Cello Symphony* with him. After intensive negotiation with Ekaterina Furtseva, the Soviet Minister of Culture, this concession was won, so Britten conducted the London Symphony Orchestra in performances of his own works in Leningrad and Moscow: the 'two Slavas', Richter and Rostropovich, performed as his soloists in the piano concerto and *Cello Symphony* respectively.

The third suite, with which Britten fulfilled the terms of the 'contract' signed on the Lincoln restaurant menu, was based on

Russian themes, and was an explicit tribute to Rostropovich as a patriot and humanist – a man who had showed the courage to defend his convictions. The third cello suite was perhaps the most personal and precious of all the works ever written for Rostropovich. After the composer's death, he could hardly bring himself to play it, for with its use of the Orthodox funeral chant, 'At Rest with the Saints', it touched on a vulnerable point, drawing both joyful and painful memories from some deep inner well of his being.

Rostropovich had long hesitated to commit his version of the Bach unaccompanied suites to record, but he finally did so when he was in his mid-sixties. He did record the first two Britten cello suites for Decca, but never overcame his reluctance to commit the third cello suite to any form of recording. He felt that this music had its own mystical existence, in some dimension beyond time.

INTERLUDE 3

Natalya Gutman

From the time I became a Conservatoire student, I had always
dreamed of studying with Rostropovich. I learnt the cello throughout
my school and Conservatoire student years with Galina Kozolupova,
who was actually his cousin, although they were not on the best of
terms. Nevertheless I occasionally slipped along to listen to
Rostropovich's classes, even though this was not encouraged.

Kozolupova taught very conscientiously: she imparted everything
necessary to achieve mastery of the cello, polishing our bow strokes
and encouraging us to produce a large sound. But I don't remember
many musical discussions during my years of study with her. In fact,
since the age of fourteen, my real music teacher and trainer was my
grandfather, Anisim Berlin. At the same time, I started attending all of
Richter's concerts. In other words I had two mentors: my musical
mentor was Richter, and my pedagogigal mentor was my grandfather.

Rostropovich heard me when I was a first-year student at the
Conservatoire in 1959. It was a strange year for me and I practised
very little; my cello usually lay unopened in its case at the flat of my
friend, who had an apartment in the same house as Richter on
Pokrovsky Street. But I desperately wanted to play the Schumann
concerto; Galina allowed me to learn it only because I was so insistent.

I then played the Schumann concerto at an exam. I didn't really
have any idea how to approach the piece, and I evidently played it
very badly. It was the first time that I failed to get an excellent mark
for cello. Galina asked Rostropovich to speak to me, as they were
both in the exam commission. He popped out of the class, and gave
me a talking to: 'We expected something better from you, you know,'
he scolded me. That was my first meeting with him.

By the time I had completed the Conservatoire training I was twenty-one. I had won the Prague competition when I was eighteen, and I played at the first Tchaikovsky cello competition two years later, where I won third prize. By then I felt that I was ready to leave Galina Kozolupova and wanted to study with Rostropovich. However, it was obvious that if I chose to do my postgraduate studies with him, Kozolupova would be mortally offended. So I developed a strategy, and told her that I was going to work in Leningrad, which would allow me to enrol in Rostropovich's class there. I prepared myself for this terribly painful conversation, and went to see her. We both wept copiously; although she was very offended, the distance involved did make it slightly less difficult for her to accept the fact that I was studying with Rostropovich. Nonetheless, Galina Semyonovna had wanted to be the one to send me into life as an artist. Although I was very fond of her, I desperately needed more stimulus and to confront new musical ideas.

The first thing that I noted about Rostropovich as a teacher was his amazing capacity to see exactly what each individual needed, and just what could be drawn out of them. When the pianist Alexei Nasedkin and I prepared for the Munich competition of 1967, we took him our whole sonata repertoire. His lessons were very intense and stimulating, and forced us to think beyond our 'ordinary' level of achievement. A lot of the teaching was concentrated in July, after the semester was over, since Rostropovich made up for his absences during the year by staying on in Moscow, where I had most of my lessons despite being officially enrolled in Leningrad.

I remember one such lesson very clearly, on the Rachmaninov sonata. Nasedkin and I hadn't had much time to prepare the work, but we were under the impression that we were playing it at quite a high level. However, once Mstislav Leopoldovich started working with us, we realised just how far we still had to go. It was a wonderful lesson, a unique experience – fortunately we still have it on tape. At one point, Rostropovich cried out at me, 'Why are you playing like that, like a policeman sitting in his booth?' This image was quite fantastic, since it precisely described my mental process, the way I sought to control everything I did to ensure it functioned on the cello, without a full emotional involvement. At the time I had thought that I was fully engrossed in my playing and in the music, but I then realised that my involvement was insufficient: it did not go beyond the personal 'I'. This image of 'the policeman in the booth' made me understand that I was too taken up with the external side of cello-playing; it really helped me sort out a lot of my problems.

What I found so interesting and enjoyable was the fantastic recip-rocal give-and-take at these lessons. Mstislav Leopoldovich would say something, then I would do my best to respond in the playing; he in turn would become more involved in the exchange and would often get quite carried away. I remember so many of the remarks he made to me, because they were so unusual, fresh and stimulating. And now when I teach, I often repeat them to my students, saying, 'This is what Rostropovich told me,' because so much of what he said has abso-lutely retained its relevance.

For instance, in Beethoven's fourth sonata, the most difficult of the five in my opinion, I remember how in the opening Andante he described the exchange of the six-note semiquaver phrase between piano and cello (this occurs, for instance, before the return of the opening theme with trills in the piano part). He turned to me and said with a sweeping movement of the hand, 'I hear it from the phrase' – a paraphrase of the Russian expression 'I hear it from a fool.' Of course, in the opening of the Allegro he talked about his experience with Richter and the way in which he had persuaded the pianist to play with the appearance of great force while still allowing the cello to come through. In the second subject of the same Allegro, I remember Mstislav Leopoldovich telling me, 'You know you are playing with yesterday's sound' – this brilliantly described my somewhat studied approach. I always think of that remark when I reach that point, and in the bar's rest that precedes the phrase I try to refresh my inner feel-ings, in order to achieve the state of mind needed to play the next phrase with a completely different impulse: it's all too easy to play that phrase passively. And in the Schumann concerto, I remember Mstislav Leopoldovich suggesting that I open out in the first phrase, like a flower unfolding towards the light – I had evidently been too tensely involved in going forward, ignoring the poetry of this moment.

Rostropovich rarely talked about the technical aspect of cello-playing, but when he did he identified some simple but fundamental things in a marvellous way. He would get irritated at the way I used my left hand, in a rather clean, violinistic way. He would upbraid me: 'Natasha, you with your sinewy stretches, your dry fingering!' He *wanted more warmth and more plasticity, a softer and more supple left hand. He asked for more glissandi, more tenderness, but at the same time his suggestions did not interfere in any way with my own interpretive approach.*

Once I brought the Brahms concerto for violin and cello to class with Oleg Kagan, who later became my husband. Rostropovich felt I was sometimes over-reticent. At a certain point in the second movement, the violin plays a phrase that is then answered by the cello. Rostropovich liked the nobility and warmth of Oleg's rhetorical expression, but after I played he turned to me and said, 'Natasha, the devil take you, can't you let go? It sounds as if you are lying in bed listening to your lover declare his sentiments, and all you do is cover your mouth with a blanket and out comes a muffled, "Yes, and I love you too."' This image made everybody laugh, but also made me change my attitude – one didn't want to merit such an accusation again!

For my part, I was only once able really to surprise Rostropovich. My first husband, Volodya, was a painter, and he thought that every true musician should know how to compose. I believed I had no talent, but he insisted: 'Just wait and see. If you exercise every day you will be able to do it.' He then set me a first exercise: 'Try and draw in sound what you see in front of you.' The idea interested me and I decided to have a go. The first thing I did was to draw the house in front of our window. Thus I wrote my first piece, a short prelude for cello solo, lasting only sixteen bars in all. But its structure conveyed the atmosphere that was in my head – Volodya was absolutely delighted.

I next wrote a series of preludes and a small fugetta. Then I started writing a little sonatina for cello and piano. Volodya absolutely insisted that I spend some time every day sitting down and composing. Strangely enough, the process of inner hearing that this involved helped me learn to listen. To begin with, when I wrote a harmony down, I would check it at the piano, and often had to correct it, adjusting what I had written against what I heard in my head. But as I practised, the process became sharper and what I heard in my head started to coincide with what I wrote down. I found it really interesting, and at one point I thought I would go and have composition lessons. I went to see Balasanyan, an excellent composer and teacher. He immediately asked me if I could improvise, and I had to admit that I did not know how. This made me realise that I did not have the talent to become a composer.

Nevertheless, a competition was announced for a solo cello piece for the Tchaikovsky competition, and Volodya insisted that I send my sonatina in. The piece had to be sent under a pseudonym, and so I yielded to Volodya's pleas. He submitted it on my behalf under the name of 'Raphael'. A commission was called to listen to all these pieces, and many cellists came and played the pieces that had been submitted. I played my own piece, and I have to say I played it very badly, as I wasn't interested in the music. When I came to the hall I discovered a lot of cellists I knew, including Tamara Gabarashvili, who asked me what I was going to play. 'Oh, just some rubbish,' I said: my authorship remained a complete secret. Then it was my turn to play, and the commission sitting there included Rostropovich, Kozolupova, Khomitser, Shirinsky and Feigin, as well as representatives from the Ministry of Culture. I thought my pieces hadn't passed, but Tamara and I decided to wait together. Suddenly the door opened and I was asked in. Rostropovich asked me, 'Tell us, do you like this work?' 'No,' I replied. Then Galina Kozolupova said, 'And would you play it?' 'No,' I said, 'I really don't want to play it.' 'But why not? If you liked it enough to play it, then the Ministry of Culture would buy it and publish it.' I was terrified that they would discover the identity of the 'author', and kept repeating, 'No, I don't like this music.'

With that I left the room. Then suddenly I heard a great burst of laughter from the other side of the door. I peeped through the door and saw that Khomitser had opened the envelope which contained the name of the composer and taken it over to Rostropovich. The whole commission was howling with laughter. Rostropovich called me in, and said, 'Goodness me, how you pulled a fast one on me!' He then asked me what I wanted to call the piece, and I told him, 'For Thursday'. In the end the outcome was good for me, as the commission arranged for the piece to be bought and published by the Ministry.

Teaching principles
Class 19 in the 1960s

In an interview given in 1966, Rostropovich stated, 'The "impossible" does not exist on the cello, there are no taboos – as long as what you do allows for the unfolding of interesting ideas and enhances the artistic value inherent in each work.'* He furthermore explained how, over the years, he had modified his approach to teaching:

Earlier I worked on every bar and polished every detail. But this inhibits the student's imagination and hinders his growth. Now I give a pupil a lot of pieces to learn, and then stand back to give him space to tackle the numerous tasks that I literally throw at him. I try not to interfere with advice. But then, at a certain point – and pedagogical intuition usually dictates when – I work in detail and depth on one particular work, dwelling on every minor point, pulling each bar apart. In this way I try to make the student fully conscious of the significance of every phrase, every bowing stroke, every pause in the music. These intensive spurts can be very effective in teaching, but need to be calculated precisely.

During the early 1960s, students who enrolled with Rostropovich found themselves playing in a high-powered masterclass system, in which lessons mostly took place in packed classrooms, and involved a significant element of performance for teacher and pupil alike. Rostropovich attracted the best talent, although he also accepted students of lower levels of accomplishment: the weaker cellists were undoubtedly inspired by the stronger ones, and it was generally agreed that the most stimulating lessons occurred when Rostropovich worked with such outstanding cellists as Natalya Gutman and in particular Jacqueline du Pré, both of whom he regarded as artists in their own right.

* *Sovetskaya Kultura* 1, 1966.

By the early 1960s, Rostropovich's classes came to rival those of the great piano teacher Genrikh (Heinrich) Gustavovich Neygauz (Neuhaus) in popularity. Neuhaus was a living legend for young Russians: an artist who represented that pre-revolutionary European culture whose humanistic traditions had been virtually destroyed by the Soviet regime. Rostropovich had got to know Neuhaus through Richter, the most famous of his pupils, and revered him not only for his musicianship and erudition, but for his 'humanity' and his warm unpretentious approach. Neuhaus taught music within a wider cultural context, constantly referring to literature and the visual arts: he was not interested in mere 'piano-playing' for its own sake. His classes were always overflowing with listeners, musicians young and old. Natalya Gutman recalls that while still a pupil at the Central Music School, she and her friend Irina Kandinskaya would play truant every Monday and Thursday morning in order to attend Neuhaus's Conservatoire classes.

Different as the two men were, Rostropovich admitted that it was Neuhaus's teaching style that he wished to emulate. I recall that in 1964, when Rostropovich suggested that I came to Moscow to study with him, he assured my parents, not without pride, that along with Neuhaus's, his classes were the most frequented at the Conservatoire. In fact, as the musicologist Manashir Yakubov vividly depicts:

The sphere of influence of Rostropovich the teacher extended far beyond the walls of his cello class. Not only was it his fame, but his incredible personal charm, his youth, energy, his easy communicative manner, his humour – in a word a certain unprofessorial 'non-solidity' that lent him such attraction and magnetism. Legends circulated about his student pranks, his astonishing witticisms and his tricks at parties and student skits. I remember in my last student year hearing rumours about a recent meeting of the Conservatoire Artistic Council, where Rostropovich, through his very 'naive' questioning, had extracted a detailed account of the 'amoral' deeds of students in the hostel and of the rather doubtful activities of the professors themselves.*

Indeed, with his love of the absurd, Rostropovich would recount with relish various comic incidents of Conservatoire life, such as the time he was upbraided by a Party activist when one of his students was caught kissing her boyfriend – horror of horrors – in the 'Krasny Ugolok' (The Red Corner), under Lenin's portrait! When Rostropovich's patience was

* M. Yakubov, 'Don Quixote', article written for this book.

strained at dreary Conservatoire staff meetings, he was likely to take the situation in hand, teasing and poking fun in a light-hearted way, provoking mirth without causing offence. Wherever he appeared at the Conservatoire, whether in class or in someone's office, he inspired an atmosphere of heightened expectancy and good humour. At the same time, like every other professor, Rostropovich was held responsible for his students' misdemeanours. Usually these concerned such insignificant offences as trying to get out of Physical Education or orchestra. Only a medical certificate could save a student from such social obligations as being sent with the 'voluntary' harvesting brigades to dig potatoes in the early autumn months. (As the Conservatoire files show, one of Rostropovich's students, Viktor Apartsev, risked being expelled for 'disruptive' behaviour in orchestra and for deliberate evasion of the potato-digging.)

Skipping the compulsory political classes, however, was a more serious matter under the Soviet regime, and in such cases no professor could justify a student's absences or bad marks. Hence when his Armenian student Vagram Saradzhan forgot to go and vote at a Party election (something that was obligatory under Soviet law), Rostropovich only just managed to save him from expulsion from the Conservatoire. As Karine Georgian remembers, Rostropovich was always willing to use his influence to help his students. When she was preparing for the Tchaikovsky competition, he urged her to take all her exams early so she would be free to practise. Then to her surprise, he appeared unexpectedly on the day of her political exams at the Faculty of Marxism and Leninism. The examining professors were flattered by Rostropovich's attention to them, and perceived the visit as a signal to be lenient to his student. Rostropovich would often make a phone call in the right place to sort out practical matters like borrowing an instrument from the state collection, or arranging the right contact to find a working position after graduation. He was also known to give certain students material aid – offering it in such a gentle, tactful manner that they would not feel embarrassed about accepting it.

Despite his high level of day-to-day involvement, Rostropovich nevertheless relied heavily on his assistant Stefan Timofeyevich Kalyanov and on the class pianist Aza Magamedovna Amintaeva to keep him up to date about his students' progress, their needs and the circumstances of their private life. Kalyanov became the class assistant at much the same time that Aza took over as class pianist, and his experience as an administrator allowed him to help students in any dealings they might have with official bureaucracy. One of the first things he did was to establish a library of cello music with Rostropovich's bowings and fingerings written into the parts. He would lend these to students to copy into their own part as they started studying the piece in question. More experienced students were expected to know how to select bowings and fingerings that reflected their own ideas and techniques, but for younger students, copying Rostropovich's solutions gave them an understanding of the 'grammar' of cello-playing. His markings had their own logic and musical 'literacy', and could easily be explained and justified.

Stefan Timofeyevich also took to writing Rostropovich's comments ('Here think of a ballerina's leap' or 'A wide expansive Russian landscape with birch trees') into the parts, and would repeat them whether or not they were applicable in a new context. Once in class Rostropovich took hold of a part when a pupil was playing the Debussy sonata. 'What's this here?' he asked '"A flying cretin"? Stefan, whatever does that mean?' 'But it is the image you gave in these bars.' 'Goodness, Tukh, I could be sent to prison for this. Just think, any normal self-respecting professor writes into his students' scores "more crescendo", or "move the tempo forward", and other such words of wisdom. And here is Rostropovich making idiotic remarks.' Rostropovich could make fun of Kalyanov's bureaucratic power, as on the unforgettable occasion when he walked into a shop near his dacha in Zhukovka with some students to buy some vodka. 'Vodka? There is no vodka to be had,' he was peremptorily informed by the shop assistant. 'That's a pity,' Rostropovich replied solemnly. 'Stefan Timofeyevich will be very dissatisfied. I don't know what Stefan Timofeyevich will do when he finds out about this.' 'Just a moment, let me see,' the shop assistant said. He went down to the store room and returned with a case of vodka. After that the words 'Stefan Timofeyevich will be very dissatisfied' took on a completely new meaning.

Aza Amintaeva was something of a mother figure to the students and would always lend a sympathetic ear to those who wished to unburden their problems. She saw all students regularly, rehearsing with them once or twice a week, as well as playing at lessons and in concerts with all the class. Aza was not only generous in giving time as was needed, but also helped students to understand Rostropovich's interpretative approach. Her total adulation of Slava was unshakeable. Sometimes difficulties arose when students wanted to do something their own way. 'Mstislav Leopoldovich plays it in this tempo, and with these fingerings and bowings,' she would pronounce, and that was that. However, the student was occasionally vindicated in class, when Rostropovich turned to him and said, 'Why play in such a fast tempo, I can see you are uncomfortable,' or, 'You have a small hand, find some fingerings that suit you, mine obviously don't.'

With her eastern temperament (she came from Makhachkala in Dagestan, on the Caspian Sea), Aza could shower a student with love and kindness, but if something went wrong she could be equally categorical in her dislike. Some felt that as Rostropovich became busier, he started to rely too much on her opinions, and that this was not always healthy.

But on the whole, Aza's warm smile and infectious laugh contributed greatly to the equable atmosphere of the class, where each student felt himself part of an extended family. Her relationship with Vagram (Vago) Saradzhan was a case in point. One of the class legends had its genesis in a rehearsal with Aza, during which Vago had difficulty coming in correctly in Prokofiev's concertino, in the recapitulation of the first theme of the first movement. He recalled that Aza was accenting the accompaniment in such a manner that he lost all sense of the beat. However often they repeated the bars in question, he couldn't get the entry right. At length Vago stopped and said, 'Aza Magamedovna, something must be done!' Aza found his plea so comical, that she recounted the story to Rostropovich. The phrase immediately became part of the class lexicon, and in almost any situation where a student came up against a difficulty, Rostropovich triumphantly produced the maxim: 'As the great Armenian illuminato and philosopher Saradzhan said, Aza Magamedovna, something must be done!'

Aza's diminutive figure – her black hair and striking features dominated by a somewhat crooked large nose – belied the force of her personality. Once, when Rostropovich happened to see her dozing on a sofa, he noticed that her profile, with its prominent nose and more than a hint of a black moustache underneath, reminded him of Stalin's. From then on he nicknamed her 'Osya' (the diminutive for Iosif or Joseph). After he left Russia, he sent Aza a gift of a Steinway piano with the letters 'OSYA' engraved over the keyboard.*

Rostropovich gave nicknames to almost all his friends, family and pupils. Kalyanov's was 'Tukh', derived from the word 'Petukh', meaning cockerel – his wavy, tufted hair probably brought to mind a cockerel's crest. Natasha Shakhovskaya was called 'Kozà' (goat), because of her stubbornness. Some of the more unflattering names seemed to come from Aza: two of her least favourite class members were 'The Trunk' and 'Rabbi'. Some students were mystified by their chosen nicknames. Vika Yagling asked Rostropovich why he called her 'ambarnaya' (barn-girl): 'Mstislav Leopoldovich, how should I understand it, barns are full of mice and rats?' 'What do you mean, Vikulya – barns are full of zerna' ('grain', with the double meaning of 'kernel').

For some reason, whenever he saw me, Rostropovich immediately sang a ditty in my honour: 'Lizanka, gde ty byla? U babushki?' (Lizanka, where have you been? At Grannie's?). Only many years later did I dare ask him what he meant by this, and he explained, 'I never quite knew where you would turn up from, whereas with my Soviet students I knew exactly where they were and what they were doing. They were out in the streets, so to speak, but you, being a foreigner, were different.' Another British student, Moray Welsh, was immediately dubbed 'Marusya', a diminutive of the female name Mariya, whereas Mariya Chaikovskaya, who was also called Lida at home, was presented in class as 'Mariya Lida Luisa Antoinette . . . but we'll not bother with all that. Any suggestions for a name? All right then, let's call her Manyunya for short.' But the generic name with which Rostropovich dubbed all his students and younger friends was simply 'starik' (old man), or 'starukha' (old woman) in the case of a woman. When Rostropovich discovered that Mischa Maisky's patronymic was Leopoldovich, like his own, he was named 'Starik Leopoldovich'. Somehow this idea of ridiculing the polarities in age served only to underline our professor's youthful vigour, even if he was some twenty to twenty-five years older than his 'old men' students. For their part, the students dubbed Rostropovich as 'Rostròp' (which in the broad-vowelled Muscovite accent came out as 'Rastràp') or as 'Chef',

* Receiving the piano turned out to be no easy matter for Aza. Soviet customs held the instrument for nearly two years, demanding an enormous sum of duty which she could not afford to pay, until Rostropovich found out and arranged for the necessary sum to be discharged.

although they always used the polite form of address with name and patronymic (Mstislav Leopoldovich) to his face.

Full-time attendance at the professor's class was an implicit obligation for his students. Rostropovich favoured the open-class system for many reasons: on the one hand, his students learnt to give performances, while on the other, they benefited from the objective observations they could make while others were being taught, without the nervous tension and self-involvement inevitable when playing oneself. Apart from anything else, hearing others play was a wonderful way of getting to know the cello repertoire; over the five-year study period, one heard an enormous quantity of music in class. Altogether, a great feeling of solidarity reigned: students gave each other tips, lent their music, compared notes, and cheered up despondent colleagues.

Often, Rostropovich would specifically suggest that one particular student helped another out. For example, he noticed one day that although I was working very hard, I seemed to be achieving little. He asked Vika Yagling to 'please go and see how Liza practises'. She did so, and was enormously helpful to me. Another time he asked Jackie du Pré to work with me on the Lalo concerto 'and impart some Spanish temperament' – I had some wonderfully inspiring sessions working with her. Rostropovich encouraged us to learn from every experience and every possible source. I soon discovered that I could gain a lot from speaking to violinists and pianists, and would ask for tips from the many talented students who lived in the same hostel. The violinist Dora Schwartzberg, for instance, helped me overcome my lack of self-assurance, imparting some of her abundantly positive confidence. I found it stimulating to think of ways to translate other instrumental processes to the medium of the cello.

New entrants to Rostropovich's class would always find their first working encounter with him a memorable experience – often it was somewhat intimidating, too. Rostropovich usually began with a general 'sounding out' of the personality, a testing of the student's reactions and an examination of his or her underlying emotional attitude towards music. Rostropovich would make his diagnosis instantaneously and give advice accordingly.

Tatyana Remenikova, a student of Valentin Berlinsky at the Ippolitov-Ivanov High School, recalls going to play for Rostropovich when she was in her last year at school:

Berlinsky took me to the Conservatoire, and when we entered Class 19, there was the usual exchange of hugs and kisses – an atmosphere I had never experienced before. Mstislav Leopoldovich seemed to me a huge man, with huge hands, who spoke very fast with a somewhat strange diction. He turned to Berlinsky, 'Well, *Starik* (old man), what has she prepared?' 'The Khatchaturian concerto.' I started playing, and after a while Mstislav Leopoldovich stopped me: 'Now, start again from the beginning, but play a half-tone lower.' I was overcome by a sinking feeling that I would mess it up and lose my chance of studying with him. But a strange thing happened: I overcame this sensation of panic, and started playing a half-tone down and went on for almost half a page until Mstislav Leopoldovich stopped me again. 'That's fine,' he said. I realised that I had overcome the first hurdle. At such first encounters Rostropovich needed to look you in the eye and check out your reactions, to see whether you were flexible. I found it highly significant that I had been able to overcome my initial feeling of paralysis, and managed to resolve the problem almost at once. Later Rostropovich set me tasks which initially seemed to me to be absolutely unattainable. Yet I somehow discovered unsuspected resources within me, an almost superhuman force which allowed me to tackle and fulfil each assignment.

At the beginning of each academic year Rostropovich would convoke the class for a meeting where he set each student his programme. By the early 1960s, he had established an 'initiation rite', where first-year students were set a new work to learn and bring to class from memory in two or three days. Passing this first 'ordeal by fire' was a signal of acceptance into the class family. As David Grigorian recalls:

The first classes were quite a shock to me. The initial class meeting took place on a Thursday. Mstislav Leopoldovich asked me, 'Balik, what works have you played?' (He always called me *Balik*, the Armenian word for 'child', since he loved Armenia, and liked to show off his few words of the language.) Under my father's tuition in Erevan, I had already built up a large repertoire. 'Goodness, what are we going to do, you've already played everything!' Mstislav Leopoldovich exclaimed. 'I know, Balik, you'll learn the Hindemith concerto, and play it from memory for Tuesday's class.' I had never even heard of Hindemith's concerto, and now I had four days to learn it. I borrowed the music from Viktor Apartsev, and went back to my room at the Kislovka hostel behind the Conservatoire. Conditions there were not easy: four students shared a room that also housed an upright piano. There were no other practice rooms, and the pianists claimed precedence in using the piano in the dormitory space. The communal kitchen was bagged by whoever got there first. Since I always seemed to arrive too late, the only place left for me to practise in was the bathroom. That's where I learnt the Hindemith concerto, working like a madman. On Monday I rehearsed it with Aza and on Tuesday I managed to play it from memory in class. And on Wednesday I played it at my first Conservatoire test. I had overcome the first trial by fire.

Like Grigorian, Remenikova entered Rostropovich's class in September 1964:

The first piece Mstislav Leopoldovich set me was the 'new' Haydn C major concerto, which had not yet been published in Russia; I was to play the whole concerto from memory and note-perfect at the next class in three days' time. I had to borrow the music from Professor Ginsburg, which was in itself not without incident, but I managed to escape his clutches. When I arrived home with the music, I felt so overwhelmed by the enormity of the task that I simply burst into tears. But there was nothing for it but to get down to work, and I managed to learn the concerto for Tuesday, under gun-point, as it were.

Now that I have taught for many years in the USA, I know that it would be almost impossible for a teacher in the West to make such demands on their students. But in those years, the general atmosphere at the Moscow Conservatoire was very exalted and there was tremendous competition and pressure. I felt I was being given a wonderful chance, and on no account could I afford to fail the challenges thrown at me.

Eleonora Testelets, who enrolled as a postgraduate in Rostropovich's Leningrad class in autumn 1962, initially did not realise what these challenges entailed:

Mstislav Leopoldovich always came up to Leningrad for a couple of days at a time, so our lessons were held in a very concentrated period. The first afternoon he gathered the class together and set us our new programmes. I was to come to class the next day having learnt Prokofiev's concertino. I went back to the hostel and studied all afternoon and evening. I managed to sort out the first movement and at least half of the second. Then I went to bed. Next morning when I came to the class it was packed full of students, not just cellists but pianists and violinists, who always flocked to hear him teach. When it was my turn, I sat down and played the first movement and got halfway through the second before coming to a halt. Mstislav Leopoldovich waved me on, 'Continue, continue, why have you stopped?' 'I'm afraid I haven't prepared any more.' He then turned round to me, 'And what were you doing last night?' 'Well I practised all evening, then I went to sleep.' He then said in a really cold tone of voice, 'Well, you shouldn't have gone to bed. You couldn't afford to go to sleep until you had finished your task. Why have you come to study with me? Under what guise do you think I'm going to teach you? Do you just want me to put bowings and fingerings in your part?' I felt so small, I wanted the earth to swallow me up. Tears welled up into my eyes, and my thoughts turned to home: 'Why have I left my lovely Riga? What am I doing here?' There I was used to being the best student in class. I went into the corridor and sobbed my heart out. Viktoria, the class pianist, came out to comfort me, and put her hand on my shoulder. 'Ellochka, didn't you see he was winking at the others, as if to say "Today she's going to get it from me." You'll see, everything will be all right.'

When I walked back into the class, Mstislav Leopoldovich beckoned me over to him. He was sitting, as was his wont, on the sofa in the middle of the classroom; he sat me next to him, and pulled my head down on his shoulder, as if to show he understood what I felt and was sorry for me. That first lesson was a lesson for life, for he showed that one should value every minute of time, and that it is possible to develop the ability to learn quickly, and prepare a piece in a matter of days. This in itself was a real training, which he continuously practised on himself. If insufficient demands are made of students, they are unlikely to discover their latent capacities. Through demanding 'the impossible' Rostropovich instilled in his students a belief in their own resources. In fact, what he asked was always possible.

This was not to say that Rostropovich's demands could not sometimes be perplexing. Sometimes he merely shoved a student's nose into a problem, leaving him to discover his own solutions. His philosophy in these cases was simple – he told the student to start thinking imaginatively, and referred him back to the score, reminding him:

The musical material has to correspond to the emotions you wish to convey. At home when you practise, you must define your task. You must be able to play the whole work through in your head, so that you understand how to search for the right sound and colour. For instance if the music conveys sadness, you have to go further in your definition of sadness: is it tenderly sad, inwardly tense, despondent, nostalgic, grieving or vulnerable? If you feel the mood in your mind, then you'll know how to reproduce it in sound; then you have only to check that the sound corresponds to what you hear in your inner ear. Your task, thus, is to organise sound within its musical framework.

Rostropovich often reiterates that his life's work consists of achieving this basic aim: 'I would say that I never attain more than half of the idea that I hear in my head! This is a weakness on my part, but I continue to live with the perspective of improvement. Of course it is a question of having the physical strength and the force of character to achieve the idea. But conceiving the idea and then implementing it represents the fundamental creative act in an artist's work throughout his lifetime.'

David Grigorian recalls that at one of his first lessons Rostropovich threw him the challenge of 'finding sound':

My lesson took place in Rostropovich's flat, where his music room had black leather padded walls, which served as soundproofing, allowing him to work late at night. Naturally the dry acoustic did nothing to flatter the sound. When Mstislav Leopoldovich rebuked me then for having no sound, I made the mistake of suggesting that it was because of the soundproofing. 'No, Balik, it's you – you don't know how to produce a good sound. If you can make the cello sound in here, it'll certainly be alright in the hall. You're to come to your next lesson with a good sound.' However, Rostropovich didn't tell me *how* I should go about it. This was a deliberate tactic, for he wanted me to rack my brains and start thinking for myself. First and foremost I had to discover what I myself wanted in terms of sound. Initially I felt lost and helpless, and the rules that I knew didn't seem to help – bow near the bridge, wide vibrato and so on. At that stage I closed my eyes and tried to conjure up the visual image of Rostropovich playing: I lowered my arm, and tried to feel the shoulder weight, particularly at the point of the bow. In the end, through experiment, I was able to improve my sound very rapidly.

Mark Drobinsky likewise recalls that Rostropovich made him question all he had hitherto learned about sound:

I came from Baku, and once when Mstislav Leopoldovich was on a tour there, he heard me play. Immediately he arranged for me to transfer from the Baku Conservatoire to Moscow while I was in my fifth year; this was very unusual, but he understood that I needed to get out of the provincial backwater. In Moscow I started off in Sviatoslav Knushevitsky's class, and only the following year, in 1962, did I start my studies with Rostropovich as a postgraduate. My first lesson took place in Rostropovich's flat on Ogaryov Street, and I played Prokofiev's sonata, which I had been longing to perform. In Baku nobody considered Prokofiev to be a worthwhile composer, they just laughed at his music, and at that of Shostakovich. I hadn't been playing for long when Mstislav Leopoldovich stopped me and said, 'You know, you are playing with such a beautiful sound!' I could tell from his sardonic look that this remark was no compliment. It was quite unsettling for me, as I had always been taught to aim for the loveliest sound possible; here was Rostropovich telling me that sound meant something else. Given that I had spent the last year studying with Knushevitsky, who was renowned for the beauty of his sound, it was even harder to comprehend. But it made me see that Knushevitsky's idea of sound actually made no concessions to the mood of the music. Already, from my first lesson, Mstislav Leopoldovich was starting to work with me on timbre and colour. I was astounded by his revelations.

When a first-year cellist arrived with wonderful instrumental credentials, Rostropovich often decided that it was a good idea to show them they didn't know everything already. Mikhail Utkin, a pupil of Kalyanov at the Central Music School, had won first prize in a youth competition in Prague:

By the time I entered the Conservatoire in 1970, at the age of seventeen, I was used to playing concerts, and felt confident that my technical level was sufficiently high to be ready to work on artistic repertoire. But Rostropovich thought otherwise, and said that I still needed to work on polishing my technique. At the first lesson, he asked me, 'Listen, old man, have you played the Davydov concertos?' I had to confess that I hadn't; somehow this stage of work had been bypassed with Kalyanov. 'Right, you are to learn all four Davydov concertos and also the *Concert Allegro*, then we can move on. Bring the first concerto to the next class from memory.' This was on Tuesday morning. I got hold of the music that afternoon and started work. The next day I rehearsed the concerto with Aza, and the day after I managed to play it in class from memory. I had passed the first test. In the end I learnt the first two concertos and the *Concert Allegro*, after which I was allowed to pass on to 'normal' repertoire.

Mischa Maisky started studying in Rostropovich's class in 1966 after winning sixth prize at the Tchaikovsky competition. He similarly recalls being set a Davydov concerto to learn in two days, as if Rostropovich wished to remind him of the distance he had to travel before becoming a concert artist. Vago Saradzhan, on the other hand, remembers being set a completely different series of tasks for his first lesson.

I first played for Rostropovich when I was a pupil of the Erevan Music School. While still at school I participated successfully in the inter-Caucasian competition (*Vsekavkazkij konkurs*), and rather against my will (and partly at Rostropovich's instigation) I played at the All-Union competition in February 1966, where I was awarded a diploma. The competition afforded the opportunity of re-establishing contact with Rostropovich, who agreed to take me in his class from the following September. I was worried that I wouldn't pass the entrance examination, because I had got behind in general school subjects after preparing for these two big cello competitions. When I came to Moscow I confided my anxieties to Mstislav Leopoldovich, who told me not to worry: 'But let me give you an important piece of advice: remember, silence is worth its weight in gold. If you don't know something, just keep quiet!' When I entered Rostropovich's class, he paid me – or rather my teacher in Erevan, Aleksandr Chaushian – a great compliment: 'Vago, you are very well prepared on the instrument, I don't have to change anything. You have your first teacher to thank for that!' Then at my first lesson he set me an unusual task. First he instructed me to visit the Tretyakov Gallery and he also gave me a list of books to read. He wanted to widen my cultural horizons: I was to go and look at paintings and to observe their different styles. I read all the books conscientiously, and afterwards Mstislav Leopoldovich cross-examined me, and asked what features I had enjoyed most, and told me to describe the plot, the character of the various protagonists and so on.

Rostropovich had a very strong intake of first-year students in the 1966/67 academic year: apart from Mischa Maisky and Vagram Saradzhan, his three other new students were Ivan Monighetti, Miron Yampolsky and Misha Milman. Miron had studied with Rostropovich since entering the Central Music School, and was on familiar terms with him through his father. There was a certain complicity between them, and one could hear Rostropovich greet Miron with strange verbal signals such as 'Oits'. Miron had actually been accepted in the Conservatoire in September 1963, but hardly had he started studying (he had been obliged to go and dig potatoes as part of a 'voluntary' student brigade) when he was forcibly enlisted for military service and allocated to a submarine unit in the Soviet navy. Having fulfilled three years' duty, he was now the oldest of the group of entrants.

The new intake was treated to some new pedagogical shock tactics that Rostropovich had been keeping up his sleeve for them. Apart from the usual new work to learn within a few days, he decided that each cellist should learn the piano accompaniment of two short pieces. The new students were paired together and were expected to play both piano and cello in the same duo combination at their first lesson. It worked for some of them, but for Misha Milman, who did not know how to play the piano, it was a very hard experience. Saradzhan recalls, 'I was asked to bring the piano part of the arrangement of Chopin's D flat major Nocturne for cello and piano. I prepared it as best I could, then at the lesson Mstislav Leopoldovich asked me to transpose it down a semitone. At a certain point he grabbed somebody's cello and told me to accompany him! This was hardly a conventional cello lesson, but was typical of the surprises he could play on us, which served to stimulate maximum flexibility in us.'

Rather than studying 'technique' as a discipline in its own right, Rostropovich preferred to develop students' technical skills through the preparation of 'study' works such as the Davydov concertos, in which musical merit was by no means lacking. He expected his students to get on with scales and various arid exercises on their own, and if in need of assistance, to study them patiently under Stefan Kalyanov's guidance. The Conservatoire curriculum required first- and second-year students to demonstrate their technical abilities at an exam that was held at the end of the winter semester, where each student played two studies and scales and arpeggios in all keys. Silvija Naruňaite remembers that one year, Rostropovich arrived back from a concert tour just in time to hear his students play at the technical exam. He was extremely dissatisfied by what he heard, and convoked the class straight away. 'I hope it's clear to you what you will be doing over the winter holidays,' he announced to the first- and second-year students. 'You'll be learning to play scales. When you come back our first class will be dedicated to scales, played in time, in tune, in every key and with every possible bowing combination.'

Scales were regarded as an essential part of a cellist's life, a daily habit like brushing one's teeth. Any technical problem encountered in a piece of music could be transferred to a scale or a study and resolved initially there. As Rostropovich would argue:

When I was younger I too played lots of studies. I consider them to be an important moment in our working life. When you play a study, you must wring everything there is out of it. For instance if it is written in triplets, you can play it in various bowing strokes and combinations. Three notes slurred to a bow is straightforward, but to play two slurred and one separate is less simple, let alone slurring in groups of two when the basic rhythmic pattern is in three. One must exercise the imagination, and invent all kind of bowing variants, with an ascending level of complexity. Thereby one develops the coordination which is fundamental to our skills. Every study needs to be played until you have squeezed the life out of it. Then you can throw it out, since by now it's nothing more than a flogged horse, which has no further use. If you start studying the musical repertoire before your technique is adequate then you risk destroying a living thing.

Rostropovich would often work with first-year students on improving their sound quality, an aspect of technique in which they frequently lagged behind. Much emphasis was placed on an even, sustained legato, requiring great bow control. Any 'bumps' or 'bulges' in the legato were ridiculed as 'making sausages' – a reference to a string of sausages connected by their skins. The task of finding a good sound, he explained, meant first and foremost developing acute inner hearing. Rostropovich noted that 'although in basic sound production the bow is of utmost importance, the left hand contributes the finer detail in an infinite spectrum of colours, with many nuances and shades, requiring an immense variety of vibrato.' In the Dvořák concerto, for instance, the opening theme requires a large 'dramatic' vibrato, whereas the second subject needs more refinement of vibrato to suit the mood of emotional nostalgia. The finale's coda requires an incredible intensity and pressure of left-hand vibrato while remaining in a very quiet dynamic, so as to evoke the impression of a heartrending farewell.

To develop their understanding of the precise relationship between the bow and the left-hand vibrato, Rostropovich would set his students short cantilena pieces in styles chosen to match their own particular needs. In the case of Tanya Remenikova, for instance, Rostropovich had identified her major defect as an excessively narrow and tight vibrato: 'He immediately set to work on this problem, and told me to strive for a wider, richer, and more luxuriantly expressive vibrato, but also to work on a greater diversity of vibrato and bowings so as to achieve an enormous gamut of colour and timbre.' Similarly, fingerings and bowings had to be thought of within the musical context. The ability to imagine sound was the crucial factor: 'For musicians it's more difficult to find a wonderful palette of colours than for a painter, who has something concrete to start with – tubes of paint. We have to create colour through the imagination. It is funda-mentally important to know how to produce variety in colours and nuances in order to become a musician, and not remain a mere instrumentalist.'

An ability to perceive and convey the music's initial impulse was essential to this process: 'A performance starts with an idea in the musician's head, but for the audience it starts with the performer's gesture. If a piece starts forte (for instance, the opening of the Dvořák concerto), then a large, energetic gesture produces an immediate effect. But you cannot start the quiet, intimate opening of Beethoven's A major sonata, for example, with a large gesture, as that would confound the audience's expectations.' As the Bulgarian cellist Stefan Popov, a student at the Conservatoire in the early 1960s, notes:

For Rostropovich, the gesture was a natural part of the music. But for us students it was not necessarily so easy. If we set out to imitate him, our performance risked seeming like a cheap reproduction. Sometimes one had to laugh, because his suggestions could be taken in the wrong way; it was difficult to refrain from imitation of such a forceful personality. I recall him once asking Mariya Chaikovskaya to make a sudden explosive attack into the second movement of the Shostakovich sonata. She had to achieve an almost theatrical effect, finishing the last slow quiet note of the first movement at the point of the bow, Then without breaking the mood, she was to lift the bow slowly off the string, hold it poised in the air, gently relaxing the right wrist so that the point of the bow dropped. There was to be no hint of what was to come. And then she was to swoop down to the nut in an energetic movement which served as the up-beat gesture to the Allegro. She obeyed everything to the letter, but the effect was comical because her gesture was totally artificial – it had not come from within her.

Rostropovich frequently used visual ideas to stimulate students, believing that an inspired choice of image could be more effective than a set of precise instructions such as 'wider vibrato, slower bow speed, nearer the bridge, more crescendo'. On occasion, of course, students failed to react as expected to the associative image, and sometimes Rostropovich had to resort to what he called 'kindergarten' methods. If this happened with his advanced students, the instruction was invariably transmitted with some irritation, and he became particularly cross with students who constantly required pedantic explanations. In his Leningrad class, as Ella Testelets recalls, he had several extremely good postgraduate students, but many of them were simply aiming to achieve a good job in an orchestra – Rostropovich used to refer to such students as 'the rationalists'. One student in particular, Mikhail Gel'fandbein, was for ever cross-questioning his professor, seeking logical rationales for his suggestions. One day Rostropovich had had enough. 'Now Misha,' he said, 'it's my turn to put a question to you. If you know the answer, then I'll agree to respond to your questions. If not, you will refrain from questioning me for the rest of the year.' Misha agreed to the conditions. 'Tell me then: why, when one comes from the street and enters somebody's house, one is invited to wash one's hands, but not one's feet?' The riddle had no logical answer, of course, and Rostropovich had made his point.

The sheer amount of repertoire that students were obliged to learn very quickly was one of the most demanding aspects of studying with Rostropovich. For example, at a series of three concerts of Soviet music given to mark the fiftieth anniversary of the October revolution, several students had to perform two difficult works within a couple of days of each other (concertos were usually divided between two students). The marathon programmes that ensued give a clear idea of the nature and the pace of work in Rostropovich's classes:

29 October 1967

Yuri Levitin, Sonata (Viktor Shpiller and Mikhail Milman)
Boris Chaikovsky, Concerto (Tatyana Remenikova and Miron Yampolsky)

Interval

Nikolay Myaskovsky, Sonata no. 2 (Elizabeth Wilson and Ivan Monighetti)
Karen Khatchaturian, Sonata (Mariya Chaikovskaya)
Dmitri Shostakovich, Concerto no. 1 (Lyudmila Koval and David Grigorian)

31 October 1967

Yuri Shaporin, Aria, Intermezzo and Scherzo (Svetlana Gornovitova)
Mechislav Weinberg, Sonata for cello solo (Victoria Yagling)
Shostakovich, Concerto no. 2 (Tatyana Dikhtyar, Mikhail Maisky)

Interval

Prokofiev, *Sinfonia Concertante* (Boris Shishkin, David Geringas)
Aram Khatchaturian, *Concerto-Rhapsody* (Karine Georgian)

1 November 1967

Kabalevsky, Sonata, second and third movements (Mikhail Milman)
Glière, Concerto, first movement (Ivan Monighetti)
Shebalin, Sonata, first and second movements (Miron Yampolsky)
Vlasov, Concerto, second and third movements (David Geringas)

Interval

Lev Knipper, *Concerto Monologue* (Tatyana Remenikova)
Tikhon Khrennikov, Concerto (Victoria Yagling)
Arno Babadjanian, Concerto (David Grigorian)
Evgeny Golubiev, Concerto, second and third movements (Mariya
    Chaikovskaya)

If celebrating Soviet music seemed like hard work for performers
and listeners alike, then Rostropovich also gave his class some unique
opportunities that were thoroughly enjoyable. In February 1966 he
organised a class evening of baroque concertos, where his students
shared a concerto between them. Rostropovich gathered together a
student string orchestra and directed concertos by Vivaldi, J. C. and
C. P. E. Bach, Tartini and Boccherini from the harpsichord.
    Later on, he developed an exchange with the Kiev Conservatoire,
and on three occasions took the entire class down to the Ukrainian
capital. In April 1969, as a fifth-year student, I participated in the
concert in Kiev, playing Beethoven's Seven Variations on a Theme
from *The Magic Flute*, and enjoyed every minute of the trip.
Rostropovich himself gave a concert with the local orchestra and held
an open masterclass for the Kiev students, and his Moscow students
played a concert in the Conservatoire hall. There was also time for

sightseeing, and together we visited the magnificent cathedral of St Sofia and saw the Kievo-Pecherskaya Lavra on the Dnieper, with the shrunken relics of monks preserved in the caves where this important monastery had originated. We were handsomely entertained to supper by the family of one of our class members, Lyuda Koval (affectionately known as 'Golusha' in class*) in their small cottage on the outskirts of town. When Rostropovich discovered that the toilet was at the bottom of the garden, he instructed us to use it before it grew dark, which was, as it happened, excellent advice. A feast had been prepared, with a table groaning with national dishes and Gorilka (Ukrainian vodka, spiced up by a hot pepper inserted in the bottle); even Rostropovich found it difficult to keep up with the toasts.

A year later Rostropovich returned to Kiev with the class. This time he conducted a concert featuring four soloists who were candidates for the forthcoming Tchaikovsky competition: Saradzhan performed the Dvořák concerto, Geringas the first Shostakovich concerto, Grigorian the second movement of Prokofiev's *Sinfonia Concertante* and Victoria Yagling Haydn's C major concerto.

Many of us also travelled to Leningrad to hear Natalya Gutman's final recital for her postgraduate diploma in June 1968, where she played three sonatas: Beethoven's Op. 102, no. 2, Brahms's Op. 99, and Britten's sonata in C, Op. 65. A party was held in her honour at Yura Loevsky's apartment on Nevsky Prospect, and the festivities continued until the small hours, when we all walked down to the Neva in the glorious white night.

In Moscow, during the second half of the 1960s, class concerts were usually celebrated at Victoria Yagling's apartment, where her parents warmly welcomed the hungry throngs of students. The post-mortem on our performances was held as we sat at table, generously supplied with food and drink. For the most part, Rostropovich refrained from scolding us too much: he was always brilliantly entertaining on these occasions, telling jokes and stories, talking of his plans, and creating a mood of general hilarity. Mischa Maisky recalls the party at Vika's house after the class concert of 31 October 1967, at which he had played the second and third movements of Shostakovich's second concerto:

* Golubushka is a term of endearment, derived from Golub (dove). But the nickname Golusha was undoubtedly also associated in our minds with the Ukrainian national dish of dumplings, known as *Golubtsy*.

This concerto loses a lot when played with piano, because many of the orchestral colours and percussion effects are completely impossible to convey. I remember very clearly how in class Rostropovich would try and imitate the percussion section at the close of the finale, emptying his pockets of coins and keys and improvising a jangling percussive effect. But one couldn't do this at a concert. However, just before I went on to stage, I had an idea. I was brushing down my suit with a wooden clothes brush, and I thought that if I hit the chair with this brush, I could imitate the effect of the clap of the *frusta* at the orchestral climax, just before the cello cadenza. I hid the brush in my pocket, and got it out at the right moment. It may have been a good idea, but unfortunately it didn't come off very well, since my jacket got in the way and muffled the sound of the blow on the chair. Later that evening, at Vika's flat, everybody discussed this effect; some said that it was an excellent idea, others that it was stupid. Mstislav Leopoldovich kept silent until somebody asked him what he thought. He replied rather slowly and deliberately, 'Well, yes, it was a rather good idea. But you know what it sounded like to me? As if Aza Magamedovna's bra had snapped open just at that moment!' There were roars of laughter, but at least I had tried!

Despite all the merriment, working with Rostropovich demanded a great deal of resourcefulness and self-discipline from his students, as easy answers were seldom on offer. As Yuri Loevsky, a postgraduate student in Leningrad during the 1960s, puts it:

Rostropovich was the most wonderful teacher in the world for those who had sufficient preparation and were mature enough to work with him. During the five years I studied with him he never once made the kind of pedagogical remark such as 'Elbow higher, wrist lower, shift on the first finger', and so on. He was the first teacher to direct our attention to the musical structure, to the form and development of the work we were studying. What was amazing was his absolute search for the truth, for the final result.

The 'artistic truth' signified that instrumental skills were subordinate to the music. If a student got too involved with a technical problem, Rostropovich would chide him: 'It's the music that's important, not the bow stroke,' and the same could be said for fingerings. As Yuri Falik observes:

Rostropovich's system of fingering was very natural in cellistic terms, very rational and very comfortable, and always served the musical idea. I would say that the underlying principle of a fingering was never conceived for its comfort, but for its fundamental expressive quality. Mstislav Leopoldovich had the same capacity to select the bow stroke which best suited the musical character of the piece. Sometimes one started by thinking that his suggested bowings were uncomfortable, but then one discovered that they fitted the articulation and aided the phrasing. I closely observed how Rostropovich played himself, and adopted certain aspects of his left-hand technique. For instance, so as to achieve a beautiful singing tone in the higher positions, he would avoid using thumb position in the conventional manner. Thus, in expressive passages he preferred not to use the thumb and taught that the thumb needed to be released from 'pressing' the string down, since it tends to make the hand rigid and impedes the production of a cantabile tone. Mstislav Leopoldovich also used the little finger in high positions, but to a lesser extent than Shafran, who in this respect had a truly violinistic technique.

Natalya Shakhovskaya recalls that in her case, Rostropovich never imposed fingerings and bowings:

Sometimes he might ask, 'Why are you doing such an idiotic fingering?' or another time he might say, 'Personally I would do a different fingering, but you can leave yours as it is, since it seems to work for you.' Any changes to fingerings and bowings were suggested exclusively for musical reasons, and colour and timbre had enormous significance for Mstislav Leopoldovich. Just looking at his edition of the Shostakovich sonata one sees that the fingerings are devised to reflect the mood: a specific dark intensity in the third movement, for instance, when he goes high up the G string in the third movement Largo. His fingerings do not necessarily cater for ease or comfort; often a passage could be played in a simpler way, using lower positions. The artistic effect, and not convenience, was what counted.

Rostropovich also paid a great deal of attention to modifying vibrato in accordance with the use of the bow, as Shakhovshaya explains:

The aim was a perfect knowledge of the reciprocal influence of bow speed, weight and vibrato. One had to develop a myriad of different combinations of these effects. Mstislav Leopoldovich liked to explain how to give expression to repeated notes of the same pitch through varying the vibrato on each note; sometimes he suggested substituting different fingers. In all the expressive cantabile passages in the Dvořák concerto – take the opening of the slow movement, for instance – the vibrato was to carry from one note to the next without ever stopping; this required the smoothest possible bow changes and imperceptible string crossings. Rostropovich demanded that the vibrato should be transmitted from one finger to another without the slightest change in sound quality. All this, of course, is a matter of instrumental skill, but it has to be totally allied to the musical concept. Mstislav Leopoldovich defined this side of technique as 'the expression of the inner hearing'.

Shifting and glissandi were other aspects of left-hand technique to which Rostropovich devoted much time in class, as Ella Testelets explains:

Mstislav Leopoldovich was always guided by the rules of good taste in shifting, and was firm about where one could permit slides on one finger, and where it would be out of place. He made a lot of reference to singing techniques, for he had a great understanding of vocal expression. For instance in the third variation of Tchaikovsky's *Rococo Variations* he favoured wide stretches to avoid too many glissandos. He was very scrupulous in his attitude to glissando, and I remember this in contexts as different as Bloch's *Schelomo* and Shostakovich's second concerto.

There were few students who consciously chose to ignore Rostropovich's suggestions about fingering and shifting, but Saradzhan was one who disliked having fingerings imposed on him:

I wasn't the normal obedient boy, and could be quite cheeky. Once Mstislav Leopoldovich asked me to play a passage with his suggested fingering. I managed to do this, but when I got home, I looked at the passage again and decided to reinstate what I did before. I preferred my own idea. When I played the piece for him again he let it pass. But when he suggested a fingering to me the next time, he also explained exactly why he wanted it this way. He realised that I wasn't going to comply without being given a reason.

Perhaps in the case of Saradzhan, Rostropovich felt that his natural facility and in-built virtuoso technique impeded his ability to think beyond the superficial effect. Once, when he was playing the Allegro from Locatelli's sonata, Rostropovich said, 'Vago, this is a very dull performance, do something with it.' Vago played the same repeated passage with three different fingerings, but the musical expression did not change in any way, to the considerable irritation of our professor.

Rostropovich worked with every student differently, and on occasion could be very tough. His greatest hatred was for laziness, but he was willing to adopt a gentler tone with those more sensitive performers who clearly suffered from nerves. He knew how to convey criticisms indirectly, often through a proverb or well-known saying. As David Grigorian remembers:

Mstislav Leopoldovich never said anything rough or insulting to me; in general he never wanted to humiliate anybody unnecessarily. If somebody's playing was dull or boring, for instance, he might use the old Russian saying '*umerlà, ne umerlà – tol'ko vremya provelà*' (She died, but didn't pass away, all she did was pass the time of day).* This way of passing comment was done with so much humour that while you had to laugh, you were also made to realise that your playing had been insipid and meaningless, and you did your best not to provoke such comment again. I recall one lesson when I failed to produce the necessary sense of climax in the central

* This particular proverb referred to the ancient village tradition in which old women would lie down in their coffins when they felt ready to die. But often they weren't ill and nothing happened, so after a while they had to get up and resume their normal life, to the derision of their neighbours.

section of a work. Mstislav Leopoldovich stopped me, saying, 'Balik, do you realise, that instead of a mountain you've just produced a molehill!' This instantly made me see where I had gone wrong in my understanding of the structure.

We all knew it was not easy to win genuine praise from Rostropovich. A student could feel pleased if at the end of the lesson he said, '*Ochen' neploxo!*' (Not at all bad!). Many aspects of the masterclass system were quite nerve-racking: students had to be ready to give a performance whatever the conditions, and needed the same kind of mental preparation to play in class as they required to perform an important concert. Many tears were shed (and not just by the female students) when one failed to meet the high standards demanded or was sent away with a sardonic remark from Rostropovich.

The unpredictability of our classes caused additional stress. Sometimes our professor was very late in arriving: perhaps he had been summoned peremptorily to the Ministry of Culture or had to sort out problems at Gosconcert. He would phone through to the Conservatoire office, leaving messages saying when he expected to arrive. Once I remember waiting in class for Rostropovich from ten in the morning until the early evening. No student wanted to miss the opportunity of a lesson, but it was quite stressful to have to wait so long. I wrote to my parents, describing this strange lesson in a letter dated 20 October 1966:

On Monday I had my lesson with 'chef Rostrop'. He started working at 7.00 p.m. and worked unrelentingly with twelve students in all until 3.00 a.m. My lesson started at 10.45 and finished at 11.30, which left me feeling like the ashy ruins of Troy, tired and hysterical. Still I had a good lesson and he helped me a lot, but I fear I continue to play like a pig.

On another occasion when the class had waited throughout the day, Rostropovich eventually appeared around seven o'clock in the evening. As a form of apology, he promptly invited the whole class to supper at the professors' canteen, empathising with the hungry, jaded look in our eyes. Afterwards he took us back to his apartment, where once again he taught through to the small hours of the morning. Rostropovich had become wary of conducting his after-hours teaching in the Conservatoire building, since on one previous occasion when he had continued into the small hours, the whole class had been locked inside the building. An enterprising student managed to open a window on the first floor, and Rostropovich led the way in making the considerable leap down into the courtyard, gallantly helping the girl students down. Since the Moscow transport system had stopped functioning, he then drove home those students who lived furthest away. With Rostropovich, nothing could be taken for granted. He could surprise us by arriving in class early, and then he would grumble loudly when the first student appeared: 'Goodness, where have you been, lazy lie-a-bed! Get your cello out at once and start playing!' Saradzhan recalls once provoking his professor's wrath through his lack of punctuality:

I usually came to the class early as I liked to warm up before the lesson. Mstislav Leopoldovich was scheduled to start teaching at ten, but seldom arrived much before eleven-thirty. Once when I was in my first year, Mstislav Leopoldovich gave me an appointment for a nine o'clock lesson. For some reason that day I didn't wake up till ten, and by the time I reached the Conservatoire it was after eleven. Even from outside the class door, I noticed an unusual hush. I walked into the class. Mstislav Leopoldovich was sitting in his armchair, but nobody was playing, and his students were all seated, waiting in icy silence. 'Ah,' he said as I walked in. 'At last. So you have decided to honour us with your presence. Excellent. And now you can go straight home. One should come to one's lesson on time.' He was absolutely furious, and a terrible scandal ensued. Rostropovich announced that he would have me thrown out of the Conservatoire and send me to the army. I was very upset, but also quite angry. I accused him of wanting to ruin my hands. 'No, old man,' he said, 'I will be sending you to be a clerk, not a soldier. I want you to learn some basic discipline, and how to get up in the morning.' It was a terrible lesson for me, and after that I was never late.

All these experiences taught us much about life as well as about the cello. Rostropovich encouraged us to learn from everything that went on around us, to exercise our musical curiosity and to develop our specific interests. He was interested in his students' hobbies: for instance, he was anxious that Ivan Monighetti would not damage his hands while indulging his passion for horse-riding. As Mikhail Utkin noted, he wanted to know his students' reactions to everything: 'Once I met Rostropovich at the Bolshoi Theatre when I had gone to see Rimsky-Korsakov's opera *The Invisible City of Kitezh*, with Svetlanov conducting. At the next class Mstislav Leopoldovich asked me what my impressions were, and then he in turn talked at length about the opera, explaining his ideas and illustrating them at the piano.'

Rostropovich's immense experience of the concert platform was a vital element in his teaching. Whether putting together interesting programmes for class evenings or giving instruction during the masterclasses, his aim was to prepare the student to view the concert platform as a place of learning and discovery. His example showed us that the intense concentration required in performance could also produce a dimension of freedom, allowing the artist to experiment with colours and timbre and to gain a greater sensation of space, which contributed a deeper meaning to silences and pauses. In a concert, he showed us, we could enter a state of mind that allowed us to create a magical atmosphere, where inspirational insights sharpened the responses and suggested new ways of phrasing. A whole new set of circumstances comes into being on stage: adrenalin brings heightened perceptions, and an acute awareness of the invisible thread that connects a performer to his audience. The intangible frisson in a hall is the result of shared experience – of a large number of people, as in a church congregation, centring their attention on the same thing. Rostropovich's personality as a performer directly showed us how liberating it was to enlarge one's horizons, and to extend one's musical thinking beyond the limitations of the instrument.

INTERLUDE 4

Karine Georgian

My first contact with Rostropovich goes back to when I studied at the Gnesins' Musical School with my father. One day I was playing at a class concert and performing quite a difficult virtuoso piece, Davydov's Concert Allegro. To my immense surprise Rostropovich dropped by to hear part of the concert. I think maybe he had heard about me and wanted to check out how I played, although I still find it difficult to believe.

I had had a rigorous training with my father, and was given daily cello lessons from an early age. At home my practice, even if not 'checked', was always 'overheard' from the next-door room. These years of preparation with my father cost me a lot in terms of my human relationship with him, but they did give me a firm technical grounding. I am sure that from a technical point of view at least, I was able to play Davydov's Concert Allegro quite well.

In the summer of 1962 I finished school and took the entry exams for the Conservatoire. I had no hesitation in putting down Rostropovich as my choice of teacher. About this time, I had my first lesson with him, which would decide whether he could accept me. I was going to play the second movement of Prokofiev's Sinfonia Concertante for him, and I was absolutely terrified.

Mstislav Leopoldovich invited me to come to his flat on Ogaryova Street. When I came through the door, the first thing he asked was whether I'd like something to eat. I was already pretty nervous, but I dared not refuse, even though I didn't feel at all hungry. So I sat down at the table on the edge of my chair, very much on my best behaviour. Then he produced a plate of fried eggs.

Knife and fork in hand, I started trying to eat them. Gradually it started to dawn on me that these eggs weren't real, but made from rubber – something I'd never encountered or even heard of before! I felt highly embarrassed at having believed the maestro had cooked an inedible meal. I don't remember if he gave me something real to eat afterwards – I suppose he did. Seeing that I was in a state of high tension when I arrived, he probably thought that this joke was a good way to relax me.

Incidentally Rostropovich played a far worse trick on Professor Lev Solomonovich Ginsburg – he must have bought several of these rubber toys when he was on tour in the United States, and amongst them was a rubber hammer. One day Ginsburg called by his flat – they were neighbours in the same block – to find Mstislav Leopoldovich standing on a ladder, pretending to fix a shelf. Turning round abruptly to Ginsburg, with a horrifying smirk, he jumped down like a gorilla from the ladder and banged the rubber hammer on the poor man's bald pate. You can imagine his shock – it was lucky he didn't have a heart attack.

After my own introductory diversion, we settled down to the serious business of the lesson. Technically, I was able to play all the notes in the Prokofiev. But Mstislav Leopoldovich rightly said that my sound production was not at the same level as the rest of my playing: he sensed that I was very tense both physically and as a person.

He decided to test me out, and see how well my mind worked. He suddenly stopped me and asked me to play an exercise in double-stops in which one voice moves in quavers and the other against it in triplets, then the same idea with triplets and quadruplets moving against each other. To do this satisfactorily you not only need great finger independence, but also quick reflexes and sufficient thought control. Just as I thought I had got it, he would ask me to change the function of the two voices. My eyes opened wide with shock, but eventually I somehow managed. What was interesting was that he needed to know what my immediate reaction was, and to see how one responded in a difficult situation. Can the brain keep working under stress?

This lesson served to tell him exactly how he needed to proceed with me. On the spot, he drew up a list of slow cantilena pieces: my first task on entering his class in September would be to work with him on problems of tone production, in order to achieve more variety and better quality in my sound. He asked me to think of the specific type of colour and vibrato I wanted for each piece, varying them to suit the music in question. Among the things he set me were Glazunov's Chant du Menestrel, *and arrangements of various piano pieces such as a Rachmaninov* Prelude *and Debussy's* Clair de Lune *and* Minstrels. *During the first three months or so, he watched carefully over my process of study, and we worked in depth on this aspect of my playing. Mstislav Leopoldovich wanted me to achieve complete freedom of the right arm, to play with an awareness of the arm's heavy mass: 'Relax, feel the weight from the shoulder.'*

He spoke about this in detail, as he wanted to solve these problems before tackling 'artistic' problems and studying the main repertoire. When I played something neatly and tidily, but without expression or character, he would tease me about playing with the 'little Gnesins' bow strokes' (Gnesinskie shtrishoshki) – this description was definitely intended to be disparaging.

This period of study with him was very interesting. He didn't say much, in fact, about my bow technique, and never tried to alter anything beyond instilling the concept of weight and freedom. But as far as the left hand was concerned, it was another matter. When I first came to him I played everything – whether fast technical passages or slow singing legato – with the same rounded position of the left hand and fingers, articulating vertically. I did so also in thumb position. He pointed out that although this worked for the technical passages, it limited the possibilities of expression. In order for me to produce a good singing cantilena, he asked me to use the pads of the fingers more, and to vary the position and weight of the fingers, elongating them where necessary.

All this produced quite a lot of conflict at home, for my father had grown up with a different concept of left-hand technique. He was convinced that Rostropovich was wrong, and I had to defend my new discoveries. After all, my father overheard my practising, and couldn't prevent himself from making comments.

Rostropovich worked insistently on expression and sound production until his ideas became second nature to me. They meant that I could play the Rachmaninov Prelude, *for instance, with an awareness of the different colours and styles of cantilena sound involved. We were soon able to transfer these discoveries to the rest of my work, and to start on the main repertoire. Mstislav Leopoldovich also helped me become aware of my tension and rigidity, showing me that it was not only a physical problem of stiff shoulders, but a matter of inner psychological tension.*

Quite soon after we joined his class, Rostropovich would usually give us a nickname, which would stick. Mine was 'Rukha', derived from 'starukha' (old woman). A little later in our studies, I was playing the Brahms E minor sonata in class. It was all good in one sense, perfectly correct. But he evidently felt that the sound I produced did not stem from any inner emotion. Suddenly he turned to me and said, 'Rukha, you haven't shed many tears in your life!' This remark quite shocked me, and stayed with me for a very long time. Of course I have made up for it over the rest of my life, with plenty of tears, but at the time he felt the need to shake me up.

There were numerous ways in which Mstislav Leopoldovich could surprise you. Once he picked up my cello to demonstrate something. My bow had a kind of rubber tube at the nut to make it more comfortable to hold. My father used it, as did all his pupils, and so, I believe, did cellists such as Cassado and Jacqueline du Pré – I didn't even know you could play without it. Rostropovich immediately turned to me and said, 'Rukha, what's this here, why have you got a condom on your bow?' I didn't know what to say or where to look, and everybody in the class had a good laugh.

When I came to Rostropovich I had already studied almost all the classical repertoire and the big romantic concertos (Dvořák, Schumann, and the Tchaikovsky Rococo Variations) with my father. I had also prepared the second movement of the Prokofiev Sinfonia Concertante with my father, who worked on it with me every day. I know how difficult I found this, but now, looking back in hindsight, I wonder what he himself must have felt about it.

When I was in my second year Rostropovich prepared his big cycle in Moscow and Leningrad. He asked each of his students to study one of the new concertos he was to perform. Perhaps it was a help to him, but most of all he wanted us to feel actively involved in what he was setting out to do. We played these pieces not just for him in class, but also at our public class concerts. I was given a concerto by the Bulgarian composer Lyubomir Pipkov. In this instance, I don't think he was too concerned how well I knew the Pipkov score – perhaps he had been unable to find a copy to give me – but I remember everybody in class laughing at me.

Rostropovich always required that you prepared everything to the maximum, which naturally meant playing from memory. There were occasions when you were sent away from the Tuesday class and told to return for the Thursday, having assimilated all his suggestions in two days. At other times, he expected you to learn a new work in two days. Nobody objected, since Rostropovich made the maximum demands of himself, and we considered it normal that he should make the same demands of us. It was part of our rigorous training.

Once when I had a lesson on the Shostakovich sonata, Mstislav Leopoldovich remained unsatisfied and told me to come back at the next lesson having learnt the piano part of the second movement from memory. I wasn't a good pianist, but I could manage it, at least slowly. In fact Rostropovich didn't really care whether I could play the piano well, but he was adamant that I should know every note of the score, and know the material inside out. His aim was for me to feel and understand things 'from the other side', as it were, having changed position in the duo – he evidently thought I was playing too egocentrically.

He always insisted that we had to completely absorb and digest the material we studied. This process of assimilation was essential to becoming a musician, rather than remaining 'merely' a cellist. He also expected us to know the orchestral score of the concertos we learnt, and would ask us here to match the sound of the clarinet or there to blend with the oboe or trumpet.

I first played in a competition when I was sixteen years old: the All-Russian competition, at which I won third prize. Later I won the All-Union competition, which allowed me to compete in the 1966 Tchaikovsky competition. This was the only international competition that I played in, and I won first prize. Mstislav Leopoldovich worked very intensively with me during the preceding months having arranged to be in Moscow almost all the time from January 1966. At his suggestion, I took all my Conservatoire exams early as an externum, so I could devote all my time to preparing the competition programme. It meant I had a few difficult months, getting up early to study political subjects that were a required part of the curriculum in those days: political economy, Marxism and Leninism, and so forth. I was amazed that Rostropovich found time to drop by the Cabinet of Marxism and Leninism when I was taking my exams, and talk to the very strict teacher called Rappaport who was going to examine me. As a result the commission was more lenient with me and I got a good mark! I would never have dared to ask Rostropovich to do this, but I was touched by his thoughtfulness, for it meant that I completed my exams by the end of 1965, and could devote my time to my playing.

For the final round of the Tchaikovsky competition we had to prepare two concertos: Tchaikovsky's Rococo Variations and another of our choice. Mstislav Leopoldovich suggested that I play Milhaud's concerto, which I loved. He worked a lot with me on obtaining a cantilena sound in the first movements, trying to extract the right mood of nonchalant charm: he gave me an image of a young Parisian girl walking down the street, gently swinging her hips. He explained how to find the right sort of vibrato by playing with the pads of the fingers. But however much I tried, I just couldn't get the tone or create the atmosphere that he wanted. It became torture for me.

While Mstislav Leopoldovich was away from Moscow for a short trip, I worked hard on the Milhaud. I thought that at last I had managed to find the right sound. As soon as he returned, I played the concerto for him in class. 'Rukha,' he said, 'I think you're going to change to the Haydn C major concerto for the final round' – he had decided that the Milhaud wouldn't show me at my best. As I loved the Milhaud concerto no. 1, I was very disappointed, but I did realise that he was right. Apart from the problems of sound, there was the piece's somewhat heavy orchestration, which in places can cover the cello. These are things that can be sorted out if you have sufficient rehearsal time with orchestra, but it would have been a very risky choice for a competition, where rehearsal time is necessarily limited. Since then I have played this concerto many times, and always with enormous pleasure.

During the preparations for the competition, I was rehearsing with our class pianist Aza Amintaeva, in her central Moscow flat in the large blocks belonging to the Composers' Union. I was supposed to go on from our rehearsal for a lesson with Mstislav Leopoldovich at his apartment, which was in a different entrance of the same block. Just as we started rehearsing the telephone rang. Rostropovich told Aza that he was not feeling well, then asked, 'Is Rukha there?' He told me to place the telephone receiver on the floor and to play. It was quite something to know that you were under scrutiny in this way. Aza and I would play for about ten minutes, then I had to pick up the receiver and he would shout and sing down the line, telling me what I was meant to do. It was an absurd, surreal experience – by *comparison, any recording session has seemed like a piece of cake! It was fortunate that phone calls in Moscow were free, because the lesson went on like this for well over an hour.*

After I won the Tchaikovsky competition, I was invited to a reception at the Kremlin given for the jury and prize-winners. Many concert agents from all parts of the world were there. Rostropovich saw me standing rather shyly by myself, so he came up to me and said, 'What are you doing? You should go and mix and talk to people, go and meet so and so.' He encouraged us to communicate and not to be bottled up in ourselves, for he believed that it was essential to have contact with the real world.

Rostropovich's idea of education involved seeing and influencing the whole personality. He was preparing us for a concert career, and our whole attitude to life and our profession was important to him. When he said that I hadn't shed enough tears to play Brahms, he was also teaching me a deeper truth – that one must know how to absorb everything into oneself, and then filter it through one's own experience.

12

Principles of interpretation

In an article written shortly after Rostropovich completed his mammoth concerto cycle, Shostakovich explained how deeply the cellist had impressed him:

I would evaluate Rostropovich's work as a phenomenon of the highest degree, comparable to the achievements of great minds, of poets, thinkers and distinguished scientists. Through his playing he reveals himself to be a fascinating and profound personality, an artist who opens up a truly infinite perspective on the world . . . His own passion for music embraces many epochs and an enormous diversity of style. Whether he plays Bach or Prokofiev, Haydn or Hindemith, we hear in his playing the taut rhythm of contemporary life, the artist's clear and bold representation of the times we live in.*

A performer in tune with his surroundings, Rostropovich was active in shaping the history of contemporary music and establishing the place of the cello within it. He did not believe in the notion that an interpretation could be fixed or 'definitive'. He compared his teaching to the work of a sculptor: first he casts the outer form of the student's interpretation, then he works with hammer and chisel to bang and coax it into the shape best suited to each individual artistic temperament. He was not interested in creating standard copies: he wished rather to convey an overall vision of a piece of music and to define the emotion that it encapsulates and the character of its sound-world. In doing this, he felt it important to distinguish between those works born as a direct manifestation of human feelings, and those created through the filter of the intellect.

For instance in a lesson with Natalya Gutman and the pianist Alexei Nasedkin on Rachmaninov's sonata, Rostropovich stressed: 'It

* In *Sovetskaya Kultura*, 12 June 1964.

is essential to get to the spirit of the music through the emotions; if you read this work according to the graph of the score, you have a composition which is really rather badly written, although it is very beautiful. You must embellish the music through the emotional tension, cram it full with emotional substance. You cannot play it in the same way as you play Bach and Hindemith.' At one point in the lesson he told Natasha that she was unsuited to Rachmaninov's sonata, advising her, 'The sonata cannot suit itself to you, you have to adapt to it. You cannot be so dry, you should start crying as you play! You know there's nothing shameful about weeping to Rachmaninov's music, just as one can cry listening to Puccini.'*

In every case, the interpreter's imagination is vital to the understanding and performance of the music. Rostropovich was adamant that 'When I play the first note of a piece of music, I already know how I must play the last note, and for the rest, my job is to build up the link between them.' Rostropovich naturally drew on his vast experience of working with living composers, and his vivid accounts of Britten, Shostakovich, Khatchaturian and many others served to illuminate their human personality, through which the music is filtered. As he puts it, 'My experience of playing over a hundred new works for cello by living composers has given me certain insights. I always try to sense the composer's presence so vividly in his music that I could draw his face. In doing so I create a bridge between the way a composer speaks, what he looks like (in other words, his complete personality) and how he expresses himself in music.' Thus in Khatchaturian's case, for example, one immediately perceives the personality as direct, passionate, and sincere, whereas Shostakovich's was multifaceted and guarded, moving between emotional involvement and ironic detachment. Britten's was a mixture of poetic sensibility and forthright conviction: as with Shostakovich, the public and private persona did not always coincide. In class we were encouraged to reflect in a similar way about composers of the past, and to see every piece of music as a living organism. Studying music by our contemporaries helped to throw light on one's understanding of music from earlier periods.

Rostropovich's first-hand knowledge of Prokofiev was a uniquely helpful guide for us: his colourful descriptions of the man, his habitual

---

* When Boris Tishchenko walked into the classroom during this lesson, Rostropovich greeted him with the words, 'Borya, come back later. We're working on some rather bad music just now . . .'

physical gestures, his direct laconic wit, his ingenuous sincerity, his love of perfume and good clothes, and his relationship with his friends, all awakened a response in his pupils and helped them bring the music to life. When talking about the sonata or the *Sinfonia Concertante* Rostropovich might illustrate at the piano, playing a scene from *War and Peace*, or a section of the fifth or sixth symphonies. On more than one occasion he referred to the denouement of the third act of the opera *Semyon Kotko** as an example of how two or more simultaneous musical lines can function on completely separate psychological levels. One of the female characters, Lyupka, is distraught on discovering that her lover, the sailor Vasily, has been brutally executed by the German occupying force. When she sees her Vasilyok 'hanging like a puppet on a tree', she loses her reason. The village has been set on fire, its houses doused with kerosene, but Lyupka mistakes the glow from the flames in the church as candles burning for her wedding day, for she does not accept her lover's death. The psychological drama is brilliantly depicted by Prokofiev through the music. Lyupka's obsessive ostinato motif ('That wasn't my Vasilyok') represents her unhinged state of mind, while we hear the real drama expressed in the voices of the other characters who are frantically trying to extinguish the fire. The six-note motif is repeated throughout the scene, starting simply and growing to an enormous climax, an instructive example of Prokofiev's mastery of orchestration. (One could point to a similar effect in the scene with the dying Prince Andrey in *War and Peace*.)

Rostropovich encouraged his students to identify the motivating factor behind every passage of music they performed: did it represent an 'atmospheric state', or did it derive from the rhetoric of a single protagonist, or from active dialogue or interaction between two or more voices? In its original version the cello concerto (later transformed into the *Sinfonia Concertante*) dates from the same pre-war 'Soviet period' as *Semyon Kotko* and *Romeo and Juliet*; these works share many characteristics, and on occasion use the same musical material. To a certain extent, the first and second movements of the *Sinfonia Concertante* borrow the principle of montage of short 'scenes' that Prokofiev had consciously adopted in *Semyon Kotko*. The dramatic coherence of the *Sinfonia Concertante* depends on

---

* Written in 1939, *Semyon Kotko* is based on Valentin Kataev's novel, *A Son of the Working People*, set in the Ukraine during the civil war of 1918–20.

finding the connections between the changing melodic interludes within the whole panorama. The actual opening of the work uses a four-note motif (E, F sharp, G, B) borrowed from *Romeo and Juliet*, where flutes play it repeatedly in a high register, creating a mysterious and hushed mood. Now transferred to full orchestral tutti in the first bars of the *Sinfonia Concertante*, the motif assumes a far more dramatic character, and acquires an important role in the development, where it is initially transferred into the cello's pizzicato chords (before figure 19). The four-note motif gains an obsessive quality as it is taken over by the orchestra against the cello's weaving accompaniment in semiquaver triplets and then demisemiquavers (these are the famous eight bars written by Rostropovich!). When the climax is reached with the return to the home key of E minor, the motif blares forth in full tutti against the desperate rhetorical appeal of the solo cello, as it reintroduces the first subject's principal theme.

The *Sinfonia Concertante* was the perfect vehicle for Rostropovich's artistry, for he magnificently controlled the large-scale structure, while investing the mosaic of shorter interludes with an enormous diversity of character. Whether in maintaining the taut spring rhythmic drive or capturing the mellow, unforced lyricism so characteristic of Prokofiev, his playing was perfectly suited to the work's expressive needs. The *meno mosso* second-subject theme in the second movement (from figure 11) is a case in point, where he shaped the phrase to great effect through careful gradation of dynamics and vibrato. He would suggest to his students that this theme was associated with the contemplation of nature: while the tremolando string accompaniment suggests shimmering light, the long melodic line evokes an endless expanse of horizon, typical of the Russian landscape.* It was essential to maintain the continuity of this line without breaking the mood of serenity, in which an extrovert display of passion would be out of place. This mood of peaceful idyll reminded Rostropovich of the woodland picnics that Prokofiev enjoyed with Nikolay Myaskovsky. He told us of one occasion where Sergey Sergeyevich teased his friend by throwing shells from his boiled egg onto the ground; Myaskovsky, armed with a special penknife, would silently dig a hole in the ground and bury the litter from the picnic out of sight.

* When teaching Jacqueline du Pré this work, Rostropovich reminded her that the wide Russian landscape had little to do with English pastoral scenery, broken up as it is into smaller divisions or 'phrases', with its criss-cross of fields, hedges and small coppices.

We are fortunate to be able to observe exactly how Rostropovich 'makes sound' in the DVD issued by EMI of a concert performance of the *Sinfonia Concertante*, filmed in Monte Carlo in 1970. During this long second-subject theme, one sees how he intensifies the expression by increasing the amplitude of the vibrato: the whole left arm becomes involved, right through to the shoulder, with the wrist free and buoyant. In the higher positions, one can observe his elongated fingers with the flattened pads holding down the string, and the finger phalanges activated in the process of vibrating.

One of Rostropovich's favourite moments, he frequently told us, was the epilogue to the third-movement Variations. In his performance, the long ascent of the preceding melody builds up such tension that it explodes into a cascade of E major broken arpeggios, which are pitted against the low rumble of bassoon and tuba, and the menacing trombone interventions. When the trumpet reintroduces the staccato theme from the second movement, the arpeggio figuration is taken over by the whole string section. At the very end, the cello 'spirals to the top of the circus dome', playing the last three bars of arpeggio figuration in its highest possible register. The whole work is brought to a halt with an imperious blow on the timpani. Rostropovich remarked on the modest means with which Prokofiev achieved the illusion of enormous force here: this economy allows the cello to emerge through the texture without detracting from the brilliance of the effect.

The use of the coda to sum up an entire cycle of movements is also brilliantly achieved in Prokofiev's cello sonata. The grandiose eloquence with which the first movement's opening theme reappears is reflected in the epigraph borrowed from Maxim Gorky: 'Man – the word resonates with pride' [*chelovek-eto zvuchit gordo*]. Prokofiev is said to have chosen this epigraph himself, although he may have felt obliged to voice such positive sentiments, given the political climate of the day – it was not printed in any of the sonata's published versions. However, it was certainly Prokofiev's decision to label the easier alternatives to the virtuoso passages '*Facilitato*' rather than the conventional '*Ossia*' – he hoped to put to shame any cellists too lazy to learn what he had written.

Rostropovich's special relationship with the music of Shostakovich forms another very important part of his life as a performer. In class, he did not need to remind his students of the composer's personal history, or the terrible events surrounding Stalin's Terror. In the 1960s, Shostakovich, despite his frail health, was a tangible presence in Moscow musical life, regularly seen in the Conservatoire concert halls where his new works were premiered.* We attended rehearsals of his music, where we saw his nervous figure, his hands always in motion, jotting down notes on the back of his pack of *papyrosy*,† and making suggestions to the performers with exaggerated politeness. Although Dmitri Dmitriyevich was outwardly shy and reserved, for musicians he remained an accessible figure.

Rostropovich conveyed his profound insights into the interpretation of Shostakovich's music through vital images rather than pedantic explanations. He was guarded in what he revealed about Shostakovich the man, respecting the composer's carefully cultivated reticence in public; on the whole, anecdote was not appropriate in this case. For instance Rostropovich never told his Conservatoire classes about Shostakovich's parody of Stalin's favourite song, 'Suliko', in the finale of the first cello concerto – such revelations could be made only to a small circle of friends.

For Russians growing up in the 1960s, Shostakovich's music still had acute relevance, but it was not interpreted in the schematically 'politicised' manner that has become a regrettable tendency of recent times. Some young composers and performers felt that Shostakovich was old-fashioned and actively opposed the musical avant-garde: for them, he remained an ambivalent figure within the Composers' Union hierarchy. Rostropovich was convinced of the music's universal significance and compassionate humanity; he shared his wonder at the composer's genius for continuous regeneration with his students.

As Rostropovich observed in his notes on candidates' performances at the 1966 All-Union competition, 'Shostakovich is not a weak figure, not a suffering victim.' These remarks were provoked by Mischa Maisky's 'over-sensitive and over-sensuous' performance of the sonata, in which, Rostropovich felt, he had misunderstood the essential mood of the third-movement Largo: 'There should be no

---

* Shostakovich observed the tradition of having his works premiered in his native city, Leningrad, but in the 1960s many works, including the thirteenth symphony and the second cello concerto, actually received their first performances in Moscow.
† Long hollow-filtered cigarettes.

relaxation of tension here. This is not a feeble lament, but a battle with clenched teeth and enormous reserves of sound.' Shostakovich's sonata was conceived following the model of classical sonata form, where the principle of contrast is fundamental. The secret of interpreting the piece lies in finding the equilibrium between emotional restraint and taut expression, and in obtaining both rhythmic drive and elasticity in the flow of the long phrases.

The principal theme of the first movement is like objective narrative, while the piano part, played with hardly any pedal ('sounding like Bach'), suggests a polyphonic subtext. By contrast, the lyrical second subject in B major (figure 6) borrows its character from the world of sentimental cinema romance, although as the theme develops it acquires expressive depth and a driving impetus. The development is underpinned throughout by a threatening anapaest figure: a rhythmic cell of two quavers and a crotchet, much used by Shostakovich. In the first pizzicato statement of this motif (figure 10) Rostropovich asked his students to use a technique more common to double-bass jazz playing, releasing the pressure of the left hand between notes to give a short, almost percussive effect, stopping dead any extra resonance of the string.

Rostropovich asked that the tension and dramatic intensity should build up relentlessly from the F minor episode (figure 12) to a climax of overwhelming strength (figure 15), where the persistent anapaest motif, thundering in the bass line of the piano, drives the music through the descending cello line into the piano's restatement of the second-subject theme. Here Rostropovich asked us to maintain both volume and tension, ignoring the *piano espressivo* marking. The tempo slackened only in the piano's ritardando bars that precede the cello's foreshortened and quieter version of the melody: the section finishes in a mood of tender, muted nostalgia, with a question mark. In the Largo section that concludes the first movement (figure 18), acting both as recapitulation and coda, the first theme is transformed into a long, quiet phrase, inert and desolate, devoid of any expression, and underpinned by the dry staccato of the piano's bass, which sounds like grotesque footsteps – or 'knocks on the door'.*

The coda requires great control, with an even, slow-moving bow: no vibrato is permitted, and a sensation of great stillness must be

---

* The word 'knock' in Russian had a slang meaning of 'to inform or grass on'. Knocking was highly symbolic: it was also a sound associated with the final nailing down of the coffin before it was lowered into the grave.

created. When the piano's threatening staccato bass-line finally gives way to legato chords (one bar after figure 19), the melodic line in the cello part is warmed with a little vibrato: it momentarily takes on the character of an expressive lament before finally retreating into gloom. As the cellist's last note died out, Rostropovich would insist on maintaining the tension, to make the sudden attacca into the second-movement Allegro more effective.

In order to convey the character of this energetic scherzo movement, he would draw an analogy with the rhythmic drive of machinery, where thrusting pistons mechanically propel the music forward. When the cello took the theme over (figure 25) the mood of irony and biting wit had to be made evident in a heavy short staccato stroke at the nut of the bow. The trio's contrasting mood of lyrical insouciance (figure 28) in the piano's simple theme – two bars of descending scale – had to be precisely rhythmic, as did the cello's accompanying figure of glissandi harmonics. Then followed a second 'military' motif (figure 30), ringing out in the piano's treble register like a toy trumpet, with an answering imitation in the cello's bass register, played up the C string to suggest the extra roughness of a tuba.

Rostropovich enjoyed telling us about Gregor Piatigorsky's 'interesting' version of the cello's harmonic passage, which involved adding a brilliant ricochet bow stroke. Rostropovich learnt the passage with this complex bow stroke in order to ascertain Shostakovich's reaction. However, the composer only laughed at this clever innovation, saying that he preferred the harmonics to be played in tempo with a simple, smooth legato bow: the fancy bow strokes were only a distraction. Similarly, he told us that it was Kubatsky (the sonata's dedicatee) and not Shostakovich who had added a bass-line to the cello part in the transition towards the second subject of the first movement. This alteration was published in the early editions, to the composer's considerable annoyance.

The heart of the sonata lies in the Largo third movement, whose tragic mood is similar to that of the final 'Siberian' act of *Lady Macbeth of Mtsensk*. The prologue (and the epilogue that mirrors it) are born of numb suffering, though every now and then a glimpse of hope is perceived and reflected through the warming up of the vibrato. In Rostropovich's interpretation, emphasis was placed on a long directional line, suggesting limitless horizons: the profound expression of the main theme (starting at figure 39) was spun out endlessly against the piano's persistent 'dry knocking' accompaniment. The movement is an early example of Shostakovich's unique ability to build a whole section on a single musical idea, driving through to a powerful culmination – an effect achieved in many of the symphonies, notably the seventh and eighth. Here in the sonata, the phrase achieves a climax of enormous power, triple *forte*, before unwinding downwards without losing dynamic force. Rostropovich urged us to ignore the *pianissimo* marking at figure 40, and only to release the tension, arriving in diminuendo at the F minor five bars later. The *pianissimo* marked in the following bar then gains that special effect of hushed, magical beauty with the unexpected modulation to D flat major.

When I asked Rostropovich how he reconciled his advice to 'respect the score' with his own departures from the dynamic and tempo markings in this movement (they are clearly audible in his recording with Shostakovich), he explained that in this instance the interpretation had 'been developed together with the composer, and as such was authorised by him'.

The opening theme of the sonata's finale is derived from the genre of urban 'street music', so typical of Soviet cinema of the early 1930s. Its underlying mood of understated sardonic humour acquires an element of caricature when the theme reappears in the cello's lower register in F minor (figure 57). Here Rostropovich sometimes gave us a vivid image of a drunk hardly able to stand up or keep his heaving stomach in order. One could imagine him pestering passers-by with the question, 'Do you respect me?' – typical of Russian drunks in this condition. The whole movement is permeated with a lively characterisation of life in the streets, its bustle and brash hooliganism so typical of the late 1920s, the period of Shostakovich's youth. When the cello first plays the opening theme, it continues with an extension of the phrase (nine bars before figure 50), whose self-conscious banality comes out in the open in its final transformation in the coda (figure 65). Here Rostropovich linked a wonderful cinematic image to the piano's legato statement of the theme in octaves, now unambiguous in its street-song character, over the cello's strumming pizzicato accompaniment. He likened this to the ending of a film – perhaps the final moments of Chaplin's *Modern Times*, where the protagonists walk away hand in hand down the road, waving goodbye and slowly disappearing out of the frame while the credits roll.

The unity and logic of Rostropovich's vision were totally convincing: the associations and images he offered, while useful in understanding the music, were less important than his structural understanding and could ultimately be dispensed with. Similarly, when teaching Shostakovich's first concerto, Rostropovich was concerned to convey his understanding of the work's construction as a single, soaring arch. His own performances offered an eagle's-eye perspective on the concerto, suggesting an all-encompassing view of the musical landscape beneath him. Like Prokofiev's *Sinfonia Concertante*, the first concerto demanded a very high level of energy from the performer. Rostropovich advised his students to calculate their strength very precisely, and therefore to identify the points of maximum strain and release of tension, in order to achieve equilibrium over the piece as a whole. He cited one of his own performances at the Edinburgh Festival, when he had come onstage bursting with energy, and started a highly charged performance. Despite the initial excitement, however, he realised that he had miscalculated, for it was impossible to sustain that level of energy throughout the piece; on that occasion, he admitted, he failed to convey a unified interpretation. He encouraged his students to think of winding up a spring, calculating how much initial tension was needed in order to allow energy to unravel throughout the duration of the piece. It was useful to have such a skeleton framework in one's mind, upon which the musical content could be hung.

One of the determining factors in defining the character of the opening of the concerto lay in finding the right bow stroke for the opening theme – a heavy, but lifted marcato played in the lower half of the bow, expressing just the right degree of sarcasm and weight. We had always to keep in mind the extraordinary character of Shostakovich's orchestration, where the percussion was limited to celesta and timpani, and the woodwind writing favoured the extreme registers of contrabassoon and piccolo, emphasising the element of grotesque. All this belied the composer's own initial description of the first movement as a straightforward March – this was probably merely a convenient camouflage. The initial four-note motif acts as a leitmotif throughout the first movement. When it sounds in the solo horn its commanding fanfare-like character dictates the quality of the cello's response. In the finale, the slowed-down augmentation of the horn's four-note theme gives it a grotesquely lampooning quality, as if the composer was sticking his tongue out at the world.

Rostropovich emphasised the importance of achieving convincing transitions, first and foremost from the slow movement into the cadenza, but also from the cadenza into the finale. Calculating these accurately gave cohesion to the whole structure. At the start of the cadenza it was necessary to enter into exactly the right state of profound meditation, so that the cello could act out its role as solitary protagonist in a long unfurling drama. The initial mood of emotional detachment later gives way to bursts of anger: one needed to gauge the impetus behind each phrase, whether it pushed forward or petered out into a diminuendo. Using an analogy with fishing, Rostropovich suggested that this depended on how we 'cast the line' with the initial gesture. The mysterious sequence of five pizzicato chords, standing like columns, sounds three times. After the third sequence, the build-up towards the end of the cadenza starts with the unravelling triplet (and later semiquaver) figuration which builds up force and tension right through to the final Allegro non troppo section. Rostropovich generally did not pull the tempo back here as indicated, but pushed on with implacable drive (and sometimes further accelerando) until the orchestra interrupted him with its short cutting chords, three times, marking the eventual transition to the finale. Rostropovich expected every student to have analysed the masterly way in which the cadenza was constructed, identifying the origins of all the thematic material in its various transformations. On more than one occasion, I saw him packing a student off home when he failed to pass a sudden interrogation on such points.

The orchestral tutti at the beginning of the finale only gives the cellist the shortest of breaks in which to gather strength for the finale. The high level of tension throughout the movement tests not only the performer, but the inherent possibilities of the instrument itself. In order to transcend its limitations, Rostropovich had no hesitation in breaking conventional rules; for example, he would grab the bow in his fist so that he could give full force to the chords in the final page of the piece where G is heard simultaneously in three different octaves. However, when David Grigorian followed his master's example on this point, he suddenly found himself a laughing-stock: having a long thumb, it protruded from under the bow which he held in his clenched fist. 'What are you doing, showing me the "f..." sign?'* Rostropovich teasingly asked.

The first concerto requires not only an intellectual grasp, but first and foremost, great physical stamina. In the second cello concerto of 1966, one might say that the priorities are reversed: it is one of Shostakovich's most interesting works in the period of regeneration following the thirteenth symphony. The concerto's genesis as a symphony with solo cello part provides the key to understanding the thematic material: its capacity for transformation and development is essential to the unity of the cycle. This is evident from the very opening, where the solo cellist plays two repeated bars made up of a dotted-minim A flat followed by a crotchet G; this semitone, for all its bare simplicity, makes up the embryonic cell whose 'DNA' contains all the essential elements of the work's structure. One had to capture the contemplative mood of these initial bars, and from there on, be able to spin out the long stretch of melody in the solo part. Underneath it there is a gradual build-up of orchestral texture, handled with Shostakovich's unique mastery (the full orchestra is only heard once during the exposition, briefly at figure 9). As Rostropovich has often said, 'One would think that there is nothing special about the way Shostakovich orchestrates the opening; just cello and low strings. But in real physical sound the effect is quite amazing.' Other interesting features of the orchestration of the second concerto include the unusual use of percussion, and the prominent part allotted to the two solo horns.

The second movement's characteristic theme, built on the Odessa ditty 'Bubliki', is also a fertile source for transformation and development. It starts in a playful and ironic exposition and eventually achieves the character of grotesque menace when it reappears in the culminating orchestral tutti of the third movement that precedes the final cadenza.

Shostakovich also used many innovative effects in the cello part, not least the use of tenths in the high register in the recapitulation of the second-subject theme in the first movement. Placing these double-stops correctly required enormous skill: more than that, Rostropovich advised that an appeal to some higher mystical powers was needed to 'snatch the chord from the air'.

* The 'sign of the fig' has the same vulgar meaning in Russian as in Anglo-Saxon countries.

Another unusual feature of the work is the prevalence of the interval of the fourth both in the construction of thematic material* and in the cadenzas. It was at Rostropovich's suggestion that Shostakovich wrote a descending chromatic passage in the final cadenza using double-stopped fourths across three strings. The concerto's sizeable cadenzas mark points of culmination and are shared between soloist and orchestra. In the first movement cadenza, the cello's high chords (based on an extension of the work's opening motif) are rudely interrupted by loud thumps of the *gran cassa*; as Rostropovich pointed out, the tension of the effect lies as much in its timbral quality as in the contrast of instrument and register.† In the central cadenza that acts as a transition between the second and third movements, the two horns have pride of place in their cascading fanfares, sounding like a call to the hunt. The challenge is transferred to the solo cello, which continues an imitation with impressive flourishes in fourths and octaves. The transition into the finale's tranquil pastoral mood is achieved through a baroque cadence, which appears a further four times throughout the movement. Rostropovich saw this as a signal of relaxation, an almost theatrical indication of a change of scene. Following on after the 6/8 barcarolle-like theme, a staccato march-like figure‡ plays a significant role in its various transformations in drawing together the various elements of the concerto.§

The whole concerto offers enormous challenges to the performer – but as Rostropovich suggested, the finale is the hardest movement to understand, with its kaleidoscopic changes and its enigmatic construction of 'boxes within boxes'. In the last moments of the piece, the cello sustains a long bass D over which the rhythmic jingling of percussion instruments lifts the work into another dimension. This seems to have little in common with the serious mood of the first movement, or the pointed irony – if not grotesque sarcasm – of the second.

---

* One could cite the third bar after figure 9 in the first movement, and (of particular significance) the playful march-like introduction to the second movement's '*Bubliki*' theme.
† Maybe it is fanciful on my part, but this extraordinary effect seems to me to presage the violent aggression of Ustvolskaya's use of the Cube (or wooden box) in her *Composition no. 2 (Dies irae)*.
‡ This is derived from the introduction to the second movement.
§ A third contemplative theme (which first appears at figure 91) is derived from the Prologue to Mussorgsky's *Boris Godunov*, although Shostakovich had already used it in a completely different context, as the aggressive opening theme of the tenth symphony's second-movement Scherzo.

Many of the images that Rostropovich offered served to shock a pupil out of a state of insipid indifference or helped instil essential character in his playing. Once, when Ella Testelets played Shostakovich's second concerto in class, our professor felt that the long glissandi up and down the interval of a ninth in the second movement (figure 44) were not achieving the necessary effect of spiky heaviness. 'Ellouisa,' he cried out, 'just think, it's as if you had drunk too much yesterday and now you have to throw up, first in this corner, then in that!' However ridiculous the image may have seemed, Rostropovich's almost graphic demonstration of it proved very effective – I doubt if anybody who heard that lesson will forget it when playing the glissandi in question!

Rostropovich could be a great tease in lessons, and I was a marvellous victim, not least because I was desperately shy, and also a foreigner without a very good grasp of the finer innuendos of the Russian language. I could never understand why, when Rostropovich kindly used a few English words to help me out, it often provoked laughter. 'Now you reach your climax,' in particular, had everybody in stitches, and I soon found out why: the Russian word 'Klimax' meant menopause. Another time when I played the Saint-Saëns concerto in class, I did not catch the dramatic character of the repeated phrase (quaver E, minim F, crotchet E) before the start of the finale. 'It's very simple, Liza,' he said. 'To begin with you must think, "*Tovàrishch, Tovàrishch*" [dear comrade], and then as the tension slackens, you play slower in the last bar: "*Ekh, tovàrishch*."' There were howls of laughter in class, since the way he said '*Ekh, tovàrishch*' sounded just like a party functionary admonishing a colleague for some ideological misdemeanour.

The tape I have preserved of this lesson shows Rostropovich's concern to draw an artistic response from me, while simultaneously trying to soothe my obvious agitation. Throughout the second movement he invented a second piano counter-melody: he talked to me continuously and told stories that fitted the light and delicate mood of this 'quasi-minuet' movement. He distracted me just sufficiently to allow me to release my tension – this was a delightful exercise in psychology. However, he was not always so indulgent or forgiving. Many tears were shed, yet more often than not, after a lesson where we had been severely reproached, he took care to give encouragement (and where possible praise) at the next encounter. In this way the overall line of progress was maintained.

It was natural that Rostropovich should demonstrate music through the prism of his own personality. As Mischa Maisky recalls, 'For us students it was extremely difficult to resist such a strong personality as his. Nevertheless he was very open-minded, and never tried to impose himself. Undoubtedly he had a great effect on us all, and I still feel his influence very strongly, even though over the years I have absorbed very many others.'

Rostropovich aimed not only to stimulate his students' imagination and develop their personality, but also to cultivate their taste. In testing a pupil's inherent likes and dislikes, he would sometimes deliberately set a work that was alien to a particular student's preferences: he believed it was essential for a musician to be able to identify with any piece of music, once he had decided to perform it.

Once, when Rostropovich set me Myaskovsky's second sonata, he could see that I was not sufficiently involved in the music. 'Liza, I am disappointed,' he said, 'I thought that this sonata had that spirit of understated noble expression so typical of the inhabitants of Albion's misty shores!' In fact it so happened that it was precisely this feature that put me off, since at that time I totally rejected English music of that period, Elgar and Vaughan Williams included. It took me some time to overcome my misguided misconceptions, and to grow to understand and value this music's wistful beauty. But for now I had failed to commit myself to the piece, and was reprimanded for letting this failure show through while I played. Rostropovich would often repeat that an interpreter cannot exercise his taste in the way a composer can: 'You must be totally in love with the work you are playing at this particular moment of time.' In addition, an artist's pride had to be maintained, and nothing but the best would do.

On occasion, Rostropovich would recommend waiting before approaching a particular piece of music. When Mischa Maisky expressed a burning desire to play Bloch's *Schelomo* for cello and orchestra, Rostropovich was against it. Ella Testelets recalls:

At the time of our preparations for the Tchaikovsky competition, Mstislav Leopoldovich spent some time discussing our programmes. As far as possible he didn't wish his various students to repeat works between themselves in the competition. He asked me which concerto I wanted to play in the final round with orchestra (*Rococo* was obligatory, but we could choose the second work). 'Probably Bloch's

Schelomo,' I said. 'Yes, that's a good choice, you have a beautiful sound that will suit the piece, go ahead.' Maisky was also dying to play *Schelomo* and although he was not yet officially Rostropovich's student, he came and played it in class. At the end of his lesson Mstislav Leopoldovich admonished him: 'Mischa, you make this music sound like some whining old Jew, grumbling away and recounting the village gossip. *Schelomo* needs a majestic spirit; you must wait. This work is not for you yet.' Mischa was over-involved and could not stand back from the drama. We all were bowled over when, around this time, Jacqueline du Pré played *Schelomo* in class. Her interpretation was truly unforgettable, and she achieved a wonderful nobility of drama while giving every ounce of her passion. When I started studying with Mstislav Leopoldovich he made it clear that he hated any kind of trivialisation or self-indulgence. He would often say, 'Play with broad strokes, broad strokes.' He wanted to convey a view of the total musical horizon.

In *Schelomo*, Rostropovich imparted a wide, generous approach, expressing a heartfelt narrative of incredible dignity through the beautifully sung solo line. In teaching it, he drew analogies to King David, to a state of meditation and prayer; he would conjure up images of camels in the desert approaching an oasis, the shepherd boy piping his flocks, and many others. As Ella points out, 'These images were not meant to be understood concretely, but they helped create a mood, and thereby indicated the inner core of the emotion behind the music. Written into the score on their own, these remarks were meaningless, unless they helped you recreate the inner condition needed to transmit the musical message.'

Rostropovich's own performance of *Schelomo* during his 1964 concerto cycle had caused a sensation, for it was effectively the first performance of the work in Soviet Russia. Its biblical subject matter and the Jewish inflections in its musical material gave the work a piquant interest for Moscow audiences – after all, anti-semitism was still an issue in the Soviet Union. Shortly afterwards, Rostropovich played *Schelomo* in New York, and was hailed by audiences and critics for his passionate interpretation. Bloch's daughter was at the performance and presented him with a score of the work with a dedication onto which she had pasted her late father's signature, probably cut out from another letter. Rostropovich also attracted a rather more peculiar compliment after the concert. On reaching his hotel room at the Park Sheraton opposite the Carnegie Hall, the phone rang. A voice speaking in Russian with a thick Jewish accent asked, 'Is that Mstislav Leopoldovich? This is Gersonsvet talking to you, the critic of the *New Russian Word* newspaper. I was at your concert.' 'I am glad to hear it.'

'You are of course Jewish.' 'Well actually, I am not.' Gersonsvet persisted, 'Mstislav Leopoldovich, you are wrong. You are not only Jewish, but you are a hassidim!' and with that he put the phone down.

Rostropovich is that rare sort of performer who is able to add stature to a work of art simply through his own performance. As one of his last Conservatoire students, the conductor Mikhail Katz observed, 'There can be no question of talking about Rostropovich as a stereotype, whether in his approach to music or to the instrument. For example, he instinctively knew what the right sound was for the piece in question. When he played Khatchaturian's *Rhapsody-Concerto*, he made it into a far greater piece of music than it was, investing just the right kind of temperament and physically exciting sound which was ideally suited to the piece. His performance of it was phenomenal!' Through the strength of his conviction, he was able to lift a mediocre work well above its level.

Rostropovich would claim that the key to his approach to interpretation lay in his ability to tune into the composer's mind, and to search for that metaphysical aspect of sound which hints at the ulterior existence of musical material in some pristine state beyond aural perception. The moment that sparked this process often lay in the opening or closing bars of a piece of music: 'Sometimes, when the ending is quiet, one must play an infinitely long last note which starts in one world and finishes in another, where the sound will continue its life in another dimension. And there are many pieces of music which start in a way where you actually cannot define the borderline between silence and the physical appearance of sound.'

This ability to switch into an endless spatial stream, in anticipation of placing the bow on the string and producing real sound, was of vital importance in a cellist's approach to such works as the Schumann concerto, Beethoven's C major sonata, Op. 102, no. 1, and Shostakovich's second concerto, to give but a few examples. Once, when working with Victoria Yagling on that Beethoven sonata, Rostropovich listened to her play the whole opening Andante before he made a single comment, but then he told her that her approach was too sentimentally expressive, too prosaic:

Well, Vika, what can I say? everything is correct, everything in time, and you played the pizzicato in time . . . But there is no aroma here. It all comes out heavy, plodding and dull. We need to feel the appearance of the opening C major in space, it should hang purely and transparently in the air, coming out of silence. Try playing it in another key, since you don't at all convey the feeling of the unusual nature of this miraculous C major. It should sound quietly, but with solemn majesty.*

Vika and Aza played the opening as suggested in A minor, and then returned to the phrase in its original key. 'Now you must play with this feeling of wonder that this music is not in A minor. You must seem to be awaiting for this magical C major, you must desire it ardently with all your heart and mind.'

Conversely, to end a piece quietly, one had to hear and 'feel' with the inner ear how to fade out the sound. In his own performances, Rostropovich could stretch the listeners' credulity in filtering a phrase in diminuendo to a hardly audible *pianississimo (pppp)*, intimating a further quality of sonority beyond our capacity actually to perceive it. For instance when performing the great Sarabande movements from the second and fifth Bach suites (which he regards as the two spiritual kernels of the complete cycle), he would invest profound significance in the transition away from physical sound, filtering off the diminuendo to a ponticello effect to arrive at quasi-silence at the end of the final note. It is an effect Rostropovich aims for no less when he conducts; for instance, one could point to the long-drawn-out tension of the *pianissimo* coda in the finale of Shostakovich's fourth symphony, where a magical resonance lingers in the air long after the orchestra's sound has ceased to be audible.

Such an attitude towards sound implied the absolute significance of silence in music – it was almost like a living organism. Rostropovich often upbraided his students for allowing the tension inherent in a pause or a rest to go slack: 'The silence in these pauses must breathe, they are also an essential part of the music,' he insisted.

In a lesson with Mariya Chaikovskaya on Kodály's solo sonata, he talked about the laws at play in such music, and the necessity of conveying a sense of improvisation in a work where the cello part is the single protagonist:

Here, in this work you are alone; you must understand that there are certain very refined laws in operation. To begin with there is silence, and silence means a temporal sound sensation. Apart from that there exists the sensation of space. A sculptor works in multi-dimensional space, and a painter, who works on the flat

---

* This and other quotations from lessons given in this chapter are taken from the extant audio tapes of the class recorded by Mischa Maisky. I have kept the copies that I took from him in the late 1960s, and have tried to transcribe them faithfully. Most of the lessons concerned date from 1967.

surface of the canvas, must do some strange things to create the illusion of multi-dimensional space that is essential to his creative process. A visual artist has to create in space, he sees the form and sees its size, a measure of the form. You are working with sound, which implies a certain character and the sensation of a stretched-out time, the duration of time.

Within this duration one had to calculate the form. As he told Mariya, one also had 'to create through the initial silence, and think what kind of sound should arise out of this silence. For in sound itself there exists the magnetism which bewitches your listeners.'

At this particular lesson he also told us why he was so preoccupied with the idea of silence, and the emergence of sound:

I am thinking how to conduct the Introduction to *Evgeni Onegin*. What am I to do to ensure that the audience doesn't shuffle around in its seats, that they stop talking? Most probably one should aim to start playing rather quietly, to produce through the character of the sound itself that invisible thread which will stretch out to the listener in the hall.

These aims were not easy to achieve. Often a student never got past the first few bars of a piece in his lesson, as Rostropovich demanded the psychological awareness and sharpened inner hearing necessary to 'capture' the appearance of sound. Moray Welsh recalls a lesson when Mischa Maisky brought Schumann's *Adagio and Allegro*:

Every time he started the first note, he was stopped and made to repeat the opening, over and over again. Rostropovich demanded the creation of atmosphere even before the sound emerged, in the thought before the gesture. The 'sound' of the silence influenced the physical gesture, and this was an integral part of the mood of the music that followed. Mischa couldn't achieve the effect, and was remorselessly made to repeat this opening note before he was allowed to go on.

Maisky himself recalls a similar occasion in class when he played the *Rococo Variations*:

At the beginning of the third variation in C major I couldn't find the sound Mstislav Leopoldovich wanted. Nothing I could do was good enough for him, however hard he tried to explain it. Then he found a fantastic argument. 'Look around,' he said. 'Just look at all those beautiful girls sitting there. Pick one and just play for her.' He knew very well that at the time I was in love with a Polish cellist, Bogumila, who was studying with Natasha Gutman. The whole class knew this too. So just as everybody expected me to do, I looked round at Bogusha. Then when I started playing again, Rostropovich exclaimed, 'You see, you see now it's a different world, that's how to play!' I can't say if there really was so much difference in my playing. Certainly in a concert you can't look around at the audience and fixate somebody with your stare (although Gaspar Cassado did do this sometimes). But you can carry an image of somebody in your mind for whom you want to play. And I have to say, that if I do this, it really has a tangible effect on the sound.

Rostropovich devoted an equally great amount of time to the very first note of the Schumann concerto: here the issue was how to find just the right sound and a seamless attack, which implied no accent, but a precise placing of the bow. In order to capture Schumann's fragile sound-world and blend into the palpitating opening orchestral accompaniment, it was essential, he would reiterate, that the performer withdrew the 'personal I' from his interpretation. As he told Karine Georgian in an intense lesson on this work, 'The Schumann concerto starts with the most intimate and profound . . . so how you play the opening bar is decisive to the success of the performance. The music in the finale is far more obvious, you can even warm your muscles up on it.' He told us that the music was like a confession of Schumann's inner poetic vision, written at a time when he was beset by mental anguish.

In the class with Karine, he spent a lot of time explaining the need for instrumental simplicity, for Schumann was not interested in composing for cello as such: he simply composed music, and his technical means were much better suited to the piano than the cello. He asked Karine to pay special attention to the function of harmony, and worked with her in particular on the long triplet figuration over the yearning orchestral chords starting on the bass G sharp pedal (bars 165–172). He asked her to forgo any exaggerated expression in the triplets: 'You are playing them like some senseless melody, but you should barely touch the strings, just play them slowly, evenly and quietly, without over-holding any note.' He suggested that she should listen to the unadorned harmony, to the 'wonderful, disappointed chords in the orchestral accompaniment. It should feel like the shattering of your happiness here.' The chords are bare, supporting columns to the straightforward narrative of triplets, shorn of expression. When Karine still played them too freely and expressively, Rostropovich reprimanded her:

Rukha, it's the harmony that matters. In beautifying the triplets, you are taking upon yourself an important role that doesn't actually exist. You are impoverishing Schumann here. You are just playing a series of bow strokes – they could have great effect in some vulgar romance, where you can show off your wonderful instrumental qualities.

He then proceeded to invent a cheap Soviet street song on the spot, with Schumann's figured triplets performed in an outrageously sentimental manner as an accompaniment, as an example of how not to play.

More usually, though, Rostropovich would illustrate his points by demonstrating how the music should sound. I cannot forget how he once played one of Schumann's most enigmatic piano pieces for us – the *Vogelprophet* from the *Waldszenen* – creating an effect of hovering ambiguity through delicacy of touch and fluid rubato, qualities that he told us were equally needed in the cello concerto.*

Rostropovich encouraged us to calculate carefully how to use rubato, paying close attention to the harmony and the tensions between intervals. An unexpected modulation, for instance, may require one to stretch the phrase, or dwell with emphasis on one or more notes that are grounded in that particular harmony. The art of rubato influences one's understanding of tempo: while 'rhythm' implies a steady beat and metronomic pulse, the notion of 'tempo' refers to speed and character, and also goes beyond it. As Rostropovich liked to remind us, tempo could be seen as a metaphor for the passage of time, which, despite its inevitable forward movement, has a malleable ebb and flow, with periods of tension and repose. An artist also had to know how to make time appear to stand still, when the music called for a state of frozen immobility.

These were the general guidelines, but there was no fixed rule for the organisation of time. Spontaneity was of foremost importance, and anything that smacked of mannerism was abhorrent to Rostropovich, just as he dismissed imitation as an act of theft, the 'borrowing of alien emotions'. In a tape recording of a lesson on the Debussy sonata with Mischa Maisky, one hears Rostropovich stopping him in the central episode of the finale. 'Mischa, your rubato is premeditated,' he admonished, 'it sounds too habitual, too studied. Rubato must be spontaneous to have effect.' He reminded his student that the elastic nature of the rubato had to remain within the framework of the rhythmic pulse, so there is no overall loss or gain of time. Rostropovich's principal aim in this lesson was to help Maisky find the right degree of freedom while remaining true to the music's character and logic.

* In particular in the G minor section after the cadenza in the finale (Bar 690).

It is sometimes difficult for a performer to know exactly how much freedom is permissible. In working with Natasha Gutman and Aleksei Nasedkin on Rachmaninov's sonata, Rostropovich had a particular set of demands for the atmospheric opening of the Lento introduction:

Your performance at the start sounds too calculated, there's not enough freedom. And you must know how to build up these small phrases, where each of them should drain itself of energy, exhausting its own impulse. It's as if the composer was looking for something new, but he can't go out of these imposed limits. These phrases are born of an obsessive idea, which keeps going round like an *idée fixe*.

In the recording that has been preserved of the lesson, one feels the tangible atmosphere of inspiration, as Rostropovich showed total involvement, speaking and singing his instructions while playing brilliantly on the second piano. His running commentary was a stream of consciousness, as well as being a reaction to this excellent duo. Throughout the lesson, Rostropovich kept asking them to create specific moods. In the opening and in the Allegro moderato's second-subject theme, he asked for 'a tired, melancholic atmosphere, so typical of Rachmaninov'. In the development's gradual build-up, he asked for more plasticity in the cello's legato phrases, which were based on the semitone motif from the introduction: 'These must sound like entreaties, but Natasha, you just bark out instructions, you must learn how to plead and supplicate.' He asked too that the cello's semitones should be almost painfully narrow, approaching quarter-tones. The typical Rachmaninov climax, he argued, was achieved more often in *piano* than in *forte* – one had to filter the expression through diminuendo to a sensuously beautiful pianissimo at the zenith of a phrase. 'In the culminations,' Rostropovich taught, 'the higher you go, the quieter it gets, and the more vibrato you need. This is a uniquely beautiful feature of his music.'

Throughout the lesson Rostropovich demanded a more generous expression from Natasha, more slides and fewer dry, 'clinical' stretches between notes; more variety and breadth of vibrato, more artistic freedom. In the second movement he demanded a warm, luxurious expression in the second subject (the E flat major theme at the *poco meno mosso* section). 'Natasha, you are as dry as a sinew,' he interrupted her.

Do you know, Rachmaninov's music occupies enormous space, you should feel the smell of the meadows with freshly mown hay . . . for he spent his summers somewhere near Tambov, staying in an estate which I think was called Satina, and there was an attractive woman, Natasha Skalon, who lived on another nearby estate . . . And there they had everything in abundance, they ate roasted piglet, with buckwheat kasha, they had everything under the sun . . . This theme could only be born from such a feeling of plenty, a laden-down table, a concept of excess. Natasha, you are playing with the air of my dog Joff when he hasn't been fed, and is longing for any old bone. Instead, you must feel a physical sensation of excess . . . and you Alyosha . . . you are playing as if you were sorry for the piano: give it all you have, as if you were fit to burst.

It was a lesson with a message for all his students: however much one thinks one is giving, one must find hidden reserves to draw on, and go beyond those restrictions that we unknowingly impose on our expressive resources.

Britten's music could not be more different from Rachmaninov's, but here too Rostropovich asked his students to search not just for the character but the emotional key to each of his cello compositions. Britten's rejection of the principle of 'constructing music' in the manner of Beethoven or Brahms meant that it was essential to feel the poetic nature behind his creative perception. The three suites for solo cello were of particular interest not only for the host of innovations in the instrumental writing, but for the considerable variety of interpretive tasks they set. No other composer understood the nature of string playing so well, Rostropovich argued; he would point to his ability to build two separate lines in double-stops, whether in the fugues and chorales of the 'Canto' movements of the first suite, or in the skilful use of bowed and plucked notes, simultaneously or alternately – in the 'Bordone' of the first suite, the 'Andante lento' from the second and the 'Andante dialogo' from the third. The 'Serenata' from the first suite, on the other hand, extends pizzicato techniques first employed in the sonata for cello and piano. The first suite's Cantos serve as pillars, whose chorale-like refrain separates the characteristic dance movements of the baroque suite. Here Britten exploited the instrumental brilliance of the dedicatee to the full. In each of the three suites, Britten includes a fugue, demonstrating a compositional technique worthy of his great predecessor, Bach. The second suite's fugue has three voices and is enormously complex: the initial theme has more rests than notes, which allows the counter-subjects to fill in the pauses in the line. There is a full-scale fugal development including inversions and a *stretto*; the cello's natural register is augmented with ample use of harmonics.

Of the three works, the first suite has achieved the greatest popularity because of its exuberant virtuosity, but the second and third suites are no less original, and explore deeper philosophical and spiritual depths. The enigmatic third suite was written as a homage to Rostropovich's courage and humanity. Britten understood the wider meaning of his support of Solzhenitsyn as a defence of freedom of expression in art, a theme dear to the composer's heart. The profound and tragic emotion that underpins the entirety of this suite thus pays respect to Rostropovich's human qualities, even more than his instrumental prowess. The interpreter needs to work his way gradually to the inner core of this music, revealing the heart of the matter in its closing pages. Here, finally, the four Russian themes that Britten chose as the basis of the suite are revealed in their simplest form, having been heard as variations in the other movements – Britten stands the conventional approach to musical structure on its head.

In my lessons with Rostropovich on the second and third suites, he asked for precise characterisation of each movement within the overall atmosphere of each suite. In Britten's music, the plasticity of line often stems from a vocal approach to phrasing and breathing. Gauging the balance in the rubato was of fundamental importance, whether in the 'Lamento' of the first suite, the rhetorical opening 'Declamato' of the second, or in the gentle rocking, so vividly suggestive of water, in the 'Barcarola' of the third. Rostropovich encouraged us to learn from Britten's unique sensitivity as a pianist and interpreter – not just of his own music, but of Schubert and Schumann.

Rostropovich demanded great attention not only to setting the mood in the first place, but to 'carrying' the music from one state of mind to another. One of the interpreter's hardest tasks, he believes, is to effect transition – whether between moods or between tempi, the change must seem an inevitable consequence of one's approach to the preceding section. Moreover, the way in which this change is managed sets up the conditions for what is to follow.

A performer begins by looking for clues as to the speed and character of the music from the composer's indications. For instance the 'Allegro con brio' marking of the first movement of Beethoven's D major cello sonata, Op. 102, no. 2, indicates that the music must be invested with a particularly energetic brilliance – in this it differs in character from the simple Allegro or Allegro vivace movements found in Beethoven's other cello sonatas.

In class, Rostropovich gave us some very striking images concerning tempo and the function of time. We were reminded that in cosmic terms, time has another weight and coherence. The everyday understanding of time was quite different, however: to explain this, he drew our attention to the functioning of an electric clock whose hands moved round the dial, jerking forward and halting at every second, as if putting up resistance to time's implacable advance. Another striking picture he liked to give was of a greyhound racing round the track, inexorably following its own nose to the finish. This association helped the student understand the directional impulse of those movements in which there could be no distraction or let-up of tension.

Rostropovich often referred to 'the conquest of space' within music, an association that served to overcome the gravitational tensions inherent in a leap, and gave the sensation of 'mass' necessary to control the pulling back of a rallentando. In the Prelude of Bach's D minor suite, he likened the arrival at the dominant pedal to a ship casting anchor: it continues to be blown hither and thither by stormy winds, but remains fixed in its anchorage of dominant harmony. It is only with the final arrival at the tonic that this anchor is released. In Bach, these points of culmination usually coincided with the 'golden section', a point within the musical architecture that could be mathematically calculated. One could sum up Rostropovich's performing principles in the simple maxim: 'It's very simple to shape the overall structure even in the largest-scale work; first you move towards the culminating point, then after reaching it, you recede from it.'

For his students, however, this was easier said than done. Of course, an intimate knowledge of the score constitutes an integral part of the performer's baggage. But knowing how to perceive the intangible elements below the surface of the musical line remains complex. To test a pupil's knowledge of the score, Rostropovich would often ask him to exchange roles, playing the piano part on the cello, or playing an accompanying figure from the orchestral score while simultaneously singing the theme. I remember being made to play the cello part and sing the clarinet part in the *poco meno mosso* section (starting at bar 143) of the finale of the Dvořák concerto. Having next to no voice, I was terribly embarrassed, for although I knew the clarinet part, my rendering probably bore little resemblance to it! At other times Rostropovich asked us just to listen to the piano line, so we were aware of the significance of the harmony or the texture of the

Natalya Shakhovskaya playing in the final round of the Tchaikovsky competition, April 1962

The jury of the 1962 Tchaikovsky competition: Maurice Maréchal, Kasimir Wilkomirsky (head turned away), Rostropovich, Gregor Piatigorsky, Aleksandr Vlasov. Hall of Columns, Moscow, April 1962

A surprise for friends of the jury: Rostropovich (in wig) conducting the 'Toy' Symphony at the Aragvi restaurant, Moscow, April 1962. Seated: Piatigorsky, Shafran, Cassado and Maréchal. Standing: Fournier, Knushevitsky and Wilkomirsky

Class 19, Rostropovich instructing Karine Georgian, *c.* 1963
Rostropovich demonstrating a point to David Geringas (David Grigorian seated on sofa),
1964

Rostropovich and Benjamin Britten acknowledging applause after the first performance of the *Cello Symphony*, Leningrad, March 1964

A radiant Jacqueline du Pré playing for Rostropovich in Class 19, March 1966

A relaxed moment in class. Elizabeth Wilson (sitting with cello) with Karine Georgian and Maria Chaikovskaya, 1967
Tchaikovsky competition winners 1966: Karine Georgian, Ken Yasudo, Eleonora Testelets. Behind: Steven Kates and Laurence Lesser in front of the Tchaikovsky statue by the Moscow Conservatoire

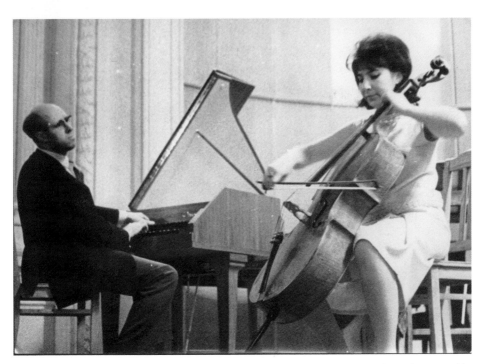

Class concert: Rostropovich directing from the harpsichord. Viktoria Yagling plays Vivaldi with the student orchestra, Small Hall of the Moscow Conservatoire, February 1966

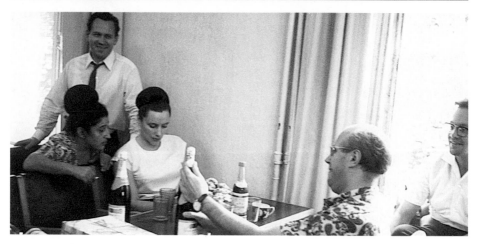

Rostropovich teaching the Rachmaninov sonata to Natalya Gutman and Alexei Nasedkin. Misha Maisky is between the two pianos recording the lesson. July 1967
Teaching Natalya Gutman from the piano, July 1967
Champagne for the end-of-year class celebration, July 1967. Rostropovich with Aza Amintaeva and Natalya Shakhovskaya (seated); behind them, Lev Evgrafov

Rostropovich with Silvia Narunaite and Aza Amintaeva, 1968
Mischa Maisky giving his all, 1970
Class 19, animated teaching. Left to right: Irina Anastasieva, Karine Georgian, Rostropovich, Stefan Kalyanov, 1970

Last concert, 10 May 1974. At rehearsal conducting Tchaikovsky's *Rococo Variations* with Ivan Monighetti, Grand Hall of the Conservatoire
Inspiration: Rostropovich conducting student orchestra, May 1974
26 May 1974, Rostropovich's departure from the Soviet Union. Outside Sheremet'evo airport with Tatyana Shchats, David Geringas, Stefan Kalyanov, Olga Rostropovich and Natalya Shakhovskaya amongst others

orchestral accompaniment. All this served to sharpen what he termed 'the listening apparatus' and helped develop mental coordination.

He also liked to develop students' perception by drawing on analogies from painting and sculpture. In the lesson with Vika Yagling on Beethoven's sonata, Op. 102, no. 1, Rostropovich suggested that the 'materials' used by different composers could be understood in physical terms:

Imagine, if you make something from plasticine, then it is soft and easy to mould. For instance how could one play Debussy from sound which is not made from plasticine, from which you can sculpt any form with the lightest of touches? Then you have material like granite, or material used in the construction industry, steel-reinforced concrete. Here in this work, for instance in the Allegro vivace, you need a different material altogether, great boulders, which have to be rudely banged and knocked into shape: to break it up you need to have an enormous instrument, a special hammer which can shatter the stone, not some feeble tool that will just leave a scratch on the table. This is Beethoven's material. And even the very quiet opening of the Andante is like a moment of reconciliation, of reflection, but even here, inside you must have at work this enormous pivotal key which acts as a spine to the structure.

Rostropovich would often liken the texture of the musical substance to marble, bronze, wood, plaster, or papier-mâché – each of which had its own consistency, malleability, weight, and tactility. Each orchestral instrument might be given a colour: 'the brown oboe' in Sauget's concerto, the 'cat-like clarinet' in Prokofiev's *Sinfonia Concertante*.

Into the 'interpretive equation' one also had to take into account the expression of the performer's personality, although it remained subservient to the composer's vision. Rostropovich was undoubtedly most interested in those students who knew how to inject their own personality into the music. He often referred to Eleonora Testelets's capacity to do this, but of course she was far from the only student to possess this ability. It was through an understanding of the sound quality, in particular, that an artist made the music his own. Without this quality one risks simply playing 'alien sounds, music that belongs to another'. There were also those who, despite an excellent level of accomplishment, lacked the 'spark' of an interesting personality, and so their playing never ignited. As Rostropovich has observed, 'Life has subsequently shown which of my former students remain *near* music, and not *in* music.'

To receive from Rostropovich, a pupil had to abandon the ego, bare the soul and be willing to react instantaneously to his ideas, momentarily pushing the analytical part of the mind into the background. They had to connect into the living musical current that flowed from Rostropovich's demonstrations at the piano and his inspired explanations. Naturally there were occasions when this contact between pupil and teacher did not materialise, and the lesson was wasted. Certainly his silence was the reaction that a student feared most of all. But as Maris Villerus describes it:

Mstislav Leopoldovich showed us the way into music, with his use of striking and picturesque imagery. Conveying the state of mind that corresponded to the soul of the music is of course a complex procedure. Some students were not able to react to his associations; they needed concrete explanations. But if you were on the right wavelength for him, then just a few words or a gesture sufficed to get the results. And this was an extraordinarily exciting experience, for one was entering into dialogue with a great artist.

INTERLUDE 5

Victoria Yagling

I was born and brought up within the Moscow artistic intelligentsia, and our family mixed with writers, artists, scientists and musicians. But despite this wealth of influences, Mstislav Rostropovich nonetheless played a crucial role in my formation. Through a kind fate, I had the good fortune to enjoy a close relationship over eleven years with this great musician.

My first meeting with him occurred in 1961, when I was just fifteen years old. I started playing the cello at the age of six, studying first at the Gnesins' Musical School with Ivan Volchkov, and then going on to the Uchilishche (high school) of the Moscow Conservatoire. The school director, Larissa Artynova, to whom I shall forever be grateful, knew Rostropovich and organised a meeting with him.

I came at the appointed hour with my parents to his flat on Ogaryov Street. Naturally I was well prepared for this occasion, and intended to play a programme that I had worked on thoroughly. But Rostropovich decided otherwise. The first thing he asked to hear was a scale with all the accompanying arpeggios, as well as double-stopped scales. Then he put me through a series of bowing combinations, asking me to make sudden changes, all in a fast tempo, which considerably complicated the task. Nevertheless I managed.

After this he surprised me again: 'Now then, let's hear you play something you haven't played for a long time.' This completely took me aback; in an effort to wriggle out of a difficult situation I started explaining that I hadn't touched these pieces for a long time, and that I had forgotten the fingerings. But Rostropovich quickly intercepted me: 'Very good, I just want to see how you forget things!' I was forced to give in.

All these demands were so unusual that tension and anxiety deprived me of the power of speech. I was convinced that this audition had been a failure and that Rostropovich would not accept me. But it turned out otherwise, and he took me into his class. Although he only taught at the Moscow Conservatoire, he told me he would give me lessons. Their frequency would depend on the interest I provoked in him and on my level of preparation. To start with he set me seven Piatti caprices, and ordered me to learn them from memory. He told me to have them ready to play in tempo for my first lesson in a week's time.

From that day a new life started for me. My professor was often away on tour, and then he would reappear in Moscow for a few days. I would diligently prepare for these rare meetings, working with an assistant – Lev Evgrafov, who at the time was studying with Rostropovich as a postgraduate. In the first year, I learnt an enormous quantity of repertoire which laid the basis for my instrumental technique and put my playing in thorough order.

The course at the high school was supposed to last four years, but Rostropovich had other ideas, and suggested that I compressed it into a three-year period. On top of this concentrated workload, I was studying composition with Dmitri Kabalevsky: I had started writing music at the age of seven, and could not conceive of life without composing.

An important event during my last year at high school was my first appearance with orchestra at the Great Hall of the Moscow Conservatoire, playing Tchaikovsky's Rococo Variations. Then in September 1964 I became a fully fledged student in Professor Rostropovich's Conservatoire class, while simultaneously enrolling in the composition faculty. Since Kabalevsky was soon to give up teaching, I worked with his assistant before transferring to Tikhon Khrennikov's class.

Early in September, all of Rostropovich's students were convoked to Class 19 on the second floor of the main Conservatoire building. Towards the beginning of the appointed time, all the students appeared (they included Karine Georgian, David Geringas, David Grigorian, Mariya Chaikovskaya, Tanya Remenikova, T. Dikhtyar). All the cellists started simultaneously warming up in the corridor outside the class, and the most terrible cacophony rang out. Quite some time before Rostropovich's actual appearance, the fragrance of his scent, Ma Griffe, wafted up the stairs, and one could hear our *professor's voice, his characteristic manner of speech with its slight impediment on the letter 'R', as he saluted and kissed his colleagues. Shortly he entered the class, energetic and ready for action.*

At my first lesson I was set the Boccherini D major concerto, which I was told to learn in four days. Naturally I was expected to play it at the next class, up to tempo and by heart. This rapid method of study was a wonderful training for the memory, a way of sharpening one's reactions.

Rostropovich taught us his own method of learning a new work. Firstly, we were to aim for a general grasp of the whole, to understand the principal ideas of its development and to analyse the compositional form. For this purpose it was useful to start by sight-reading the work, as far as possible in tempo, and on the piano as well as the cello. If the piece was a concerto, then we were to study the orchestral score and know it to perfection: only then was one ready to start working at the instrument in detail. This method allowed us to preserve a feeling of the entire form during performance, transmitting the character and substance of the work without getting bogged down in inessential detail.

In class Rostropovich sat at the piano, of which he had perfect mastery, often playing along with the class pianist at the second piano. He knew the piano parts of the whole cello repertoire from memory. Since I was a competent pianist, he would sometimes ask me to play for another student; I was expected to be able to sight-read the accompaniment.

The atmosphere in Class 19 was quite special. Usually there were some twenty to thirty people in attendance, including students from other faculties, Conservatoire teachers and professors, and also outsiders, attracted by Rostropovich's personality. Our teacher's magical influence exerted itself on all present, and he entertained us through his lively imagery and riveting discoveries, his unfailing sense of humour evident all the time.

At the time, Haydn's C major concerto had recently been rediscovered, and all of us were entranced by this music. Rostropovich worked on it in class with enthusiasm and a spirit of adventure: 'You must play this music as if you were reading a Dumas novel, when you can't wait to turn over the page and discover what befalls the hero next.'

I remember how Rostropovich worked with me on extracting a suitable colour for the opening of the Schumann concerto; he paid particular attention to the way the soloist's first note emerged against the palpitating strings in the orchestra, demanding that it imperceptibly blend into the orchestral backdrop. He seemed to use sorcery in demonstrating how to achieve the kind of vibrato that would create a fragile and poetic sound-world.

For the very difficult opening of Beethoven's sonata in C, Op. 102, no. 1, his approach was fascinating. He asked me to imagine an invisible thread of melody, to hear it in the inner ear before its real appearance in the opening bars of the solo cello line. My task was simply to listen, tune in, pick up this inaudible melodic filament and produce its real-life continuation. In this way, he enormously facilitated what had seemed for me a difficult interpretive problem.

Rostropovich made a completely different set of demands when interpreting Prokofiev's Sinfonia Concertante. *We were told not to spare our strength or the instrument itself: we were to aim for a large-scale expression of the expansive melodic lines and to reveal the overall concept of the whole. His own interpretation of this work was ideal and unique; we were left with heart in mouth!*

We attended all our professor's lessons: by listening to him teach others, we benefited from his suggestions, which were directed not only at the cellist playing, but at us all, for we could adapt them to our own needs when playing. Mstislav Leopoldovich spoke a great deal about the flow of time in music, of the significance of pauses, of silences and breathing, of the need to calculate every culmination precisely, and of the necessity sometimes to sacrifice some superfluous decorative detail or nuance in the interest of the overall concept. He inculcated good taste and a sense of proportion in us, and in my case, he also worked a great deal on acquiring a singing cantilena.

If Mstislav Leopoldovich was interested in a student's playing, then he could work unstintingly for two or three hours, investing his whole spirit and his enormous force of temperament into his work. If, on the contrary, he was bored by the student, he might sit in complete silence in his armchair for the whole duration of the lesson. Such lessons were considered a complete catastrophe.

Naturally, we attended all Rostropovich's concerts, and at that time he was performing a huge number. It's enough only to mention his cycle of more than forty concertos, of which a large part were written for him and dedicated to him. Although all Rostropovich's concerts were events in themselves, certain ones remain particularly strongly etched in the memory. For me such a concert was his recital in Moscow with Benjamin Britten, and in particular their unforgettable rendering of Schubert's 'Arpeggione' sonata – it was an interpretation of genius.

I also attended all the rehearsals before the premieres of new works. Before the first performance of his second cello concerto, Shostakovich was very anxious. As was his wont, Dmitri Dmitriyevich sat discreetly in the middle of the stalls of the Grand Hall of the Conservatoire, biting his nails. His rare comments were uttered in a soft voice and were hardly audible, so when he did speak, a tense silence could be felt. He always started with an apology, followed by praise for the orchestra, Rostropovich and the conductor, before rather bashfully expressing his demands – or to be more precise, his wishes. The premiere of the second concerto created a devastating effect.

I also remember Aram Ilyich Khatchaturian at the conductor's podium rehearsing his new creation, his spirited, passionate Concerto-Rhapsody for cello and orchestra. The composer was not always able to follow his soloist; despite the fact that the work was new to him, Rostropovich had mastered all its difficulties with complete freedom, and could display his wit and tease Aram Ilyich as he played.

One should note that in those years, the atmosphere of the Moscow Conservatoire was filled with a sense of purpose and a heady creative spirit. Next to Rostropovich's classroom were those where David Oistrakh, Leonid Kogan, Yakov Flier, Emil Gilels, Lev Oborin, Yakov Zak, and Yuri Yankelevich taught. Naturally we never missed any performances by any of those musicians, let alone those by Richter, Yudina, or the joint recitals where Richter partnered either Rostropovich or Oistrakh. The overwhelming mastery of this constellation of great artists served to awaken our imaginations, stimulate our fantasy, and stretch our artistic horizons.

The class concerts were special events in our student lives, and were held in the Small Hall of the Conservatoire, with its beautiful acoustics. The hall was always full to bursting, and an atmosphere of great excitement reigned, so that our nerves were not spared. Rostropovich usually created the programmes of these class concerts in accordance with particular themes. For instance, he might programme all five Beethoven sonatas or all the Bach suites, dividing them up between the students, or perhaps he would set a series of contemporary cello concertos, and so on. On three occasions, Rostropovich took his class to Kiev for concerts. The second time he put together a student orchestra on the spot, so we could perform concertos which he himself rehearsed and conducted. In this concert I performed Haydn's C major concerto under his direction.

A few years earlier he had organised a similar event in Moscow, a class concert dedicated to baroque concertos, where he again created a student orchestra and directed it, this time from the harpsichord. On that occasion I performed Vivaldi's G major concerto.

Rostropovich always encouraged me in my composition studies. For the celebrations of the Conservatoire's centenary in 1966 I performed my second cello sonata. Before the concert, Mstislav Leopoldovich worked on it with me in class and his comments were extremely interesting and perceptive.

Another absolutely unforgettable occasion was Jacqueline du Pré's performance of the Haydn C major concerto, which Rostropovich conducted at the Grand Hall of the Conservatoire in June 1966. On this occasion I played in the specially formed student orchestra. I was very friendly with Jacqueline and she often came round to my apartment, together with another friend and Rostropovich pupil, Liza Wilson. Without exception, we all recognised and hailed the unique nature of Jacqueline's talent. Our professor worked with her with the greatest attention and care.

From my first year at the Conservatoire, I was elected as class representative; among my various responsibilities I was delegated the important task of organising the celebrations after our class concerts. These parties almost always took place at our apartment, where my mother Emine Yagling and my stepfather, the well-known poet Ilya Fraenkel, hospitably opened their doors. Ilya Fraenkel was friendly with Georgi Sviridov, and it was on the latter's advice that I started to study music. My stepfather was also acquainted with Dmitri Shostakovich, and they once planned to create a song together, but alas, this project was never realised.

My parents were always happy to welcome the crowd of students with Rostropovich at its head. By that time they had befriended Mstislav Leopoldovich, and used the familiar 'Thou' when addressing each other. We would assemble late at night at our flat in Lavrushensky Lane, in the Writers' House near the Tretyakov Gallery, where many celebrated Soviet authors lived, including Yuri

Olesha and Valentin Kataev. Boris Pasternak's flat was situated in the same entrance as ours.

Once Mstislav Leopoldovich and his horde arrived late in the evening, quite unexpectedly for my parents. 'Emi, I'm hungry, I want to eat,' the maestro announced to Mother. She opened the fridge and showed him its meagre supplies. Rostropovich couldn't hide his disappointment. Then Mother ran upstairs to the writer Boris Kozhevnikov who lived on the floor above. On discovering that the famished visitor was none other than Rostropovich and that we had nothing to feed him with, his wife, with true generosity, handed over a pot full of pilaff. Taking possession of this treasure, the professor shut himself into the kitchen with my parents, and ate the whole contents straight out of the pan with a spoon, downing it with a glass of vodka. Then rubbing his hands in delight, he said, 'Well, I'm off to rub shoulders with the People!' By 'the People' he meant us, his students, who were waiting impatiently for him in the sitting room.

As a rule, though, these gatherings were accompanied by a well-laden table with plenty of food and wine. The climax of the evening was always the discussion of the class concert itself, when Rostropovich would give his evaluation of each of us, pointing out not only our shortcomings, but also the good features of our performances: he was always sincerely delighted when somebody had played particularly well.

Preparations for international competitions were a fundamental part of the Conservatoire training, and were to be taken very seriously. First of all we had to play at internal auditions within the Conservatoire, before being selected for the team that was sent abroad. Given the extremely high level of young Soviet musicians at the time, Conservatoire students could reasonably count on winning a high prize in these contests. Behind the Iron Curtain, 'stewing in our own juice', the optimum conditions for the perfection of young talent were created: for instance, a month before the start of the Tchaikovsky competition, the participants were sent to Serebryany Bor on the outskirts of Moscow where, at the government's expense, they were housed in separate cottages, fed and watered. Before the Munich competition I went to the 'Writers' House of Creativity' at Maleevka, where I diligently prepared for the contest. Unfortunately our group was prevented from leaving the country, since the competition took place in September 1968, shortly after Soviet tanks had invaded Czechoslovakia. In this situation, the authorities considered it inappropriate for us to travel abroad.

In 1969, after overcoming a considerable number of difficulties, I was allowed to travel to Florence to participate in the First International Gaspar Cassado competition. Rostropovich came to my defence at a meeting of the Conservatoire Party Unit, where they took issue with my not being a member of the Komsomol – at the time this was considered a grave crime. Today, young people in Russia find it well-nigh impossible to comprehend the climate we lived in, the rules and regulations that governed our lives – our very existence was subject to the iron grip of authority and the ruthless logic of Soviet bureaucracy, which each of us experienced to our cost. Rostropovich also travelled to Florence as a jury member, accompanying me and Tanya Remenikova, the two Soviet participants. He drew up a detailed schedule for us, mapping out a daily timetable for the duration of the whole competition, in which he allocated time not just for practice and rehearsal, but for rest, walks and sight-seeing. Interestingly, he forbade us to go and listen to the other participants – in my opinion, this was absolutely the right advice.

I remember that our rehearsals before the second round took place in a convent. The lovely young nuns sat along the walls along the side of the hall where we played. They looked demure in their white headdresses, but reacted with spirit and vivacity to all that was going on, and considerably distracted our professor! For me the competition had a successful outcome, for I was awarded the first prize as well as the special prize for the best woman cellist, given by Antonio Janigro, one of the jury members.

On our return to Moscow from Italy, Rostropovich presented me to Gosconcert, which was the only international concert agency in the Soviet Union in those days. From that day, I started my independent concert career, and in the same year (1969) I completed my Conservatoire studies and enrolled on the postgraduate course.

With my prize money from Florence, I bought my first car, a Moskvich, which seemed to me the very best automobile in the world, an unimaginable luxury. Once, Rostropovich proposed a race with me on the outer ring road of Moscow. We decided on the starting point, and each was to drive as fast as we could. Mstislav Leopoldovich was as happy as a child, and allowed me a head-start of several kilometres, while he waited, the engine of his Mercedes *ticking over at the side of the road. I pressed my foot right down on the accelerator, pushing my Moskvich to its limits; but my initial advantage was soon lost, as after a few minutes' wait Mstislav Leopoldovich launched into the attack, and soon his Mercedes glided effortlessly past me. You should have seen the mischievously triumphant smile on his face as he overtook me with a friendly wave of the hand.*

A year later I also participated in the Tchaikovsky competition in Moscow, where I won second prize. For a while, Mstislav Leopoldovich continued to guide my progress and helped me select concert programmes.

As the years passed by, Rostropovich's worldwide triumphs continued. While he continuously renewed his enormous repertoire on the cello, he also started a new career as a conductor. How he found time for all this will always remain a mystery to me. One must also mention his concerts with Galina Vishnevskaya, whom he accompanied brilliantly at the piano, and always from memory. Once he invited me to the first closed showing of the film of Shostakovich's Katerina Izmailova, *where Vishenevskaya sang and acted the title role quite splendidly. The showing was in the enormous cinema Rossiya, and Galina Pavlovna, Mstislav Leopoldovich and I were the only three spectators.*

In autumn 1973 Rostropovich rang me from Volgograd, and asked me if I would fly out at once to take his place in a performance of Khrennikov's first cello concerto. He and Galina Pavlovna were travelling down the Volga giving concerts: it was a difficult time for my teacher, as he had fallen out of favour with the authorities due to his support of the disgraced writer, Aleksandr Solzhenitsyn. The drama of his fall from grace unfolded before my eyes, leading to the banishment of this unique artist from his own country. The Volga town administrators were not always happy to host such a famous couple, and in some cases even arbitrarily cancelled their concerts, pasting over the posters – this is what happened in Volgograd. Of course I flew down there and played, as Rostropovich asked me, but I was very nervous as I had so little time to get the concerto back into my fingers. At the same time, of course, I was glad to have another opportunity to meet my professor. Later I recorded Khrennikov's first concerto for Melodiya.

Events hurtled forward at lightning speed. Shortly afterwards, Rostropovich was banned not only from playing but from conducting, and soon I learnt of his decision to leave the country. I will never forget his last concert at the Grand Hall of the Conservatoire, where he conducted Tchaikovsky's sixth symphony. I sat next to Aram Khatchaturian, and we both wept openly. As the last sounds of the symphony died away, the whole hall rose to its feet, with everybody chanting in rhythm, 'Come back, come back'. We all understood perfectly well whom we were about to lose. I said my goodbyes to Mstislav Leopoldovich in the courtyard of the Melodiya record firm.

Rostropovich's departure was like a bereavement for us: without him, Russian musical life seemed orphaned, pallid and insipid.

13

The late 1960s

Rostropovich's mammoth concerto cycle of 1963/64 demonstrated his unique capacity for continuous artistic development and self-renewal, as well as for a ruthlessly strenuous pace of work. Not content to rest on his laurels, he continued to search out new works to enrich the repertoire. By now composers from all over the world were besieging Rostropovich with requests to play their music, and he had to use considerable discretion in selecting which of them to perform.

In October 1964, he gave the first performance of Khrennikov's cello concerto, a debt carried over from last season's cycle, for the composer had failed to produce his new work on time. Tikhon Khrennikov was a force to be reckoned with in Soviet music, due to his long-held position as First Secretary of the Composers' Union. Having started in the late 1930s as an interesting talent, one of Shebalin's best pupils, he had made his career through allying himself with official Communist policy. In 1948, he oversaw the attacks on Shostakovich, Prokofiev, and other major figures in Soviet music. His own compositions predictably reflected the style and aesthetic of socialist realism; without ever being memorable, his music never fell below professional standards of competence. (It was often rumoured, however, that as he became busier in his role as first secretary, Khrennikov farmed out the work of composing his music to various assistants.)

Around the same time, Rostropovich was informed by his older Conservatoire colleague, Professor Lev Ginsburg, that an 'excellent young composer' from Uruguay, by the name of Soriano, wished to write a concerto for him. Rostropovich trusted Ginsburg's recommendation and agreed to learn the work. Soon, however, he learnt that this proposal came directly from the musical department of SSOD, the Friendship Society responsible for cultural contacts with foreign countries, who organised meetings and concerts in the florid pseudo-baroque 'House of Friendship' near the Arbat. SSOD was responsible for promoting Soviet art and importing culture from abroad – not just from Third World countries, but also from the West, when political discretion allowed. Unfortunately this meant – as Rostropovich was to discover to his cost – that Soriano's qualifications as a composer were chiefly ideological: 'When I received the score of the concerto from Uruguay, I saw at once that it was written by a musical illiterate; there was no way I could serve up such shit to audiences,' he recalls.

Now Rostropovich faced a dilemma, for the composer was shortly due to arrive in Moscow. Eager not to disappoint, the cellist realised that some kind of performance was essential, so the question was how to limit the damage. His first step was to give Soriano's concerto to his second-year student Mariya Chaikovskaya (whom he always addressed by the nickname 'Manyunya'). Rostropovich set her a threefold task, to be performed within two days: to write out the cello part, to reduce the orchestral score for piano, as no piano score had been sent, and to learn it immediately. After she had stayed up two nights, slaving away, writing out the piano part, and putting a blanket round her cello to muffle the sound of her nocturnal practice, she came looking somewhat exhausted to Thursday's class. 'Mstislav Leopoldovich, I have managed to write out two and a half movements into piano score, I didn't quite finish the finale.' 'That's all right, Manyunya,' he replied, 'the piano score has just arrived in the post. Here it is.' Manya was struck dumb, and thought with anguish how much time she had wasted reducing the orchestral score for piano. Afterwards she realised that in the process of writing and copying, she had actually absorbed much of the music, and consequently it became easier to memorise. In her view, the concerto, though written in a contemporary idiom, lacked any evident musical logic, and hence there was nothing to latch on to when learning it. She was gratified that her reduction of the orchestral score coincided for the most part with the composer's piano score; as she recalls, 'If I succeeded in this task, it was because I knew Mstislav Leopoldovich believed I would manage to do anything he asked me.'

That day Rostropovich also informed Mariya that Soriano had postponed his trip to Moscow for the time being. He suggested that she should nevertheless play the concerto at the forthcoming class concert: 'We'll start work straight away.' The lesson began, and with it the fun. As Mariya recalls, Rostropovich more or less 'reinvented' the work with her on the spot. All the other students were amazed at how their Professor could find so many brilliant solutions to pep up the many grey, inconsequential passages. 'Manya,' Rostropovich directed, 'try an arpeggio passage here, now a passage across to the G string, try this fingering, now slide down to a low A. And this passage would sound better in double-stops, why not play it in thirds? Now finish with a flourishing four-part chord. Here let's invent a virtuoso bowing stroke' – and so on. By the end of the class a composition had indeed materialised. This in itself was instructive to all those listening. Mariya played the work in its new version a few days later at a class concert.

Some months later, Mariya came home to the hostel to find an urgent message to ring Rostropovich. He informed her that Soriano had just arrived in Moscow. 'Now it's my turn to have to learn the work, but you can help me by buying time. Tomorrow we will invite Soriano to an open class at the Conservatoire, and you will give him a nice surprise by playing his concerto.' When she expressed doubt as to whether she could remember it so quickly, he retorted, 'Manyunya, you have the whole evening ahead of you.'

This second masterclass was also something of a comedy, for Mariya had to pretend to be playing the concerto for the first time, as Rostropovich tentatively offered the 'improved' passages as a possible alternative to the composer. They were, for the most part, accepted without hesitation. Rostropovich's next step was to arrange a play-through concert with the conductor Gennady Rozhdestvensky at the House of Friendship for the SSOD employees – after all, SSOD had been responsible for Soriano's invitation. Rozhdestvensky, who was also an excellent pianist and brilliant sight-reader, accompanied Rostropovich at the piano, reading directly from the orchestral score. At their only rehearsal, the two men agreed on a set of signals, allowing them to take turns in inventing the music. A monologue on the cello would be followed by a development on the piano (representing the orchestra), and so forth. Their performance at the House of Friendship went ahead as planned: Rostropovich started with a rhetorical solo passage, then after a hefty nod to his conductor, landed on an open string, staying fixed while the 'orchestra' played the next section. Then in turn, Gennady gave a sign to Slava and they reversed the roles. Soriano, a large imposing figure of a man, was delighted with the result; at the end he kissed Rostropovich on stage, whispering in his ear, '*Mucho bien*' – whether this referred to his own work or the artists' performance nobody could tell. Rostropovich had salvaged the situation with honour intact, and spared himself the indignity of performing the piece with orchestra.

Such miscalculations, however, were rare. Rostropovich was very open-minded, and he was happy to learn new works not only by established composers, but by young, unknown talents, provided that they had interesting ideas and a professional attitude. He kept his ear to the ground, garnering information from many sources. When his student Aleksandr Knaifel played a new work by Gennady Banshchikov, himself still a student, Rostropovich was so impressed that he asked the young Leningrad composer to write a concerto for him. Banshchikov did so (it was actually his fourth cello concerto) and Rostropovich duly kept his promise and performed it in Leningrad early in 1966. In the mean time Banshchikov also wrote an effective set of four short pieces for cello and piano, entitled *Visions fugitives*, which he dedicated to Rostropovich's student, Viktor Apartsev. Without telling the composer, Apartsev presented them in a contest for the set work to be played at the second round of the 1966 Tchaikovsky competition. To Banshchikov's amazement, the *Visions fugitives* was chosen ahead of all the other entries.

At a similar time, Rostropovich heard many good reports about an extremely talented young Estonian composer, Arvo Pärt. He had established a reputation as an 'avant-gardist', a dubious privilege in the Soviet Union of that time, where this was almost a term of abuse – the musical equivalent of being a 'dissident'. When visiting Tallinn on a concert tour in May 1966, Rostropovich sought Pärt out, and found him in poor health, living in very difficult conditions, earning money as a sound engineer at Estonian radio. Pärt accepted Rostropovich's invitation to write a concerto for him, and by the end of the year he had completed *Pro e Contra*, a highly original work loosely based on the model of a baroque concerto grosso, with soloist, concertino group and ripieno. As in so many of Pärt's works of the time, he pitted the tonal element of its historical model (with direct references to Bach) against elements of serialism and atonality, setting up an opposition between nostalgia for an idealised past and the brutal reality of today's world. Unfortunately, any work smacking of dodecaphony and 'modernist' experiment was considered suspect by the authorities at the Composers' Union. While Rostropovich did succeed in performing *Pro e Contra* in Tallinn on 16 February 1968, his efforts to bring it to Moscow were thwarted.

Later in 1968, however, Pärt's *Credo*, an important work for solo piano, choir and orchestra, was performed, creating a huge scandal. Through some bureaucratic oversight, its openly religious title had been overlooked;* this in itself was enough to provoke criticism, and Pärt found himself in direct conflict with the Composers' Union. Shortly afterwards he underwent a severe creative crisis, and apart from occasional inspired interludes, he wrote no music for seven years. After a long voyage of self-discovery, Pärt recommenced composing in 1976 in a radically changed compositional style which he named 'Tintinnabuli'. This implied a complete repudiation of his modernist past, and at that stage he was not interested in having his earlier works played – this is why *Pro e Contra* lay unperformed for so many years after its initial hearing.

While on his travels, Rostropovich always made enquiries about the contemporary music scene of each country he visited. In this way he discovered that an Argentinian composer, Astor Piazzolla, wished to write a work based on tango. *Le Grand Tango* for cello and piano was actually written without Rostropovich's prior knowledge, many years before Piazzolla became a household name throughout the world.

On his first trip to Japan with the Leningrad Philharmonic in April 1958, Rostropovich met Kosa Yamada, the doyen of Japanese composers, who presented him with a signed copy of his transcriptions of Japanese folk songs. On one of his next visits, Rostropovich found himself playing under the direction of the conductor Yuzo Toyama, who was also an excellent composer, as he discovered:

I asked Toyama to write a concerto for me which would capture some of the colour and atmosphere of Japanese folk music. An interesting feature of Japanese music is their predilection for slow tempi. Fast music lies outside their normal sphere of musical thought. I would say that in this concerto it is almost impossible for a Western ear to predict the sequence of pitches; the Japanese have their own logic of musical thinking.

* Its text was not taken from the liturgical creed, but after the opening – 'I believe in Jesus Christ' – the lines are taken from the Gospel according to St Matthew. Relevant to those times were Christ's words, 'But I say unto you, do not resist evil.'

Toyama came to Moscow and conducted the first performance of his concerto in the Tchaikovsky Hall. Although the hall was only about half full, his performance was enthusiastically received.

Similarly, when on tour in Portugal Rostropovich met one of the country's best-known senior composers, Ferdinand Lopes-Graça. As was his wont, the cellist immediately coaxed him to compose a new work for him. The result was an attractive work entitled *Concerto da camera*, which Rostropovich premiered in Moscow in October 1967, in a concert series dedicated to the 'development of the cello as a solo instrument'. Like Toyama's concerto, Lopes-Graça's work was a worthwhile addition to the cello repertoire, although Rostropovich himself did not return to either work after their premieres. He learnt both pieces 'almost entirely for my own pleasure', and there was no thought of recording them at the time. However, it later transpired that in those years, the radio network had microphones permanently placed in Moscow's concert halls. This meant that many concerts were recorded live without the knowledge of the artists concerned; in a country where commercial considerations counted for little, nobody bothered with legal contracts, and there was no question of the radio organisation paying extra broadcasting fees. After the collapse of the Soviet Union, it emerged that the radio tapes had been lovingly and carefully preserved at the sound archives in Ostankino. Though Rostropovich's name had been taboo in the Soviet Union between 1974 and his return in 1990, the archivists understood the historical significance of these performances, and concealed his name to ensure the tapes would not be destroyed.*

I was curious to discover whether Rostropovich had played concertos such as those by Toyama and Lopes-Graça without music. His answer was simple, and corresponded to what I remembered: in those years he played everything from memory, even works he learnt for a single performance. He admits that the most difficult work he has ever had to memorise was the concerto by Lucas Foss, which he performed in his cycle in New York during January 1967. The piece was constructed in an interesting manner: certain sections of improvised variation were to be played in an order arbitrarily established by the conductor. The work also contained aleatoric

---

* Many of the performances discussed in this chapter were issued by EMI to mark Rostropovich's seventieth birthday in 1997, in an album entitled *The Russian Years*.

passages, and in the composed sections there was a series of complex, numerically calculated combinations. Retaining the concerto in his memory required a fantastic degree of concentration, as Rostropovich recalls:

I decided not to speak to anybody from morning onwards on the day of the concert. It seemed to me that if I had to say so much as 'Good morning' or 'How do you do', the whole work would have flown out of my memory. In the evening I managed to play the concerto with the London Symphony Orchestra without a single mistake; in fact one small slip would have cost me the whole performance!

Shortly afterwards he gave a second performance out of town, under Foss's direction, but this time he decided to play from the music, rather than undergo such stress a second time. Rostropovich confesses that in his considerable experience of memorising new works, only Schnittke's second cello concerto could begin to compare in difficulty.

In general Rostropovich's philosophy was simple: he lent prestige to a new work by launching it into the world, then it was up to other cellists to pick up the challenge and perform it elsewhere. He hoped that Japanese, Portuguese and American cellists respectively would programme the concertos by Toyama, Lopes-Graça and Foss in their own countries. Being given a first performance by Rostropovich was regarded as a guarantee of quality and feasibility for the instrument, and naturally it enhanced a composer's CV.

The more established composers with whom Rostropovich worked included the highly regarded French composer, André Jolivet, who wrote his second cello concerto for him, and he played it several times after giving the first performance in Moscow on 7 January 1967. A few years later, in 1970, Rostropovich learnt a concerto by Sir Arthur Bliss, who was at that time Master of the Queen's Musicke. Bliss (whom Rostropovich somewhat mischievously dubbed 'Sir Author') had been rather lukewarmly recommended by Britten. On this occasion, however, Rostropovich went to the trouble of learning a work (by memory, naturally) for only a couple of performances in Britain.

Back at home, in May 1969, Shostakovich had prepared an unusual present for his student Boris Tishchenko in the form of a new orchestration of his first cello concerto. He aimed to make Tishchenko's unusual scoring for seventeen wind instruments and percussion more transparent, by removing the brass instruments and adding strings. Tishchenko regarded this not only as a great compliment from his teacher, but also as an instructive example. However, the lesson apparently went unheeded, for later that year Tishchenko completed a second concerto for Rostropovich with an orchestration far more radical than that of the first. As he explained:

I conceived the work at a time when I was trying out my powers in a compositional style, which I decided to call '*stile robusto*' – that is to say, in a 'strong, powerful style'. My choice of the formation of the orchestra was polemical: forty-eight cellos, twelve double-basses and percussion . . . The emotional and imaginative content of the music was dictated by the fact that I was totally in love with the overwhelming genius of Mstislav Rostropovich. On presenting him a gift copy of the score I put it to him in as many words: 'This is a concerto for *Rostropovich* and orchestra.'*

Unfortunately, the 'polemical' scoring doomed the work to silence, until a few years later Tishchenko decided on a compromise version arranged for cello and string orchestra. Rostropovich himself never played this concerto as soloist, since it was presented to him at a time when he had many different problems and preoccupations. Nevertheless, some thirty years after it was written, he programmed the world premiere of the concerto in its original version as part of the Second World Congress of Cellists in St Petersburg in July 1997. He conducted the piece, and invited one of his favourite students, Ivan Monighetti, to be the soloist – over the years Ivan had become a great champion of new music in his own right, and he had in fact played the revised version of Tishchenko's concerto some fifteen years back. Monighetti and Rostropovich recorded the work in Moscow the following year.

Rostropovich once told me that new works often came in a sequence of 'waves': usually about one wave in seven brought something outstanding. He would generally play modern concertos only if they had been especially written for him – thus he never played Alfred Schnittke's first cello concerto, which was written for Natalya Gutman. However, in the late 1980s, he asked Schnittke to write for him both as cellist and conductor. This resulted in a series of splendid works, including the second cello concerto, the *Concerto*

* CD programme notes for Tishchenko and Boris Chaikovsky concertos, Artel Vostochny Veter Moscow, 2004 (Monighetti, Rostropovich, Russian Symphony Orchestra).

*for Three** (written for Gidon Kremer, Yuri Bashmet and Rostropovich), the opera *Life with An Idiot*, and his sixth symphony. Walton's fine cello concerto was another work that Rostropovich never played, for the same reason, although he did promise the composer that he would consider playing it as soon as he wrote another one for him. Walton did not live to compose the hoped-for second concerto, but he did write a Passacaglia for solo cello towards the end of his life, and heard Rostropovich play its premiere at the Royal Festival Hall in London, shortly before he died.

Of the large quantities of works written for him, many he only played once, and others a handful of times. Fewer than a dozen of the concertos written for him became part of his central repertoire, but those he performed as regularly as he could. These concertos have become classics of the cello repertoire: the names of their composers – Prokofiev, Shostakovich, Britten, Lutoslawski, Dutilleux, Penderecki and Schnittke – speak for themselves. When I recently asked Rostropovich which other composers should be included in this list he replied without hesitation. 'Boris Chaikovsky.† If his genius is not recognised today, this is in part because of his modesty and unwillingness to promote himself. Don't worry, his time will come!'

From the late spring of 1967, Rostropovich devoted a large part of his energy to a new musical activity, which would increasingly dominate his life. He had accepted an invitation to conduct Tchaikovsky's *Evgeny Onegin* at the Bolshoi Theatre; the then director of the theatre, Mikhail Chulaki, had supported Rostropovich's talent from the age of fifteen, when he had taught him composition and given him many kinds of help during his difficult years of evacuation.

Ever since his father had taken him to see Gounod's *Faust* at the age of eight, Rostropovich had always adored opera, and this passion was naturally reinforced when he married Galina Vishnevskaya, the principal soprano of the Bolshoi Theatre. As he recalls:

---

* The English title does not convey the joking quality of the Russian *Na Troikh*, which refers to the national tradition of buying and consuming a bottle of vodka on the street in groups of three people. 'Do you want to be the third?' was a question often asked in these circumstances. Shostakovich's famous response to this query was, 'No, I want to be the first!' – he was scrupulous about hygiene and liked to be the first to swig at the bottle!
† Rostropovich was certain that sharing a surname with the illustrious Pyotr Ilyich had not helped Boris at all.

Once I went to hear *Onegin* at the Bolshoi when Galina was singing. It occurred to me that what I was hearing did not coincide with what Tchaikovsky had intended. This was only an intuition, but when I came home that evening (of course I could remember the performance perfectly) I got out the score and had a good look at it. What I saw there was completely different from the 'traditions' which had become a standard convention in the Bolshoi's interpretation.

Rostropovich declared that he wanted to cleanse the score of these false traditions, which were effectively nothing but bad habits: senseless rubati, wrong tempi, even errors in the text. Chulaki agreed that Rostropovich would work on a new production with his friend, the experienced director Boris Pokrovsky. They were given a rehearsal period of several months – the subsidised Bolshoi could afford this, and it far exceeded the time generally given in Western opera theatres.

One of the indirect consequences of this new project was that Rostropovich decided to cut back on his teaching activity at the Conservatoire. He announced that he would be reducing his class numbers from sixteen to eight.* Naturally, those who were excluded were still welcome to attend as listeners. If Rostropovich gave less time to his class, this was compensated for by the fresh enthusiasm and renewed energy that he brought from his new job and shared with his students. He was totally immersed both in Pushkin's great poem and Tchaikovsky's music: he often came on to the Conservatoire directly from the opera rehearsals, and would excitedly recount his own impressions of the work in hand, talking with delight of the finer details of Pokrovsky's production. It was a fascinating time, not just for Rostropovich and the musicians of the Bolshoi, but also for his pupils.

For instance, he told us that to start with he could not get the orchestra to play the introduction with the right degree of veiled nostalgia: their sound was too hard and direct. He then asked if the heavy velvet stage curtain with the Soviet hammer and sickle embossed on it could be removed, and replaced by a transparent tulle backdrop. 'And do you know, there was already an improvement: the orchestra was suddenly able to think back to different times, and they captured a completely different sound-world.'

---

* The eight students left were in fact eleven, by my recollection: David Geringas and Mariya Chaikovskaya (both in their last year), David Grigorian, Victoria Yagling, Tanya Remenikova, Ivan Monighetti, Vago Saradzhan, Misha Maisky, Lyudmila Koval and myself. He also worked with two postgraduates, Karine Georgian and Rasim Abdulaev, who came especially from Alma-Ata for instruction.

Much of what he said had direct relevance to his teaching; for instance, when he worked on the *Rococo Variations* with Jacqueline du Pré, I recall how Rostropovich deplored any kind of direct sentimental expression in the slow variations, something that he felt was endemic to 'certain Western performers':

Despite Tchaikovsky's homosexuality, his acclamation of female beauty was unique in musical literature. Perhaps because he did not know women, and regretted not being able to know the warmth and comfort of a family, he could eulogise them through the mist of his imagination. Any hint of direct blatant sexuality in the sound is totally alien to Tchaikovsky's music.

Anybody who listens to Vishnevskaya and Rostropovich's superb interpretations of Tchaikovsky's vocal romances will appreciate this restrained quality of expression and their sensitive revelation of the heartache and nostalgia inherent in the music.

In *Evgeny Onegin*, Rostropovich reiterated, Tchaikovsky was true to the spirit of Pushkin:

A hint or suggestion could be more exciting than the blatantly explicit fashions of our age. The glimpse of a lady's ankle, which so excited Pushkin, leaves more to the imagination than the short mini-skirts worn today, which expose all to the eye and destroy the chance to fantasise!

Similarly, Rostropovich was implacably opposed to productions of *Evgeny Onegin* that did not respect the social conventions of Pushkin's times. He deprecated a certain Western opera director's 'clever idea' in the scene of the quarrel between Lensky and Onegin, where the two men started pushing each other and fighting. 'No, in Pushkin's age, men stood on their dignity. It was enough to throw down the gauntlet, a quarrel meant a duel, not a brawl!'

The opening of the new production of *Evgeny Onegin* at the Bolshoi on 12 January 1968 was Rostropovich's official conducting debut in the capital. He arranged for all his students to get tickets to one or another of the performances. The opera and the production were eagerly discussed in class; it was generally agreed that the Bolshoi orchestra had never before sounded so good. The following year Rostropovich started preparing his second opera production at the Bolshoi, Prokofiev's *War and Peace*.

In a sense, Rostropovich was acting on his declared intention of overcoming the limitations of his chosen instrument. As he once stated in an article, 'I have always dreamt of a cello with one hundred strings. I have envied conductors who inspire orchestral musicians in an artistic vision for which no single instrument possesses sufficient means of expression.'* With this new enlarged 'instrument', the orchestra, Rostropovich was able to use and extend the methods he had developed in his Conservatoire class, conveying his ideas through inspired images and conjuring up magical sound-worlds.

Although Rostropovich had never studied conducting in a conventional sense, he had had plenty of experience of conductors. Interestingly enough, he recalls that as far back as 1959, long before he had thought of realising his dream to conduct, Leopold Stokowski had came backstage with Sol Hurok after one of his concerts in New York. After complimenting Rostropovich on his playing, Stokowski told him, 'You don't know it yourself yet, but you are a wonderful conductor!' It took a veteran to recognise the cellist's potential as a conductor. In fact, Rostropovich had been learning about the craft of conducting in his own way:

When travelling round the world playing concertos, I always closely observed the conductor. I found it fascinating to see how each one approached the same work, say the Dvořák concerto, and how they brought completely different musical qualities to their interpretations. I always tried to understand how they transmitted their ideas and how they achieved results.

He had no hesitation in asking advice from his various conductor friends, and Kirill Kondrashin was particularly helpful. Revealingly, when he put the same question to Kondrashin and Herbert von Karajan – 'How am I to show the quality of sound I want in my upbeat?' – their answers were identical: 'Well, just as you would when you are playing; think of the gesture you make with your bow in an upbeat!'

Quite apart from his conducting debut, 1968 was a highly significant year for Rostropovich – indeed, it marked a point of no return. During the autumn celebrations of the fiftieth anniversary of the 1917 Revolution, Rostropovich, like many of his Soviet colleagues, toured the large provincial cities throughout the Soviet Union. On 3 and 4 November 1967, he played two concerts with orchestra under Kondrashin in the town of Ryazan. He learnt that the writer Aleksandr Solzhenitsyn had been in the audience, although he had not come backstage to greet him. The next day Rostropovich found the house where the writer lodged, and rang the bell. An old lady answered the door,

* *Vecherniy Leningrad* (Evening Leningrad), 27 January 1968.

who turned out to be his mother-in-law. Rostropovich was invited in, and sat and talked with Solzhenitsyn for several hours. At the end of their meeting the writer complimented Rostropovich on the richness of his spoken language, with its unusual use of metaphor, and asked if he could visit him whenever he happened to be in Moscow. The two men soon established a friendship, and Rostropovich was an interested and anxious observer of the events that shortly unfolded in the literary world, directly affecting Solzhenitsyn's life.

Many had hoped that his latest novel, *Cancer Ward*, would escape official censorship and be passed for publication in the influential literary journal, *Novy Mir*. However, the authorities lost their nerve, and moreover forbade any further publication of Solzhenitsyn's works in the Soviet Union. This decision made it inevitable that sooner or later, his writing would be published – illegally, as far as the Soviet government was concerned – outside his own country, and this was just what happened when the British publishing house, Bodley Head, published *Cancer Ward* in Russian in May 1968. After this act of disobedience, the authorities were determined to find a way of punishing Solzhenitsyn.

In summer 1968, Rostropovich spent a great deal of time in Britain, giving the first performance of Britten's second suite at the Aldeburgh Festival in June. While at Aldeburgh I discovered that Rostropovich had played a large part in influencing Britten to dedicate his new 'church parable', *The Prodigal Son*, to Dmitri Shostakovich. (The following year saw the compliment returned when Shostakovich dedicated his fourteenth symphony to Britten.) That year's festival also included Vishnevskaya giving the UK premiere of Shostakovich's new song cycle, *Seven Verses of Aleksander Blok*, with Britten at the piano, Emanuel Hurwitz playing the violin, and Rostropovich the cello. All these concerts were given at the newly opened Maltings at Snape, which was immediately appreciated by musicians and audiences as a glorious hall with a fabulous acoustic.*

Rostropovich suggested that my family came to Aldeburgh, since he wanted to introduce us to Britten. He had been delighted to learn that my father, Sir Duncan Wilson, had just been appointed as Her Majesty's ambassador to Moscow. As Rostropovich had hoped, this

---

* The following year the Maltings burnt down at the beginning of the festival. Rostropovich sent Britten a telegram of condolence from Paris, and offered to come and 'rebuild it with my own hands'.

was the start of a friendship between Britten and my father, which would also have important consequences for the next few years of the cellist's life.

Later that summer, my parents and I also accompanied Rostropovich to St Andrews University, where he received his first honorary doctorate – Willy Brandt, then Mayor of Berlin, and shortly to become West German Chancellor, was among the others on whom the honour was conferred at the same ceremony. I recall that my parents and Victor and Lilian Hochhauser (the British impresarios who looked after all the renowned Soviet artists) were highly amused to discover the Soviet cultural attaché prowling around the Salvation Army headquarters, in what appeared to be a futile attempt at espionage. That summer, Rostropovich announced to my brother David that he wished to buy a car, perhaps a camper, that would suitably match a car horn that he had already acquired – it emitted a startlingly loud, bovine moo. David succeeded almost immediately in tracking down a Land Rover, already fitted out with beds and camping gear – Rostropovich bought it at once.

The christening ceremony of the new car, 'Buttercup', was held at The Red House in Aldeburgh: Britten marked the occasion with an off-the-cuff 'farewell cantata' a few bars long, which included a part for the mooing horn. Rostropovich and Vishnevskaya left in triumph and drove back to Moscow in 'Buttercup'. Before long they travelled back to the UK for concerts in London, Harrogate and Edinburgh. The night after his return, Rostropovich was due to play Dvořák's concerto with the USSR State Symphony Orchestra at the Proms. But on the day of the concert, 21 August, he and Galina were shocked to learn the news that Soviet troops had invaded Prague. As Vishnevskaya wrote, 'There could not have been a sadder coincidence in London: on a day that was tragic for the whole world, a Soviet festival was opening with Dvořák's concerto at the head of its programme.'* Demonstrators with placards surrounded the Royal Albert Hall, shouting 'Soviet fascists go home', and in the hall itself an air of open hostility reigned. Only when Rostropovich came out onto the stage in a state of obvious tension did the audience quieten down; when he finished his heartfelt performance, into which he had injected all his pain and compassion for the Czech people, the hall burst into

* G. Vishnevshaya, *Galina: A Russian Story*, pp. 385–86.

applause. Indeed, he commanded such love and respect from London audiences that, as one London newspaper suggested, even if he had ridden into the Albert Hall on the back of a tank, he would still have been greeted with an ovation.

These few days saw the collapse of Rostropovich's loyalty to his Soviet homeland. Vishnevskaya put it succinctly: 'Without our suspecting it, the events in Czechoslovakia had slammed shut the book on what had been our good life.'* Rostropovich elucidated his position further when he told me:

Up until then I had two separate and unconnected lives; the first was in the Soviet Union and the second outside it, when I went on tours abroad. Everything was different, audiences, ordinary people and the whole structure of society. In Russia, one could find oneself drinking with some ordinary person who might stop you on the street, who was not impeded by inhibitions. He might say, 'Listen, I saw you playing away. It was quite something. No, I don't think I could manage to do that!' In the West there existed a feeling of respect for the individual, but also more reserve. Then with the Soviet invasion of Czechoslovakia, these two lives suddenly crossed over and could no longer be separated.

To his Conservatoire students Rostropovich seemed to lead far more than the one life in which they took part – that of teacher and cellist. Of course, his students were aware through his own stories of Rostropovich's other existences, of his vast range of interests and his large circle of acquaintances from all walks of life. As a foreign student, I perhaps had a somewhat different perspective, for I had observed how Rostropovich was fêted in London and Aldeburgh, and I had seen his state of shock and his tears at the 1968 Edinburgh Festival, where the anti-Soviet demonstrations continued, and the Usher Hall was besieged by angry protesters. All this deeply affected the Soviet soloists and orchestral players; I remember David Oistrakh asking Lilian Hochhauser to film these demonstrations, to prove to his friends back home the strength of Western reaction against the Soviet military action. At one of Rostropovich's concerts, a young man even disrupted the performance itself, standing up ostentatiously and making a noisy exit from the Usher Hall while shouting loudly, 'Viva Casals!'

In 1968, the Edinburgh Festival made a special feature of Britten's music, and on 24 August Rostropovich played his cello symphony with the USSR State orchestra directed by Svetlanov. As Conrad Wilson wrote in *The Scotsman* the day after, 'One has heard

* Ibid.

Rostropovich give more finished performances, but rarely can he have made the first movement sound lonelier, the scherzo more spectral, the cadenza more intense, the music more generally nervy and brooding . . . In the circumstances, it could hardly have been otherwise.'

The tensions were of a completely different nature than those experienced in the 1964 festival when Rostropovich and Richter had performed the complete Beethoven sonata cycle under extraordinary circumstances. I had witnessed the tragi-comedy of the enforced postponement of this recital due to the pianist's indisposition. The festival director Peter Diamand persuaded the artists to reinstate the recital on 31 August, but the only time left available at the Usher Hall was at 10.30 pm. Getting the two Slavas together proved problematic since they had both taken offence; neither would take the first step to arrange a meeting. (Rostropovich borrowed my copy of the LP recordings of the sonata to remind him of their interpretation). It took some ingenuity on Lilian Hocchauser's part to engineer a 'chance' meeting in the hotel lobby on the morning of the concert. Once they got going, Rostropovich and Richter rehearsed more or less right up till the start of the performance. Conrad Wilson wrote of the concert's 'furnace-like atmosphere',* certainly the knife-edge tension added an incredible dimension of excitement to their unique Beethoven interpretation.

I also recall Rostropovich's mock indignation when, in the early days of September 1968, he heard Jacqueline du Pré's televised performance of the Dvořák concerto at the Albert Hall given in aid of Czechoslovakia. While she was changing a broken string, the BBC announcer solemnly told viewers, 'Tonight Miss du Pré will be exorcising the ghost of the Soviet artist Rostropovich who only two weeks ago played this work as Soviet tanks invaded Prague.' As far as Slava was concerned, this was below the belt!

At one of his next lessons on the Dvořák concerto in class, Rostropovich confessed to having found elements of that particular du Pré performance to be over the top, including the cello's long up beat bar (an ascending scale in octaves) in the first movement leading to the orchestra's triumphant recapitulation of the second subject. Jacqueline had taken an exaggerated amount of time, stretching the passage to its limits. He now instructed his student to play this bar

* *The Scotman*, 1 September, 1964.

strictly in time. He too wished to exorcise a musical indulgence that had veered dangerously near the border of bad taste.

*

The political situation in Europe changed irrevocably after August 1968. The Soviet Union lost its moral standing, even amongst those in the West who were sympathetic to Communism, and at home the brutal beating into submission of a 'brotherly' country shocked not only the intelligentsia but many ordinary people.

Even at the Conservatoire, the aftermath of the Soviet invasion was felt. Vika Yagling and Tanya Remenikova, two students who had been chosen to participate at a cello competition in Munich that September, were refused permission due to the political tensions. West Germany had been heavily criticised by the Soviet government for their apparent support of Dubček's reforms during the 'Prague spring' – such concessions to liberty formed a highly dangerous precedent for Moscow, and even more so for neighbouring East Germany. I recall that by September, a little white book was on sale in the streets of Moscow, offering an ideologically correct explanation of the Soviet occupation of Czechoslovakia and justifying to Soviet citizens the military intervention in a brother country. The book claimed that the Soviet action saved Czechoslovakia from Germany's aggressive intentions. Of course, politics were ardently discussed, usually in the privacy of Muscovites' kitchens, over a cup of tea or a glass of vodka. The Soviet invasion of Czechoslovakia also saw protest at home – for instance Pavel Litvinov, who had led a small demonstration in Red Square, was arrested for his pains. All this gave impetus to the dissident movement.

As it was, the Soviet system put an enormous number of obstacles in the way of ordinary citizens in everyday life. Many students were discriminated against, if not punished, simply for remaining firm in their intention not to join the Komsomol or the Party. A recommendation and character reference from the Komsomol Unit in the Conservatoire was essential for any student who wished to travel abroad to partake in a competition.

Graduation year was always a critical time for students, since they had to deal with the hurdle of '*raspredelenie*' (job distribution). Each student was sent to some work position chosen by the State authorities: the posting was regarded as a repayment for sixteen years of free education. Theoretically it made sense to improve the cultural level throughout the country, while in reality it also represented an attempt not to overload the crowded cities with young people. Resident permits were a legal necessity in the Soviet Union, and it was next to impossible to move to Moscow and Leningrad unless a permit was guaranteed. Many of the posts offered by the job-distribution commissions were in some far-off backwater; given the enormous size of the Soviet Union, this meant that musicians who took these postings risked disappearing from the artistic scene for ever, and most students tried very hard to evade their assignations. Various strategies were used to achieve this. The final year of studies often became something of a marriage market, as 'provincial' fifth-year students tried to find a suitable Moscow resident to marry: marriage to a resident allowed one to stay in the city, a useful loophole which was exploited to the full.

The individual problems caused by professionally inappropriate postings were often acute. For example, David Geringas wished to apply for a postgraduate place at the end of 1968, but the Conservatoire job-distribution commission offered him a new position as cello teacher in Frunze, the capital of the Kirghiz republic. He was given to understand that his postgraduate place depended on accepting the offer; it was argued that as an external student, he could travel the several thousand kilometres dividing Frunze and Moscow for his lessons. In the event, the Kirghiz authorities themselves decided they had no need for any music teacher, let alone a cello teacher. However, David's initial refusal was not forgotten, and he was consequently barred from applying for a postgraduate place. All this drama was played out in Rostropovich's absence, and by the time he returned to Moscow, it was too late for him to influence the decision. He agreed that he would continue teaching David as a *stageur*, until he was finally permitted to enrol as a postgraduate. In the event, this only happened after he had won first prize at the 1970 Tchaikovsky competition: at a reception for participants and jury members, Rostropovich presented 'the conquering hero' to Ekaterina Furtseva and told her of the problem, enabling the matter to be resolved at the highest ministerial level.

In June 1969, together with three of Rostropovich's other students, I graduated from the Conservatoire. My friends jokingly asked whether I had a job allocation in London – in fact, I divided my time between London and Moscow, having more lessons with

Rostropovich as a *stageur*. David Grigorian was allocated to a job in Novosibirsk, a town with an excellent musical life, and travelled as an external postgraduate for lessons to Moscow. Together with David Geringas and Vago Saradzhan, he participated successfully in the All-Union competition, held in Baku in December 1969, and consequently took part at the 1970 Tchaikovsky competition, where he won fifth prize. In late June 1969, Vika Yagling and Tanya Remenikova were both sent to participate in the Gaspar Cassado competition in Florence, where Vika won first prize. After that they both remained in Moscow as postgraduate students of Rostropovich. The fifth student from our year, Tanya Dikhtyar, was by now married and had a child, and therefore postponed her graduation, though she later chose to specialise in quartet playing. Rostropovich gave her his blessing, and assured her that loving the cello would make her do everything in life better, whether cooking dinner for her family or playing chamber music. I found it very touching that as he sent his graduate students out into the world, our professor would invariably beg us, 'Please do not forget the work we did together.'

In July 1970, to the shock of his Conservatoire colleagues, Mischa Maisky was arrested on charges of 'speculation'. This charge implied that he had been caught with dollars or currency certificates for which he did not have the required special permit. Maisky wished to acquire a beautiful second-hand cello bow, but it transpired that the vendor would only sell for some form of technical equipment available exclusively in the hard-currency shops. The rouble effectively had no purchasing power, and this in turn resulted in a thriving but illegal black-market system in Moscow. Mischa must have known what a grave risk he was undertaking, but he wanted the bow rather badly. After all, plenty of his colleagues had acquired instruments, tape recorders, and other equipment under similar circumstances, even if others had managed it by exercising their legal right to keep a small part of their convertible currency earned abroad and to spend it in the special hard-currency shops in Moscow.

Mischa, not the most disciplined of students, and a great talker, had evidently allowed his intentions to become known to several Conservatoire students, one of whom then informed on him. The identity of the student in question seemed to be commonly known; in a story worthy of Dostoyevsky, he was reputed to have married a prostitute in order to redeem her while in the mean time living off her earnings. This was probably a wild exaggeration, but it was typical of the legends that circulated round the Conservatoire. Whatever the truth, the informer certainly seemed to personify treachery and evil and was consequently avoided by other students.

The fact that the word of an informer could jeopardise the lives of innocent and decent people was a horrible reminder of the cruel totalitarian system we lived in, an inheritance from the years of Stalinism. It seemed to me that at this time these divisive issues surfaced more and more frequently, as the political climate changed. However, it was important to distinguish infringement of the laws about currency dealings and the black market from the more serious matter of real political dissent, which was growing rapidly as the 1960s approached their end.

A feeling of unspoken gloom pervaded the class at the beginning of that academic year, for we knew that Mischa was locked up in the notorious Butyrki prison, awaiting trial. A few of his braver friends tried to help by attesting to Mischa's honest character and talent, but the only person from the Conservatoire staff actively to speak up for him was Natalya Gutman. Apart from supporting Mischa's distraught mother, she met with his lawyer, to see what measures could be taken to help. Now a young teacher on the cello faculty staff, Natasha went to see the Conservatoire authorities and suggested that there should be a united effort to help this young student. The ruse backfired, for the Conservatoire Party organisation, headed by a 'loyal' trumpeter by the name of Usov, started threatening Gutman, telling her to keep silent and stop 'defending a speculator'. She refused to be intimidated, and accused the Conservatoire of abandoning a student who needed its support. She herself spoke up in his defence at Maisky's trial in October 1970, as did David Geringas, who testified to his classmate's talent and good character. These actions were immediately reported to the authorities, usually by 'anonymous' denunciators, and in both cases the consequences were felt.

Gutman's support of Maisky was undoubtedly one of the reasons that the start of a brilliant career in the West was rudely interrupted. In December 1969, Natalya had made a highly successful US concerto debut under Stokowski, and was due to return to America for a second trip the next season. But now the necessary 'character reference' from the Conservatoire Party organisation was withheld. By the end of 1970, despite the many invitations issued to Natalya, she became 'nevyezdnoi' (a new, typically Soviet word, denoting 'one who was not able to travel out of the country'). This label was soon also attached to her husband Oleg Kagan, and to many other musicians of similar calibre, often for no ostensible reason. Natasha's problems were compounded when her former husband, Vladimir Moroz, was also arrested for similar reasons: 'speculation' covered a whole spectrum of offences.

Viewed from the outside, these were undoubtedly difficult and unhappy years in the Soviet Union, yet for those who remained untouched by corruption, and who did not sell their souls to the Party, life within this closed society still offered many interests and spiritual rewards – not least among them, a deep understanding of the value of true friendship and a disinterested love of culture. Nevertheless, the temptation to make a career by playing the system led to the reign of mediocrity in those years of Brezhnev's stagnation. In musical circles, the artists who were allowed to travel were not always the best or the most honest, but those who observed the rituals required by the Party or who cultivated the right contacts.

Natalya Gutman was finally allowed to travel abroad again at the very end of 1978. It was like starting again: permission was granted first to play in a socialist country (her first concert was in Timosoara, Romania), then in a neutral Western country, Finland (this occurred through the persistence of Seppo Kimanon, founder and director of the Kuhmo festival), and then finally a capitalist country (for concerts in Vienna). Many of Rostropovich's former students, however, had already left the Soviet Union during the second half of the 1970s. Some had managed to secure an official 'invitation' to Israel: these included David Geringas, Mischa Maisky, Tanya Remenikova, Miron Yampolsky, and Yos Fegelson.

Rostropovich himself had managed to attain his position without ever joining the Party. As he recalls, when asked by the Conservatoire Party branch to participate in a meeting called against Boris Pasternak at the TseDRI (the Central House of Artists), he found an expedient way out of it. The campaign against the writer had assumed mammoth proportions after the award of the Nobel prize for literature in October 1958 and the publication of *Dr Zhivago* in Italy – illegally, in Soviet eyes. The meeting was called on a Monday, but Rostropovich was due to play a concert in Ivanovo, a textile town, the preceding Saturday – he decided to stay on at any cost, rather than participate in a spectacle of treachery against a great writer. As he recalls, he had not even read *Doctor Zhivago* at the time. He told the local concert organisers that he liked Ivanovo so much that he wanted to continue performing for the 'weavers', and he also mentioned that a young lady weaver had caught his eye, to make his excuse seem more plausible. When he arrived back in Moscow on Tuesday morning he went straight to the Conservatoire, where the Party activists hauled him over the coals: 'Where were you? You let us down yesterday.' Rostropovich immediately produced his train ticket from his pocket and said, 'Look here, you can see I've just got back from playing concerts in the Ivanovo factories.'

Such manoeuvres allowed him to live with a clear conscience. One could say that Rostropovich managed to maintain his neutral position only through using his foresight and through his clear-headed perceptions of the world. By now, like all members of the Soviet intelligentsia, he was very familiar with the publications of *samizdat*.* I recall an occasion when he was driving to pick up some parcel at Vnukovo airport. He had invited some of us students to come with him, so we could have a long chat about this and that. He started retelling a story which he had just finished reading in *samizdat*. It was, he told us, 'undoubtedly written by one of our writers'. He started recounting in detail the contents of a book which I immediately recognised as Orwell's 1984. I cried out, 'But no, you are wrong, this book is by a famous English writer. It's so famous that it's a set book in most British schools!' I don't think anybody present was much convinced by my claim.

Rostropovich also tried to alleviate Maisky's situation and went to see the Procurator, but unfortunately, given the trouble that he himself was in for other reasons, his influence in official circles was no longer as strong. There was little he could do beyond writing a glowing recommendation of Mischa's musical talent, and insisting that he should not be given work that might injure his hands. The Procurator responded by accusing Rostropovich of being a corrupting influence on Maisky. A young person who saw that his professor owned a colour television or a Western hi-fi set, it was argued, was confronted by the

---

* Meaning 'self-publication', *samizdat* came into being in the mid-1960s as a means of distributing typescripts of proscribed literature. The system of circulation was simple: after having been read, the typescript was passed on to the next person.

evil temptations of capitalism. Despite his public loyalty, Rostropovich did in fact have some private criticisms of Mischa's behaviour and lack of discipline. He felt that it was necessary for a student in a Soviet institution to respect the rules, and to observe certain unwritten codes of behaviour – this could be done without losing one's honour.

Maisky was eventually sentenced to eighteen months' 'enforced labour' in Pravdinsk, a small settlement outside Gorky, working in the factory that manufactured the paper for *Pravda*.* (Since he had served four months in the Butyrki prison, the sentence was commuted to fourteen months.) Within a few months, however, we learnt that he had been allowed to form a small amateur musical ensemble as a substitute for hard manual labour. We even got to see Mischa when he was allowed back to Moscow under the pretext of collecting material for the ensemble. Few people knew that Rostropovich had been instrumental in making this happen.

---

* His stories of life there were hair-raising. For the most part, the citizens drowned their sorrows in alcohol. When he emigrated to the West, Maisky wisely decided not to refer to these events in his autobiography, since he wanted to make his career on his musical merits, and not because he was perceived as a victim of political repression.

INTERLUDE 6

Ivan Monighetti

First impressions and first meeting

In the eleven concerts that constituted his great concerto cycle of 1963–64, Rostropovich premiered more than twenty new works, most of them dedicated to and written for him. Here we witnessed something more than the making of cello history – rather the invention of twentieth-century music. It was the start of an era of cellistic discoveries and conquests, where Rostropovich was the prime mover, not merely creating a new epoch, but inventing his own unique biography.

Both for me, a fifteen-year-old student of cello at the Gnesins' Musical School, and for my unforgettable teacher A.K. Fedorchenko, Rostropovich was an absolute idol and the highest authority. Not one of his Moscow performances was to be missed! His personality, his musical genius, his whole manner and style of existence all had an incomparable, hypnotic effect. My far-off and seemingly unattainable dream – just the very idea of it excited my spirit – was to join his class and become his pupil.

Fedorchenko was absolutely convinced that I should study with Rostropovich.

Our first meeting in the spring of 1966 had a decisive effect on the rest of my life. By happy coincidence Mstislav Leopoldovich's sister Veronika and Fedorchenko's mother lived in apartments in the same newly built block on the Smolensk embankment. After some complex diplomatic negotiation, Fedorchenko managed to arrange that after lunch at his sister's, Mstislav Leopoldovich would come down the two flights of stairs to Fedorchenko's mother's flat, where I waited in fear and trembling. When the maestro appeared, he exuded excellent spirits – and the fragrance of expensive perfume. Evidently the family lunch had gone well.

We had come without an accompanist, so I had to start cold into the second movement of Prokofiev's Sinfonia Concertante, *which I was to play that same evening at an end-of-school concert at the Gnesins' Hall. Rostropovich threw himself into an armchair, while I sat in front of him, cello in hand. 'Well, let's start, old man,' he said – his speech was rapid, and he swallowed his 'r's. I hardly had time to play the first head-splittingly difficult passage when he interrupted me, 'Have you ever been anywhere apart from Moscow?' He listened to my answer and then told me to start from the beginning. At the same place he stopped me with the words, 'And what are you reading now?' Three times I started off playing, and three times he interrupted me. Checking out one's reactions and stamina in this way was a favourite device of his.*

And then a completely incredible thing happened. Suddenly he jumped up, plunged towards the piano, and without hesitating for as much as a second he played the orchestral introduction. For the fourth time I started off on the opening passage. Then without drawing breath or ever stopping, we played through the whole movement. I had never experienced anything like it in my life: an inexplicable sense of freedom, of fantasy, a miracle. After the concluding chord, he looked at me attentively again, with his penetrating, almost mesmerising stare, and said laconically, 'Let him enrol in the Conservatoire, I'll take him in my class.'

In the summer of 1966 I took the entrance exams for the Moscow Conservatoire. Together with me, Mischa Maisky, Vagram Saradzhan, Miron Yampolsky and Mikhail Milman were accepted in Rostropovich's class. Miron was older than the rest of us, for he had done his military service in the submarine unit. Coming from a renowned Moscow family of musicians, he had known Mstislav Leopoldovich for a long time: he was always optimistic and possessed a sharp wit and an innate sense of humour, which allowed him to be somewhat irreverent with 'Chef' – as Mstislav Leopoldovich was called behind his back. He was aware of this, but raised no objections.

At the first general meeting of the class, he told his first-year students: 'I want to discover your interests, to read the books that you are reading, to peer into your souls, so that I can help you develop in as many ways as possible.'

Lensky and the *Tribune*

Chef was a teacher of genius. Possessing enormous practical experience, a phenomenal memory, and a unique and profound intuition, he himself greatly enjoyed the whole teaching process. This is not surprising. In Class 19 he was surrounded by an atmosphere of rapturous admiration, if not complete adulation. Whatever he did or said was received with delight and accepted without question. For him, the class was a 'creative laboratory', an extension of the Grand Hall of the Moscow Conservatoire where he regularly performed in concert. An amazing and unique feature of the class was the quantity of new music played; practically everything he performed was studied and brought to class. Occasionally several students were given the task of learning the same new work simultaneously. At one point, he even went as far as to bestowing his 'brilliant' formula of success: ten new concertos will make an old programme at least twice as good as before.

In class he could experiment, check out and develop his creative thoughts, enjoying himself in the process while entertaining those present. Maybe in some other existence Chef had been a brilliant actor – his musical demonstrations were often transformed into something theatrical, with inimitable grimaces; whole scenes were mimed, with jokes and stories bandied about with the speed of gunfire.

It was striking how even a fairly small number of outside listeners sufficed to provide his inspiration. What was all the more amazing was just how apt his comparisons and allusions were, and how his incredibly rich perception of the surrounding world was organically connected to the works being performed, finding therein adequate reflection. It is a futile task to try and reproduce his lessons in detail. What he said was in fact completely inseparable from how he said it: each time his words sounded new, creative and inspired. It might seem a paradox, yet he did not teach 'cello-playing'. The cello was in the first instance, for him, a means of transmitting grandiose ideas, hypnotic images, profound spiritual states of being; it was an instrument through which one could influence masses of people. This concept lay behind his own performances, and this is what he taught. Of course we never missed any of Chef's concerts; here, on the stage of the Grand Hall of the Conservatoire, we witnessed his spontaneous displays of the art of cello-playing.

From autumn 1966 to spring 1974 I rarely saw him in class with a cello; at most three or four times, and usually then it was an instrument that he had grabbed from one of his pupils. After that, for several days one could still detect on the fingerboard the smell of his magical touch – the perfume he used, Ma Griffe, *had an unusually persistent smell. 'That's how I sweat,' he used to joke.*

Quite often he could work with his students on the day of one of his own concerts, appearing in class between the morning rehearsal and the evening performance. He never showed the slightest sign of tiredness or fatigue; on the contrary it seemed that he drew strength from his teaching.

In Class 19 one can still see the low-slung leather armchair where Rostropovich sat or half lay during lessons. His other favourite position was at the second piano. He played wonderfully, and knew the whole cello repertoire from memory. He would frequently illustrate the lessons with hundreds of examples from the symphonic repertoire, from violin and piano concertos; he could equally well cite from chamber music and the vocal literature. Sometimes the sounds of somebody else teaching or practising would waft in through the open window or down through the ceiling. Immediately recognising the music, he might play along – to 'help out' a colleague.

The atmosphere in Class 19 was absolutely special. Students were expected to attend all the classes, and apart from that, special guests would come, as well as interested students from other classes and disciplines. Sometimes the lessons were recorded, and a student might find himself playing with one or even two microphones under his nose. They were what today would be called masterclasses, but often these lessons resembled more the work of a great conductor with a first-class orchestra at his disposal, ready from the first rehearsal to absorb new, endlessly varied musical ideas, and to enter into the spirit of creative collaboration. All the hard preparatory work lay behind, the piece was ready for performance, and full interpretive freedom allowed for spontaneous changes of tempo, mood, character, bowings, dynamic. The role of the ideal orchestra was played by the pupil, the conductor by Chef, *who could play the whole repertoire from memory on the second piano. In his choleric tempi, the words spill out at incredible speed, as he quotes and refers to music by other authors, teases, parodies and mocks the student. He produces a veritable firework display of imaginative similes and associations, drawing on an enormous arsenal of material: music, painting, plastic arts, rhetoric, as well as sensual and tactile perceptions, and culinary allusions – all this cascades onto the student, who has to be able to*

*comprehend and absorb it all immediately, at this very moment . . .
and to translate it into cello-playing.*

*At these lessons the quality of instant response and reaction was the
thing that mattered most; the student had to be malleable material in
the hands of the sculptor who bestowed upon it a magical and
brilliant form. Those who were unable to react immediately, who got
lost or confused, risked severe punishment in the form of public
ridicule. Often in the process of his work the 'conductor' transmuted
into a theatre or opera director, who demanded various transformations from his student-actor – the instant capturing of an image, an
artist's improvisation.*

*This creative space was not just to be realised through the perceptible
world, but would be elevated to the level of a universal and humanistic
concept. Chef expressed the ideas of beauty, goodness, justice and self-
sacrifice with a precise and compact formula: 'The performer must
simultaneously be Lensky and the Tribune' – in other words, both a
poet and a prophet who ignites people's hearts from his art.*

*In September 1966 Chef decided to pair off his four first-year novice
students, and set them a double task of learning two new pieces on the
cello and preparing two piano accompaniments. I was paired with
Mischa Milman, who confessed with open-hearted candour that he
hardly knew how to play the piano. This did not deter Chef one bit:
'Well, you have two weeks ahead of you to learn how to play!' I was to
play the piano parts of Clair de Lune and Minstrels by Debussy
(arranged for cello and piano), while on the cello I was to play Fauré's
Arabesque and Papillons. I brought the original versions of my pieces
to the lesson, earning Chef's praise; I even managed to play these
accompaniments quite decently on the piano.*

*These amazing sessions were neither cello nor piano lessons, but
were something quite out of the ordinary. One can only term as
miraculous the way Rostropovich himself demonstrated on the piano.
His supernatural, phenomenal grasp of time, his palpitating, animated
sense for musical fabric being produced in front of one's very eyes – all
this at the distance of a stretched-out hand, not on the concert platform, but right here, manifestly under my nose. Never in my life had I
experienced anything like it.*

*For his part Chef expected some comeback: a brilliant reaction, an
instant switching into the process of spontaneous, sophisticated
creativity. I felt completely shattered and disheartened, and was*

unable to give anything back in return. Most probably at the time I could only make a promise to remember this for the rest of my life, and hope that some time in the indefinite future I would be able to retell in words and on the cello all that he was so generously giving to us first-year students on that day. As for Chef, he himself was delighted at his new pedagogical method. 'What a good teacher I am,' he observed as an aside, as way of taking his leave after the lesson.

In summer 1967, Chef remained in Moscow; amongst other business, he wanted to do some good work with his students, since he had been absent a lot in the preceding months. But after completing my first year at the Conservatoire, I had formed the impression that summer meant holiday time and with habitual light-heartedness I set off for the Crimea. In doing so, I brought the justifiable wrath of our teacher upon myself. I would pay for it in the autumn, when Chef decided to programme three class concerts in honour of the fiftieth anniversary of the October Revolution. The programmes would be made up of works that had been written for him. By way of punishment, I was given the 'hard labour' of having to learn Glière's concerto, an incredibly long work, difficult and boring – throughout my life I have never come across a more tedious opus. It was usually given to those who had been guilty of negligence. Through an irony of fate, the following year the same Glière concerto was assigned to Mischa Maisky for performance at a class concert.

In October 1967, on the eve of the concert, Chef worked with his students at home, lying on the sofa and complaining of his indisposition and of the evil fate which had sent him such useless mediocrities – this outburst was a most unusual occurrence, in view of his phenomenally strong health and optimistic disposition. My fate hung by a thread. Tomorrow the class concert was to take place, where I was to play the concerto's first movement, and I was barely able to weave my way through the debris of passages; I would stumble, raise myself up, only once again to collapse into the abyss. Chef's resolution was unshakeable: 'Tomorrow you are to play. In whatever form. And don't you dare think of falling ill!' It was clear that I would put an end to everything if I adopted the latter solution. Just as in ancient Sparta, the lazy, the weak, the untalented were all to be thrown to their death over the cliff.

For the rest of the day and night I practised in a state of numbness, having decided that I wasn't going to give up without a struggle. I reached a turning point just a few hours before the performance. I lay at home on the sofa, and Glière's music spun round in my head like a tropical fever. Again and again, I played the concerto through in my head from beginning to end, trying to gather up its threads and unravel the passagework. And suddenly I had a moment of clarity: I could see the whole work from beginning to end, as if one looked out of a plane window on a clear day and beheld underneath the whole landscape with its rivers, mountains and lakes. At that moment it became absolutely clear to me how I would play.

That evening everybody was amazed, Chef included; yesterday I couldn't put two notes together, and today I was playing, and quite decently at that. He was very pleased and was sincerely delighted at my success, my first accomplishment of a superhuman feat. For him this endless process of self-perfection through the continuous achievement of apparent miracles was not simply a means of existence. To this day, I am always amazed at his ability to absorb new music from the moment of his first contact with it. It is not merely a question of memorising in a cold manner, but in some mysterious way of fusing with it, becoming its co-author. Depending on the complexity of the new work, this process of assimilation could take a few hours (as happened, for instance, with concertos by Babadjanyan and Khrennikov), or several days, as with Shostakovich's first concerto and Boris Chaikovsky's concerto.

After the concert we all gathered at Vika Yagling's home. Chef had recovered and was in excellent spirits, joking and entertaining us with a host of interesting stories. I arrived a little late, since before coming on to the party I had seen home my future wife, Tanya. In justification I mumbled something about my mother not feeling well. Without hesitating a second, Chef retorted, 'I am afraid that it's not your mother who feels unwell, but you who feels too well!' Gauche and embarrassed, I wished the ground would swallow me up, while he looked on triumphantly.

Towards the beginning of November, one could see on the streets of Moscow long columns of tanks and military transport preparing for the Red Square Parade in honour of the October Revolution, held on 7 November. The city centre was closed to traffic during these hours. Mstislav Leopoldovich complained that he had been made to wait for the tanks to pass while driving out to Vika's. At this our 'grey cardinal' Stefan Kalyanov, who formally acted as class assistant, *decided to put in a word of banter: 'All you had to do was to say who you were, and they would have let you through.' Chef rejoined instantly, 'That's just what I did, I shouted "I'm Kalyanov, let Kalyanov through!" But even this didn't have any effect!'*

The farewell concert

My years as a postgraduate (1971–74) were the time of my closest contact with Rostropovich. Locked within the frontiers of the former Soviet Union, he had never before worked so intensively with me, and never before had he showed such warm, almost paternal feelings towards me.

By chance, this period coincided with the time of the intensive building works at his dacha at Zhukovka, when Rostropovich was erecting a concert hall as an extension of his house. All this occurred during his fall from grace. The authorities started to be obstructive, and tried to bring his building activity to a halt. This deliberate obstruction was evident even within the lowest levels of bureaucracy, such as the local councils and architectural offices to whom Mstislav Leopoldovich had to apply in connection with his building plans. Waving his red Lenin Prizewinner's booklet in front of officials' noses no longer produced the magical effect it used to. No longer were doors thrown open or red carpets unrolled in front of him. Instead, Rostropovich came up against those blank walls so familiar to the ordinary Soviet citizen. There was even a moment when one of the local authorities proposed demolishing the nascent concert hall on the grounds that planning permission had not been granted. This threat was probably merely a 'try-on', a ruse to intimidate. But Mstislav Leopoldovich was not so easily deterred, and his resolve to complete the building was merely reinforced, even if he now had to resort to the more humble methods of ordinary Soviet man, searching out and procuring all the materials himself. During one of my lessons, he recounted to Aza with great passion how he had gone to collect some cement, and had himself loaded the heavy bags into his car. His determination paid off, for the hall was completed and graces its environment to this day.

In December 1973, I participated in the All-Union competition which took place in Riga. Mstislav Leopoldovich took the preparations very seriously. Shortly before my departure for Riga I performed the whole competition programme in a two-part solo concert at the White Hall of the Conservatoire. Rostropovich arrived at the beginning of the concert and stayed till the end, listening to it all. At ten o'clock the next morning he called me for a lesson, where he reviewed the whole concert and worked on various parts of the programme. This in itself was a fairly unusual occurrence, since he rarely listened to his students play the same work more than once. But in my case at least, while preparing me for the competition he departed from this rule, and he did so again not long before his departure in 1974, before the Tchaikovsky competition. I was fortunate to be able to play the whole contest programme no fewer than three times for him. Each time he was able to reveal a completely new viewpoint on each familiar work. This creative method had universal value, for the artistic truth, especially in the performing arts, is incredibly volatile; should it become fixed, it stagnates, turning into routine or banal platitude.

For many years Rostropovich had acted as chairman of the jury of both the All-Union and the Tchaikovsky competitions, but he did not preside at either the previous or the present All-Union competitions. I think he himself had decided not to go to Riga, although it is also very likely that he was expecting to be asked – if not implored – to go. But when nobody invited him, there was no alternative but to stay at home.

Thus it was Daniil Shafran who assumed the role of chairman of the jury, as he had done in Baku in 1969. Shafran was more than willing to take on the task. I myself learnt of the outcome of the competition from the violinist Philip Khirshhorn. The competitors were lounging around in the foyer of the Riga Philharmonic, waiting for the results to be announced while the jury were still locked in session. Philip somehow found out their decision ahead of everybody else. 'Congratulations, you outstripped the others,' he informed me. 'You've won the first prize, they aren't giving a second at all, and Demin and Zagurskiy will share third prize.'

Rostropovich was delighted at the news and did not hide his joy. 'Your victory is of enormous importance to me,' he said, and he repeated these words more than once.

This was in December 1973. He still lived in hope that things would change for the better, that the authorities would forgive him, and that in their eyes his 'achievements' would outweigh his 'sins'.

Shortly after the All-Union competition was over, my mother arranged a small party for the inner family circle in the communal flat on the Arbat street in Moscow where I had grown up. Apart from my mother, myself and my wife Tanya (who was, as was all too evident, just about to produce our first child, Denis), only Mstislav Leopoldovich and Aza Amintaeva were present. He arrived straight from the christening of Ermolai Solzhenitsyn, his godson, so to begin with he was not hungry and refused our offers of food.

That day, it was as though all his troubles and conflicts with the authorities were taking place on another planet. It was clear that my encounters with him touched only one of his many simultaneous existences. For me, Rostropovich lived on a special, completely different dimension to any I had experienced.

We students followed the events and humiliations that he underwent, even if we never talked about them in the Conservatoire. Soon we learnt of his decision to apply to Brezhnev in person for permission to leave the country for two years. By April 1974 it was common knowledge that he would be leaving, although many expected him to stay on for the Tchaikovsky competition. But once permission had been granted, things moved with great speed.

I clearly remember Easter 1974, when Mstislav Leopoldovich came to the Conservatoire having stayed up to attend Vespers and the All-Night Vigil at church. We exchanged the traditional Orthodox Easter greeting, kissing three times. I was about to utter the words 'Christ has risen!' but half joking, half serious, he interrupted me: 'Be silent, be silent!'

At the time, this was a forbidden phrase, but we understood each other without words. He left on 26 May 1974, and his last farewell concert, in which he conducted rather than played, took place in the Grand Hall of the Moscow Conservatoire on 10 May. It was an unforgettable occasion: the orchestra that he had gathered together included many of the Conservatoire's best students, including the viola player Yuri Bashmet. Mstislav Leopoldovich chose to perform an all-Tchaikovsky programme: the suite from The Nutcracker *and the* Rococo Variations *in the first half, the sixth symphony in the second. He invited me to play as his soloist: it was his final gesture as my teacher, and a truly generous gift to me on the eve of the Tchaikovsky competition, which was due to start in early June, after his departure.*

The whole of musical Moscow came to the concert on 10 May: people were standing in the passageways and sitting on the floor. Before the beginning of the concert, the audience rose to its feet to give Rostropovich a long standing ovation. Many had tears in their eyes. Everybody felt themselves to be a participant in an event whose significance extended far beyond music. I remember my own anxiety, and Chef's words of encouragement, and the untransmittable enthusiasm of the orchestral musicians and the audience. As for Chef himself, although one felt his incredible agitation, he radiated a superhuman energy, which in a way comprehensible only to him transformed his suffering into an unforgettable performance.

A few days later I came to say goodbye; it seemed then that this was a final parting, that Mstislav Leopoldovich was leaving for ever. We quickly said our farewells, then he embraced me tightly, kissed me, and said, 'Ivan, believe in God!' My tears welled up and stuck somewhere in my throat. I left as in a daze and wandered aimlessly through the streets for a good while. I had the feeling that through this forceful embrace, Mstislav Leopoldovich was trying to transmit part of his own strength, his own energy, something of his own persona to me.

Not long before the concert on 10 May, Rostropovich took me to the State Collection of Musical Instruments on his own initiative. Thanks to his intervention, I was given a wonderful instrument: 'his' instrument – considered to be an Amati or Bergonzi – which he had played on for several years before acquiring his legendary Storioni cello.* I had the good fortune to play on this instrument for the next eight years.

With it I travelled as far as Kamchatka and Sakhalin, made four LP recordings, and played my first concert at the Warsaw Autumn festival in 1979. But I performed on this cello for the first time on 10 May 1974. One could easily read something symbolic into all this: the precious cello, received from the master's hands, my participation in his farewell concert. Performing under his direction was like the passing down of a spiritual mantle. To this day I treasure a photo taken at one of the rehearsals at the Grand Hall of the Conservatoire, which Mstislav Leopoldovich signed on the day of the concert: 'To my dear pupil Vanya Monighetti, from his loving and devoted accompanist.'

* Rostropovich bought his cello by the renowned Cremonese instrument-maker Lorenzo Storioni (1751–1801) from an orchestral cellist in Kiev in the late 1950s. It is the cello on which he made most of his recordings. In his hands the cello had an unusually rich and noble sound and a unique projecting quality. Only after he left the Soviet Union, did he acquire the famous 'Duport' Strad in New York in 1975. This cello is generally acknowledged as one of Antonio Stradivarius' best instruments.

14

The final years in the Soviet Union

Shortly after Shostakovich bought his dacha in Zhukovka in 1960, he suggested to Rostropovich that he should look for a property in the same settlement and helped him in his search. For Rostropovich, the house in one of Moscow's most exclusive areas of dacha-land – Zhukovka was originally built for the privileged class of Academician-Scientists – meant more than just a lovely family home in the quiet of surrounding forests. It became an ongoing project: the house was renovated and extended, fences and hedges went up, a tractor was acquired, a Spanish bar and modern gadgets installed, a garage erected and two large Newfoundland dogs set to guard it. Finally a new wing was constructed, housing a large concert hall. During his trips abroad, Rostropovich spent his spare time acquiring the materials needed for these improvements. I remember once helping him acquire an enormous quantity of brass door hinges in Grays, his favourite hardware shop in Edinburgh. They seemed to weigh a ton, and he quickly calculated that paying overweight would triple the cost of each hinge. Undeterred, he decided to take them as hand luggage on board the plane. Nobody knows how he managed to carry his cello in one hand, and the small bag of door hinges in the other – I believe it weighed about seventy kilos! By the end of it all, he could boast that if the house was not exactly built by his own hands, it was constructed almost entirely from material he had sourced himself from around the world.

When building his garage, Rostropovich decided to add a service flat which could be useful for a live-in handyman or custodian. This was originally intended for his Leningrad pupil, Valeri Kravchenko, and his family. As a teenager, Valeri had suffered acute depression when his parents divorced, and had attempted suicide: he ended up with permanent injuries to his legs, and his walking was considerably crippled. When Rostropovich started teaching at the Leningrad Conservatoire, the director Pavel Serebryakov had told him about a young boy who was his biggest fan in town; the walls of his room were completely covered by Rostropovich memorabilia. The young professor was sufficiently intrigued to pay a surprise visit to Valeri, during which he asked him to get his cello out and play. From then on, he always took an intense interest in the boy and his family, and gave him lessons every time he came to Leningrad. Seeing that the boy's mother and stepfather lived in very difficult conditions and had difficulty in scraping together a living, he conceived the idea of transferring the whole family to Moscow as custodians of his dacha. Kravchenko's family was initially delighted by Rostropovich's generous proposal, but for some reason had a change of heart and decided to refuse the offer. This was why Rostropovich found himself with spare accommodation that he could offer to Aleksandr Solzhenitsyn.

Some time in October 1969, Rostropovich received a phone call from Lydia Chukovskaya, informing him that Solzhenitsyn was probably dying of cancer. The writer was living in an unheated summerhouse on the eighty-third kilometre of the Mozhaisk Highway. Rostropovich had no hesitation as to what to do, and drove off in his car to see for himself:

I found Solzhenitsyn lying in bed, wrapped in cabbage-like layers of old rags and blankets . . . 'What's up with you?' I asked. He answered, 'I think I may have acute sciatica.' 'Well, if that is the case, you can come and live in a small flat I had built for a special purpose in the grounds of my dacha. It has heating in it, and it's warm. If it's a question of sciatica then you'll get better soon. If it's cancer then it doesn't matter where you die.'*

Solzhenitsyn was convinced of the sincerity of the offer and accepted it straight away.

The writer's move to the flat within Rostropovich's dacha happened to coincide with an intensification of the authorities' campaign against him. In autumn 1969 he was ousted from the Ryazan branch of the Writers' Union, and in November he was expelled from the central All-Union organisation. Soon reprisals were also taken against the editor of the famous *Novy Mir* literary journal, Aleksandr Tvardovsky, who had succeeded in publishing Solzhenitsyn's story *One Day in the*

* Spektor, *Mstislav Rostropovich*, pp. 66–67.

Life of Ivan Denisovich in 1962, but had recently failed to get *Cancer Ward* past the censorship. Rostropovich found himself unwittingly housing an enemy of the People. Ekaterina Furtseva, the Minister of Culture, and Shchelokov, the Minister of the Interior, contacted Rostropovich and Vishnevskaya personally to instruct them to get rid of the writer. Rostropovich replied sternly that should the ministers provide a heated room for Solzhenitsyn elsewhere in Moscow, then the writer would leave of his own accord: 'But a good host wouldn't drive a dog out into the frost, let alone a human being.'

The news spread around Moscow like wildfire that Rostropovich was housing the country's most famous dissident writer. He immediately informed my family and his other foreign friends that we could no longer be invited to his dacha, which for obvious reasons was under KGB surveillance. In these circumstances, the presence of any foreigner in Zhukovka could easily be misconstrued. We were well aware that any thoughtless action on our part could compromise Rostropovich and his family.

My parents recalled that when they visited Rostropovich at his flat in the Composers' Union building on Ogaryova Street, the suspicious thugs lurking around the lift-well and the corridor outside his flat did not bother to hide the purpose of their mission. Slava's visitors would joke with him about these 'young composers' seeking inspiration from the Muses in such strange places. Microphones were almost certainly installed not only in foreign embassies, but in the apartments of many Russians. It was generally assumed that all telephone lines were 'bugged': my Russian friends would automatically unplug their phones at home when they wanted to speak about any sensitive issues.

During the 1969/70 season Rostropovich's musical life was largely unaffected by political events, and he continued travelling abroad. On 25 July 1970, he gave the first performance of Henri Dutilleux's new concerto *Tout un monde lointain* at the Aix-en-Provence Festival, in the beautiful outside space.* Each movement of the work takes lines from Baudelaire's verse as an epigraph, which the composer proceeds to illustrate with unique skill, creating a sound-world of enormous delicacy and luminous beauty. At the premiere, as Rostropovich recalls, he repeated the entire concerto as an encore. As he embarked on the opening phrase for the second time, it seemed that the trees joined in

---

* Rostropovich gave the Paris premiere on 30 November 1971.

with the percussion, shaking their branches in the wind in time with, and imitating, the sonority of the swishing sound of the cymbals. For the cellist, 'it was an extraordinary, mystical experience'.

The students of Class 19 were well aware of what was going on in Rostropovich's life outside music, although they never talked about it openly. As Mischa Utkin remembers:

Early in the autumn of 1970, when I was in my first year, we were astounded to see Solzhenitsyn appear with Aza Amintaeva at the Conservatoire. They came upstairs to Class 19 where Mstislav Leopoldovich was teaching. Aza beckoned to Rostropovich to come out into the corridor where Aleksandr Isayevich was waiting for him. A minute or two later Mstislav Leopoldovich popped back in and announced, 'Children, that's it for today, I have to go now.' I stupidly enquired whether he would be coming back to finish the lessons. He turned to me with a sardonic smile, and said, 'Old man, don't spoil my holiday.' The next day we found out that Solzhenitsyn had been awarded the Nobel Prize for literature.

There was much speculation in Moscow as to whether Solzhenitsyn would be allowed to go to Stockholm to pick up the prize. As Rostropovich explained to my father in those anxious days of mid-October, even if permission were granted, it might well not be wise for Solzhenitsyn to travel, in case the Soviet authorities refused to allow him back into the country. One day in class Rostropovich called me over, and whispered that he might need to transmit an urgent message about this matter to the British Embassy. Given that I was about to go to London, I suggested that if I wasn't there he might use Moray Welsh, his other British student, as messenger. I must stupidly have failed to warn Moray, and he was rather astonished when Rostropovich did indeed request his help, but he duly went to the British Embassy to pass on a somewhat garbled account of the message that his teacher had hurriedly whispered in his ear.

In the mean time, Rostropovich was preparing to travel to London to give the first performance of a concerto by Witold Lutoslawski, which had been commissioned for him by the Royal Philharmonic Society. While he was there he would also be awarded the Society's Gold Medal. Just a few days before he was due to leave, he called my father at the Embassy to say that the Soviet authorities had forbidden him to travel. He asked for help, and suggested that my father write to Britten, to see if he could use his influence. In the event Rostropovich managed to talk his way out of the situation at the last minute, and left for London as planned.

He had asked Lutoslawski to write a cello concerto as long ago as the late 1950s, as the composer recalled:

Every time we met Rostropovich reminded me about [his request]. Once he came to visit us with his cello and played for us the third [sic] Britten cello suite.* I put on for him recordings of my string quartet and *Paroles tissées*. He said nothing about the quartet, but on listening to *Paroles tissées* he exclaimed, 'This is the music I'd like to play, I want something like this!' The years passed and I could find no way to write the cello concerto – it was always squeezed out by more urgent plans. Then in 1968 Chester Music phoned me from London and proposed that I write a cello concerto as a commission for the Royal Philharmonic Society . . . When Slava discovered this, he said, 'Write without thinking about the cello. I am the cello!' But actually I had to think about the cello rather a lot and I made a graph model of the four strings so as to be able to understand the instrument's possibilities. When he received the first fragment of the concerto, Slava exclaimed, 'I've been playing the cello for over thirty years and now I must assimilate new techniques and methods.' My concerto makes use of quarter tones: Slava invented a wonderful fingering for the solo part, and proposed a way of marking it; the ordinary intervals were designated with large numbers and the quarter-tones with small. It was practical and also looked decorative!†

The concerto was to be performed with the Bournemouth Symphony Orchestra under Edward Downes, so preliminary rehearsals were held in Bournemouth even though the concert would be at the Royal Festival Hall. Rostropovich invited me to come down with him and the composer to attend these rehearsals, thereby giving me a fantastic opportunity to understand this complex music better. Just before our departure from Waterloo station, a journalist from one of the British newspapers burst into the train compartment, and started questioning Rostropovich: Is it true that Solzhenitsyn is living at your dacha? What can you tell us about the writer's reaction to the Nobel Prize? The only thing that a Soviet citizen could do in this situation was to keep silent, and Rostropovich instructed me to ask the journalist to leave at once. Lutoslawski and his wife were unable to disguise their indignation at such lack of sensitivity by a member of the 'free' press.

It was fascinating to see this concerto come into being in rehearsal. I remember Edward Downes explaining to the orchestra at length how

* Given that the third suite was written after the Lutoslawski cello concerto, Rostropovich probably played Britten's second suite.
† Nikolskaya, *Witold Lutoslawski*, p. 59.

the aleatoric passages should function; these were all quite novel techniques for musicians at the time. The work was immediately successful at its premiere, and was given an inspired and entirely convincing performance by Rostropovich. However, I sensed that despite his pleasure in the concerto's success, Rostropovich's nerves were actually quite shaken. The strain did not show on the surface, but much was going on at the back of his mind. Shortly afterwards, he went up to St Andrews University where he had promised a concert to the new friends he had made there. During these days he had time to reflect on recent events at home: he decided that he could no longer remain silent, and resolved to write a letter in defence of Solzhenitsyn. After his return to Moscow, Galina initially tried to dissuade her husband from sending such a provocative document to the authorities; she saw all too clearly what the consequences would be. However, when she saw that her husband's resolve was unshakeable, she lent him her full support, helping him correct the letter. Galina Vishnevskaya is a woman of enormous strength and courage, and Rostropovich could rely on her as his staunchest friend and helpmate. He left for a six-week trip abroad on 31 October – on the way to the airport, he posted four copies of his letter, addressed to carefully selected Soviet newspapers.*

Initially there was no reaction from any quarter, and his concert tour of Austria and Germany proceeded normally. When he phoned his wife at home, she too reported that everything was as usual. Then one day, on arriving in Bregenz, Rostropovich saw a huge crowd of journalists and television cameras outside the concert hall, and realised that news of his letter must have broken. This was confirmed just before the concert when he was handed translations of his letter into English and German; the Soviet authorities seemed to have allowed the document to be 'leaked' to the Western press. On returning to his hotel after the concert, he noted a black Volga car parked outside it. Soviet Embassy officials were waiting for him in the hotel lobby, and asked for an immediate interview. Rostropovich willingly confirmed that he had indeed written this letter, and for the rest of the trip, the officials treated him with solicitous care, clearly anxious that he would be tempted to seek political asylum. In fact, he had absolutely no intention of doing this, and in any case, with his wife and children in Moscow it would not have been possible.

* Namely: *Pravda, Izvestiya, Literaturnaya Gazeta* and *Sovetskaya Kultura*.

Back in the Soviet Union, Rostropovich's return was anxiously awaited. The authorities were stepping up their campaign against dissidence, using virulent and hysterical language that reminded people of the worst years of Stalinism. A leading article from the 17 December 1970 issue of *Pravda* spoke of the 'cesspool' into which Solzhenitsyn had slithered: imperialist propaganda represented him as a 'great' Russian writer, he was in fact 'an internal émigré, alien and hostile to all that is held dear in Soviet life'.

Rostropovich knew that some form of punishment for his action was inevitable, although he did not know what form it would take. He no doubt calculated that his prestige at home and abroad would shield him and his family, and allow him to continue performing. The influential contacts he had made abroad would also help protect his position: his acquaintances in the West included the British Prime Minister, Ted Heath (who was of course a well-known music-lover), and Willy Brandt, the West German Chancellor. Many saw this as shrewd planning on Rostropovich's part, but in fact his outgoing nature meant that he always spontaneously collected friends, both great and humble, rich and poor, in every part of the world. Nonetheless, Rostropovich was rare among Russian musicians in having relationships with politicians. At home, his public defence of Solzhenitsyn had undoubtedly greatly increased the political consciousness of the normally uninvolved musical community. Even the most politically apathetic member of the musical elite, however, could hardly have failed to notice the greatly increased number of arbitrarily cancelled foreign trips, which affected many Soviet artists.

In December 1970, all musical Moscow was celebrating the bicentenary of Beethoven's birth. A solemn ceremony took place at the Bolshoi Theatre on the actual birthday, starting with a long roll-call of speeches referring to Beethoven's revolutionary heritage, democratic fervour and foresight. Shostakovich opened the proceedings, reading out a prepared text parrot-fashion, followed by politicians and workers' representatives from throughout the Eastern bloc. The occasion ended with a performance of the ninth symphony conducted by Svetlanov, in which Vishnevskaya was the soprano soloist. To the amazement of the press and diplomatic community, the whole Politburo turned up in the government box for this performance. As my mother told me, the diplomats and journalists wondered what this signal meant. Were Soviet troops about to enter Poland to squash the Gdansk strikers? Or was some horrible punishment going to be meted out to Rostropovich, who had yet to return home? My mother, who was acutely aware of the pressures on Vishnevskaya, was full of admiration for her regal stage behaviour: she swept onto stage, giving the Politburo the most condescending and disdainful nod possible as she passed.

Rostropovich arrived home a few days later and was immediately scheduled to play two performances of Beethoven's 'Triple' concerto with Richter and Oistrakh under Svetlanov's direction on 28 and 29 December, having recently recorded the work with the Berlin Philharmonic under Karajan. They played the work again in March 1972.

The Ministry of Culture abruptly informed his colleagues that Rostropovich was not permitted to play; he was to be declared indisposed, and was told to announce a 'fictitious' cold, while the other two soloists were commanded to find a replacement. Neither Oistrakh nor Richter would even contemplate such a solution. Even if they had been willing to agree to such treachery it was in any case impractical, for there was no time for rehearsal with a new partner. Eventually, because the whole event was acquiring the proportions of a political scandal, only the first concert of the pair was cancelled. All those present at the second (myself included) can testify to the extraordinary atmosphere of the performance. Despite the overall excellence of the interpretation, much of the stormy applause was directed towards Rostropovich, a token of public support for his civic courage. As was noted in the *Guardian* of 31 December 1970, the seven minutes of standing ovation at the end were 'a double triumph for Rostropovich'.

In the early months of 1971 it was made clear to the cellist that he would not be allowed to go abroad for six months, a ban that was later extended. (Exceptionally, Rostropovich was permitted to perform Dutilleux's concerto in Paris in November 1971.) Instead he was to take his Art around the vast territories of the Soviet Union. He did so with zeal, clocking up some 117 concerts that year. Initially, he continued conducting at the Bolshoi, while appearances in Moscow and other big cities were reduced.

One day in early 1971 when Rostropovich came to the British Embassy to see my parents, he saw the recent English editions of Solzhenitsyn's works in the bookshelves of the small private sitting room. He quietly picked them up and took them away with him. Within a few days he returned them to me with the addition of

Solzhenitsyn's signature and dedication – *Cancer Ward* for me, *The First Circle* for my parents.*

My father was in constant touch with Rostropovich at the time, not least in connection with the forthcoming 'Days of British Music' in April 1971. The highlight of this festival was to be the visit of the London Symphony Orchestra with their chief conductor, André Previn. Both William Walton and Benjamin Britten had also been invited on the tour, and the latter was to conduct programmes of his own works. Even before Rostropovich had written his letter defending Solzhenitsyn, Britten had made it clear that his main reason for coming to Moscow was to lend support to his Russian musician friends – 'to Slava and Galya in particular', as he told my father.

On a visit to London in early January 1971, my father met Ben to discuss the new situation. At this stage it was agreed that Britten should make his own position explicit, and impose as an absolute condition to the Soviet Ministry of Culture that his visit depended entirely on the participation of the 'two Slavas' in his concerts. The inclusion of Richter, who at this point remained in favour with Furtseva, meant that Britten's choice of soloists would be understood to have been governed by artistic, and not political, considerations.

The 'Days of British Music' opened with the London Symphony Orchestra's programmes in Leningrad. Here, at the Grand Hall of the Philharmonia, Britten conducted the last of four programmes, in which Richter performed his piano concerto, and Rostropovich the *Cello Symphony*. As my father reported to the Foreign Office, the desperately overcrowded hall and the police cordons outside reminded us of a Beatles concert at the height of their popularity:

An expert estimate given to me in Leningrad suggested that there were four thousand people packed into a hall that is not meant to accommodate more than two thousand. This may well be an exaggeration, but both in Leningrad and Moscow the concerts were being observed (listening could hardly have been possible) from a height by students who had climbed on to the roof of the hall. In Leningrad [Britten's] concert marked the end of a long boycott by Rostropovich himself, who had quarrelled bitterly with Mravinsky, Chief Conductor of the Leningrad Philharmonic Orchestra, about the latter's attitude to Shostakovich, and for over

---

* Mine, which I own to this day, has the inscription 'To one of the favourite students of my friend Rostropovich'; and in the dedication to my parents, the author wrote 'I have heard many good things about you from Stiva Rostropovich.' Stiva, supposedly derived from the character of Stiva Obolensky (Anna Karenina's brother), was Solzhenitsyn's nickname for Slava.

five years had made no 'official' solo appearance in Leningrad. Britten told me that, on this occasion of Rostropovich's reappearance, the tension in his performance was remarkable and disturbing, but it earned him a tremendous ovation. In Moscow the corresponding concert ended with a similar ovation, deserved on purely musical grounds, but no doubt accorded with Rostropovich's political record also in mind.*

In Moscow I attended the concerts and was able to act as interpreter for Britten and Pears. Two particular occasions during their visit stand out in my mind. The first was when we visited Dmitri Shostakovich and heard his recent thirteenth quartet performed in his sitting room by the Beethoven Quartet. Then, at a similarly moving and equally private occasion at Rostropovich's flat, Ben presented Slava with his newly composed third suite for solo cello: a personal tribute to a 'great Russian musician and patriot', as he wrote in the preface to the first published edition. Britten played it through on the piano to a small audience of Rostropovich, Dmitri and Irina Shostakovich, Peter Pears, Sue Phipps (Peter's niece) and myself. At the end of the performance Shostakovich pointed out to Britten that he had used the Kontakion from the Orthodox Liturgy (one of the four Russian themes on which the suite is based) in a different version from the one he knew. Ben was visibly upset, as although it would be easy to change the theme itself, he did not see how he could change the preceding variations based on it. On his return to London he checked with Bishop Pimen of Saratov and Volgograd, who confirmed that the version in the suite was the one usually used in the liturgy. Nevertheless, Britten ensured that Dmitri Shostakovich's version of the Kontakion was given as an alternative in the printed score.

During the 'Days of British Music' festival Rostropovich was conspicuous by his absence from the official receptions given in honour of the British musicians. In Moscow, we soon discovered, the invitation to the British Embassy's luncheon in honour of the British concert artists and composers was simply not delivered to Rostropovich and Vishnevskaya – a minor but typically annoying example of the regime's displeasure. (Rostropovich was also a notable absentee from the reciprocal 'Days of Soviet Music' held in Britain in November 1972. An array of the best Soviet artists (Oistrakh and Shostakovich amongst them) performed in London, and Maxim

* G. Bennett (ed.) *Documents on British Policy Overseas*, p. 335.

Shostakovich conducted the premiere of his father's new fifteenth symphony. The absence of Rostropovich and Vishnevskaya was acutely felt by their loyal London audiences.)

On 23 April, Britten went to hear Rostropovich conduct Prokofiev's *War and Peace* at the Bolshoi Theatre. It was to be their farewell meeting on this visit, for Slava was obliged to depart immediately for a tour of Central Asia. As my father recorded, he had only recently come back from a tour of Kamchatka, presumably intended for the benefit of the 'music-loving eskimos'. It seemed, though, that Rostropovich had actively embraced the policy of playing throughout the Soviet Union, hoping to earn himself a reprieve. The next time Britten and Rostropovich met was in the summer of 1974. Both men's lives had changed radically; Britten had undergone heart surgery and was an invalid, and Rostropovich had effectively been thrown out of his own country.

The performance Britten attended was one of Rostropovich's last appearances at the Bolshoi. The theatre was a hothouse of ideological orthodoxy, and neither the singers nor the administration wished to be further associated with an artist whose political record had been so seriously contaminated. Furthermore, the new director of the Bolshoi, Kirill Molchanov, had demonstrated his own outlook at the start of his career in 1948, when he zealously supported the Party's policy against formalism in music. No one was surprised, then, when Rostropovich was asked to step down from conducting *Onegin* and *War and Peace*.

One of the more unexpected results of the campaign against Rostropovich was that he had far more time for his students. Deprived of his foreign tours, and with his concerts also cut back, his position at the Moscow Conservatoire seemed to be the only fixed point in his working life – it was the one institution that never withdrew its support from Rostropovich. Mischa Utkin remembers that from the beginning of 1971, our professor took to appearing regularly in class every Tuesday and Thursday, arriving punctually at ten o'clock: 'Given that Mstislav Leopoldovich's performances were increasingly restricted, he really had no other opportunity to express his creative personality except in teaching.' This new pattern meant that the pressure on his students was further increased. Previously, Rostropovich had worked with them intensively and then gone away on tour, leaving time to absorb his instruction and prepare new repertoire. As

Vagram Saradzhan recalls, the lack of space between lessons now made it hard for students:

The intervals when Mstislav Leopoldovich was away on tour were very useful. Others would lament, 'What are we going to do without him?' but I needed the time to digest his remarks, and work quietly, so as to reinforce everything he had given us in the lessons. We could not possibly absorb all he told us or react to it immediately. After each lesson I would take the score and read through it with my eyes, away from the instrument. In the light of his suggestions I would try and put the music into perspective.

The class representative during this period was Misha Utkin, nicknamed 'Shchatsky' by Rostropovich, after a character from Griboyedev's *Woe from Wit* who, like Misha, had long sideburns.

It fell to me to organise the class timetable, and to decide who was to play at which class. Now the students started to ring me and say, 'Please tell Mstislav Leopoldovich that I am ill.' Or they would explain, 'I can't cope; I haven't had time to prepare any new repertoire. I've already played everything to him that I have been working on over the last month.' Even David Geringas, a postgraduate and first-prize winner of the Tchaikovsky competition, once rang me and said, 'Listen, I played in the last three classes. I haven't got anything else ready. Sorry, but I can't play tomorrow.' Students still flocked to his classes and had to stand or sit on the windowsills, since there weren't enough chairs for everybody. Sometimes the actual teaching was over by eleven-thirty, nobody else had anything to play. Then *Chef* would start recounting many stories and incidents from his life. He told us about his childhood, his parents, the evacuation years, and his first concert tours. He would often talk about music. Even though he had been driven out of the Bolshoi Theatre, he would still go and listen to opera, as he loved it, and would talk to us at length about what he had seen.

Rostropovich's state of official disgrace had an impact on the lives of all his students. Saradzhan recalls once being called up and interrogated by the KGB: 'What were you talking about with Rostropovich the other day?' Vago replied, 'As a matter of fact, we discussed whether it's better to start the Brahms E minor sonata with the third finger or the first.' He refused to be drawn into giving any other kind of information. Others, such as Karine Georgian and David Geringas, first-prize winners of the Tchaikovsky competition, were told specifically not to mention Rostropovich's name in public interview. Naturally neither of them would countenance such a betrayal.

For the first time since Rostropovich had started teaching, being his student did not confer an automatic advantage; he no longer had the same influence at competitions and other such events. However, this reduced public status did not affect the number of students who wished to learn from him, nor the crowds who packed out his classes. Mikhail (Misha) Katz had only one year's instruction in Rostropovich's Conservatoire class, although he had been playing for him since he was a boy in Rostov-on-Don, where his father Leonid was chief conductor of the symphony orchestra. As he recalls:

I was a very lively lad, a typical Rostov 'hooligan'. When I came to Moscow to study at the Conservatoire I hadn't calmed down much, and I was always getting into trouble. First of all I was really more interested in girls than in the cello, and I even missed lessons. Rostropovich was wild with rage when he saw I wasn't working, and even rang up home to complain about my behaviour, telling my father, 'Misha could have been my best pupil, but I see that he couldn't care a damn about me!' In fact I got thrown out of Komsomol and was even expelled from the Conservatoire, so I was hardly an exemplary student. But notwithstanding, I learnt an awful lot from Mstislav Leopoldovich. Most of all he had an enormous influence on me as a thinker. His own gifts as a cellist were quite unique and very natural. He was for ever searching, and discovering, and perhaps for this reason he actually was not good at explaining cello technique; in any case it didn't interest him greatly.

Eventually, after emigrating from the Soviet Union, Mikhail gave up the cello to become a conductor. Much of Rostropovich's instruction could be immediately applied to his new métier:

What he conveyed was a large-scale structural thinking. He had a perfect grasp of form, and he could calculate very precisely how tempo works within the structure, the flow of rubato and the timing of the culminations. He paid great attention to articulation and tempo, as well as having a wonderful sense of rhythm. It seems to me that Mstislav Leopoldovich's principal achievement was to release the cello from its limitations, and to evolve new attitudes to the instrument. The principles he applied in the art of cello-playing are actually universally valid in every branch of music.

One of the classes that made an enormous impact at the time was a lesson on Henri Dutilleux's *Tout un monde lointain*, which Rostropovich asked David Geringas to learn. This was in spring 1971, and the piece was unknown in the USSR. David was effectively the second person to play the concerto after his professor, and offered the first opportunity to Muscovite musicians to hear it. Rostropovich lent him his own manuscript copy, and the task of photocopying it was entrusted to me. (Photocopying machines simply did not exist in Moscow, and I therefore asked my mother to help out at the Embassy, which she did.) David asked the brilliant pianist and composer

Aleksandr (Alec) Rabinovitch to accompany him; Alec had such extraordinary skill that he could sight-read the orchestral score on the piano from sight. An enormous number of people squeezed into Class 19 to listen to one of Rostropovich's best postgraduates work with his professor on Dutilleux's extraordinary new work. It was an important experience not just for David, but for the other students present who were thirsting to hear new music, and who likewise benefited from Rostropovich's revelations and insights into this wonderful new score.

Rostropovich was occasionally allowed to give concerts in Moscow but, much as he tried, he could not gain permission to play Dutilleux's masterpiece anywhere in Russia, so it had to wait many years for a premiere there. It was surprising, then, that the authorities should have allowed Rostropovich to give the delayed Russian premiere of Lutoslawski's cello concerto under Gennadi Rozhdestvensky's baton in December 1972. This was effectively the cellist's first performance of an important contemporary work in the composer's presence since his concert with Britten in April 1971, and it was greeted with much excitement. The programme actually included two other cello concertos (Haydn's C major and Dvořák) in addition to the new work – it was almost like a return to old times for Rostropovich!

He had been attempting to programme Lutoslawski's concerto for over two years, and had asked the Union of Composers of the USSR to use its influence, and to issue an invitation to Lutoslawski. His request, however, was systematically ignored. As the Polish composer recalled:

In the end I came to Moscow on a private visit at the invitation of Rostropovich. I was very glad that receptive Russian audiences had a chance to get to know this work. I knew that my music was of importance to Russian listeners, many of whom loved it. So it was a very significant event from lots of points of view. And Slava, of course, played marvellously.*

In Lutoslawski's view, Rostropovich's interpretation was typically Russian in that it was rooted in extra-musical associations:

When Slava performed my cello concerto in Moscow with Rozhdestvensky, his sister, Veronika, who was playing in the orchestra, ran up to her brother full of animation and exclaimed, 'Slava, you must tell me the content of this work.' It was impossible for her to imagine that this music could have no specific subject, and indeed, Slava himself had related it in his mind to an extra-musical programme. Identifying himself with the solo part, he said that it represented his life-story; the

* Nikolskaya, *Witold Lutoslawski*, p. 58.

heavy brass were the enemies who persecuted and hindered him. Several times in a row, the trumpets or trombones interrupt the cello line, and again and again the soloist has to start all over again from the beginning. In the slow cantilena section, the cello is gradually augmented by the addition of the string group, which eventually fuses into a single unison line. The soloist, aiming to bring the work to a climax and leading with a strong sense of confidence, drags the whole orchestra in his wake. At this point the brass enters – 'That's the whole Central Committee,' Slava would say. And before the coda there is a small, pitiful phrase, which Slava told me always makes him cry. 'Why is that?' I asked. 'Because this is where I die.' 'But then in the coda you arrive at your triumph . . .' I intervened. 'Ah yes, but that is already in the other world,' he remarked philosophically.

I myself try in every way to avoid propagating this approach. Music for me has its own intrinsic value, it can have its own drama without recourse to extra-musical analogies.*

Despite Lutoslawski's own reluctance to see his work as programme music, the cello concerto does seem to invite an almost pictorial dramatic interpretation, and this may well have contributed to its popularity among Russian audiences. The rhetoric of the solo cello line veers from the studied indifference of the opening – with the apathetic, constantly repeated note D, to passages of noble eloquence and outbursts of frenzy and angry frustration. Many listeners heard it as a fable of life under communism, where the individual is reduced to a puppet, controlled by evil forces. It is in this sense that one should understand the comment of the Polish critic, Tadeusz Konchinksi, that the work represents 'the conflict of the individual and the crowd'. More concretely, Galina Vishnevskaya described the work as a 'twentieth-century equivalent of the *Adventures of Don Quixote*' – perhaps giving a hint of how she views her brilliant husband's character, since he so closely associated his own complex biography with the solo cello's role as protagonist. But as Irina Nikolskaya, an authority on Lutoslawski, has succinctly put it, 'The fable lies so close to the surface that critics and musicians tend to interpret the work too simplistically, seeing only the primary level of meaning.' The composer himself, while acknowledging its theatrical quality, insisted that the concerto had to be understood as a purely musical structure:

The cello concerto is completely unique to my output, for it was created under the strong impression of Rostropovich's personality as a performer. But there is no extra-musical programme which critics kept seeking out; this was not at all what I wanted. It goes without saying that certain life situations can be reflected in the

* Ibid., p. 58.

principles of the structure of the musical form. I do not deny this, but it is another aspect of the problem.*

During this visit to Moscow in December 1972, Lutoslawski also attended a recital given by Vishnevskaya and Rostropovich at the Small Hall of the Conservatoire:

At that concert Galya and Slava first performed some arrangements of folk songs by Prokofiev. After each piece, people from the public would walk up to the stage and present Galya with flowers. What a wonderful Russian tradition! And while the flowers were being brought up, Slava was feverishly learning the other new pieces, barely touching the keys of the piano. He is such a brilliant person, that he can even sight-read at a concert. Of course he had not had enough time to delve into the interpretative depths, as he usually did.†

A few months later, Rostropovich succeeded in putting together an orchestra of students and young professionals to perform Shostakovich's fourteenth symphony, with Vishnevskaya and Mark Reshetin as soloists. He had been longing to conduct the work from the moment he first heard it. Rudolf Barshai had recorded it shortly after the premiere with the Moscow Chamber Orchestra and different soloists, but despite the high level of Barshai's performance, Rostropovich felt that many aspects of the score had still to be uncovered. Shostakovich attended Rostropovich's rehearsals and performance, and approved his spacious reading, which brought out the work's inherent drama as well as underlining its profound tragedy and metaphysical quality. An arrangement was made to record the concert, held in the Large Hall of the Moscow Conservatoire: Shostakovich had been struck by many of the new details brought to light in Rostropovich's interpretation, and used his influence with Melodiya to enable an LP of the performance to be released. Now available on CD, the recording remains a remarkable document.‡ Despite the small errors inevitable in live performance – some moments where the orchestral playing is ragged or the intonation imperfect – the extraordinary tension and excitement of the performance more than compensates. Vishnevskaya's superb interpretation conveys the music's enormous emotional impact, and her beautiful singing encompasses an extraordinarily wide range of dynamics. The control she shows is

* Ibid., p. 111.
† Nikolskaya, *Witold Lutoslawski*, p. 57.
‡ The CD issued by Elatus of his recording of the fourteenth symphony notes that it was 'recorded in the Great Hall of the Conservatoire', February 1973.

remarkable, particularly in the penultimate movement, 'Death of the Poet', where she achieves a 'white', detached sound.

Rostropovich felt himself ousted from the capital to ever less important venues; likewise he was unwelcome in such regional capitals as Kiev, Tallinn and Leningrad. Yet of the 81 concerts he played during 1972 in 19 Soviet cities, six dates were actually in Moscow. These included on 30 March another performance, captured on video, of Beethoven's Triple Concerto with Oistrakh and Richter, conducted by Kondrashin. In 1972 he performed 130 concerts as a cellist in 27 towns including six in Moscow, figures collected by the KGB,* which probably did not take account of concerts cancelled without any prior warning. When Seiji Ozawa visited Moscow with the San Francisco Orchestra in June 1973, he made it clear that he would not go on stage without Rostropovich, his soloist in the Dvořák concerto.

The cellist's greatest satisfaction came from tours of Transcaucasia, and he was always warmly welcomed in Erevan and Baku in particular. Rostropovich has the fond memories of a tour undertaken during this period with Aram Khatchaturian, performing under his direction the *Concerto-Rhapsody*. But there was no guarantee that his concerts in smaller provincial centres would not be cancelled arbitrarily, even after he had arrived or while he was making his way to the town in question. Frequently there were no notices of his performances in the press and no posters were to be seen, and so he often played to practically empty halls. Sometimes his name disappeared altogether from concert programmes, reviews and publicity, when the organisers lost their nerve: in one tragic-comic instance in Ulyanovsk, the poster of Rostropovich's concert was deliberately concealed by another poster announcing the town's forthcoming exhibition of rabbits. However, the rabbits were not quite enough to obliterate his rather long name, and its first and last syllables protruded visibly on either side of them.

Whenever she was able, Galina joined in with her husband's projects, even if they took place far from the capital. During the tour of the Volga he conducted and she sang Puccini's *Tosca* in a concert performance in Saratov. However, her diary was considerably busier than his at this stage: as principal soprano of the Bolshoi, she continued to sing in Moscow, and was also able to travel abroad with the theatre.

* V. Shauro, 'Notice of Rostropovich's performing and pedagogical activity', *Muzyka vmesto Sumbura*.

Throughout this difficult period, Rostropovich's friends in the West tried to maintain contact with him and show their support. Britten was of course among these friends – but after the huge pressure of completing his opera *Death in Venice*, he had his own problems of ill health to contend with, and was advised to have heart surgery. The London impresarios, Victor and Lilian Hochhauser, were other loyal allies: they continued to travel frequently to Russia, and were able to carry news to and from Slava. Our family also maintained close contacts with Moscow and helped to keep the lines of communication open. In March 1973, my mother visited Moscow in connection with her work in lexicography. Rostropovich invited her to accompany him to the Bolshoi to hear Galina sing the premiere of Rachmaninov's *Francesca da Rimini*. The following day, on 22 March, she wrote a hurried, somewhat telegraphic letter to Britten with an important message.

Galya sang superbly, [she looked] younger and more beautiful than ever . . . I'll tell you what I got in whispers [from Slava] before the overture. The day he turns Solzhenitsyn out of his house, he can go anywhere, till then nowhere. You can imagine his answer! But clearly he has no hope. His message to you is this. In whatever town he is in Russia on 15 June this year he will give the world premiere of your third cello suite and he will play it every day for a week. In the mean time you should think of – and find – a cellist who will play it after 15 June in Alde-burgh this year. He doesn't think it should be held up any longer as he sees no prospect of getting [out of the country] himself. He says he suffers much but is strong. It was the first time he had been to the Bolshoi for six months, sitting with me in the audience, not in the official box, just as Galya's husband.

My mother must have found it hard to control her sense of outrage, for she was given to speaking her mind. True, diplomatic life had trained her somewhat to restrain her lively and impulsive reactions. She exclaimed in her letter, 'It really is all so shaming. I just couldn't take in the opera feeling what a Man was sitting beside me! HOW can people behave like that! . . . I'm sure like me you'll feel like weeping.' She concluded her hastily scribbled letter with the words, 'Slava needs all our support.' However, Britten would not contemplate another performer, and eventually the third suite received its premiere in Alde-burgh in December 1974, after Rostropovich had left the Soviet Union.

Despite the assurances of the authorities, Rostropovich's situation was in no way alleviated by the fact that in the late spring Solzhen-itsyn left his Zhukovka refuge and took up residence in his second wife's Moscow flat. The writer put it thus, 'The question stands: is it right for one great artist to wither away so as to allow another one to grow'.* The promise that once the writer left his house he could start travelling abroad proved to be completely worthless: the petty persecution and humiliation continued. He soon discovered that for the Soviet bureaucrats, Lenin's maxim of 'Who is not for us is against us' could be applied in a most haphazard way. Rostropovich was called up by Demichev, a high-up secretary of the Central Committee responsible for culture, who quoted those famous words to his face. 'How do you know I am against you?' Rostropovich replied. 'When I play the Dvořák concerto, which I play very well, can you tell whether I am for you or against you? Don't you just need excellent musicians and writers, whether or not they are for or against you?'†

In the Conservatoire files, I found two 'character references' signed by the director Aleksandr Sveshnikov. In them there is no mention of Solzhenitsyn or any reference to his current situation of disgrace. On the contrary Rostropovich is described in the stock phrase, as 'morally dependable and politically literate', and praised for his many musical achievements, notably for his propagation of Soviet music. These character references, a necessity in obtaining permissions to travel outside the country, relate to the only three occasions during three and a half years when Rostropovich was allowed to perform abroad. The first trip was to Paris to play the Dutilleux concerto, the next to Austria between 14 and 30 April 1972. Thanks to Yehudi Menuhin's intervention, he was allowed to travel to Paris for chamber music concerts between 4 and 10 January 1974. Menuhin was at the time President of the Music Sector of UNESCO, and invited Rostropovich to play at the organisation's annual gala concert in Paris with himself and Wilhelm Kempf. The invitation was issued in the normal manner through Gosconcert and the Ministry of Culture.

Now the Soviets were in a quandary, for they could hardly refuse to boycott an event organised by UNESCO. After initially agreeing to Rostropovich's participation, a few days before he was due to depart the authorities informed the concert organisers in Paris that the cellist was ill and couldn't travel. Yehudi immediately phoned his friend at home. Galina answered the call, and told Menuhin that Slava wasn't in. But no, he was not ill, in fact he was perfectly fit, indeed, he had never felt better. There was no reason why he couldn't travel to Paris. Armed with this news, Menuhin exerted pressure on Furtseva and Gosconcert. In this manner Rostropovich was 'released' and enabled

* M. Spektor, *Rostropovich*, p. 75.   † M. Spektor, *Mstislav Rostropovich*, p. 73.

to travel to France and play with Menuhin. I travelled over to Paris to hear the concert; I recall in particular a remarkable performance of Beethoven's 'Archduke' trio by Kempf, Menuhin and Rostropovich.

Immediately after these concerts, Rostropovich was allowed to make a private visit to Aldeburgh, he specifically wished to see Britten. My parents and I also met Rostropovich there, and we, like his other friends, were amazed at his buoyant good spirits and his cautious optimism, despite his many tales of horror at home. He never complained, even when giving us an extensive list of troubles, humiliations and concert cancellations. Slava recounted everything with habitual humour (we heard the story of the rabbit poster on that occasion) and left others to express their feeling of outrage at the authorities' wretched behaviour. My father was surprised to hear that he was unaware of the recently created Helsinki Watch Group, and told him that it could be helpful to his case.

Solzhenitsyn was shortly to be expelled from the country. In autumn 1973, a copy of his *Gulag Archipelago* was discovered and confiscated, a decision that led to tragedy when the friend entrusted with its safe-keeping committed suicide. Within weeks, copies reached the West and the writer gave permission for its instant publication. By the early New Year, we were already reading excerpts from it in the Sunday newspapers. The revelations in *Gulag Archipelago* were distressing and painful to read. Solzhenitsyn had gathered evidence from all over the Soviet Union documenting the fate of thousands of innocent people, who had been executed or had languished for years in the camps. This exposure was more than the Soviet regime could tolerate, and in February 1974 the writer was bundled out of the country without ceremony, soon to be followed by his wife and children.

Shortly afterwards, in the company of his friends (amongst them as always Dmitri and Irina Shostakovich), Rostropovich celebrated his forty-seventh birthday. For the first time in three years there was reason for optimism. With Solzhenitsyn out of the country and the apparent source of the trouble thus removed, people believed that things would improve for Rostropovich. In fact, just some weeks earlier he had been granted permission to conduct and stage Johann Strauss's *Die Fledermaus* at the Theatre of Operetta. It was a piece Rostropovich adored, so there was nothing surprising in his accepting this invitation, despite the fact that levels of performance at the Operetta were not particularly high. Rostropovich decided to invite young musicians from the Conservatoire – students and recent graduates – to help stiffen up the orchestra. The producer and artistic director S. Ansimov, elated by the consequent transformation of the orchestra's sound, would cry out during the rehearsals, 'Slava, you are a genius! It's brilliant!' He also attended the birthday party, where he raised his glass to Rostropovich and expressed his delight to the gathering with an extravagant toast: 'I have the good fortune to have arrived at Communism. Having the great Rostropovich conducting at the Operetta is the realisation of a dream.' ('Arriving at Communism' was, one might say, a Soviet equivalent of 'entering paradise'.)

Events seemed to have taken an upward turn when the Rostropoviches were given the chance to start work on a cherished project: a recording of *Tosca* with the Bolshoi Theatre singers and orchestra, with Vishnevskaya in the title role. The opportunity came about in a rather unorthodox manner. In mid-March Galina learnt that the Bolshoi Theatre was embarking on a second recording of the opera with Tamara Milashkina cast as Tosca. Milashkina had already recorded the opera a few years back, and it appeared difficult to justify her doing it a second time with the same forces. Galina was extremely offended, and justifiably so, for she was the theatre's leading soprano and had clearly been snubbed. Apart from anything else, it was a role that she sang superbly.

Vishnevskaya decided to make a personal phone call to Demichev, as her husband recalls:

Galya cried down the phone, asking why she had not been considered for the recording, and saying that if it went ahead she would leave the Theatre. Demichev was genuinely upset and said that she would be contacted very shortly. And fifteen minutes later Furtseva rang: 'Of course, Galina Pavlovna, you must record *Tosca*. There will be no problems.' 'And who will be the conductor?' Galya asked, 'Is there any reason why Slava cannot conduct?' We had just performed the work in Saratov with great success. Furtseva agreed at once.

A somewhat strange situation thus arose, with two recordings of the same work made simultaneously at the same theatre, using different casts and conductors (Mark Ermler conducted the other). Within days of the conversation with Furtseva, Rostropovich and Vishnevskaya went to the studios. The Bolshoi Theatre orchestra were delighted and welcomed Rostropovich back as a long-lost friend. As he remembers, 'The first session took place on a Monday, which was always the Theatre's day off. This was on 25 March, just before my birthday. I asked the musicians not to give me too demonstrative a welcome, and told the orchestra we would begin at a certain point well into the first act.' Rostropovich did not want the authorities to misconstrue his behaviour as provocative, and wished it to appear that they were not starting their work from scratch. During that first day they recorded most of Act I, after which there was a pause of a few days before they were due to record the rest of the opera. Rostropovich continues the story:

We were due back in the studios on 28 March, the day after my wonderful birthday party. That morning, Galya told me not to answer the phone, as she had an intuition that things were not right. The phone did indeed keep ringing, and in the end I picked up the receiver. It was the producer from the studios: 'Thank goodness you answered. You don't need to come in today, the recording won't be going ahead.' I understood immediately that the order to stop it had come from a much higher authority.

Nevertheless, Rostropovich decided to seek out the director of the Melodiya studios, Pokhomov, in person. When he arrived at his office, the secretaries told him that the director was busy: he was engaged in an important meeting and could not be disturbed, and would be out the rest of the day. Tired of lies and excuses, Rostropovich insisted on his rights, and barged into Pokhomov's office. 'What are you doing here?' he was asked.

'Just tell me one thing: is it true that the recording has been stopped? Is it just this session or the whole thing?' With a certain air of regret, Pokhomov confirmed that the project had been cancelled. It was obvious that the decision had been taken out of Melodiya's hands. Rostropovich could not disguise his true feelings, and remarked bitterly: 'You have left me with a clear choice: either I have to leave the country for ever – or commit suicide.' With that, he stormed out of the office and slammed the door.

Both he and Galina were certain that something lay behind this sudden volte-face – unusual even in the Soviet Union – but they only discovered the truth some six months later. It emerged that five leading singers from the rival Bolshoi cast, angered to learn of the Rostropovich recording, had worked out a plan to put a stop to it. They arrived unannounced at Demichev's office, and demanded an audience. The surprised Demichev was probably astounded to hear the singers announce that they were here to carry out a civic duty. The tenor Atlantov announced, 'It is as communists, not as singers, that we have come to denounce Rostropovich.' Although his musicianship was not questioned, they insisted that his ideological impurity would contaminate the Bolshoi Theatre's singers and orchestra. The recording had to be stopped! Vishnevskaya rightly condemned her colleagues as spiteful and envious, determined to repel their rivals by whatever means were necessary.

In these circumstances, Demichev was powerless to follow his better instincts by defending Rostropovich. An attack on ideological purity was dangerous: not even a senior official could be seen to be disregarding it. Unfortunately such treacherous behaviour was not uncommon in that period. For example, the conductor Evgeny Svetlanov, who had frequently worked with Rostropovich and had no reason to resent him, denounced him in public as a 'musical gangster' – a remark he would sincerely regret in later years.

It is difficult now for us to believe that such non-musical judgements could have so much impact, but this very combination of a lack of artistic reasoning from the authorities and cynicism from colleagues, all too prevalent in the Soviet era, could reduce a musician's life to misery. The cancellation of the recording of *Tosca* was the final straw for both Rostropovich and Vishnevskaya. There and then they decided to write to Brezhnev, asking for permission to travel abroad for two years, and they delivered their letter (dated 29 March) immediately to Demichev whom they knew would pass it on without delay. Though normally unwieldy, the Party machinery could act speedily when needed, and within hours Rostropovich was given a positive response to his request – the decision was made by Brezhnev himself.

Rostropovich had hoped until the last that he would be implored to stay, but he perceived the alacrity with which the authorities reacted as a sign of their complete lack of respect for his lifelong musical achievements. In early April, I came out to Moscow on a short trip to visit friends. I immediately rang my dear professor, and was invited to family breakfast in the flat on Ogaryova Street. Sitting over our plates of kasha (buckwheat porridge), Mstislav Leopoldovich and Galina Pavlovna filled me in on all these recent developments. They were going to come to London, they told me – their lovely teenage daughters, Elena and Olga, could not hide their excitement. I showered my teacher with questions: 'Mstislav Leopoldovich, what will you do, where will you stay, and when are you arriving?' 'I'm coming at the end of May and I'll stay for the first days with your family in

Cambridge.'* This is indeed what happened.

Now that permission had been granted, it was just a question of organising their departure. Furtseva, the Minister of Culture, had told Rostropovich that he had to leave before 4 June, the date when the Tchaikovsky competition was due to begin. He had headed the international jury for the cello category ever since its inception, and Furtseva realised that if he were forbidden to participate while still living in Moscow, the foreign jury members would withdraw – after all, most were close friends of Rostropovich. However, this judgement would not apply if he had already left the Soviet Union, and could be represented as having gone of his own volition. Rostropovich decided to travel ahead of Galina at the end of May, in order to prepare the ground; she would remain with their daughters, who had still to finish the school year, and they would travel to join him in July.

I had observed that the flat in Ogaryova street was in a state of chaos. Antique furniture and various pieces of broken porcelain occupied most of the living space, despite the fact that the family had now acquired the adjoining apartment as an extension to their own. Rostropovich had recently taken up the hobby of collecting pre-Revolutionary furniture and valuable porcelain; this soon developed into a passion that absorbed much of his abundant energy during the increased amounts of free time that he had available. After breakfast that morning, he offered to drive me to my next appointment, and asked me to wait while he changed. It turned out that he had mislaid his shoes, and a hunt started involving the maid Rimma, Galina, Olga and Elena. One shoe was found. 'Where have you women hidden the other one?' he asked irritably. Tempers were frayed, hot words flew, until suddenly Olga cried out, 'I've found it!' – she had opened a broken refrigerator to find the missing shoe on one of its shelves. It occurred to me that never before had I seen my professor lose his temper or show visible signs of stress. It was entirely to Galina's credit that she was able to diffuse the situation by treating it as a comedy – which of course it was – but the incident gave me a small insight into the strain the family had been living under.

Even having decided to leave the Soviet Union, Rostropovich undertook to fulfil his remaining engagements in the two months that remained. In April he travelled to Lithuania and to Chukotka with his

* My father had taken up the position of Master at Corpus Christi College, Cambridge, in September 1971.

erstwhile partner, Aleksandr Dedyukhin. One day they gave a concert in a school in Uelen, only five miles from the border with Alaska – Rostropovich joked that if he had played a little bit louder he would have been heard in the United States. On his return to Moscow he was busy with his students at the Conservatoire and continued rehearsing *Die Fledermaus* at the Operetta. For those young musicians who played in the orchestra, it was an unforgettable experience. Masha Yanushevskaya, who was leading the cellos, recalls how Rostropovich brought out all the humour and brilliance in the score; every day there were new inventions and surprises, all conveyed with his habitual energetic élan:

In working with the orchestra he extended the techniques he used when teaching in class. His ideas were so unusual, so unpredictable, and for this reason his whole attitude to music and to life was fresh and wonderful. One was carried along in the current of his music-making, which gave one a sense of freedom, as well as having its own force and logic.

One of his students, Maya Predel, also played in the orchestra, an experience she vividly remembers:

We were all infected by Mstislav Leopoldovich's enthusiasm, his total involvement with all the details of the production. Already by the first rehearsal he had marked in all the bowings and fingerings. He directed the music with so much joy, it sparkled and bubbled over. All this was in such contrast to the conditions we lived in. Overall he immersed us in the mood and emotions of the work. Then because of his search for the Truth, everything collapsed. All his work at the Operetta was obliterated, they even rubbed out his markings, his bowings and fingerings.

This period at the Operetta proved to be the briefest of respites. On 6 May the management informed Rostropovich that he had been removed from the production and that his scheduled performances had been cancelled. The same Ansimov who had expressed such delight at his genius now told him coldly, 'You have degraded as a musician. We don't need you.' For once Rostropovich was lost for words. Silently he went into the theatre's courtyard and stood alone under an arch, weeping like a child.

I had noticed that during this period Rostropovich was observing the strict Orthodox Lenten Fast. Religion had become of increasing importance in his life, for it gave him the spiritual strength to remain steadfast in his resolve to live by his conscience and not to compromise himself. Shortly before his departure, a service of thanksgiving and farewell was held at the small church in Nezhdanova Street near his home. The officiating priest was a personal friend, and his confessor. The service was attended by a small circle of close friends, and several students also turned up. Rostropovich was moved to see Nina Makarova, Aram Khatchaturian's wife; the couple had always been totally supportive, and if money was needed would lend it gladly. He was equally surprised and touched to see Tatyana Gaidomovich in the congregation – she was the only representative of the Conservatoire administation.

A far more public farewell took place on 10 May at the Grand Hall of the Conservatoire, the scene of so many of Rostropovich's triumphs, where he had made musical history by giving first performances of Prokofiev's *Sinfonia Concertante*, Britten's *Cello Symphony* and Shostakovich's second concerto, to mention but a few key works. The Conservatoire director, Sveshnikov, gave his blessing to the venture, and Rostropovich collected together a student orchestra – he knew that he could no longer rely on any professional orchestra to honour an engagement with him. But the cream of Conservatoire students were delighted to have the chance to play under his direction: the leader of the viola section, for instance, was the young Yuri Bashmet. His all-Tchaikovsky programme consisted of the *Nutcracker* suite, the *Rococo Variations* and the sixth symphony. Ivan Monighetti, his eldest student at the time, and favourite to win the Tchaikovsky competition, was the soloist. All who were at this emotional occasion remember it vividly, in particular the passionate and heart-rending performance of the Pathétique. Many in the audience openly wept, and as the last note died away, it rose to its feet as one. Soon the whole hall was chanting, 'Do not leave, do not leave!' – but nobody was deluded into thinking Rostropovich would be back any time soon.

Meanwhile, Soviet musical life continued to move on without him. Preparations for the Tchaikovsky competition were reaching fever pitch. Over the last year, Rostropovich had been preparing three students for the contest. Apart from Monighetti (officially considered a student of Lev Ginsburg in cello theory, since there were not enough postgraduate places for cello in the year he enrolled), he had taught the Bulgarian cellist Seta Baltayan and Joseph (Jos) Fegelson, who came from Riga. Jos had met Rostropovich as a boy through his uncle Boris Khaikin. The great cellist encouraged him to finish school two years early so he could enrol in his Moscow class in 1971. 'Aren't you bored with school anyway?' he had asked Jos, and with that the matter was decided.

Jos was amazed how nothing, important or unimportant, would escape Rostropovich's attention: 'His comments in class would range from purely musical questions to everyday situations, jokes and comedy. It would seem one thing fed off the other. But in all this he gave everything maximum attention. This quality, together with his unique energy supply, allowed him to put "mind over matter".' Rostropovich was quick to observe that Jos's passion for the cello was somewhat overshadowed by his interest in girls, not an unusual thing for boys of his age given their first taste of independence:

Mstislav Leopoldovich sensed it and sometimes he got wind of some details of my life. On occasions he would cheer me up, and once he saved me from being expelled from the Conservatoire for 'bad morals'. As one can imagine, the quality of my playing began to lag behind as the hours I spent at the cello got fewer. Nevertheless, I managed to learn new works quickly and Mstislav Leopoldovich admired me for it. But when I auditioned for the forthcoming Tchaikovsky competition late in 1973, I wasn't really prepared. He was absolutely mad at me! Only then did I wake up. I begged him for another chance, for I desperately wanted to participate. Finally, he agreed, and I made good strides forward. Closer to the date of the competition, despite his imminent departure in late May and a lot of other pressures, Mstislav Leopoldovich spent a good deal of time working with me at his flat. Those last lessons were unforgettable. Sometimes he would teach me and simultaneously listen to his daughter Olga practising on the other side of the wall! It was both comical and sobering that he would care so much for his daughter's playing.

The Tchaikovsky competition of course took place without Rostropovich, but his students did well considering the circumstances. Seta Baltayan, a very talented cellist and a hard-working student, performed very well and received third prize. For Jos the competition went by as if in a dream, but he was nevertheless included amongst the prizewinners. He recalls that most people imagined that he too would be emigrating abroad. Vanya Monighetti might have won the competition had he not presented himself as a Rostropovich pupil, which of course he was, but to call himself a pupil of Ginsburg was not an option. In the event, the first prize went to Boris Pergamenshikov, an excellent cellist from Leningrad, and Ivan was placed second.

Other students who enrolled with Rostropovich – Alfiya

Napibekova, Robertas Urba, Maya Predel – may have studied with him for a shorter time, but his influence remained with them. For Maya, who had come to Moscow from Riga, it was Rostropovich's understanding of the spiritual value of music that left the deepest impression on her:

What was so special about Mstislav Leopoldovich as a teacher was how his imagination was tied to the life experience. He was very closely connected to the mysteries of the world. It seems to me that he felt the idea of God very strongly, and made us aware that there is always something higher than us, and that through music we can come into contact with a higher spirituality.

Shortly after the farewell concert, Rostropovich gave his last class in the Conservatoire. Maya Predel played Beethoven's fifth sonata. 'The lesson went well,' she recalls. 'I remember when I played the chorale theme in the second movement, he turned to me, and said, "Maya, it's God who is tickling you here." When he left we had the sense that our lives had come to a standstill.'

Rostropovich still had some farewells to make. He visited the Moscow cemeteries to pay his respects to the dead, amongst them his mother, who had died in 1972, and Sergey Prokofiev. Then he took his courage in hand and went to see Shostakovich, fully aware that this would be a final parting. Dmitri Dmitriyevich was in very poor health, although he managed to keep composing. He could not restrain his tears when Slava, his one-time student and the most passionate champion of his music, told him that he was shortly to depart. 'But Dmitri Dmitriyevich, over there I will be able to play your music and record Lady Macbeth of Mtsensk and all your symphonies.' Through his tears, Shostakovich said, 'Well, if you're going to record the symphonies, then please start with the fourth.' During the conversation Shostakovich kept repeating an enigmatic phrase: 'Slava, if over there you receive a strange anonymous parcel, don't throw it out – who knows, it might have a good score inside!' Rostropovich did not cross-question him on this at the time. However, the riddle was recently solved when the curator of the Shostakovich archive, Manashir Yakubov, discovered a manuscript with the instrumental line of Shostakovich's final work, the viola sonata, written out in the bass clef.* This hint that the work was probably originally intended for the cello (and specifically for Rostropovich) is reinforced by the quotation in the last page from Strauss's *Don Quixote* – a work in which the chivalrous knight is represented by the cello. The quotation comes from the moment in Strauss's work when Don Quixote dies and his spirit is transported into a different dimension. Of course, this quotation – along with the many others in the viola sonata both from Shostakovich's own work and that of other composers – probably also refers to the dying composer himself, who composed the piece aware that it would be his swansong.

Dmitri Shostakovich died on 9 August 1975, and Rostropovich became the most ardent champion of his music in the West. He naturally kept his promise and recorded the symphonies, including the rarely performed nos. 2 and 3; even before that, however, he made what is widely regarded as the definitive recording of *Lady Macbeth of Mtsensk* in London, with Galina Vishnevskaya singing the title role.

On Sunday 26 May 1974, a handful of close friends, family and a few students accompanied Rostropovich to Sheremet'evo airport – among them were Irina Shostakovich, Natalya Shakhovskaya, David Geringas, his wife Tatyana Shchats and Mariya Yanuchevskaya.† He was travelling with one large suitcase, two cellos and his enormous, handsome Newfoundland dog, Kuzya. He had informed us in advance through the councillor of the British Embassy Jo Dobbs that he intended to bring the dog, so that quarantine arrangements could be set up in Britain. Apparently Kuzya did not want to go through customs at all, and Galina had to lie down on the floor with him to persuade him.

Galina and Irina Shostakovich were the only people allowed to accompany Rostropovich through customs, while other friends and students had to wait disconsolately behind the glass doors. A short while later, Galina walked back carrying a small bundle on her shoulder. 'These', she announced loudly, 'are Rostropovich's medals. If they had been made of pure shit he could have taken them with him. Given that they are made of gold, he has been told to leave them behind.'* During these last minutes in his own country, Rostropovich

---

* The viola sonata was written in July 1975, within weeks of the composer's death. It was in fact arranged for cello quite soon after its publication by Daniil Shafran.

† The KGB had a precise list of all those at the airport farewell. It included two diplomats, the Ambassador of Luxembourg (an excellent pianist who had befriended many Muscovite musicians) and Jo Dobbs, Councillor of the British Embassy. See M. Spektor appendix.

had undergone the humiliation of a thorough frisking from the customs officials, with a stern admonition for trying to smuggle gold out of the country. As far as Rostropovich was concerned, the medals were not constituted of gold, but of life work – his own blood, sweat and tears.

Four hours later, on the tarmac of Heathrow airport, a small party of friends awaited Rostropovich: Victor and Lilian Hochhauser, my parents, Betty and Duncan Wilson, and me. Because of the special circumstances, we were allowed to come right up to the aircraft steps. We were all moved to tears to see Rostropovich, pallid and tense, descend the steps with two cellos in one hand and leading his Newfoundland dog in the other.

Unfortunately, British law states that foreign dogs cannot walk off a plane and touch the ground. Rostropovich was abruptly instructed to go back into the plane while the van from the kennels, which had been waiting by the aircraft hold, drove round to the front of the steps. The kennel authorities had assumed that the dog would be in a crate in the hold, rather than travelling first class with his master. It was my job to go up into the plane and explain. 'What's happening?' Rostropovich asked me anxiously. 'Mstislav Leopoldovich, they were expecting Kuzya to be in a cage; it's because of the quarantine rules; a van is coming to pick him up, they ask you kindly to wait two minutes.' 'And where do you suppose I could have got a cage for a dog who weighs ninety kilos?' he asked me. 'Was I to go to Moscow Zoo and ask for an elephant cage?' When the signal was given, Rostropovich led his dog down the plane steps for a second time; Kuzya obediently stepped into the van that was waiting at the bottom.

Rostropovich himself began his new life in the West with no material possessions other than his two cellos and a single suitcase of clothes. When he eventually returned to Moscow after sixteen years of exile, he had fulfilled many of his musical ambitions, and was at the peak of his international fame. Meanwhile Russia, on the threshold of democracy, had been changed beyond recognition by the collapse of Communism and the demise of the Soviet Union.

---

* He was actually allowed to take with him two rather tacky-looking medals, made from simple metal: one marking his achievements in the 'Virgin Soil' campaigns and the other from the City of Moscow. See Vishnevskaya's book *Galina: A Russian Story*, pp. 471–2.

Epilogue

'An artist's living nature is not simply an object of imagery but the metaphor and breath of his inner world . . . He can never find enough in reality, therefore he is forced to invent it.'* This definition of the artist's quest for the truth by Andrei Sinyavsky (whose *nom de plume* was Abram Tertz) could be seen as a succinct statement of Rostropovich's philosophy of life. In retrospect, our lives at the Moscow Conservatoire under his guidance provided a haven, where music isolated us from the grim reality and drab routine of the outside world. This passionate quest for artistic truth had enormous significance in the repressive political atmosphere of the Soviet Union. After Rostropovich's departure, an immense void was felt in artistic circles, although his influence lived on in the hearts of many – his former students in particular.

The story of Mstislav Rostropovich's life after leaving the Soviet Union lies beyond the scope of this volume: it could easily provide material for several books in itself. Suffice it to say that he and his family were unable to return to Russia for sixteen years. In March 1978 they were deprived of their Soviet citizenship for 'actions incompatible with remaining Soviet citizens'.† Only at that point did they stop living out of suitcases and bought an apartment in Paris, their first real home in the West. Rostropovich and Vishnevskaya received travel documents from the Principality of Monaco, but despite many offers, they did not accept any other nationality. In effect, they became and remained citizens of the world, refusing Mikhail Gorbachev's early offer to reinstate

* Abram Tertz, *Golos iz Khora* (A Voice from the Choir), London: Stenvalley Publishing House, 1973, p. 9.
† The edict of the Praesidium of the Supreme Soviet of the USSR was dated 14 March 1978 and signed by Leonid Brezhnev.

their Russian citizenship, even after most of their interests and residences were transferred to Moscow and St Petersburg.

When Rostropovich arrived in the West in May 1974 he did not have a single engagement fixed, but it was only a matter of days before he was inundated with invitations – both to play the cello and to conduct – from impresarios, concert organisations and the world's best orchestras. His thirst to perform music, combined with his energy and incredible capacity for hard work, produced quick results, and his career flourished in every sphere. In 1977 he accepted the position of chief conductor of the National Symphony Orchestra of Washington DC, remaining in that position for seventeen seasons. Simultaneously, he developed close contacts as a conductor with many European and Japanese orchestras. From the late 1980s, Rostropovich built on an important association with the London Symphony Orchestra, performing frequently at the Barbican Centre in London, where he organised festivals dedicated to the music of Shostakovich (1988), Prokofiev (1991) and Britten (1993).

Not surprisingly, Rostropovich's name became closely associated with Russian repertoire, and most particularly for his authentic and acclaimed performances of the music of Prokofiev and Shostakovich, the two great Russian composers with whom he was so intimately connected. It is significant that on his return to Russia in February 1990 at the head of Washington's National Symphony Orchestra, Rostropovich placed Shostakovich's Eighth Symphony (generally considered his greatest work) at the Grand Hall of the Moscow Conservatoire. His searingly emotional interpretation emphasised the work's intrinsic tragedy and all-embracing humanity. To mark the exact centenary of Shostakovich's birth – 25 September 2006 – he conducted the same work at the same venue, this time with the Russian State Orchestra, in what proved to be his last Moscow Concert. In December he gave his last concerts in Japan.

Rostropovich last appeared in public – in extremely fragile health – at a grand reception at the Kremlin given by Vladimir Putin in celebration of his eightieth birthday on 27 March 2007. Here he was presented with Russia's top award, the Order for Services to the Fatherland, first class, in recognition of his unique contribution to music. Exactly a month later Rostropovich died in Moscow's Blokhin Oncological Clinic. After a civic service at the Moscow Conservatoire and a religious funeral liturgy at the Church of Christ The Saviour, he was buried in the Novodevichy Cemetery. His grave, in simple marble decorated with a large Orthodox cross, is just opposite that of the famous dancer, Galina Ulanova, which in contrast is embellished by a statue of the ballerina in tutu!

Rostropovich no doubt merits a place in the *Guinness Book of Records* for his many feats as a cellist. He gave the premieres of nearly two hundred works for cello – of which he was almost always also the dedicatee. His last such premiere was in Vienna on 19 and 20 June 2005, when, at the age of seventy-eight, he performed Krzyzstof Penderecki's new *Largo* for cello and orchestra under Seiji Ozawa, at what was intended as his last public appearance as a cellist. Rostropovich also premiered some ninety works for orchestra as a conductor. He received over sixty honorary degrees from universities throughout the world, and over one hundred awards and medals, including the Soviet Union's Lenin Prize (1964), the Presidential Award for Freedom (1987, USA), Grand Officer of the Légion d'Honneur (1997, France) and an Honorary KBE (1987, Great Britain).

As a believer in human rights, Rostropovich could not remain indifferent to the collapse of Communism. On hearing that the Berlin Wall had fallen, he flew to the city on 12 November 1989 with his cello, selected a place near Check Point Charlie in front of the Wall (against painted Mickey Mouse graffiti), and played Bach's solo Cello Suites. This spontaneous act was not only a way to remember those who lost their lives attempting to escape from East Berlin to West, but served as a symbolic reconnection of the different parts of his own life divided by politics. Similarly, when he learnt of the putsch in Moscow in August 1991 that threatened to reinstall Communist dictatorship, Rostropovich immediately flew there without so much as warning his family. After talking his way through passport control – he had no visa – he rushed to the White House to join the fight to defend democracy and lend support to Boris Yeltsin. The famous photograph of the young guard asleep on his shoulder while Rostropovich held his rifle has been reproduced all over the world – it transpired that neither of them knew how to shoot!

Rostropovich never slackened in his mission to promote the cello. In 1977, the first Rostropovich Competition was held in La Rochelle, and was specifically dedicated to contemporary music. Thereafter the competition was held in Paris (with the collaboration if the city of Paris) on a more or less four-yearly basis, with the last competition taking place in 2009. The quality of the prize winners now embarking on important international careers ensured the visibility and status of the competition. As a matter of principle Rostropovich did not sit on the jury, but his influence was tangible in the commission of a special work for solo cello from a renowned composer. In 1997 the Rostropovich Cello Foundation was created in Kronberg, followed seven years later by the Kronberg Academy. Rostropovich also initiated with Raimund Trenkler the Cello Masterclasses & Concerts – an event still held biannually. All this, he claimed, made the small German town near Frankfurt into 'The World Capital of the Cello'.

In the last decade of his life Rostropovich dedicated a large part of his energies to philanthropic activities, and to helping young people. In 1997 he created the Mstislav Rostropovich Foundation, which supported a selection of talented young musicians through stipends, as well as organising their participation in masterclasses and public performances. Twenty-three years later, a total of 350 concerts have been performed by the scholarship-holders in Moscow and other Russian cities, as well as in prestigious halls abroad such as London's Wigmore Hall, the Salle Gaveau in Paris and the Kaufman Center in New York.

Under the auspices of the Rostropovich Foundation for Cultural and Humanitarian Programmes (director: Olga Rostropovich), a variety of projects have been set up. First and foremost the Mstislav Rostropovich Festival was created in Moscow under the directorship of his daughter Olga in 2010. In its ten years of existence, it has become one of Russia's most important musical events, hosting prestigious European orchestras with renowned conductors and soloists, many of whom were personal friends of Rostropovich. The Festival, which always opens on his birthday on 27 March, has been brought to other cities, notably St Petersburg, and also provides under its umbrella a platform for young talent. The 2020 Festival – to have been the eleventh – was cancelled because of the Covid-19 pandemic. Olga Rostropovich has also been instrumental in founding other Rostropovich Festivals, in Baku (the maestro's birthplace), and more recently in Orienburg, as well as concert tours on the Volga, where performers and audience travel by boat to its various cities (one of the cruise steamers even boasts Rostropovich's name).

His birthplace, Baku, was particularly favoured by Rostropovich during the last years of his life. He visited the city annually, giving performances and masterclasses, with the aim of raising the standard of music-making and encouraging young talents. In 2006 he organised a music festival dedicated to the centenary of Shostakovich's birth. The Museum of Leopold and Mstislav Rostropovich was opened in the house in Baku where he was born and spent his childhood years. A similar museum is to be opened in the house where the Rostropovich family lived during the Second World War under the auspices of the Orienburg Fine Arts Museum.

Perhaps nearest to the cellist's heart was the creation in 1991 of the Rostropovich–Vishnevskaya Foundation (RVF), a humanitarian project founded in reaction to the appalling state of children's health care in Russia at the time. With its base in Washington DC, the Foundation initially provided essential medical equipment and instituted a vaccination programme against Hepatitis B; during Rostropovich's lifetime it had already immunised more than two million children in Russia and in neighbouring former Soviet countries. After the death of Rostropovich, and in 2012 of Galina Vishnevskaya, Elena Rostropovich (their younger daughter) was appointed President of the RVF, with Thomas Pickering acting as Chairman of the Board. With intensified programmes for MMR Vaccination, Pneumococcal Vaccination and Rotavirus vaccination as well as screening programmes for congenital heart disease, and intestinal parasites as well as HIV/Aids, the RVF is today active in an expanded area, including Azerbaijan, Armenia, Georgia, Kazakhstan, Uzbekistan and in the Middle East, notably in the West Bank, the Gaza strip and Egypt. The Foundation is strictly a non-political institution that aims for sustainability, and works with and trains local public health care staff.

In 1993 Rostropovich and his wife Galina Vishnevskaya started the purchase of a large mansion on the Kutuzov Embankment in St Petersburg with the intention of making it the home of their official archives, as well as for themselves. The archive became active in January 2001 under the curatorship of Larisa Chrikova, who has sorted, identified, and catalogued thousands of boxes of documents, scores, programmes, letters, press cuttings, and recordings. This scrupulous research is used in almost every existing project to do with Rostropovich, whether CDs, documentary films, books, articles and festival and concert programmings.

After Rostropovich's death, lasting tributes have been made to his life and musical achievements through the issue of CDs and documentary films. Warner Classics released an album in honour of what would have been Rostropovich's ninetieth birthday with forty-three CDs reissuing the recordings that appeared originally on the EMI label (some of them reissues of Melodiya) and which leaves testimony to the large number of new concertos by a large variety of composers played, some of them performed only once or twice.

Various other festivals to honour him have been held, notably at Berlin's Konzerthaus in 2017. Several seriously researched and brilliant documentary films have paid tribute to Rostropovich's unique legacy. Notable among them are John Bridcut's *The Genius of the Cello* (2011), winner of the Vaclav Havel award; Bruno Monsaingeon's *The Indomitable Bow* (2018), and Svetlana Terner's *Mstislav Rostropovich – Prosto Slava* (Mstislav Rostropovich – Simply Slava) (2019). After leaving the Soviet Union, Rostropovich never sought another teaching post, although he taught several talented cellists privately and frequently gave masterclasses to both students and young professionals. He never limited these classes to cellists, for he enjoyed work-ing with pianists and chamber groups, particularly in repertoire by his friends Prokofiev, Shostakovich and Britten.

Necessarily this involved adapting his teaching style to the context of the masterclass, where contact is established with the student for a single isolated occasion. Rostropovich knew how to pare down his didactic methods to the essential: making a quick 'diagnostic' analysis, praising a student's qualities so as to give something to build on, and pointing to weaknesses that often need long-term attention. While a masterclass generally precludes work in depth, it provided immense stimulus not only to the students involved, but also to audience members.

As for the graduates of Class 19, today they are scattered to the winds throughout the world. Many left Russia in the diaspora of the 1970s, when emigration to Israel provided an officially accepted route to leave the Soviet Union – and not only for Jews. Later, when *glasnost* and *perestroika* hastened the final collapse of the Soviet Union, Russians started to enjoy the opportunity to travel freely, and many ex-students took teaching jobs in the West. With the deaths of Natalya Shakhovskaya and Anatoly Nikitin in 2017, Vagram Saradzhan in 2019 and the retirement from teaching posts of many of the eminent cellists who were one-time students of Class 19, we can today look to Rostropovich's cellistic 'grandchildren' and 'great-grandchildren' to keep his legacy alive. Undoubtedly, they all benefit from looking back to that inimitable example that Rostropovich gave. Above all they should be motivated by 'musical and human conscience', which he believed lay behind musical greatness.

Appendix 1

Rostropovich's cello students, 1947–74

Central Music School (TseMSha), 1947–55

I have not traced the full list of pupils at TseMSha. The book refers only to his first students, whom he began teaching in 1947:
Alla Vasilyeva
Tatyana Priymenko
Kira Tsvetkova
Georgi Ivanov

and to a few of those who studied with him at the school between 1948 and 1956:
Viktor Apartsev
Lev Evgrafov
Miron Yampolsky

Moscow Conservatoire, 1948–74

Rostropovich began teaching at the Conservatoire as Kozolupov's assistant, a position he held between 1948 and 1953. He was given his own class at the Conservatoire in 1953 and remained as an 'independent teacher' until he left Russia in 1974. The following list includes all Conservatoire students in this period for whom Rostropovich was their principal teacher:
Boris Korshun (1949–54)
Georgi Ivanov (1949–54)
Efim Meerson (1950–55)
Alla Vasilyeva (1951–56)
Illarion Sheishvili (1951–56; postgraduate 1956–60)
Medeya Abramyan (1953–56)

Lev Evgrafov (1953–58)
Alla Khatsko (1953–58)
Valery Zelenyak-Kudreiko (1955–60)
Viktor Apartsev (1955–60; postgraduate 1960–63)
Kseniya Yuganova
Aleksei Yesipov
Galina Sosnovskaya (1956–61)
Lyubov Pyatnova
Anatoly Nikitin (postgraduate)
Peter Zimmerman
Stanislav Appolin
Seppo Laamanen
Dzhemil Mamedov (1958–63)
Aleksandr Damurjan
Evgeny Altman (student and postgraduate)
Maris Villerus (postgraduate 1960–63)
Tamara Gabarashvili (1961–66) (transferred during
    fourth year, continued as postgraduate)
Aleksander Knaifel (1961–63)
Natalya Shakhovskaya (postgraduate 1960–63)
Stefan Popov (1961–65)
Aleksandr Kovalyov (1962–67)
Elena Kharkovskaya (1962–65)
Karine Georgian (1962–68; postgraduate 1968–71)
Mark Drobinsky (postgraduate 1962–65)
Silvija Narunaite (1962–66)
David Geringas (1963–68; postgraduate 1970–73)
Mariya Chaikovskaya (1963–68; postgraduate 1968–71)
Tatyana Dikhtyar (1964–70)
David Grigorian (1964–69 postgraduate 1969–72
Tatyana Remenikova (1964–69; postgraduate 1969–72)
Elizabeth Wilson (1964–69; stageur 1969–71)
Victoria Yagling (1964–69; postgraduate 1969–72)
Viktor Shpiller (1965–70)
Vika Mateison (1965)
V. Kupin (1965)
N. Zagrekov (1965)
Rasim Abdulayev (post graduate)
Jacqueline du Pré (Jan–June 1966)

Miron Yampolsky (1966–71)

Vagram Saradzhan (1966–71; postgraduate 1971–74)

Ivan Monighetti (1966–71; postgraduate 1971–74, officially studying with Ginsburg)

Mikhail Milman (1966–68)

Mikhail (Mischa) Maisky (1966–70)

S. Gornovitova (1967–68)

Boris Shishkin (1967–68)

Lyudmila Koval (1967–72)

Kovchargin

Moray Welsh (stageur 1969–71)

Mikhail Utkin (1970–75)

Seta Baltayan (1970–75)

Josif (Yos) Fegelson (1971–76; with Gutman from Sep 1974)

Maya Predel (stageur)

Alfiya Napibekova (1972–77)

Raimo Saraiola (1972–74)

Misha Katz (1973–78)

Robertas Urba (1973–78)

Tatyana Zavarskaya (1973–78; completed studies with Shakhovskaya)

Daniel Veis (1974–79)

Leningrad Conservatoire, 1961–66

Yuriy Falik (1961–63)

Gennady Gennovker (1961–63)

Arkadi Orlovsky (1962–64)

Mikhail Gel'fandbein (1963–66)

Yuri Loevsky (1964–66)

Yuri Tsiryuk (1964–67)

Eleonora Testelets (1964–66)

Natalya Gutman (1964–68)

Boris Talalaya (1965–69)

Appendix 2

An Open Letter from M. L. Rostropovich, to the Editors-in-Chief of the newspapers *Pravda, Izvestiya, Literaturnaya Gazeta* and *Sovetskaya Kultura*

Dear Comrade Editor

It has long since ceased to be a secret that A. I. Solzhenitsyn spends a large part of his time at my home near Moscow. I witnessed his expulsion from the Writers' Union at the very time he was working intensively on his novel *August 1914*, and just recently I witnessed his receipt of the Nobel Prize and the subsequent press campaign against him. It is in connection with this last point that I am writing to you.

As I recall, this is the third time that a Soviet writer has received the Nobel Prize. In two of the three cases we regarded the award of the Prize as a dirty political game, whereas in the third case we saw it as just recognition of a literary figure of world importance. If, at the time, Sholokhov had refused to accept the prize from those who awarded it to Pasternak 'for considerations connected with the Cold War', I would understand that from now on I should call into question the objectivity and integrity of the members of the Swedish Academy. But now it turns out that in an arbitrary manner we sometimes accept the Nobel Prize with gratitude and at other times disparage it. What if next time the Prize is awarded to Comrade Kochetov? It would undoubtedly have to be accepted.

Why, only one day after the award of the prize to Solzhenitsyn, did our newspapers publish a strange account of a conversation between correspondent X and a representative of the secretariat of the Writers'

Union, to the effect that the entire nation (including, of course, all scientists, all musicians and so forth) actively supported his expulsion from the Writers' Union?

Why did *Literaturnaya Gazeta* tendentiously select from the Western newspapers only the statements made in the American and Swedish communist newspapers, bypassing such incomparably more popular and significant communist newspapers as *L'Humanité*, *Les Lettres Françaises* and *L'Unità*, not to mention the commentary of the non-communist press? If we can trust the words of a certain critic named Bonosky, what, then, about the opinion of writers as outstanding as Böll, Aragon and François Mauriac?

I well remember our newspapers in 1948, and I would like to remind you of what they wrote. How much claptrap was printed then about S. S. Prokofiev and D. D. Shostakovich, who today are universally recognised as giants of our musical culture. Take this example: 'Comrades Shostakovich, Prokofiev, Shebalin, Myaskovsky! Your a-tonal cacophonous music is ORGANICALLY ALIEN TO THE PEOPLE. Formalist tricks come into play when there is little talent, but much pretension to innovation . . . The music of Shostakovich, Prokofiev and Myaskovsky is totally unacceptable. It has no harmony, no order, no tunefulness or melody.'

Today when you look at the newspapers of those years, the shame of many things is unbearable : the fact that the opera *Katerina Izmailova* was not heard for three decades, that Prokofiev was unable during his lifetime to hear the final version of his opera *War and Peace*, or the *Sinfonia.Concertante* for cello and orchestra; that there was an official list of banned compositions by Shostakovich, Prokofiev, Myaskovsky and Khachaturian.

Can it really be that after living through such times we still have not learnt to take a more cautious attitude toward the crushing of talent, to refrain from speaking in the name of the entire nation, to stop forcing people to utter opinions about things they have never heard or read? I remember with pride that I did not appear at the meeting at the Central House of Workers in Art when Pasternak was being hounded; in the speech I was expected to make I was instructed to condemn his novel *Dr Zhivago*, which at the time I had not even read.

In 1948 there were lists of banned works. Today verbal bans are preferred, in the form of suggestions that 'an opinion exists, stating that such and such is not recommended . . .' However, it is impossible to ascertain where and from whom that OPINION originates. Why, for example, was Galina Vishnevskaya not allowed to perform Boris Chaikovsky's brilliant song cycle based on texts by Joseph Brodsky in her Moscow recital? Why were performances of Shostakovich's song cycle based on texts by Sacha Chorny obstructed on several occasions, even though the text had been published in this country? Why those strange difficulties attending the performances of Shostakovich's thirteenth and fourteenth symphonies?

Again, obviously, 'there was an opinion'. Who conceived the 'opinion' that Solzhenitsyn had to be expelled from the Writers' Union? I have been unable to ascertain this, despite my keen interest in the matter. It is hardly likely that five Ryazan 'writer-musketeers' would have dared do that without the mysterious existence of an 'opinion'. Plainly, OPINION has prevented my compatriots from seeing Andrei Tarkovsky's film *Andrei Rublyov*, which was sold abroad, and which I was lucky enough to see along with the enraptured Parisians. Obviously it was OPINION that prevented the publication of Solzhenitsyn's *Cancer Ward*, which had already been set up in type at *Novy Mir* journal. Had it been published in this country, it would have been widely and openly discussed, to the benefit of both readers and author.

I shall not touch on our country's economic or political problems, since there are people who understand these things better than I. But explain to me, please, why in our literature and art is the decisive word always spoken by those who are absolutely incompetent in these matters? Why are they given the right to discredit our art in the eyes of our people?

I am stirring up the past not to grumble, but so that in the future, in some twenty years from now, we will not be compelled to hide today's newspapers in shame. Every person must have the right to think and express views fearlessly and independently about things that are known to him, that he has personally thought out and experienced – and not simply to offer watered-down variants of OPINIONS imposed on him. We will certainly arrive one day at free discussion without prompting or rebuffs.

I know that this letter will certainly provoke the appearance of an Opinion about me too; but I am not afraid of it, and I am saying openly what I think. The talents that are the pride of our nation must not be subjected to attack in advance. I am familiar with many of

Solzhenitsyn's works. I like them, and I feel that he has earned the right through suffering to set down the truth on paper as he sees it. Nor do I see any reason to conceal my attitude towards him when a campaign has been launched against him.

Mstislav Rostropovich
31 October 1970

List of sources

INTERVIEWS

The author conducted interviews with Mstislav Rostropovich in London, Paris, Amsterdam, Parma, Turin, Pracatinat, Bologna, Moscow and St Petersburg during a ten-year period between 1996 and 2006

Between 2003 and 2006 the author conducted interviews with the following:

In Moscow
Veronika Rostropovich
Valentin Berlinsky
Tatyana Gaidomovich
Alla Vasiliyeva
Lev Evgrafov
Natalya Shakhovskaya
Yuri Loevsky
Galina Sosnovskaya
Mariya Chaikovskaya
Mikhail Utkin

In St Petersburg
Aleksandr Knaifel
Anatoly Nikitin
Yuri Falik

In Latvia (Riga)
Maya Predel
Eleonora Testelets
Maris Villerus

In Italy (Cervo, Cremona, Torino Bolzano)
David Geringas
Natalya Gutman
Mischa Maisky
Tatyana Remenikova
Vagram Saradzhan
Mariya Yanuchevskaya

In UK (Argyll, London)
Karine Georgian
Moray Welsh
Stefan Popov
Alfiya Napibekova (Bekova)

In Switzerland (Basle and Lugano)
David Grigorian
Ivan Monighetti
Mark Drobinsky

By telephone, email and correspondence

Tatyana Priymenko
Medeya Abramyan
Valery Zelenyah–Kudreiko
Tamara Gabarashvili
Silvija Naruňaite (Sondeckien)
Tatyana Dikhtyar
Misha Katz
Mikhail Milman

Jos Fegelson
Miron Yampolsky
Arkadi Orlovsky

Articles were written especially for this book by

Ivan Monighetti
Victoria Yagling
Manashir Yakubov

PUBLISHED SOURCES

Baldock, Robert, *Pablo Casals*, London: Viktor Gollancz, 1992

Bennett, G. and Hamilton, K. A. (eds.), *Documents on British Policy Overseas: Britain and the Soviet Union 1968–1972*, London: The Stationery Office, 1997

Campbell, Margaret, *The Great Cellists*, London: Viktor Gollancz, 1998

Carpenter, Humphrey, *Benjamin Britten: A Biography*, London: Faber and Faber, 1992

Danko, L. G. and Broslavskaya, T. V. (eds.), *Peterburgskiye stranitsy russkoi muzykal'noy kulturoy* [St Petersburg: Pages of Russian Musical Culture], St Petersburg: Rimsky-Korsakov Conservatoire, 2001

Gaidomovich, Tatyana, *Mstislav Rostropovich*, Moscow: Sovetskiy Kompozitor, 1969

Gaidomovich, Tatyana, *Nezatyvaemoe – Shtrikhi k portretu L. Rostropovich a* [The Unforgetable – Strokes for a portrait of L. Rostropovich], Stornik Petersburgshihn Stranits, Vol. II, St. Petersburg, 2001

Ginsburg, Lev, *Mstislav Rostropovich*, Moscow: Sovetskiy Kompozitor, 1963

Ginsburg, L. S., Kandinsky, A. I., Nikolayev, A. A., Protopopov, V. V. and Tumanina, N. V. (eds.), *Moskovskaya Konservatoriya 1866–1966* [Moscow Conservatoire 1866–1966], Moscow: Izdatel'stvo Muzyka, 1966

Glikman, Isaak, *Story of a Friendship: the letters of Dmitri Shostahovich to Isaah Glikman*, trans. Anthony Phillips, London: Faber and Faber, 2001

Grum-Grzhimaylo, Tamara, *Rostropovich e ego Sovremenniki v legendakh, bylyakh i dialogakh* [Rostropovich and his Contemporaries in Legends, Tales and Dialogues], Moscow: Agar, 1997

Gusev, V. A., Vargaftik, M. A., Fikhtengoltz, M. B. and Oksimets, V. N. (eds.), *Daniil Shafran Violonchel' solo* [Daniil Shafran, Solo Cello], Moscow: Izdatel'stvo ACT, 2001

Ho, Allen B. and Feofarov, Dmitry (eds), *Shostakovich Reconsidered*, Toccata Press, 1998

Ivashkin, Aleksandr and Oehrlein, Josef, *Rostrospektive – zum Leben und Werk von Mstislaw Rostropowitsch* [On the Life and Achievement of Mstislav Rostropovich], Schweinfurth: Reimund Maier Verlag, 1997

Khentova, Sofiya, *Rostropovich*, St Petersburg: Kult Inform Press, 1993

Kirk, H. L., *Pablo Casals: A Biography*, New York: Holt, Rinehart and Winston, 1974

Kovnatshaya, Lyudmila (compiler), *D. D. Shostakovich: Anthology of articles for the ninetieth anniversary of his birth* [D. D. Shostakovich: Sbornik Statei k 90-letiye so dnya rozhdeniya], Kompoeitor St Petersburg, 1996

Mansaingeon, Bruno, *Richter, Ecrits, Conversations*, Éditions Van de Velde, Aches Sud Arte Éditions, 1998

Nikolskaya, Irina, *Witold Lutoslawski Stat'i Perevody i Vospominaniya* [Articles, Translations and Reminiscences], Moscow: Tantra, 1995

Pears, Peter, *Travel Diaries 1936–1978*, Aldeburgh: Britten–Pears Library/Boydell Press, 1995

Rostropovich, Elena and Tartini, Stefano, *Mstislav Rostropovich*, private publication, 1997

Rubtsova, Valentina, *Tikhon Khrennikov: Thus it was on his times and himself* [Tak i bylo: Tikhon Khrennikov o vremeni i o sebye], Moscow, 1994

Shauro, V., *Spravka ob Ispolnitel'skoj I pedagogicheskoj deyatelnosti Rostropovicha Dlya TsK KPSS 11 Aprelya 1974* [Notice of Rostropovich's performing and pedagogical activity, written for the Central Committee of the CPSS 11 April 1974]

– Article in *Muzyka vmesto Sumbura: Kompozitory I Muzykanty v Strane Sovetov 1917–1991* [Music Instead of Muddle: Composers and Musicians in the Country of Soviets]; editor: L. Maksimenko, International Foundation Democracy, 2013

Shlifshteyn, S. I. (ed.), *S. S. Prokofiev, Materialy, dokumenty, vospominaniya* [S. S. Prokofiev, Material, Documents, Reminiscences], Moscow: Gosudartsvennoye Muzykal'noye Izdatel'stvo, 1961

Spektor, Mikhail, *Mstislav Rostropovich: Vekhi zhiznennogo i tvorcheskogo puti* [Mstislav Rostropovich Landmarks of his Life and Work], Jerusalem: Tarbut, 1997

Teplitskaya, V. M., *Dar Bestsenniy: Dialogi s V. A. Berlinskim* [An Invaluable Gift: In Dialogue with Valentin Berlinsky], Voronezh, 2004

Vasiliyeva, Alla, *Ispoved' muzykanta – Moi uroki* [Confessions of a Musician – My Lessons], Moscow: Moskva Muzyka, 1996

Vasiliyeva, Alla, *Moy Opyt, Moya Vera* [My Experience, My Faith], Moscow: Net Graphics, 2000

Vedernikova, O. Y. (ed.), *Anatoli Vedernikov: stat'i i Vospominaniya* [Articles and Reminiscences], Moscow: Kompozitor, 2002

Vishnevskaya, Galina, *Galina: A Russian Story*, London: Hodder and Stoughton, 1984

White, Eric Walter, *Benjamin Britten: His Life and Operas*, London: Faber and Faber, 1983

Wilson, Elizabeth, *Shostakovich: A Life Remembered*, London: Faber and Faber, 2006

Wilson, Elizabeth, *Jacqueline du Pré*, London: Faber and Faber, 1998

Articles in newspapers and journals are referenced in the footnotes.

Index